Palgrave Studies in Economic History

Series Editor
Kent Deng
London School of Economics
London, UK

Palgrave Studies in Economic History is designed to illuminate and enrich our understanding of economies and economic phenomena of the past. The series covers a vast range of topics including financial history, labour history, development economics, commercialisation, urbanisation, industrialisation, modernisation, globalisation, and changes in world economic orders.

More information about this series at
http://www.palgrave.com/gp/series/14632

Albert Carreras • Xavier Tafunell

Between Empire and Globalization

An Economic History of Modern Spain

palgrave
macmillan

Albert Carreras
Department of Economics
and Business
Pompeu Fabra University
Barcelona, Spain

Xavier Tafunell
Department of Economics
and Business
Pompeu Fabra University
Barcelona, Spain

ISSN 2662-6497 ISSN 2662-6500 (electronic)
Palgrave Studies in Economic History
ISBN 978-3-030-60503-2 ISBN 978-3-030-60504-9 (eBook)
https://doi.org/10.1007/978-3-030-60504-9

Cover illustration: Panther Media GmbH / Alamy Stock Photo

This Palgrave Macmillan imprint is published by the registered company Springer Nature Switzerland AG.
The registered company address is: Gewerbestrasse 11, 6330 Cham, Switzerland

Preface

Has Spain grown in the last two centuries? Yes, a lot. Has Spain converged on its neighbours, the countries of Western Europe? It depends. The time period under consideration is essential. Within the last sixty years convergence has been spectacular. If we go back two centuries or more, not at all. In this book we deal in detail with economic growth and convergence and the permanent tension between the two when assessing historical experience since the industrial revolution. The central issue of the Spanish economy from the late eighteenth century to the early twenty-first century is the convergence or divergence with respect to the Western European pattern.

The basic problem is, of course, that of non-convergence. Despite all the growth, which allows Spain to be much more prosperous than in 1800—twenty times—Spaniards are as far away from their neighbours as they were more than two centuries ago. The torturing sense of "failure" or "backwardness" has dominated generations of Spaniards. From the romantics to the regenerationists, from the right to the left, from the capitals to the peripherals, and for many economic historians from all around, the question remains: why has Spain not come to homologate to Western Europe? Our judgement will be nuanced, as there have been periods of strong convergence. We aim to clarify which policies have not helped to converge, and which ones have. Our main characters are five: institutional change, capital formation (physical and human), structural change, internationalization and State action. All these factors and trends force attention to be drawn to the economic policies deployed throughout the modern age and force a chronological approach, because human action unfolds over time.

We propose, indeed, a rigorously chronological journey through the economic history of modern Spain, always with an eye opened to what happens in the international economy. Chapter 1, "The Economic Growth of Spain: A Very Long-Term Perspective", is dedicated to a long-term overview, and justifies our chronology. The rest is the temporary flow of the economy. The chapters on the first periods—Chap. 2, "From Empire to Peripheral Economy (1789–1840)", during the crisis of the Old Regime and the Liberal Revolution; and Chap. 3, "The Impact of European Industrialization: the Double Failure of Agrarian and Industrial Strategies (1840–1890)"—are longer, in line with the chronological framework considered—about fifty years each. From 1890, the next half century, until the outbreak of the Civil War, is covered with two other chapters of similar length and chronological spread: Chap. 4, "Spain in the First Economic Globalization (1890–1914)"; and Chap. 5, "The Spanish Economy During Great War and Interwar Years (1914–1936)". The next five chapters study shorter periods, between eight and fifteen years long, from 1936 until 1998: Chap. 6, "The Isolation from the International Economy: Civil War and Autarky (1936–1951)"; Chap. 7, "Import Substitution Industrialization (1951–1959)", Chap. 8, "Spain in the Golden Age: Reintegration into the International Economy (1960–1973)"; Chap. 9, "Economic Crisis and Political Transition (1973–1985)"; and Chap. 10, "Integration into the European Economy (1986–1998)". The last piece of the chronological sequence is longer as it deals with the twenty years of the Spanish economy without monetary sovereignty, which is dealt with in Chap. 11, "Spain in the Euro Area (1999–2017)". The final chapter, Chap. 12, "Balance of Two Centuries: Growth Engines and Economic Policies", formulates a balance of long-term results in terms of growth factors and economic policies. It includes a reminder of our main interpretative lines: the importance of commercial policy—as the greater the opening the better the performance of the Spanish economy—and the importance of State's action as a propellant or brake of growth, depending on its financial equilibrium. Monetary policy has a crucial role in addressing the recurrence of twin deficits. A final consideration is made on the distributional impact of Spanish growth and policies and we close with a reminder of institutional changes along the whole time span considered, from Empire to globalization.

To give coherence to the temporal sequence, we have prepared a quantitative appendix with twenty-four very significant macroeconomic series to which we repeatedly resort, such as GDP per capita, prices, investment quota and degree of openness, to name a few, that in some occasions are compared with most of Western Europe (those countries that for the years before 2004—the East enlargement—formed the European Union). In economic history this information is continually being reworked, but in the Spanish case it has acquired an enviable solidity that allows us to bet on the stability of the overall vision. The changes may come—and are coming—from the international coupling of the Spanish experience. Indeed, we underline that the economic history of modern Spain is forged in the collapse of the American empire, and that this starting point, of an intrinsically international nature, is essential to understand everything that happens later, as is the industrial revolution and the subsequent diffusion of industrialization, the first economic globalization, the great world wars of the first half of the twentieth century and the strong trend towards economic isolation, the impact of European economic growth and integration or the strong economic globalization in which we are fully immersed and that completely conditions the future of the Spanish economy. Between that great imperial space, completely protected, and this current world space in which distance barely counts, all parameters have changed, starting with the fundamental represented by the change of expectations about what the future can hold for us. All these great historical phenomena require a better fitting of the Spanish economic history into the European and world economic history. It is worth mentioning that the comparison with the average world experience provides the more optimistic comparative assessment of long-term economic performance, even if this new-century developments are disappointing for Spain.

Our text is focused on the presentation of the economic history of Spain in response to the challenges that have seemed central to us, namely economic growth and convergence or divergence. We have been interested in the mechanisms that drive growth and the problems of economic stability that can derail growth policies such as the price level, the public finances, the foreign sector and the market for factors. This does not mean that we despise other themes, quite the contrary. In several cases we have left them aside because there were very satisfactory texts already available. This is the case, for instance, regarding the regional approach and the sectoral approach. For the regional we have a complete regional economic history of Spain, in addition to other works on similar themes.[1] We have consciously set aside this approach, mentioning it only briefly at some relevant moments and in some bibliographical notes. The studies on sectors, both agricultural and industrial, have been numerous and of high quality, as is the case, for example, of the Industrial Atlas of Spain and the huge literature on agrarian history.[2] In our text we have focused our attention on specific sectors only according on the intensity of the contribution of each sector—whether positive or negative—to growth and stability. Nor have we incorporated more than exceptionally business history, which enjoys excellent academic health reflected in texts such as a business history of Spain using a regional approach.[3]

Inevitably, we concur with other texts that aspire to cover the same field and in the same language. Those of Joseph Harrison (1978), Nicolás Sánchez-Albornoz, ed. (1987), Pablo Martín Aceña and James Simpson, eds. (1995), David Ringrose (1996), Gabriel Tortella (2000) and Joseph Harrison and David Corkill (2004) are particularly significant.[4] We offer our point of view and our content organization, but we have taken them fully into account in our more chronological argument. The reader will not find everything he or she would like to know about the economic history of modern Spain. The bibliographical essays at the end of each chapter offer some indications of where you can continue studying and learning,

[1] Luis Germán, Enrique Llopis, Jordi Maluquer de Motes & Santiago Zapata, eds., *Historia económica regional de España. Siglos XIX y XX*, Editorial Crítica, 2001, and Alfonso Díez-Minguela, Julio Martínez-Galarraga and Daniel A. Tirado-Fabregat, *Regional inequality in Spain: 1860–2015*, Palgrave Macmillan, 2018.

[2] Jordi Nadal, Josep Maria Benaül & Carles Sudrià, dirs., *Atlas de la industrialización de España, 1750–2000*, Fundación BBVA y Editorial Crítica, 2003. Both industrial history and agrarian history have well established specialized academic journals: *Revista de Historia Industrial* and *Historia Agraria*.

[3] José Luis García Ruiz & Carles Manera, dirs., *Historia empresarial de España. Un enfoque regional en profundidad*, Editorial LID, 2006.

[4] Joseph Harrison, *An economic history of modern Spain*, Manchester University Press, 1978, Nicolás Sánchez-Albornoz, ed., *Economic modernization of Spain, 1830–1930*, New York University Press, 1987, Pablo Martín-Aceña and James Simpson, eds., *The economic development of Spain since 1870*, Edward Elgar, 1995, David R. Ringrose, *Spain, Europe and the "Spanish Miracle", 1700–1900*, Cambridge University Press, 1996, Gabriel Tortella, *The development of Modern Spain: an economic history of the nineteenth and twentieth centuries*, Harvard University Press, 2000 and Joseph Harrison and David Corkill, *Spain: a modern european economy*, Ashgate, 2004.

especially in those areas that are being subject of intense research such as territorial inequality or inequality in income distribution. In both cases we acknowledge the main contributions that are being published in major international journals of economic history, but we do not introduce them in our central argument. On the other hand, and from many points of view our book is complementary to that of Leandro Prados de la Escosura, *Spanish Economic Growth, 1850–2015*, 2017 in this same publisher and collection.[5] The continuous production of new data, new series or updated series by Leandro Prados de la Escosura has challenged and inspired us and we have provided interpretative frameworks in which to fit, explain and make sense of his systematic historical quantification. Many other colleagues have produced extremely valuable research or synthesis, and we refer to them in our bibliographical essays.

The book is intended for a non-expert audience. We have shunned the erudition—the book is not annotated—and the debates, except in some sections that report and assess the different existing interpretations on particularly controversial aspects that have continued to be so despite the new research carried out. As there is a longer version of the original edition in Spanish, we have shortened the contents on which we could not be as conclusive as in the basic convergence/divergence scheme and its causes, or that were less relevant to this object. We have also compacted the texts, tables and figures, lightening them whenever possible. The contents of first and last chapters have been reorganized.

The authors have always been committed to propose to the readers new visions of the economic past of Spain based on the principle of quantitative and chronological continuity between the remote past and the more recent experience, even if they seem so distant to be incomparable. We are convinced of the possibility and the need for comparison over time, which is our basic task as historians of the economy. The problem of falling from imperial power to economic backwardness and the quest for modernization from the late eighteenth century to the early twenty-first is fascinating and a permanent issue for reflection for the Spanish society and for other societies. We hope that the interpretations we present, which we believe are widely shared, form the basis of educated opinion. Moreover, we aspire that certain interpretations that we think are not well founded, will be

[5] Leandro Prados de la Escosura, *Spanish economic growth, 1850–2015*, Palgrave Macmillan, Palgrave Studies in Economic History, 2017.

cornered. Progress consists in abandoning wrong beliefs even more than adopting new, sounder, beliefs. For all these reasons, we have found it essential to take our history to the most recent possible past even at the risk of not properly interpreting this reality of which we are all contemporary; that is, at the risk of being rectified by the historians of tomorrow. It is unavoidable to run the story of the transformation experienced by the Spanish economy from the dawn of the modern era to the present, without a solution of continuity.

The original Spanish text was completed early 2018. Nothing special was to be changed even by early 2020 when we completed the English version, but the coronavirus pandemics has changed everything, putting a sudden stop to the undergoing trends. The Spanish economy, as many others around the world, has been obliged to interrupt or reduce its activity for an unknown period of time. We should recognize that our book displays Spanish economic history up to the very recent present, but that we are entering into a completely different epoch.

We are very grateful for the support received by Professor Kent Deng, director of the Palgrave Studies in Economic History, and by the editorial staff, as well as the excellent suggestions received from two anonymous referees.

Barcelona, Spain
April 2020

Albert Carreras
Xavier Tafunell

Contents

List of Figures

List of Tables

CHAPTER 1

The Economic Growth of Spain: A Very Long-Term Perspective

This chapter offers the reader two introductory pieces to the whole book: a geographical overview of the natural constraints of the country, and a quantitative overview of the process of economic growth experienced by Spain over the last three centuries. The quantitative overview starts by examining the growth patterns of the Spanish population. It then shows what has been, in broad terms, the economic evolution of the country in the very long term, resorting to GDP per capita, and its comparative performance taking, first, Western Europe as a standard, and afterwards, the whole world. Later on it pays attention to alternative measures of well-being, as heights and human development. A final section of the chapter is devoted to the long-term movements of the basic nominal variables: prices and exchange rates, as well as their fundamental determinant, the quantity of money.

Of course, it would be possible to use a much larger number of economic indicators to decipher the long-term evolution of the Spanish economy. Nevertheless, we do not do that here so as not to overload this chapter. In the remaining chapters of the book, other indicators will be used to analyse the successive stages of the Spanish economy, where the emphasis will be on the cyclical and conjunctural component, always in comparative perspective.

A. Carreras, X. Tafunell, *Between Empire and Globalization*, Palgrave Studies in Economic History,
https://doi.org/10.1007/978-3-030-60504-9_1

1 The Natural Constraints

It is not possible to fully understand how a particular economy has developed in modern times by decontextualizing it from its natural environment; especially for the more or less distant past, given the predominantly agrarian character of economic activity. The physical environment has conditioned the economic possibilities of countries and regions. It is clear that the degree of economic development achieved by each of them has not depended exclusively or mainly on natural conditions. To argue otherwise would be to defend a crude geographical determinism, which economic history has long since overcome. The list of nations that, being rich or very rich in natural resources, are not part of the most advanced group of economies is very long. It is equally easy to invoke the economic success stories of countries that are very poor in natural resources. This does not deny the importance of geographical elements. The endowment of natural resources and the ease of transport and communication depend on the characteristics of the natural environment.

An understanding of these features, however elementary, requires considering five different aspects: the geographical situation of the Peninsula; the relief and natural communications; the climate and hydrography; the conditions of the soil and its agricultural use, and, finally, the characteristics of the subsoil. We will devote a couple of paragraphs to each of these aspects. Our main conclusions are the following. The physical environment has clearly played against the economic development of Spain, in comparison with the rest of Europe (and the United States). The unfavourable natural conditions of the peninsular territory, in terms of physical relief and climate, have been a basic cause of the relative poverty of Spanish agriculture and the deficient system of transport and communications. The extremely peripheral geographical position of the Peninsula has kept Spain apart from the main economic flows and networks established among Western European countries. For all these reasons, it is difficult to refute that the physical conditions have to do with Spain's economic backwardness in relation to Western Europe.

The geographical location of the Iberian Peninsula within the European continent is unique. Two opposing forces have acted. One of them entails a natural tendency to isolation; the other provides stimuli to the relationship with the outside world. In some historical periods the first has dominated, while in others the opposite has occurred. However, both are not equally important. The force that drives isolation has been more powerful.

The propensity to isolation is given by the very eccentric position of the Peninsula within the European continent. It's at one end. And it is at a double extreme: it is the southernmost of the European territories (apart from some islands) and at the same time it is the most western (again, apart from some island countries: Iceland and Ireland). It is difficult to exaggerate the importance of this fact, which is still a factor of marginalization today. Spain is very far from the heart of Europe, which is situated between the Netherlands and the Po Valley and is linked to the Rhine. Such a great distance from the epicentre of transport, commercial, financial and exchange networks of all kinds has deprived Spain of invaluable possibilities for economic development. Moreover, this markedly peripheral geographical position is strongly accentuated by the difficult connection of the Peninsula with the Continent. The strip of territory that acts as a link is crossed from one end to the other by the Pyrenees, a mountain range that represents a formidable natural barrier. It has no transversal valleys, it only loses height at the ends and it does not consist of a single mountain alignment but of several parallel ones. The Pyrenees have clearly been a wall that has made the transit of goods and people between the Peninsula and the rest of Europe extremely difficult.

However, the geographical situation of the Peninsula has stimulated the relationship of its inhabitants with the outside world. The Peninsula is the natural bridge between two continents—Europe and Africa—as recent waves of North African and sub-Saharan immigrants remind us. It is also the bridge between the Mediterranean Sea and the Atlantic Ocean. Spain is literally the gateway to the Mediterranean—the only one in existence, until the opening of the Suez Canal in 1869. Spain's geographical location is strategic, or, what is the same, especially favourable for its inhabitants to maintain relations with other peoples by sea. Its markedly peninsular character contributes to this: it has almost 4,000 kilometres of coastline, not counting the island territories. Greater historical importance has had its natural advantage in transatlantic communications. The southwest coast of Spain is part of one of the natural navigation circuits of the Ocean, circuits that are marked by the direction of the marine currents and the dominant winds. If this is added to the geographical position, it is understandable that Portugal and Spain exercised an overwhelming leadership in the discovery and conquest of West Africa and the Americas.

Regarding the relief and its impact on internal transport, the Peninsula, on a morphological level, can be described as a complex physical unit made up of several pieces poorly assembled together. It is dominated by a large central plateau—the *Meseta*—, around which there are many areas that are difficult to fit together. The *Meseta* is isolated from the two great coastal depressions—the Ebro and the Guadalquivir—by two remarkable mountain ranges—Iberian System and Sierra Morena—that form a belt. Between the *Meseta* and the Cantabrian coast there is a colossal wall: the Cantabrian range. In turn, the *Meseta* is divided into two parts by another respectable mountain range, the Central System. That is not all, since between the different areas of the periphery there are great natural barriers. In summary, and without going into greater detail, the Spanish territory is characterized by its great orographic complexity and by a very abrupt and rugged relief. The mountainous alignments have a wide spatial development and high peaks abound. The topography of Spain is radically different from the topography of continental Europe, which is characterized by very extensive plains at a height close to sea level. The dominant feature, at the orographic level, of the Continent is the great plain that extends from Atlantic France to the Urals in Russia, north of the monumental mountain range of the Alps. The contrast with the relief of the Spanish territory is absolute.

Obviously, this makes communication between the interior and exterior of Spain very difficult, as well as between some geographical regions. With the outside because the country is surrounded almost entirely by mountain ranges that unfold longitudinally on the periphery, leaving a very limited space for the coastal plains. The contrast could not be more marked with the European continent. The various regions are generally separated by great physical obstacles. Natural communication routes are limited to corridors through narrow valleys or, often, mountain passes. The road network has been greatly conditioned by such harsh physical constraints: the national road and rail networks follow in large part the old Roman roads (Spaniards only partially freed themselves from this yoke with the current network of motorways and highways, by means of very expensive engineering constructions, without counting, of course, the extraordinary liberation represented by air navigation). Transport and communication routes have had to be adapted to the tortuous relief, seeking the easiest access and passage through the mountain ranges. Having to cross mountain systems, the movement of people and goods was slow and very costly. This is why an integrated internal market did not exist until much later than in most European countries.

The climate is, together with the relief, the physical factor that most influences the possibilities of agricultural exploitation of the soil. There are three determining climatic elements: temperature, degree of sunshine and rainfall. Of these, the third is the critical factor. Agricultural yields depend directly on the amount of rainfall and its distribution throughout the year. Wet Spain occupies a small part of the territory, less than a quarter of it. The wetlands that are particularly suitable for agricultural use are highly concentrated spatially: they are all located, with the exception of the most mountainous areas, in a narrow northern strip that stretches from Galicia to the Basque Country, and does not extend further south in the Cantabrian mountain range. Practically all the rest of Spain belongs to the dry Spain. The amount of rain that falls there is not only insufficient, but it is also distributed very unevenly throughout the year. The latter marks a fundamental difference with most of the European continent. While the most humid Europe receives rain uniformly throughout the year and in Central Europe it is concentrated in the hottest months, Spain, with the exception of the Cantabrian coast, suffers an acute drought in the summer months. The rain that irrigates its soil often falls in a few downpours. There is another difference added to the previous one, determining both the aridity of the soil: the temperature and the degree of sunshine. In almost all the Spanish territory the cloudiness is very scarce. The latter is caused by the peripheral mountain barriers, which prevent the masses of humid and warm air coming from the Atlantic from penetrating inland. The result is a very high degree of sunshine and, in the interior, a great thermal amplitude. In summer the temperatures are usually very high and in winter the cold is severe. The sunshine provides a very important absolute advantage for the tourist activity, but on the other hand it means a serious disadvantage for agriculture.

The climate, together with the relief, determines the hydrographic regime. Spanish rivers are generally torrential and their beds are usually narrow. Their flow, besides being scarce, is tremendously variable, which logically derives from the rainfall regime. The torrential nature, which is a consequence of the fact that a large part of their course runs through mountainous areas, makes the rivers unsuitable for agriculture and unsuitable for use as waterways. The encasement of the river beds makes irrigation very difficult. The irregularities and inadequacies of the flow prevent navigation. It is important to emphasize that Spain does not have, in any way, the minimum natural conditions indispensable for the creation of a river communication network. It is inevitable to recall at this point that naturally navigable rivers and canals were the means by which the most advanced industrial countries provided themselves with an efficient and cheap transport and communication system before the railway era. It is true that the hydrographic regime has not in all circumstances entailed a major disadvantage. From the energy point of view, the relief and the hydrographic regime have given Spain a relatively privileged situation: a good natural endowment for the production of electricity from hydraulic sources.

We have pointed out that the climate and topography impose harsh conditions on the agricultural exploitation of the soil. Let us look at this issue—the land and its potential agricultural use—a little more closely. The main conditioner is the aridity of the soil. In most of the Spanish territory there are several months of land humidity deficit. This deficit derives from the combination of the level of rainfall and water losses caused by evaporation, which in turn are basically given by the average temperature and altitude. Spain is clearly at the margin of the great European fertile area, which coincides with that of the great plain. Moreover, it is in a worse situation than other countries in the Mediterranean basin. Portugal and Italy are much less arid territories.

The deficit of humidity in the Spanish lands is such that it entails a very low natural fertility, hardly counterbalanced by the most recent technical advances, such as artificial irrigation, thermal protection, etc. The agricultural yields of the crops that have historically been predominant—dryland cereals—are still significantly lower today than in almost all European countries. Agriculture is still poor today where—inland—temperatures in winter are low. The more temperate places—the Mediterranean coast, the Guadalquivir valley—have been able to escape the agricultural poverty resulting from the natural aridity of the land. They have had the appropriate natural conditions to devote it to Mediterranean tree or shrub crops—vineyards, olive groves, fruit trees—or, if they have had irrigation, to irrigated vegetables, tubers and cereals.

Nature has been more generous to Spain in the resources it has accumulated in the subsoil. At least the country is, or has been, well endowed with the metallic minerals (lead, iron, mercury, copper) most used in the first industrialization. It lacks, however, the minerals of the second industrial revolution (oil, bauxite, nickel, chrome, silicon, etc.), and has suffered from the shortage of the key non-metallic mineral of the first: coal. We are not going to go into the history of mining now. We will do so at the right time, when we will analyse the challenges of industrialization. The point here is simply to take a quick stock of the relative endowment of natural resources and to set out the physical constraints on the exploitation of mining reserves.

Taking stock of mining, in global terms, is more complicated than in the case of agriculture, since if we refer to the last two centuries, the situation is clearly ambivalent. On the one hand, Spain benefited from the extraordinary reserves of metallic minerals it possessed. But, on the other hand, Spanish industrial development was seriously slowed down and delayed by the shortage of abundant and good quality coal. In addition, the physical configuration of the Peninsula did not generally favour mining. The tectonics, that is, the geological evolution of the Peninsula, has resulted in mining being almost always difficult and expensive. In the same way, and for the same reason that the relief of the ground is very rugged and tortuous, so is the subsoil. Foldings and faults abound, often on a large scale. As a result, the veins of the minerals being mined are often vertical or very steep, as well as fragmented. The minerals therefore contain many impurities and are difficult to extract.

2 The Demographic Transition

In the European context, Spain is still a relatively sparsely populated country. The demographic shortage is a genuinely historical product: it is the result of mediocre and late economic development. Comparative historical experience shows that, with a few exceptions such as France, the process of industrialization was accompanied by a strong and sustained expansion of the population, a "demographic explosion". If Spain has not known it, it is precisely because its economic modernization took place slowly and with a great delay with respect to most of the surrounding nations.

Table 1.1 shows the magnitudes and rates of population growth. The population has increased more than sixfold in the last three centuries (between 1717 and 2017). The rise has been progressively accelerated. From an annual rate of increase of 0.47% in the eighteenth century, it rose to 0.52% in the nineteenth century, to reach 0.83% in the twentieth, extending it to 2017. Is this little or much? The answer is: rather little. The Spanish population increased at approximately the same rate as the continent as a whole throughout the eighteenth century, but it lagged behind markedly in the nineteenth century (the European population grew at an annual rate of 0.76%). In the twentieth century (extended to 2017) the opposite has happened, Spain has been demographically more

Table 1.1 Spanish population, 1717–2017

Years	*Population (thousand)*	*Annual growth rate (%)*	*Annual growth rate (%)*
1717	7500		
1787	10,393	0.47	1717–1787: 0.47
1821	11,662	0.34	
1857	15,463	0.79	
1900	18,584	0.38	1787–1900: 0.52
1930	23,583	0.75	
1950	28,000	0.64	
1970	33,878	0.98	
1981	37,764	1.02	
2001	40,766	0.36	
2017	46,549	0.82	1900–2017: 0.83

Note: Growth rates are measured by exponential adjustment, except before 1857, when they are among the pairs of known values

Source: From 1850 onwards, Appendix, column 1. Before: R. Nicolau (2005): "Población, salud y actividad", in A. Carreras and X. Tafunell (coords.), *Estadísticas históricas de España. Siglos XIX y XX*, Madrid, Fundación BBVA, vol.1, and V. Pérez Moreda (1988): "La población española", in M. Artola (dir.): *Enciclopedia de historia de España*, vol. 1: *Economía. Sociedad*, Madrid, Alianza

dynamic than Europe as a whole. However, from a comparative perspective, the acceleration of the twentieth century has not compensated for the relative stagnation of the nineteenth century. Spain did not experience a "demographic explosion" like that experienced by other European countries at the time of their industrial revolution. What most closely resembles the explosive population growth that Spain has experienced is the boom of the first decade of the twenty-first century, caused by a massive influx of immigrants that swelled the population by nearly five million.

What are the causes of the remarkable moderation and gradualness of the growth of the Spanish population until the end of the twentieth century? The causes can be summarized in one: the delay of the demographic transition. If the Spanish population increased slightly during the course of the nineteenth century, it was because the mortality rate remained at very high levels, the highest in all of Western Europe. As G. Tortella has pointed out, the main factors involved were those characteristic of a situation of economic underdevelopment: an insufficient and deficient diet; unhealthy housing; and serious deficiencies in private and public hygiene. With regard to the first aspect, we must bear in mind that the backwardness of agriculture condemned the Spanish people to suffer periodically from extreme shortages of basic foods. In each decade of the nineteenth century the Spanish suffered the ravages of the notorious subsistence crises. Malnutrition of the population was aggravated in the years of bad harvests, which favoured the transmission of infectious diseases. The other two factors mentioned above also contributed strongly to the spread of pathogens. The public supply of drinking water and the efficient disposal of waste water through adequate sewage infrastructure are of crucial importance in combating them. In the nineteenth century, public administrations did not invest enough in water and sewage networks; even less in health services, even in such basic areas as preventive vaccination against diseases that were the main causes of infant mortality. In short, throughout the nineteenth century Spain remained almost on the sidelines of the progress made by other nations in the fight against death.

The consequence was a late demographic modernization. As is known, historically this has consisted of a radical change in the patterns of the two vital variables—fertility and mortality. Populations under the old regime are characterized by high mortality and birth rates. As a result, they experience extremely weak long-term vegetative growth. Modern populations have extremely low vital rates. Consequently, natural population growth is equally low, or even non-existent (zero or negative). Historical experience tells us that, sooner or later, all societies end up moving from the first state to the second. In the process of transition, called "demographic transition", the mortality rate is drastically reduced—first, by the fall and disappearance of catastrophic mortality; then, by the gradual decrease of ordinary mortality, especially exogenous child mortality. The birth rate adjusts with delay to the secular decline in mortality, through the diffusion of voluntary mass fertility control. The time lag between the secular decline in both rates is what causes very strong population growth.

The starting point of the demographic transition in Spain can be dated to the last five years of the nineteenth century. As shown in Fig. 1.1, from that time onwards there was a trend towards a continuous decrease in the mortality rate. The most demographically (and economically) advanced countries had entered it a century or more ago. Reaching demographic modernization so late will mean burning out stages quickly, as the figure reveals. During the first third of the twentieth century, the mortality rate fell by nearly 40%. It went from a level of 27.9 per thousand to 17.2 per thousand, an extraordinary advance. It translated into an increase of more than 15 years in the average life span. After the Civil War, in a couple of

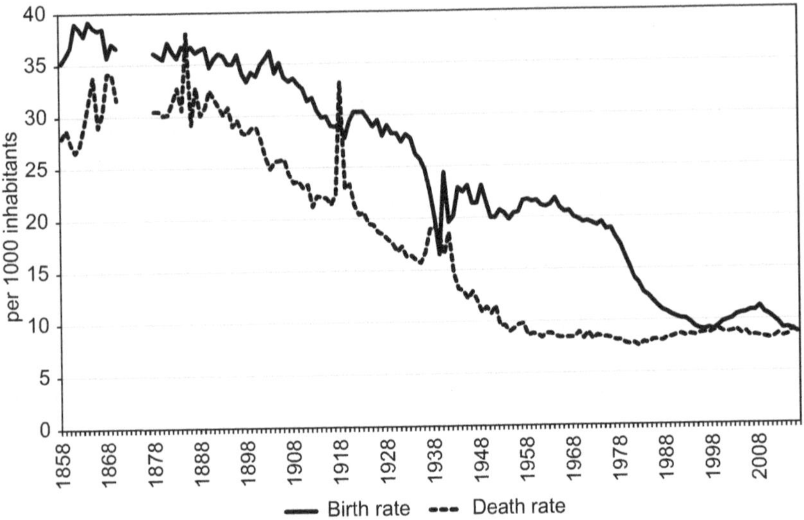

Fig. 1.1 Birth and death gross rates, 1858–2016. *Sources*: R. Nicolau (2005): "Población, salud y actividad", in A. Carreras and X. Tafunell (coords.): *Estadísticas históricas de España. Siglos XIX y XX*. Bilbao: Fundación BBVA, vol.1, and own preparation based on INE data

decades, the mortality rate would again be reduced by half, adding twenty years to life expectancy at birth. This gain is surprising, since it occurred during a period of serious difficulties for the Spanish economy. Advances in medical care and in the spread of sulphonamides and antibiotics were decisive. Since then, progress has been slower, although it has not stopped until the present.

The most distinctive feature of the Spanish demographic transition is that the secular decline in the death rate began almost simultaneously with the decline in the death rate, with hardly any gap between the two trends (see Fig. 1.1). During the first two decades of the twentieth century, there was a slight decrease in the drop in the birth rate. Then, until the eve of the Civil War, the decline was more pronounced. This reduction in fertility was linked to the advance in the process of urbanization of the population and the emigration from the countryside experienced by Spanish society in the interwar period. The decline in the birth rate accelerated during the years of the civil conflict and the immediate post-war period, which must be attributed to the exceptional circumstances caused by the conflict. Once this situation was overcome, it did not return to the previous levels, but the downward trend in the birth rate was interrupted for a very long period: between 1941 and 1976 it remained stationary at relatively high levels (around 21 per thousand). This is a new peculiarity of the Spanish demographic transition. The abnormal pattern of Spanish fertility disappeared abruptly in the last quarter of the twentieth century. With the advent of the current democracy it collapsed, reaching in a few years very low levels, completely comparable to those of the rest of the Western European countries. As the birth rate rapidly approached the death rate, vegetative growth slowed down sharply. Table 1.1 shows the slowdown in the last two decades of the twentieth century. In short, around 1980 Spain completed the process of demographic transition initiated when the nineteenth century was about to end. The rise in the birth rate—and also the slightest drop in the death rate—that has taken place since 1999, caused by the massive arrival of immigrants, will hardly open a new page in the process of demographic modernization.

3 The Increase in GDP and GDP Per Capita: A Comparative Perspective

The history of the European economy over the last two centuries, after the end of the Napoleonic Wars and up to the present day, is dominated by an unprecedented economic expansion. This is what is often referred to as modern economic growth—a notion coined by Kuznets to refer to the process of continuous and self-sustaining increase in per capita income in which industrialization and economic development have materialized. The feature common to all Western countries has indeed been this: per capita GDP has been increasing steadily since the beginning of the nineteenth century (except for setbacks in specific years, either due to war or severe recessions). What interests us now is when Spain was immersed in modern economic growth and with what intensity this process has developed. To do so, we need to look at the secular evolution of Spain's GDP and per capita GDP.

Fortunately, we have a reliable estimate of the Gross Domestic Product since 1850, prepared by Prados de la Escosura, which we reproduce in the statistical appendix (column 3 for GDP; column 4 for GDP per inhabitant). It should be noted that this statistical reconstruction has a similar reliability to that of the existing historical national accounting series on other countries. Before 1850, we have a fascinating estimate of per capita product by Álvarez Nogal and Prados de la Escosura, which goes back to 1280. We will take advantage of their estimate of the century and a half before 1850 to capture as best as possible the moment of the start of economic growth in Spain. These data should be taken with great caution. If we were to give them credit, we could say that Spain did not exceed the maximum per capita GDP reached in the mid-fourteenth century until the third decade of the nineteenth century. In these five centuries only the population would have grown, but not its material well-being. The stagnation hypothesis is corroborated, for the seventeenth and eighteenth centuries, by all the evidence mobilized in recent historiography to characterize the "small divergence" (in contrast to the "great divergence" between Western Europe and the other civilizations) within the same Europe, according to which Spain would be part of the stagnant Europe as opposed to the growing Europe, led by the Netherlands and Great Britain.

In Fig. 1.2 we reproduce both estimates linked as a single series but marking with a vertical dashed line that they are not of the same nature. Also, the figure is crossed vertically by the dividing lines of the periods that we distinguish in the economic history of Spain, to each of which we will dedicate a chapter in this book. We have defined them according to the economic trends that characterize them, the political and institutional framework, the international environment and the relationship of the Spanish economy with the international one and, last but not least, the historiographic tradition.

In the annual series that we represent in the figure since 1787 (and, in Table 1.2, with a previous cut in 1717, to better compare with the demographic trajectory) we can detect that the secular stagnation of the levels of material welfare does not begin to be overcome until the years of the War of Independence (1808–1814). In a twenty-year period, approximately from 1808 to 1827, the GDP per capita grows a little more than 10%, as a result of a strong agrarian expansion, facilitated by the collapse of transhumant cattle farming that freed many pasture lands from the Mesta bonding. A stagnation of some fifteen years followed, but already since the early 1840s, per capita GDP has been gently growing again, reflecting now the first impact of the expansion motivated by the liberal agrarian reform and the first—incipient—steps of industrialization. From 1850 to 1880 there is a significant acceleration that marks a visible

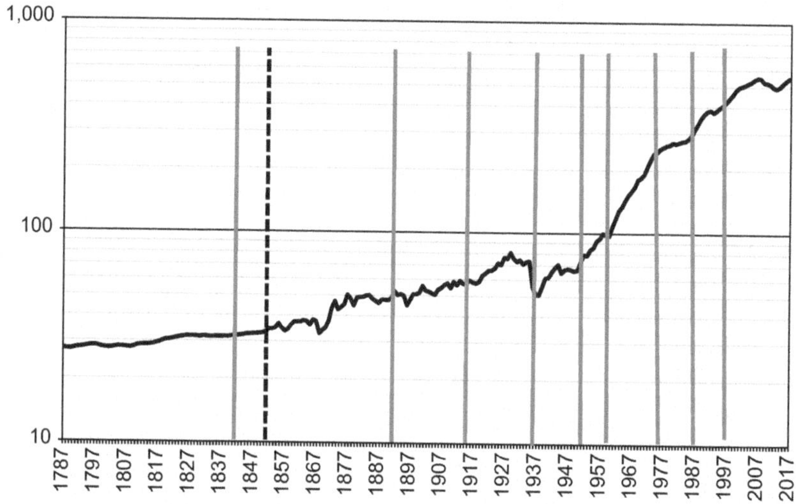

Fig. 1.2 Per capita GDP, 1787–2017. *Note*: The series up to 1850 is a centered moving average of eleven years. This eliminates the strong year-on-year variability of the original data. The vertical dotted line divider remind us of this difference and also that estimation procedures before 1850 are not at all comparable with those after 185. *Sources*: 1787–1850: geometric mean of the three indices calculated by C. Álvarez Nogal and L. Prados de la Escosura (2013): "The Rise and Fall of Spain, 1270–1850", *Economic History Review* (66), 1. Since 1850, Appendix, column 3

turning point in the series (Fig. 1.2). Over the rest of the century—taking it to 1913, which is its true historical end point—GDP and GDP per capita grow at a moderate but persistent rate. During the second long half of the nineteenth century (1850–1913) the Spanish economy expanded, on average, at a rate of 1.4%. The population increase reduces by half a percentage point a rate that was already low, so that the GDP per inhabitant increases every year at a rate of 0.9%. This means that the level of economic well-being of Spaniards more than doubled throughout the entire nineteenth century (1808–1913).

The twentieth century has been a very different story. Between 1913 and 2017, the GDP has grown at an average annual rate of 3.6%, and the GDP per capita of 2.7%, in other words, the Product has multiplied by a factor of 21.4 and the average real income of the Spaniards has multiplied by a factor of 9.3. Contrast these records with those of the previous

Table 1.2 GDP and GDP per capita growth rates, 1717–2017

Years	*GDP growth rates (%)*	*GDP per capita growth rates (%)*
Panel A		
1717–1787	0.6	0.1
1787–1850	0.6	0.3
1850–1913	1.4	0.9
1913–2017	3.6	2.7
Panel B		
1808–1913	1.3	0.7
1850–2017	2.5	1.8
Panel C		
1913–1950	1.0	0.2
1950–1975	6.3	5.3
1975–2017	2.9	2.2
Panel D		
1913–1929	3.0	2.2
1929–1950	0.2	-0.5
2007–2017	-0.1	-0.2

Source: Same as in Fig. 1.2. Growth rates have been calculated based on the linear trend adjusted to the logarithms of the values

century (1808–1913), namely: 3.9 and 2.1, respectively. Obviously, such a spectacular increase in income in the twentieth century is unparalleled. It reflects that Spain became industrialized and achieved a high level of economic development. In the figure above, it is clear that between the nineteenth and twentieth centuries there has been another fundamental difference. In the section of the series prior to 1914 we can easily draw an imaginary trend line, from which the short- and medium-term movements do not deviate too much. The twentieth century has been, in this sense, another story. If the previous one was characterized by its regularity, this one is recognized by the marked discontinuities of the growth process. The stages of great dynamism alternate with others of stagnation. Thus, between 1914 and 1929 the Spanish economy experienced a period of prosperity. It grew each year a little more than twice as much as in the period 1850–1913. The two following decades—from 1930 to 1950—are of completely opposite sign. In this fateful period, the contemporary Spanish disaster took place. In 1950, the GDP barely recovered to the level of 1929. In terms of per capita income the picture was even more bleak: that of 1950—more than ten years after the end of the Civil War—was still 17% lower than that of 1929 (see col. 4 in the appendix). The years between 1930 and 1950 are the longest period in the last century and a half in which Spaniards have suffered a significant decline in their standard of living.

After the disaster, and after the 1950s characterized by recovery and overcoming pre-war levels, came the boom. This is what the propagandists of the Franco regime proclaimed as the Spanish "economic miracle" of the 1960s. A miracle that, interestingly, they recorded in the assets of the dictatorship, ignoring the liabilities that the first Francoism had represented. In fact, more than talking about the Spanish miracle, we must talk about the European post-war miracle. Nevertheless, there is no doubt that the meteoric rise of the Spanish economy was an extraordinary phenomenon. For a quarter of a century, GDP increased annually at a cumulative rate of 6.3% and GDP per capita at 5.3% (see Table 1.2). This meant multiplying the first macro-magnitude by 4.7 and the second by 3.6. The figures are so eloquent that they do not require much further comment. Behind such high rates lies not only the recovery of lost ground during the Spanish "great depression" of 1930–1950. Spain definitely completed its industrialization in this period.

Let us say, finally, to conclude this quick reading of the long-term path of total and per capita product that from 1975 onwards a new stage of less vigorous and more volatile growth was inaugurated. The rate of increase in GDP between 1975 and 2017 (2.9%) may be, at first sight, quite appreciable. What lies behind it (see Fig. 1.2) is a very slow progress in the decade of very hard crisis—1975–1985—a strong expansion between 1986 and 2007 in the heat of the incorporation to the European Community and the euro, and a deep depression between 2008 and 2013, not fully overcome yet by 2019.

Once we have made our mind, broadly speaking, on the long-term macroeconomic development, we should ask ourselves: did the Spanish economy perform similarly to its neighbouring economies? Fortunately, we can find the answer to this fundamental question thanks to estimates by Maddison and Prados de la Escosura, which allow us to calculate the level of Spain's real income in relation to that of other countries, both expressed in 1990 dollars adjusted for purchasing power parity. Based mainly on the series of the first author cited, we have calculated the average income of the countries that made up the European Union before the enlargement to include Eastern European countries (EU-15) for the period 1787–2017 (see Fig. 1.3 and column 5 of the Appendix). We warn the reader to accept this statistical reconstruction with caution, as it is not

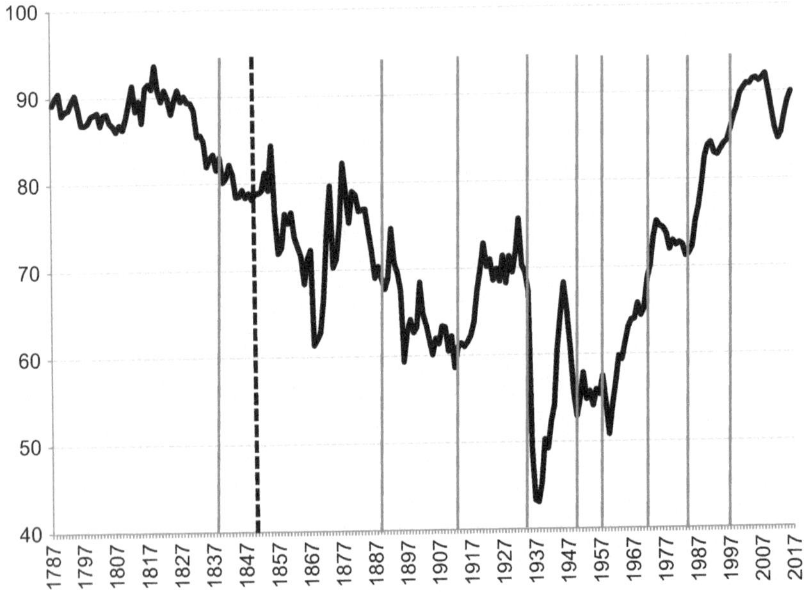

Fig. 1.3 Spain's GDP per capita compared to European Union (EU-15), 1787–2017 (in %). *Sources*: Appendix, Column 5, for the period 1850–2017. Before 1850 is our own estimate based on the Spanish GDP per capita (see Fig. 1.2) and that of an EU restricted to the six national cases for which annual series are available (Netherlands, England, Italy, Sweden, and, since 1820, France and Denmark). The series for the first four nations mentioned up to 1800 have been collected by R. Fouquet and S. Broadberrry (2015): "Seven Centuries of European Growth and Decline", *Journal of Economic Perspectives* (29), 4; for the period after 1800 they are in the Maddison Project database (https://www.rug.nl/ggdc/historicaldevelopment/maddison/). The GDP per capita of this restricted European Union is the ratio of the aggregate GDP and population of the above-mentioned countries, which we have calculated from the data in the above-mentioned databases and, for the population, from B. R. Mitchell (2007): *International Historical Statistics Europe 1750–2000*. New York: Palgrave/Macmillan. We have estimated annual population figures where necessary by means of appropiate exponential interpolations

exempt from certain methodological problems that may distort the results, especially for the period prior to 1850. As in the previous figure, the vertical dashed line alerts us that the two sections of the series are not entirely comparable, while the remaining vertical lines mark the chronological limits of the historical stages the Spanish economy has gone through, as we analyse them in this book.

What lessons can be drawn from this direct measurement of the degree of real convergence of the Spanish economy? The first and fundamental lesson is precisely that it has not converged. At the initial point—at the end of the eighteenth century and in the first thirty years of the nineteenth century—the income of the Spaniards was 10% below the average income of Western Europeans. Afterwards, it has not managed to grow faster than they have in the long term. Today it is at exactly the same level as at the end of the eighteenth century (89.9% in 2017, compared with 90% in 1787–1789). The balance of the two centuries would therefore be that Spain has not have converged at all. This fact is so important that it will be the focus of the analysis that we will develop throughout this work. The entire history of the contemporary Spanish economy must be studied, in our opinion, from the perspective of the difficulties it has faced in order to overcome the state of relative backwardness and its inability to overcome them.

It is necessary to make an important nuance to what we have just stated, regarding the different signs of the different periods. At the risk of oversimplifying—we will clarify this throughout the book—we can say that the divergence concerns the central century and a half. It was from 1820 to 1960, approximately, when Spain's delay was consummated. In its course, the average income of its population declined from a level of around 90% of the average income of Western Europeans to a level that was 43% in the middle of the Civil War, or 51% in 1961, the lowest in peacetime. The second half of the Spanish Twentieth Century and the first years of the new millennium have been characterized by an effort to converge. Unlike the previous century and a half, the effort has not been in vain. But neither has it yielded the desired results. The country's late industrialization has allowed it to converge... halfway. Spain has climbed from the 51% in per capita income in Western Europe to the 92% in 2009, just when the last major crisis was erupting, and then dropped to the 85% in 2014, a level from which it has climbed again in recent years. Covering the remaining percentage points is the challenge of the coming years. The perspective offered by the secular series does not suggest that the gap can be closed soon.

Other interesting lessons about the divergence and convergence alternatives experienced by Spain can be drawn from reading Fig. 1.3. The 1850s and 1870s saw an effort to bring the country closer to European welfare standards. In the early 1880s there was a shift towards a trend of sustained distancing from those standards, which lasted until 1914. In the first half of the twentieth century, the years of World War I and the interwar years seemed to stably correct the trend of divergence with a significant relative advance during the Great War and then a stabilization at a level of 70%, ten points above the pre-conflict level. In that war cycle the level of welfare of the Spanish people did not actually increase, the relative improvement being due to the fact that the welfare of the Europeans decreased. But when the continent recovered the path of growth in the 1920s, Spain managed to consolidate the relative position it had previously achieved. After the collapse of the Civil War, the recovery of the first half of the 1940s was only due to the European collapse during World War II. Its subsequent meteoric recovery brought the Spanish economy back to approximately 55% of the Western European average.

The 1961 minimum was quickly exceeded. The hyper growth registered between 1960 and 1975 paid astonishing dividends in terms of approximating to the levels of well-being of the most developed nations. In spite of this, it did little more than neutralize the dramatic decline of the years 1936–1950. The oil crisis and the imbalances it opened up in the Spanish economy caused practically a decade of regression. Integration into the European Economic Community and then into the euro zone led to almost a quarter of a century of convergence, with a brief pause following the recession of 1992–1993. The crisis that began in 2008, which ended up affecting the Spanish economy more intensely than its European neighbours, meant five years—until 2014—of sharp decline (seven and a half points).

If the causes of the relative backlog were to be briefly stated, the following could be said. The relative stagnation of the nineteenth century, from shortly after the end of the Napoleonic Wars to the eve of the First World War, was caused by the difficult adaptation to the loss of the colonies combined with the slow agony of the State of the Old Regime. In its journey from "Empire to Nation", following Prados de la Escosura, Spain did not succeed in finding the path of modernization easily and entered the industrialization race with a bad foot. The agrarian bet, pretty intense, did not give the expected results. The industrial bet, timid, could not give them. When the first globalization arrived, Spain bet, with great internal consensus, on the reinforcement of protectionism and economic nationalism, which accentuated the backwardness. During the years 1936–1959, when the country was very closed to the international economy, the backwardness acquired unknown proportions. If the Spanish economy then diverged in a more extreme way than in any other historical moment, it was due to the policy of isolation and asphyxiating intervention applied by the Francoist authorities. There was another time when Spain had to bear the cost of the failures of Franco's economic policy: the decade 1975–1985. In between, from 1960 to 1974, Spain converged at full speed, opening up to the outside world and liberalizing its economy to take advantage of the exceptional momentum of the international economy. The subsequent wave of opening up to the outside world had a more consistent pro-convergence effect. Integration into the European common market provided Spain with opportunities for growth that enabled her to make good much of the relative backwardness she had been suffering since the time of the industrial revolution. The second globalization has offered additional opportunities, but at the same time constitutes a threatening environment for the Spanish economy.

4 The Spanish Economy between Empire and Globalization: Another Comparative Perspective

In the last three decades the world has witnessed the triumph of the second globalization. It was the result of the set of liberal measures that were imposed on the Western world, and which also impacted on the Soviet bloc and China, creating a new international economic environment that is much more conducive to market expansion. This makes it necessary to place the Spanish economic history in this global context. The following figure fulfils this objective. The available data allow us to make a comparative analysis over several centuries. The statistical information produced by economic historians has already provided, since 1820, very significant coverage of the GDP per inhabitant of this planet.

It is easy to detect that the Spanish trajectory has almost always been well above the world average. In fact, it is only below the average during the years of the Civil War, and below the minimum pre-Civil War (the value of 1910) from 1940 to 1960, which confirms the extraordinary nature of the autarkic years. From 1820 to 1935 the trend is slightly downward, but much less than it appears in the comparison with Western Europe. Once the pre-war levels were surpassed in 1961, the Spanish economy—its per capita GDP—would live forty extraordinary years, jumping, in several steps, from 134 to 282% of the world average. The progressive opening up of the Spanish economy to the European and world economy allows it to take full advantage of the development that had taken place outside its borders and to become incorporated, already within the European Economic Community and the European Union, into the successive waves of foreign trade liberalization and the international movements of capital and labour that have fuelled the growth of the world economy after the Second World War.

But the success fades towards the year 2001. Despite continued economic convergence with Western Europe (see Fig. 1.3), the possibility of further growth above the world average is running out. Since the beginning of the twenty-first century, the world average per capita GDP has been growing much faster than in Spain. That level 282 is reduced in 2016 to 211 (26% lower), which is not bad at all, but it is a vivid image of what the rise of China and the emerging economies is bringing to the economies of the European Union. Already before the start of the depression in 2008, they had lost 31 percentage points. In fact, the trajectory since 2001 barely makes it possible to distinguish either the great recession of 2008 or the euro crisis. This would be a powerful convergence phenomenon never seen before, but now with respect to Spanish GDP per capita levels. Certainly, the crisis has accelerated it, but not by much. If the Great recession and the crisis in the Eurozone have meant that the push for integration into the Euro has been exhausted, globalization has meant the evaporation of the advantages of all kinds obtained through entry into the European Economic Community. The comparative level with respect to the world average in 2016 is almost the same-something lower-than that which the Spanish had in 1986. A hammer blow (Fig. 1.4).

While most of the following text is devoted to understanding the patterns of divergence and convergence of the Spanish economy with Western Europe, we also call the attention on the sustainability of the advances made with respect to the world average. During the first globalization (see Chap. 4) Spain missed opportunities for convergence, especially visible in the comparison with Western Europe. The second globalization has been more forceful. European integration has allowed for excellent performance until the turn of the century, but afterwards the impetus of the emerging countries has completely changed the pattern of comparison. Spain maintains a comfortable cushion of advantage over the world average, but has once again moved away from the Western European average. A chill shakes Spain: are we repeating the trajectory of the

Fig. 1.4 Spain's GDP per capita compared to world's, 1820–2017 (in %). *Source*: Appendix, column 6

southern cone—Argentina and Uruguay—a century ago? They went from being among the world's richest countries to declining economically, sometimes faster, sometimes slower, to the world average.

5 Welfare: Looking for Better Assessments of Well-being

The study of the population's well-being should not be limited to real per capita income, or any similar measure derived from the National Accounts. Human welfare is expressed in other areas, which complement and qualify the image that emerges from the income and consumption figures resulting from the calculations of aggregate production of goods and services. In this section we will pay attention to two of the approaches to human welfare most frequently used by economic historians and other social analysts: the average height of the population and the human development index.

5.1 *Stature*

In recent decades anthropometry—the measurement of the human body—has provided very important advances in the description and understanding of the material results of well-being. In the past, we relied solely on demographics (see Sect. 1 in this chapter), which allowed us to understand basic life phenomena. Anthropometry adds the knowledge of the evolution of the human body. The historical study of the heights (of the young, typically when they were carved to fulfil their military obligations) has revolutionized our understanding of the historical evolution of material goods. Heights around the age of nineteen (approximately: the age of carving varied slightly between nineteen and twenty-one, depending on time and country) incorporate information on nutrition, disease, physical effort and rest, synthesizing into a single figure all these factors that are very expressive of material well-being. The information is very massive.

The series corresponding to Spain as a whole in Fig. 1.5 are unofficial but come from the Ministry of Defence, starting in 1953, extended back sixty years by statistical sampling by G. Quiroga. The growth in height that has taken place with notable continuity since after the Civil War, accelerated from 1960, is captured in detail. The more moderate and irregular growth from 1893 to the years of the Second Republic is also detected. A fall caused by the war and the immediate post-war period is perceptible.

The figure also reproduces the series reconstructed by J.M. Martínez-Carrión and J. Puche on five provinces in southeast Spain, which has the virtue of starting much earlier, with the carvings of 1856 (those born in 1837). This series shows that the growth that began in 1893 did not come from an earlier trend. From 1856 to the middle of the last decade of the nineteenth century, the trend was unquestionably towards a reduction in height, a feature confirmed in other local studies, which once again shows that the growth in GDP in those years had to be achieved through greater physical effort—working harder—as in the worst periods of the industrial revolution. It is suggestive to relate this result to the simultaneous fall in the level of studies documented, later on in this book, in Fig. 12.3. Growth that began in the late nineteenth century seems to have been vigorous until the Civil War. The subsequent decline is much more visible in this series and the effects extend into the late 1940s, suggesting that the first post-war period was not suffered equally everywhere.

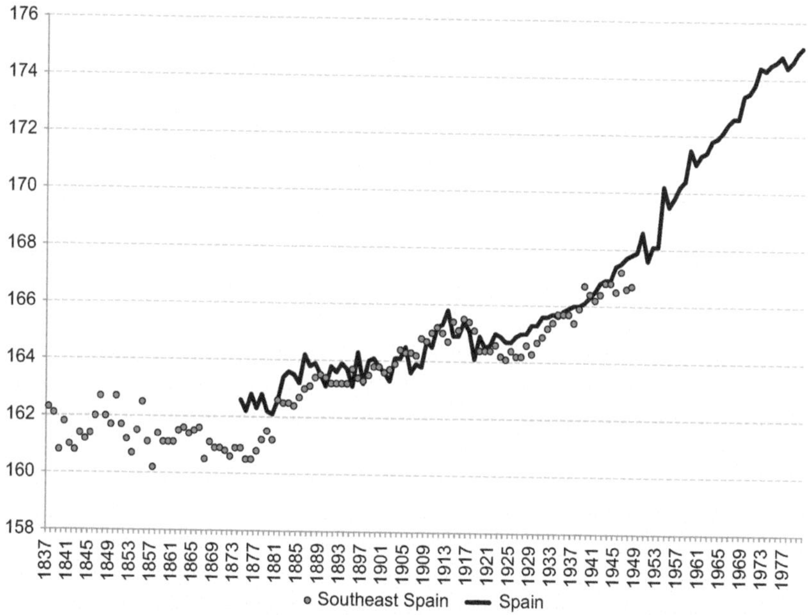

Fig. 1.5 Average height of recruits (in cms.) according to age at recruitment, 1856–1999. *Source*: R. Nicolau (2005): "Población, salud y actividad", in A. Carreras and X. Tafunell (coords.): *Estadísticas históricas de España. Siglos XIX y XX*. Bilbao: Fundación BBVA, vol. 1

The data collected for the eighteenth century point to levels similar to or slightly higher than those of the initial years of the series we have just presented, but with the peculiarity of showing an intense fall, of between two and three centimetres, in the carvings made in the late eighteenth and early nineteenth centuries, including the years of the Napoleonic occupation.

There is nothing that surprises us in the information provided by the statures. The known trends are confirmed, but the diagnosis of a stable or slightly declining nineteenth century height is worrying. It gives an alarm signal about the welfare costs of the first steps of economic growth in Spain-practically all of the nineteenth century. The twentieth century, as already detected in the demographic data, is all bullish (in terms of height and welfare) with the only negative interval being the end of the Civil War and the first decade of the Franco regime.

5.2 *Human Development*

The human development index (HDI), which expands the range of constituent elements of human well-being, has had a great predicament. It not only considers economic well-being, approximated by GDP per capita, but also combines it, with equal weighting, with life expectancy and the degree of literacy of the adult population. Despite all its limitations, the HDI per capita can go beyond GDP. L. Prados de la Escosura has recalculated the HDI, correcting its main operational limitation: as they approached higher levels, they tended to slow down to the point where comparisons were difficult. The new HDHI (human development historical index) solves this problem by valuing absolute increases in variables such as life expectancy and adult literacy. The result, visible in Table 1.3, focuses on the proportions between the Spanish results and those of the EU-15, the USA and the world.

The Spanish HDHI has grown a lot in the long term, and practically without interruption (except for the Civil War). As a relative indicator, the most interesting thing is to compare its trajectory with that of the surrounding countries. Column 2 of Table 1.3 shows the significant progress made in the HDI with respect to Western Europe even in periods of economic divergence. Convergence in the HDHI began in 1913 and lasted until 1933. It starts again in 1950 and will not stop until 1990, when the gap closes completely. If we compare with the world leader—the United States—from which Spain is so far away in terms of GDP per capita, we also observe a complete convergence since 2000. The HDHI shows us a history of resounding success, and shows it even for periods of economic divergence.

Among the features worth highlighting is the fact that Spain's trajectory since 1870 has always been above the world average—and at very similar levels to GDP per capita, as shown in Fig. 1.4, and that the trajectory compared to the EU-15 or the United States has been one of complete convergence. Looking more closely, we can observe that neither in relation to the EU-15 nor in relation to the world there is any relative variation before 1913. Neither convergence with Western Europe nor divergence from the world average. Nor is there any change in relation to the world average between 1925 and 1965. All of these are features that reinforce or nuance some of the indications that we will develop throughout the chronological chapters of the work. The complete convergence in human

Table 1.3 Human development historical index, 1850–2007

Year	*Spain*	*Spain/EU-15 (in %)*	*Spain/USA (in %)*	*Spain/world (in %)*
1850	0.077	59.5	43.3	
1860	0.093	64.1	45.5	
1870	0.100	62.6	45.5	131.7
1880	0.111	62.6	50.9	133.2
1890	0.126	63.0	49.8	132.9
1900	0.140	62.9	49.6	131.1
1913	0.162	63.8	52.5	132.6
1925	0.202	70.9	55.2	143.3
1929	0.229	75.0	59.8	146.1
1933	0.242	76.4	64.6	148.3
1938	0.238	71.0	56.9	128.7
1950	0.296	76.4	62.2	141.1
1955	0.333	79.4	66.4	141.7
1960	0.382	84.9	73.0	145.1
1965	0.414	88.6	73.9	144.7
1970	0.472	94.8	80.9	153.7
1975	0.496	93.6	83.4	153.6
1980	0.528	94.9	85.3	158.2
1985	0.558	96.3	86.2	160.8
1990	0.612	99.5	90.1	166.7
1995	0.666	96.6	91.3	171.7
2000	0.702	96.5	94.7	168.8
2005	0.778	100.1	101.3	173.3
2007	0.802	101.4	103.5	174.3

Source: Own elaboration based on L. Prados de la Escosura (2015) "World human development: 1870–2007", *Review of Income and Wealth*, 61, 2

development with the most advanced countries in the world is worth emphasizing.

The series homogenized by L. Prados de la Escosura goes up to 2007. The United Nations Development Programme (UNDP), deeply inspired by A. Sen, has continued to produce results, and to innovate comparatively. Limiting ourselves to the traditional HDI ranking, the UNDP series alerts us of the deterioration of the Spanish position since 2007. At that time, its position in the international ranking was 15th, just two positions and one thousandth behind the United States. In 2010, which is the following figure, the United States moves up to 4th and Spain moves down to 20th. In 2013, Spain has dropped to 27th position (USA, 5th), where it still is in the index corresponding to 2015 (USA, 10th). Considering that in

2005 Spain had been in 13th position, immediately behind the United States, the deterioration has been significant and matches with the GDP per capita series displayed in Fig. 1.4.

6 Prices, Money and Currency

As is well known, variations in prices have a great influence on productive activity and aggregate demand. So, once it is known, in broad terms, what path GDP and GDP per capita have followed, it is now convenient to know how the fundamental nominal variables (prices, including the exchange rate) have evolved and their main long-term determinant, the quantity of money. The aim is to capture the magnitude of large movements and long-lasting trends. We leave it to the following chapters to observe the situation in more detail.

The Spanish reality of the post Second World War years has encouraged a topical view according to which Spain has always been an inflationary country and has systematically suffered higher inflation than the neighbouring countries. Both clichés are false, as we soon shall see. Inflation affected the Spanish economy only from 1936 onwards, not before. For the rest, Spain has not been a more permanently inflationary country than most advanced countries. If we make a global balance of the twentieth century, the result is that it has been less inflationary than the whole of the European Union (EU-15). We draw the same conclusion if we consider only the first half of the century. Western Europe suffered much more severe inflation during the First World War and the immediate post-war period. It again suffered higher inflation in the 1940s because of the Second World War, despite the inflationary pressures accumulated by the Spanish economy during its civil strife and in the first post-war decade of pure self-sufficiency. The cliché we allude to comes from the fact that the evolution prior to 1950 has been lost sight of. What is certain is that from this date until 2010 prices in Spain have continuously increased more intensely than in most developed nations.

Figure 1.6 provides an overview of price behaviour in a time perspective similar to that of GDP per capita, from 1789 to 2017. It is the consumer price index, although the data with which it has been compiled do not always refer to the same concept of prices of goods and services purchased by consumers.

The beginning of the long nineteenth century (1789–1913) was marked, first, by the intense but brief inflation unleashed by the French

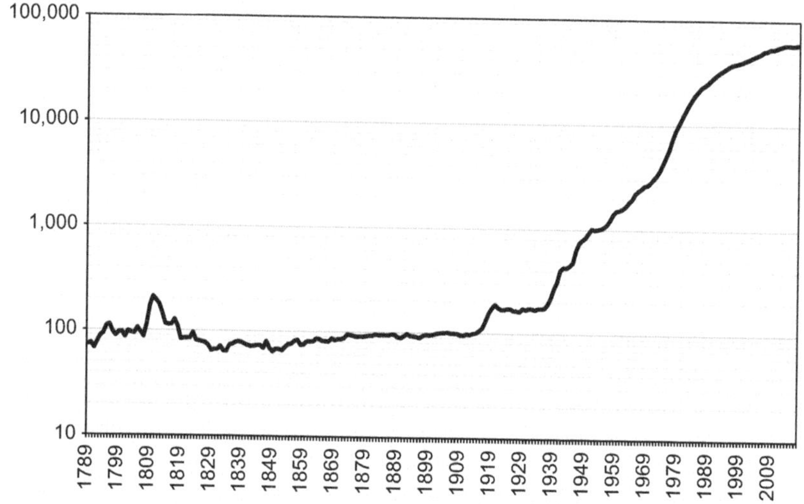

Fig. 1.6 Consumer price index (CPI), 1789–2017 (1913=100). *Source*: Own elaboration based on the data of P. Nogués (2005): "Análisis de la deflación española de la primera mitad del siglo XIX: Una comparación internacional", *Revista de Historia Económica*, 2; J. Maluquer de Motes (2013): *La inflación en España. Un índice de precios de consumo*, 1830–2012. Madrid: Banco de España

occupation; then, by the more intense and prolonged deflation (1812–1830) caused by the loss of the Empire and its sequel of monetary contraction. Once the effects of these depressive forces subsided, an era of long-term price stability was ushered in. The picture that emerges from Fig. 1.6 for the period 1815–1913 is one of almost perfect horizontal secular trend. The price level in 1913 was in fact approximately the same as a century earlier; indeed, it was the same as in 1700. In this respect, Spain did not differ from other neighbouring countries.

The fact that there was no inflation or deflation in the long term did not prevent prices from rising or falling at shorter intervals. The price index represented in the figure shows that prices fluctuated widely. The year-on-year changes were often very sharp. Generally, they developed cyclical movements. The figure also shows that these were more extensive and intense during the first half of the century, which would have to be explained by the economic upheavals caused by the loss of the Empire and by the still overwhelmingly agrarian nature of the national economy.

The First World War was a shock comparable to that of the Napoleonic occupation: prices almost doubled in the space of six years. In Spain, however, the inflationary impact of the conflict was limited. It happened in a short time span and did not trigger an inflationary spiral. In other words, the world war had a mere step effect on prices. It did not alter the nineteenth century dynamic. The period 1920–1935 was dominated by stability.

The radical change took place following another war, that of 1936–1939. Here is the real historical break. In 1936, Spain entered a new era in the history of consumer prices, the defining feature of which is continuous and intense inflation. We can summarize it in one fact: between 1936 and 2017, consumer prices have multiplied 342 times, that is, they have increased at an average annual rate of 7.5%. But some nuances need to be made. The rise has not been linear. Some periods have been more inflationary than others. Table 1.4 provides data adjusted to a periodization that can be perceived from a careful inspection of the figure. The Civil War and autarky caused very intense inflation. The golden age of economic growth in the 1950s and 1960s was characterized by relatively moderate inflation. In contrast, in the 1970s and the first half of the 1980s the

Table 1.4 Consumer price index (CPI) and money supply (M1) average growth rates, 1936–2017 (in %)

Years	*CPI*	*M1*
1936–1951	12.2	14.5
1951–1970	5.4	12.9
1970–1985	15.6	15.3
1985–1998	5.2	9.4
1999–2008	3.3	–
2008–2017	1.1	–

Source: Author's elaboration based on column 20 of the Appendix, and on Carreras and Tafunell (2010): ***Historia económica de la España contemporánea (1789–2009)***. Barcelona: Crítica, column 18 of the Appendix, calculating the rates on the trend adjusted to the logarithms of the values. We do not provide the money supply growth rates for the period after 1998 because they are meaningless following the transfer of monetary sovereignty to the ECB

Spanish economy suffered from sharp price increases that caused serious imbalances and economic problems. Since the mid-1980s there has been a marked disinflation (reduction in the rate of inflation), which has intensified since Spain ceded its monetary sovereignty to the European Central Bank (1998). Twenty years later, the data we have allow us to argue that the evil genie of inflation has finally been locked in the bottle from which it escaped during the Civil War.

What caused such a radical and profound change in the pattern of price evolution since 1936? The answer is simple, if we look at the long-term trends in the main economic variables. The origin of inflation lies in the excessive increase in the amount of money. You don't need to have any particular faith in the monetarist creed to agree that, in the long run, inflation is caused by an increase in money supply greater than the increase in money demand. It is enough to examine the secular series of prices and monetary magnitudes to confirm that the inflation that Spain has suffered since the Civil War is of monetary origin. It was precisely then that it began to have a purely fiduciary monetary pattern. For sixty years, the government was able to use it almost without restriction, which it took full advantage of to finance excess public spending. The appeal to the Bank of Spain by the Treasury led to an excessive growth of the amount of money, causing the intense inflation registered by the price indexes.

Indeed, the money supply (M1) grew at a very moderate rate between 1874 and 1935, except in the context of the First World War. Specifically, between 1874 and 1913 it increased at an annual rate of 1.5%. As GDP grew at the same rate, prices remained stable. In the period 1920–1935 monetary aggregates expanded very little (0.9% per year), less than GDP. As a result, the Spanish economy was subject to deflationary pressures, although these were much less intense than those suffered by most economies. It was only between 1914 and 1920 that the money supply grew unbridled—it was multiplied by 2.5—as a result of the enormous accumulation of foreign reserves thanks to neutrality and also due to the monetization of the public deficit, which overflowed as military expenditure soared and tax revenue fell in real terms. As real output increased very discreetly in those years, the sharp increase in the amount of money led to high inflation.

On the monetary front, the Civil War marked a radical departure from the past. The monetary system broke all ties with the metal—silver—standards. Lacking a nominal anchor, it was subordinated to the financial demands of the Government. The financing of the war tripled the money supply. During almost the entire period of Franco's regime, it continued to expand at a rapid pace (see Table 1.4). Obviously, such excessive money creation had a remarkable, yet differentiated, inflationary impact. During the war and in the 1940s, demand for real balances remained stagnant, due to the economic depression. In contrast, in the 1950s and 1960s there was a very strong economic growth that greatly increased the demand for money. Hence, inflation was much higher in 1936–1951 than in 1951–1970 (see Table 1.4). In the 1970s–1985 monetary expansion accelerated further. This reflects the lax handling of monetary policy by the Spanish authorities in dealing with the public deficit and the severe macroeconomic problems that plagued the country from 1974 onwards. The amount of money increased almost explosively while GDP hardly grew at all, thus exacerbating inflation (see Table 1.4). In the 1990s circumstances changed dramatically again, to the extent that we can safely say that an entirely new era was dawning. The process of monetary union led to monetary independence for the Bank of Spain (1994) and, finally, to the transfer of monetary policy to the European Central Bank (1998) when Spain joined the euro zone. It is crystal clear that these momentous events have completely changed the historical pattern of the preceding half-century. Nor is there any doubt that they will mark the future of Spanish economy.

So far we have talked about the internal prices of goods. It is of the greatest interest now to analyse the evolution of the price of a very particular good, the national currency. We are referring to its quotation with respect to the most important currencies at an international level and in Spain's foreign transactions. The variations in the exchange rate are closely related precisely to the evolution of prices. According to the theory of purchasing power parity—which no economist doubts governs in the long run-exchange rates fluctuate according to the variation of domestic prices in relation to international prices. The exchange rate of the peseta therefore clarifies the question of the importance of differential inflation. The exchange rates also reveal other things, since their alteration is determined by the state of the balance of payments. When a country enjoys a favourable balance, the exchange rate of its currency tends to appreciate, as it is more in demand than in supply, and vice versa. Naturally, the balance of payments deficit or surplus can have many causes. If it occurs in the current account, it is usually related to prices and productivity. If it occurs in the capital account, it may be related to more conjunctural or volatile factors, such as expectations regarding macroeconomic developments, free mobility of foreign investment or socio-political stability.

Figure 1.7 shows the exchange rate of the national currency from 1821 to 1998. Three large and long-lasting movements are immediately apparent and dominate the profile of the curve as a whole. The first is the almost straight horizontal line from 1821 to 1888; the second is the inverted V-shaped arc from 1888 to 1930; the third draws a steeply descending line. This last movement began with the Civil War and did not stop until the disappearance of the peseta in 1999. Two data summarize the secular evolution of the foreign exchange rate of the Spanish currency. Its level in 1935 was the same as at the beginning of the nineteenth century. On the eve of the replacement of the peseta by the euro, the exchange rate was only 5.3% of the 1935 value. The loss in value of the last sixty years is so devastating that it may give rise to gloomy interpretations of the performance of the Spanish economy. It is dangerous to accept this conclusion before undertaking empirical comparative analysis. A quick

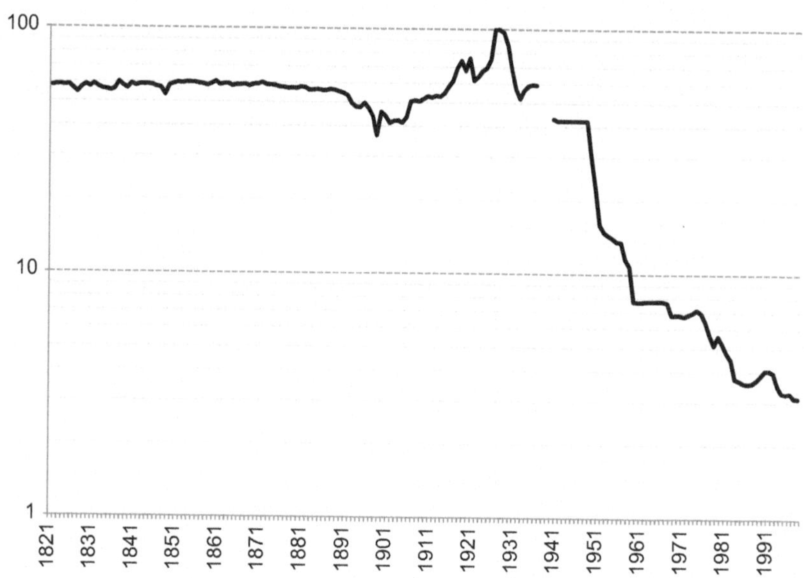

Fig. 1.7 Peseta nominal effective exchange rate compared to most developed countries, 1821–1998 (1927=100). *Source*: See Appendix, column 18

review of the parities between currencies in the days when countries' monetary systems were based on metallic standards would allow us to discover that although the peseta has devalued enormously against certain currencies (the pound sterling or the dollar), it has suffered a smaller loss in value than some of the currencies of stronger and more developed economies (the French franc, the German mark, the Italian lira).

The most outstanding feature of the exchange rate's nineteenth-century trajectory is, as we pointed out, its great stability. There were certain oscillations, but none were really important. This pattern of almost unchangeability was perfectly normal at that time. It is typical of a monetary regime based on metallic money of full content, in which bank money is still secondary and the cash in the hands of the public grows slowly. Now, the figure clearly shows that from 1888 the pattern changed. Until 1904 the peseta suffered a persistent depreciation (of 26%), which reached its maximum intensity in 1898, due to the so-called "Cuban disaster". What was the reason for this? The answer is clear: because Spain did not enter the gold standard. The authorities did not decide to take the step, aware that belonging to the gold standard was incompatible with a substantial chronic public deficit such as that carried by the Treasury. They chose to remain in a bimetallic monetary system, when the price of silver in relation to gold was sinking. This resulted in the country running out of gold reserves in a few years. As it became disconnected from the international monetary system, the peseta tended to depreciate because it was considered a weak currency. But the devaluation was not primarily dictated by expectations. The evolution of relative prices weighed more heavily: the prices of countries in the gold standard tended to decline in relation to those of Spain. From 1905 onwards, the opposite happened, and that is why the peseta was revalued. The inflow of capital caused by the expectations raised by the programme to clean up public finances carried out by Fernández Villaverde must also have contributed to its appreciation. By 1913, the peseta was not far below its theoretical parity with gold.

The cycle of the First World War had a spectacular effect on exchange rates. Neutrality yielded good dividends. The peseta appreciated strongly against the currencies of the surrounding countries, which were involved in the conflict. Less intense inflation and a huge surplus on the external balance raised the peseta. Its position was so solid that in the mid-1920s there was a massive influx of capital from abroad, discounting Spain's incorporation into the gold standard. The Bank of Spain failed to meet these expectations, so that speculative foreign capital was withdrawn. The Great Depression and the establishment of the Republic led to an abrupt intensification of the fall. However, on the eve of the Civil War, the effective exchange rate was at the same level as fifty or a hundred years earlier. Until that moment, the Spanish monetary system was anchored by the will to belong to a metallic standard, even if Spain never adhered to the gold standard, unlike all her surrounding countries.

The Civil War, as we know, opened a new era. It is difficult to perceive this in the types of changes that took place before 1950 because the Franco regime wanted the peseta to maintain an unalterable value. The authorities established an iron-clad exchange control, which made it possible to keep the official exchange rate artificially fixed. The intervention led to a strong, and growing, overvaluation of the peseta. The foreign trade balance and the reserve account came under great pressure, which became unsustainable in 1949 when the generalized devaluation of European currencies took place. Franco's regime used the very complicated multiple exchange rate mechanism to carry out covert devaluations, which the series we are examining faithfully reflects. Differential inflation and the malfunctioning of the autarkic model forced the Government to apply successive devaluations, always in a disguised way. When, in 1959, the autarkic model was liquidated through the Stabilization Plan, the true situation of the peseta was clarified by the establishment of a new official and unified exchange rate that implied a devaluation of more than 80% over the rate in force in 1939.

The Stabilization Plan meant the reincorporation of the Spanish economy into an international economy whose monetary regime was governed by the Bretton Woods agreements. Being a regime of fixed, although adjustable, exchange rates, the peseta tended to maintain a very stable level until the collapse of the system in 1971 (the peseta was only devalued once, in 1967). From 1974, when the world was faced with a flexible exchange rate regime in a deeply recessive situation, the Spanish currency began to depreciate. In a quarter of a century it lost more than half its value. This is a good reflection of the difficulties that Spain encountered in carrying out adjustment and structural reform policies to eliminate the serious external and internal imbalances that arose during the decade of crisis (1975–1985) and in the cycle of integration into the Community (1986–1993).

We end our tour of Spanish monetary history where Spanish monetary sovereignty ends. In 1999, Spain joined the Euro Zone. The figure reminds us of this. Chapter 11 will be devoted precisely to studying the performance of the Spanish economy when its monetary policy has been governed by the European Central Bank and not by the Bank of Spain. As can already be anticipated, being in the euro one loses the capacity to devalue one's own currency and one loses the capacity to conduct its appreciation or depreciation.

Bibliographic Orientation

On the natural constraints we follow the excellent work of A. Cabo, "Condicionamientos geográficos", in M. Artola (ed.) (1973), *Historia de España Alfaguara*, vol. I, Madrid, Alianza, which masterfully condenses the geographical knowledge on the subject.

The most complete reference on the evolution of GDP, population, GDP per capita, structural change and prices is L. Prados de la Escosura (2017): *Spanish Economic Growth 1850–2015*, London, Palgrave/Macmillan. We have used his latest update until 2019 available on the website https://espacioinvestiga.org/bbdd-chne/. All his series are annual. On population, R. Nicolau (2005): "Población, salud y actividad", in A. Carreras and Tafunell (eds.), *Estadísticas históricas de España. Siglos XIX y XX*, Madrid, BBVA Foundation. For a general interpretation, J. Nadal (1988), *La población española (siglos XVI a XX)*, Barcelona, Ariel. Specifically on mortality and health, V. Pérez Moreda, D-S. Reher and A. Sanz Gimeno (2015): *La conquista de la salud. Mortalidad y modernización en la España contemporánea*, Madrid, Marcial Pons. The estimate of GDP and GDP per capita for before 1850 is in C. Álvarez Nogal and L. Prados de la Escosura (2013): "The Rise and Fall of Spain, 1270–1850", *Economic History Review*, 66, 1, pp. 1–37. Physical well-being, as measured by height, has been presented in several works by J. M. Martínez Carrión. Very useful is his review of (2016): "Living Standards, Nutrition and Inequality in the Spanish Industrialisation. An Anthropometric View", *Revista de Historia Industrial*, 25, 64, pp. 11–50. Human development can no longer be studied without reference to L. Prados de la Escosura (2015): "World human development: 1870–2007", *Review of Income and Wealth*, 61, 2, pp. 220–247. On the behaviour of prices, J. Maluquer de Motes (2013): *La inflación en España. Un índice de precios de consumo, 1830–2012*, Madrid, Banco de España. On money supply and exchange rates, P. Martín Aceña and M.A. Pons (2005): "Sistema monetario y financiero", in A. Carreras and Tafunell (eds.), *op.cit.* On the exchange rate, J. Aixalá (1999), *La peseta y los precios. Un análisis de largo plazo (1868–1995)*, Zaragoza, Prensas Universitarias de Zaragoza.

For general interpretations, it is still necessary to read J. Nadal (1975): *El fracaso de la revolución industrial en España, 1814–1913*, Barcelona, Ariel, and L. Prados de la Escosura (1988): *De imperio a nación. Crecimiento y atraso económico en España (1780–1930)*, Madrid, Alianza. There is an executive summary of it: L. Prados de la Escosura: 'Economic growth and backwardness, 1780–1930', in J. Álvarez Junco and Adrian Shubert (eds.) (2000): *Spanish History since 1808*, London: Arnold. The various references to G. Tortella correspond to G. Tortella (2000): *The Development of Modern Spain. An Economic History of the Nineteenth and Twentieth Centuries*, Cambridge (MA): Harvard University Press. In its last revised Spanish edition of 2011 the authorship is by G. Tortella and C.E. Núñez. An alternative quantitative overview is by J. Maluquer de Motes (2016): *España en la economía mundial. Series largas para la economía española(1850–2015)*, Madrid, Instituto de Estudios Económicos.

To put the Spanish experience in a systematic European perspective, start with S. Broadberry and K. O'Rourke (eds.) (2010), *The Cambridge Economic History of Europe*, Cambridge, Cambridge U.P., 2 volumes, starting from 1700. A twentieth century European account consistent with this book is A. Carreras, "The Twentieth Century", in A. Di Vittorio (ed.) (2006), *An Economic History of Europe: from Expansion to Development*, London, Routledge. A European focused statistical sketch in A. Carreras and X. Tafunell, *Western European Long Term Growth, 1830–2000: Facts and Issues*, Barcelona, CREI, Opuscles del CREI, 20.

CHAPTER 2

From Empire to Peripheral Economy (1789–1840)

In our opinion, the history of contemporary Spain began in 1789. The outbreak of the French Revolution will produce an immediate impact on Spain and a number of profound effects that will be felt in the medium and long term. Moreover, this impact will be deployed simultaneously with the British industrial revolution. During what Hobsbawm called the "double revolution", the Spanish economy will suffer greatly. Both revolutions will be challenges to Spain's imperial pre-eminence. The challenges took the form of wars, first against France (1793–1795), and then against England (1796–1801 and 1805–1808). It was on the latter occasion that Spain suffered the historic defeat of Trafalgar (1805), losing the bulk of its large fleet and the ability to control the transatlantic routes. Finally, in 1808 Spain was invaded by the Napoleonic troops. The war then went on for six years on the Peninsula. The collapse of the monarchy was also the collapse of the Empire. Between 1810 and 1826 all the Spanish possessions in mainland America became independent.

After the war and the restoration of the monarchy in the person of Ferdinand VII, there were six years of strict restoration of the Old Regime (1814–1820). As if nothing had happened. But the novelties weighed heavily and eventually led to a successful military pronouncement, which resulted in the liberal triumph (1820–1823). The Cadiz Constitution of 1812 was once again in force and the king became constitutional. In 1823, with the help of the French army, Ferdinand VII reinstated the absolutist

A. Carreras, X. Tafunell, *Between Empire and Globalization*, Palgrave Studies in Economic History,
https://doi.org/10.1007/978-3-030-60504-9_2

regime, which was in force until his death in 1833. The succession was very conflictive and led to a war (1833–1840)—the first Carlist war—during which a series of measures were deployed that can be characterized as a true liberal revolution.

1 The Collapse of Colonial Trade

Between 1810 and 1826, as we said, Spain lost its entire continental American empire. Some 12 million subjects and some 12 million square kilometres. A very hard blow, which represented the end of the Empire in its current dimensions since the Treaty of Utrecht (1713). Cuba, Puerto Rico and the Philippines remained until 1898. We will first study the impact of the loss on foreign trade and then on the Treasury.

Trade with the American colonies was of major importance in the expansion of Spanish foreign trade during the second half of the eighteenth century. But, wars with France and England weakened the control of the colonies. American independence took place, de facto, from 1808, when Napoleon's armies occupied the Peninsula. By the time they were expelled in 1814 and an absolute monarchy was restored, the possessions of the American continent had already escaped the economic and political control of the metropolis.

The breakdown of colonial trade had a profound impact on the Spanish economy. It occurred in four different macroeconomic domains, which should be distinguished. First, in the levels and structure of foreign trade. Second, on the external balance of the Spanish economy. Third, on the evolution of national income. Fourth, in the productive structure and the allocation of resources. We will address these aspects, one after the other, in the following paragraphs.

We do not know precisely what the magnitudes of foreign trade were during this period. In Spain, no official statistics were compiled, except for a few isolated years, until 1849. In addition, a significant volume of foreign articles was imported by smuggling. The figures in Table 2.1 are the result of a laborious estimate based on different sources, which cannot be expected to quantify foreign trade accurately. They can be used to give an approximate idea of how it has evolved.

The most striking feature of Table 2.1 is the contraction suffered by exports and by trade with the Americas as a whole. Total exports declined by 40% in real terms (36% in nominal terms), or an average annual rate of -1.8%. Due to this severe fall, overall foreign trade fell (15% in volume,

Table 2.1 Spanish foreign trade, 1784–1820

Average annual value, in million reales de vellón

	Current values		*Constant values*	
	1784–1792	*1814–1820*	*1784–1792*	*1814–1820*
Exports of Spanish products				
America	205	109	276	106
Abroad	361	404	532	477
Total	566	513	808	583
Reexports				
America	266	38	208	47
Abroad	158	84	203	98
Total	424	122	411	145
Total exports				
America	471	147	485	153
Abroad	518	488	735	575
Total	989	635	1219	728
Net imports				
America	94	105	168	123
Abroad	478	644	406	672
Total	573	749	574	795
Total foreign trade				
America	566	252	652	276
Abroad	997	1132	1141	1247
Total	1562	1385	1793	1523
Trade balance				
America	111	4		
Abroad	-118	-241		
Total	-7	-236		

Note: Rounding off prevents final adjustment of the sums

Source: L. Prados de la Escosura (1993): "La pérdida del Imperio y sus consecuencias económicas", in L. Prados de la Escosura y S. Amaral (eds.), *La independencia americana: consecuencias económicas*, Madrid: Alianza

11% in current values), despite the increase in net imports—foreign products consumed in Spain. The contraction of Spanish foreign trade contrasts with the evolution followed by the foreign trade of most of the surrounding countries, which underwent a great expansion after the Napoleonic wars.

The table shows that the sharp decline in exports was caused by the loss of the Empire. Almost half (48%) of total exports were destined for Latin

America. Of these, 43% consisted of transit trade: re-export of foreign products overseas and re-export of colonial products abroad. In 1814–1820, this was 70% lower than in 1792, while the former had fallen by 86%. In the course of the following years, with emancipation secured, trade flows with Latin America and transit trade weakened further. The independence of the colonies meant for Spain the loss of captive markets for its products and also for foreign products imported by the colonies through the metropolis. The monopoly of the colonies' trade was based on pure coercion and not on any competitive advantage. The services offered by the Spaniards, as well as the goods they sold, were not competitive. Once the colonial pact was broken, the goods sold by the Spanish to the Latin American republics and the services offered to them were soon displaced by those provided by agents from other more advanced countries, particularly Great Britain. In 1827, Spain exported 42 million to the region, less than 10% of the 1792 figure.

One last aspect of the table mentioned above deserves to be highlighted: the deterioration of the external accounts. The balance of payments depended on colonial trade. For centuries, the Spanish economy suffered from an unfavourable balance of goods with the rest of the world (excluding the colonies). The large excess of exports of goods and services to the Indies over imports of goods from there made it possible to settle the overall trade balance without a deficit. Table 2.1 reveals the irreparable breakdown in the balance of the external sector from 1814 onwards. The traditional trade surplus with Latin America disappeared. The balance with the rest of the world worsened considerably. For the time being, the Spanish economy was unable to increase its export capacity to the rest of the world to compensate for the closure of the American markets. The economic chaos and disorganization caused by the wars against France and Great Britain, the Napoleonic occupation and the loss of the American continental empire led to an increase in net (smuggled) imports. For all these reasons, the balance of goods evolved from a situation of equilibrium in 1784–1792 to one of strong deficit in 1814–1820. In addition, there was a drastic reduction in private silver remittances from the Americas. As a result, the Spanish economy incurred a huge trade and balance of payments deficit since 1814, which had to be settled with silver and gold extractions. As the current monetary system was based on these metals, their large-scale drainage caused an intense drop in prices.

How did the collapse of colonial trade impact on national income? It is not easy to give a clear answer to this question. The latest estimates of

GDP, to which we referred earlier (see chapter 1), do not reveal any appreciable contraction in those years. It is possible that this was the case for the Spanish economy as a whole, still very much outside the market. But it is equally plausible that the loss of the colonies would have very negative economic effects in the short term for the most dynamic regions and sectors, which produced for the market and gave preference to colonial demand. The same deflation caused by the external imbalance resulting from the collapse of exports must have had a strong depressive impact on business circles. The ruin of the merchants and other entrepreneurs on the Spanish periphery was able to coexist with a revival of agricultural production in inland Spain. We will return to this question later.

The economic consequences of the breakdown of colonial trade were far-reaching because of the externalities of that trade. Its existence allowed for a productive specialization, from which substantial profits were derived for the economy of the metropolis. The Indies represented a market reserved for Spanish manufacturing, while supplying it with commodities. The colonies could have had great importance as consumers of the products made by the most developed productive sectors of the Spanish economy, as we have just pointed out. This issue has been the subject of a lively historiographical debate. It seems that the colonial demand only absorbed a minority part of the production. However, this fraction of production was sold under very remunerative conditions and could be an element of support and stabilization of the income of the manufacturing sector and of export agriculture. Industrial exports plummeted when the colonial traffic ceased (in 1827 their current value was equivalent to 13% of that of 1792). This put in serious difficulties the most advanced and generally most dynamic productive branches of the Spanish economy, those that exhibited a level of productivity and a propensity for innovation clearly superior to the rest. They only could overcome these obstacles with the formation of a national market, which had been incipient until then.

Indeed, the closure of the American market and the imbalance of the foreign sector forced the Spanish economy to undertake a profound process of adjustment and adaptation. The balance of payments deficit of the years 1814–1820 was unsustainable. Spain could not expect automatic equilibrium to be restored by the fall in domestic prices, since the price level of Spanish products was much higher than in other countries. Consequently, it would be necessary to reduce imports and, at the same time, increase exports. In addition, the absorption capacity of the domestic market should be increased in order to place on it the production which was previously placed on the colonial market and which did not find any other alternative market.

The composition of imports and exports in 1827, compared with that of 1792, shows the effort of adaptation, still ongoing at that date, carried out by Spain. As can be seen in Table 2.2, the structure of foreign trade underwent profound changes during the period, in response to the emancipation of the American colonies.

The mutation in imports is notorious. The strong reduction in the relative weight of food products is remarkable. They declined not only in relative terms, but also in absolute terms. It is noteworthy that in 1827 cereal imports ceased, which at the end of the eighteenth century were purchased in huge quantities to supply the periphery. The disappearance of these purchases was imposed by prohibitionist tariff legislation, enacted in 1820. The country's agriculture was able to produce enough grain to feed the population, except in years of natural disasters. Food self-sufficiency required the configuration of grain trafficking axes, through which the grain circulated from the cereal-producing areas of inland Spain to the deficit areas on the periphery. In exchange, the latter had the opportunity to sell to those areas the industrial or agricultural products in which they had specialized and which they could no longer place on the American market. Following this argument, the reader will be surprised by the strong increase in imports of manufactured goods. The figures in Table 2.2, which compute smuggled goods, seem to contradict the import substitution strategy. The extremely protective, prohibitionist tariff policy enacted in 1820 was extended to all major manufactured goods. What happened is that the ability of the Administration to effectively control the borders was constantly challenged by foreign traders. This did not prevent indigenous

Table 2.2 Foreign trade structure in 1792 and 1827, in percentage points

	Exports			*Net imports*		
	Food and beverage	*Raw materials*	*Manufactured goods*	*Food and beverage*	*Raw materials*	*Manufactured goods*
1792	29.1	39.9	31.0	43.0	12.4	44.6
1827	44.5	42.5	13.0	26.9	13.8	59.3

Source: The same than Table 2.1. The 1792 percentage has been estimated at 1778 prices, and 1827 at current prices

manufactures, at least the cotton and wool fabrics industry, from increasing production and sales.

The composition of exports in 1792 and 1827 reveals an extraordinary modification in the specialization pattern of the Spanish economy. The loss of the colonial market led to a marked decrease in the relative weight of manufactured exports, which became very modest. Conversely, primary products became overwhelmingly dominant. By 1827, Spain had become a typical backward export country. It was in the process of integrating into the international economy, specializing in the production and export of those primary products in which it had comparative or absolute advantages and which were increasingly in demand by countries in the process of industrialization. Olive oil, wine, citrus fruits, raisins, cork and lead were the main exports.

The process of substitution of basic food imports and the productive specialization in crops with strong foreign demand opened up great prospects for expansion of Spanish agriculture. But this horizon of growth and modernization of the sector required that the agricultural exploitations developed their activity under conditions that could hardly occur in the institutional framework of the Old Regime. The small family production units, predominantly in the countryside, which were subject to very burdensome censuses and lived outside the marketing of the harvest, had to be fully integrated into the market. The vast territorial patrimony of the Church and other institutions, uncultivated or very poorly exploited, would have to pass into the hands of agents with resources and incentives. Otherwise, agriculture could not successfully meet the demands of the internal and external market.

2 The Bankruptcy of the Absolutist Treasury

At the end of the eighteenth century, the Spanish Treasury depended, as it had for centuries, on the income linked to the maintenance of the Empire. Remittances of precious metals transferred by the colonial *haciendas* (treasuries) to the metropolitan *hacienda* and customs revenue, the return on which was closely related to the volume of colonial trade, were two main sources of income. In 1788–1792 they provided about half of the regular income (see Table 2.3). The interruption or breakdown of trade relations with the colonies would therefore lead to a large public deficit. And if it were the case that the cancellation of these external

Table 2.3 Treasury net income (1788–1820) * (annual average, in million *reales de vellón*)

	(1) Customs revenues	*(2) Colonial remittances*	*(3) External revenues (1+2)*	*(4) Debt*	*(5) Caja de Amortización revenues*	*(6) Total net revenues*
1788–1792	176	100	276	25	–	645
1799–1807	111	110	221	482	153	1211
1815–1820	99	0	99	254	–	806

Notes: (*) Income of the Tesorería General (the Treasury) after deduction of salaries, administrative expenses and charges, plus income of the Caja de Amortización,the entity in charge of the management of the new State debt (the "vales reales", see main text) after deduction of interest payments on "vales reales" and income from disentailment; (1) "rentas generales" (income from customs and Crown monopolies) plus wool rights; (4) extraordinary income (debt placement); (5) income from redemption of church property and taxes levied on the Caja de Amortización; (6) total income of central government less previous year's inventory plus net income of the Caja de Amortización

Sources: Own elaboration, based on J.P. Merino (1981): "La Hacienda de Carlos IV", *Hacienda Pública Española;* J.P. Merino (1987): "Las cuentas de la Administración central española, 1750–1820", *Instituto de Estudios Fiscales,* and J. Cuenca (1981): "Ingresos netos del Estado español, 1788–1820", *Hacienda Pública Española*

revenues were combined with an increase in public expenditure, the real treasury would be thrown into a critical situation.

This is precisely what happened in the last decade of the eighteenth century and the first two decades of the following one. The revenues linked to the Empire failed just when spending skyrocketed, as a result of the war conflicts that repeatedly pitted Spain against Great Britain and France. The Spanish treasury then suffered a huge budget deficit, which, not being able to be wiped out in the short periods of peace, dragged it into an unstoppable spiral of debt. The final outcome of this story was the bankruptcy of the Treasury.

The fiscal crisis began in 1779, when Spain went to war with Great Britain in the struggle for independence of the American colonies; it worsened in 1793, due to the armed conflicts that the Spanish Crown engaged in, first with revolutionary France and then, without respite, with Great Britain. It passed a point of no return around 1798. The extraordinary fiscal resources then mobilized would delay bankruptcy for a decade. From 1808 onwards, the Spanish Treasury was struggling with manifest insolvency and extreme hardship. The last governments of the absolutist monarchy were unable to restore financial equilibrium. With no possibility of continuing to get into debt, they were forced to cut public spending so drastically that the State ceased to provide the pure public goods indispensable for its own legitimacy and political survival.

Between 1785 and 1807 there was a sharp increase in public spending, caused by the cost of the military campaigns on which Spain embarked. Between both years, public expenditure doubled. In contrast, ordinary income remained stable; to be more exact, it decreased during the battles against Great Britain. His Armada managed to impose in all of them (1779–1783, 1796–1801 and 1804–1808) the suspension of all foreign commercial traffic. This had a dramatic impact on public accounts. Tariff revenues dropped to zero. The same was true for the silver revenues on behalf of the viceroyalty estates. And domestic tax collection tended to contract as a result of the economic recession engendered by the paralysis of foreign trade.

Other means aimed at increasing the tax burden were activated. A first line of action was to raise existing tax rates and fees. In this way, the public treasury obtained considerably more money until 1808, at the cost of facing growing social discontent and greater fiscal resistance. The rulers also created a large number of different taxes, with disappointing results. The tax system became almost unmanageable. A final route used to increase tax collection was to incorporate as taxpayers public institutions and social groups that were exempt from paying direct taxes, i.e., the privileged classes. This reflected the absolutely desperate situation of public finances, although the monarchy did not dare to subject the privileged classes to the payment of regular taxes.

But the strenuous efforts of the rulers to counteract the decline in Empire-linked income met with little success. Domestic tax revenues hardly increased until 1808 (see Table 2.3 for the difference between column 6 and the sum of columns 3, 4 and 5). Since inflation was present in this period, the Treasury was faced with a decline, in real terms, in ordinary domestic income. On the other hand, expenditure rose sharply, as mentioned above. From the growing gap between payments and receipts, a large cash deficit arose. The accumulated one between 1793 and 1807 represented more than half of the total tax revenues.

How could this deficit be financed? From 1780 to 1798 it was done by issuing debt. The State resorted to foreign savings. But with the French Revolution and the Napoleonic Wars, the doors were closed to foreign investment. From 1789 to 1814, each nation had to bear the burden of its public finances alone. So the Spanish treasury financed the deficit with domestic debt. The securities, called "vales reales" (royal vouchers), were legal tender, although with limited liberating power. No one, except the government, was obliged to accept this money in payment of economic transactions or debts incurred. As financial assets, they bore fixed interest and were repayable over twenty years.

Royal vouchers had a clear advantage for the State over other types of public debt. It could put them into circulation without trading on the stock market, simply by paying its suppliers with those securities. However, they were a risk for the Treasury. The government had to accept vouchers presented to it for tax payment at face value. On the other hand, when the Treasury exchanged vouchers for cash to cover its current expenses, it had to sell the securities at their current market value. They were immediately depreciated. The State's demand for capital was excessive. It exceeded the supply. To make matters worse, the State proved to be a bad debtor from the very beginning: it did not respect the voucher redemption schedule. Naturally, investors became increasingly suspicious of the government and prices fell even further. The rulers did not manage to stop such a dangerous dynamic even with the creation (1782) of a bank linked to the Government, the Banco Nacional de San Carlos—the remote predecessor of the Bank of Spain. The Bank was unable to perform its function of stabilizing the voucher market, which was over-supplied with securities. The Bank witnessed, unable to react, the collapse in prices resulting from the massive debt issues carried out. Since 1799, the price of vouchers has been so low that it has made it impossible to launch new issues.

The collapse of the market for royal vouchers pushed the Treasury to the limit. Financial distress threatened to paralyze the State machine, i.e. a collapse of the political system, as had just happened in France. In this critical situation, the monarchy chose to take a politically radical fiscal measure: the expropriation and sale of part of the Church's assets. The process of disentailment of church property in Spain (and in the American colonies) began. This first disentailment had a considerable scope. In 1808, according to estimates by R. Herr, the government had sold about 1/6 of the Church's properties. The authorities placed all their hopes in the disentailment being the panacea of the fiscal crisis. It was not enough to save the Treasury from bankruptcy. The mass of living debt continued to increase rapidly. Servicing this debt absorbed around 40 percent of ordinary income. Being impossible to fulfil, it brought the Treasury to the brink of bankruptcy.

The War of Independence (1808–1814) delayed it, while making it even more inevitable. Occupied by the Napoleonic army, the old machinery of the Bourbon State was completely broken down. The amounts paid in by the treasury decreased brutally (by almost 80%). Obviously, expenses were not reduced, quite the contrary. Where did the money come from? How was the war financed? In part, from credit, thanks to loans granted by the British, now allies of Spain against the French emperor, as well as through internal debt. The remaining funds needed to finance the war and the State were collected from the population directly by the armies themselves, usually in kind.

The War of Independence thus aggravated the imbalance in public finances. The volume of recognized accumulated debt almost doubled between 1808 and 1813. In order to pay the interest and repay the overdue debt, it would have been necessary to allocate no less than 80% of the non-financial income. To make matters worse, silver remittances and a substantial part of customs revenue could no longer be counted on (see Table 2.3). Obviously, in these circumstances, the Treasury had no choice but to suspend the payment of the debt. But even that would not solve the burden on the public purse. How could the State finance such a deficit if it failed to pay the debt it had incurred, or if it repudiated it? It is clear that a fiscal adjustment that would eliminate the primary deficit could not be postponed. Either a drastic increase in revenue was achieved, or expenditure was reduced to the level of revenue.

The persistence of absolutism during the next two decades—under the reign of Ferdinand VII (1814–1833), with the brief parenthesis of the Constitutional Triennium—made the fiscal crisis irresolvable. The institutional model of the restored Old Regime closed the way to a tax reform. There was no way to really carry it out without extending the tax burden to the privileged classes, the social groups that owned most of the national wealth. This option was ruled out for political reasons, and projects to modify the tax system were doomed to failure, as J. Fontana has shown.

If it was imperative to balance the public accounts and the rulers were unable to increase revenues, they had no alternative but to spend less. This is what they did. According to F. Comín's calculations, the actual payments made by the public treasury were almost halved in 1813–1819 compared to 1801–1807. In part, by reorganizing the tax administration, improving and rationalizing its management and keeping a strict and efficient control of disbursements. Hence, the annual elaboration of the Budget was established in 1827. This instrument contributed to the clarification of public accounts. However, the greatest savings were achieved by another route: the neglect of the major expenditure items. The State stopped paying all its creditors. It also stopped paying its suppliers of goods and services. Public employees and troops did not receive their salaries either, or they received them with great delays and partially. The most serious thing for the very survival of the political regime was that abundant funds were spared in Defence, the only public good provided by the Spanish State at that time. The scarcity of the budget allocation broke the strength of the Army to the extent of being unable to put down armed conspiracy. Insurgent movements sprang up everywhere from 1830 onwards, in the heat of the revolutionary wave that swept through Europe. The bankruptcy of the Treasury paved the way for the revolutionary liberals to take power.

3 The Crisis of the Old Regime and the Liberal Revolution

The word "revolution" may give the wrong idea about the way in which liberal Spain was forged. Some authors have emphasized the liberal movement's inability to create a stable political system. We will not discuss this idea, here we cannot entertain ourselves in the details of political history. What we should bear in mind is that if political liberalism was fragile, liberal economic legislation was not. We can speak of a liberal Spain, in the economic field, which, born between 1833 and 1839, lasted until 1936. It succumbed only at the outbreak of the Civil War, and not in any of the many previous periods in which the constitutional regime was suspended. Let us make a brief note of the basic chronology of the liberal revolution.

The general attack on the Old Regime started in 1808, but the liberal system did not triumph until 1839, when there was the defeat—not definitive—of the irreducible defenders of absolutism. In 1808 the State and institutions of the Old Regime collapsed. As it happened in the whole of Europe invaded by the Napoleonic armies, the military occupation of the country led immediately to a power vacuum as the old administrative and political organization was dismantled. National sovereignty fell on new institutions, born from the popular uprising against the French occupier and which had a vaguely representative character. At this propitious juncture, the liberal movement designed a complete revolutionary programme, sanctioned in 1812 in the Cortes de Cádiz (one of the first Constitutions in the world, a true masterpiece of liberalism). The restoration of absolutism did not allow the implementation of this revolutionary programme until 1835, when the liberals came to power in the midst of the Civil War of 1833–1839, the first Carlist war.

The direction taken by the liberal revolution in Spain was marked by the compromise between the revolutionary bourgeoisie and the landowning aristocracy. A different orientation to that taken by France, but analogous to that of many other Western European countries, such as Germany or Italy. It claimed some victims. The main losers were the lower layers of the peasantry, the Church and the municipalities. The economic and social power of the peasantry and the Church explains the enormous political resistance that the liberal regime encountered, resistance that was not definitively overcome until 1876, when the last Carlist war ended. For its part, the local administration, which had a very notable patrimony of real estate and land—badly managed—suffered such plundering that from then on it lived in hardship and was unable to adequately supply public goods necessary for economic and social development. Primary education—provided by the local councils and, to a lesser extent, by the Church—was plunged into a desolate state of affairs, which it did not abandon until 1901, when the government took over its financing. On the other hand, the social model of triumphant liberal revolution had other long-term negative effects on economic growth. The expropriation and proletarianization to which a large mass of the peasantry was subjected constituted a brake, instead of a stimulus, to the progress of agriculture and, ultimately, of industry. The abundance of labour postponed technical change on farms for a long time. The low purchasing power of the bulk of consumers was, as we shall see, a major obstacle to industrial development. Finally, the power of the rural oligarchy—an amalgamation of the old aristocracy and the new landowning bourgeoisie—meant that agricultural interests took precedence over industrial ones.

In the rural world, the liberal revolution consisted of a change in land ownership rights. This required, in many cases, a change of hands. According to the principles of economic liberalism, only a regime of individual ownership of the factors of production in which the holders can freely dispose of such factors guarantees an adequate allocation of resources and, therefore, a sustained increase in production and economic well-being. Consequently, the legal regime of agricultural property under the Old Regime, in which ownership was usually shared, or not individual, or bonded or entailed, was demolished. By means of the liberal revolution it would become an individual, full and liberalized property. In order for this transformation to take place, the liberal rulers carried out an agrarian reform whose essential elements were: the disentailment, the abolition of the seigniorial regime and the unbinding of the possessions of the nobility, the suppression of the tithe and the annulment of the restrictive rules on the use of the land. We will now briefly describe these legislative measures and their impact on agricultural production.

The civil and ecclesiastical disentailment affected 40% of the arable land (and a smaller but significant portion of the urban land). With the confiscation operation, a volume of land was privatized that represented the same area that was under cultivation in 1800. The disentailment consisted of a nationalization of the lands belonging to the Church and the municipalities, followed by their privatization through an orderly sale by public auction to the highest bidder. What repercussions did the disentailment have on the agrarian economy? It tended to polarize the distribution of property. The small farmers lost out with the confiscation, not only because they did not gain anything by not being able to bid at the auctions, but also because many small farmers were no longer viable because they lost access to Church and communal lands for free or at a reasonable price. But beyond the distributive effects, what consequences did the confiscation have on agricultural production? Thanks to it, the area under cultivation was greatly increased, to the detriment of pastures and forests, which led to a significant increase in the supply of food. On the other hand, the disentailment contributed to an increase in the supply of labour, by proletarianizing the lower layers of the peasantry.

The abolition of the seigniorial regime was, together with the disentailment, the main measure of the liberal agrarian reform. The liquidation of the seigniorial regime was indispensable for the establishment of capitalist property rights. About half of the population lived under this regime. Both the lords and the peasants had property rights to the same land. This had no place in a capitalist economy: every piece of land had to belong exclusively to one of them. In general, where feudal property rights were not perfectly specified, the abolition of the lordly regime was resolved in favour of the lords, so that the peasantry was plundered without receiving almost anything in return—only the abolition of feudal taxes, which were small in amount—while the noble class expanded its already very considerable wealth. In short, the liquidation of feudalism had an important redistributive effect, notably worsening the social inequality in the distribution of property.

The unbinding of the patrimony of the noble houses can be conceived as a complementary measure to the abolition of the seigniorial regime because it made it possible for the lands of the nobility to enter fully into the market and for their owners to freely dispose of them. In the Ancien

Régime, the wealth accumulated by noble families was never diminished or fragmented because the heritage was "bonded". The bonding was, therefore, equivalent to the entailment of the ecclesiastical and municipal lands. But, unlike disentailment, disassociation did not entail a transfer of possession of the assets. It simply allowed them to be mobilized, which made it possible for them to be put to more productive use.

As for the tithe, its legal abolition had a positive indirect effect on the expansion of agriculture. The tax burden on farmers did not change in intensity, but in nature. They now had to pay higher taxes to the government, partly in order to cover the public budget to support the Church. Since the payment of the taxes had to be made in money, as opposed to the payment of the tithe, which was made in kind, the farmers were forced to market their production to a greater extent, which favoured agricultural development. In order to produce for the market, farmers learned to react to market signals, prices and demand.

Regarding the abolition of restrictive land use regulations, we should mention the following. One of the most important was the elimination of the *Mesta* and its privileges. This medieval institution, which defended the interests of the owners of the transhumant cattle herds, had for centuries conditioned the use of enormous extensions of land. The owners of the lands once devoted to grazing the *Mesta* cattle regained control of their lands, which they would then devote to cultivation. A second and no less important legal measure was the closure of all the farms. This is a legal closure, whether or not it is accompanied by physical closure. As we know from the British experience of enclosures, legal closure of farms was essential for more intensive land use. Substantial increases in agricultural yields should be achieved first through new crops and crop rotation systems, rather than through the introduction of more efficient tools. As long as farms remained open, the introduction of such innovations was impossible. Thus, agricultural production and productivity had to be increased as a result of the closure of farms, as well as the measures that put an end to the endless administrative regulations of agricultural operations that constituted a highly restrictive public intervention, at the municipal level, of agricultural activities. In the rural environment, individual initiative had been constrained by all these traditional restrictions on land use. Finally, the legal protection of the right of the owner to use his property without any limitation was completed with the introduction of the freedom to lease the land. For all these reasons, from the 1830s onwards, capitalism was able to develop unhindered in the Spanish agrarian world.

So far all that has been said concerns legal-institutional changes in land ownership rights and the use of such rights. What happened to the property rights of the other two production factors—labour and capital—and outside the agrarian world? In the labour market, liberalization had been undertaken by the enlightened rulers (1767), restricting it to the hiring of agricultural labourers. As for the markets of non-agrarian productive factors, the free hiring of labour came with the disappearance of the guilds, which also brought about the free use of capital. Two of the key principles of the liberal order were the free exercise of any commercial and industrial activity and that markets should function in a perfectly competitive manner. A law established the "freedom of industry and commerce", by virtue of which all citizens were free to exercise any profession or establish any type of company. Another legal provision abolished the powers of the guilds. They were reduced, with the exception of a few cases (liberal professions), to mere associations of entrepreneurs in a given sector, deprived of any capacity to influence or disturb the free operation of market forces.

The liberalization of product markets took place essentially through the abolition of price rates and the free movement of goods throughout the national territory. In 1834, the Government decreed the free internal movement of agricultural products—non-agricultural products already enjoyed this—which was accompanied by the abolition of official price ceilings. Shortly afterwards, the remaining internal customs, the so-called "dry ports", were eliminated. All of these measures were transcendental for the integration of the economic spaces. The articulation of the internal market was also enhanced by the establishment of a single system of weights and measures (1849) based on the metric system, which replaced, not without difficulty, a multitude of measurement regimes that complicated transactions and entailed costs for intermediaries and consumers.

Researchers have not yet sufficiently clarified whether the commercial networks dominated by monopolies and privileges that prevailed until the end of the Old Regime were dismantled by the legal measures we have mentioned. But there is no doubt that in the 1830s liberal rulers managed to legally establish a regime of competition in the goods and factor markets, which, without being perfect, had revolutionary effects on long-term economic growth. Suffice it to say that, with the new rules of the game, the integration of the internal market received a powerful boost. As Adam Smith demonstrated, the wealth of a nation, rather than being fed by technical change, is given by the development of exchanges and a market economy free of constraints.

4 Between Agriculture and Industry: The Formation of the National Market

The economic balance of the tempestuous half century that separates the placid succession of Charles III by his son Charles IV, in 1788, from the end of the first Carlist war, in 1840, after having liquidated the institutions of the Old Regime, lost an empire and carried out a liberal revolution, can be outlined thanks to an estimate of the behaviour of the real GDP per capita for the whole period (see Fig. 1.2). What we have to retain from it is the leap forward of a 10% of the real GDP per capita that we can locate between 1808 and 1826 and that will not be lost in the future.

According to all indications, the growth is the mirror image of the expansion of cultivated land—the "clearing tide" to which E. Llopis refers. How could extensive growth—expansion of cultivated land—lead to intensive growth—growth of the product per inhabitant? How many economic laws are we skipping? It happened that, as we have mentioned, during the Napoleonic occupation the barriers that the eighteenth-century Enlightenment had denounced as impediments to the cultivation of abundant and fertile land fell. The *Mesta*, with its transhumant livestock, was fulminated by the repeated looting of its herds by all the troops that were travelling around the Peninsula. The soldiers, regular or irregular, French, Spanish or British, ate the sheep. Many pastures and cattle tracks were freed from the control of the *Mesta* and were broken up by the peasants, who were hungry for land. As the Napoleonic armies were representatives of a new political order that had put an end to the Old Regime by excellence, which was French absolutism, the peasants felt released from paying—or paying less—tithes to the Church, rents to the lords, occupying communal lands and, in general, bypassing the established order. The occupied lands had not been cultivated since time immemorial and gave excellent harvests for many years. The worst served to cultivate a tuber (the potato) of high yield per unit area, that until then had been considered barely usable for human consumption. All of them, whether they were grasses or forests, intensified their use. As the war ended, the break-ups continued, new families were formed and more children were begotten. For a few decades the Spanish population grew faster than anyone could remember. The improvements in welfare that came from higher yields and fewer liabilities had to be used to purchase manufactured goods. Manufacturers who had lost their colonial markets must have appreciated the emergence of greater domestic demand. Clearly, this was the case with the Catalan cotton textile industry, which mechanized spinning to cut costs and pressed for tariff bans.

Certainly, peasant welfare, diffused throughout the central *Meseta* area, did not extend in the same way to the periphery. The latter suffered severely from the loss of the colonial empire and the collapse of trade with America. For a long time historiography considered that this factor had to be the dominant one, but probably the agrarian growth, more diffuse in the interior of the Peninsula than in the periphery, had more than compensate the colonial crisis in terms of GDP growth. Another thing is whether the model of extensive growth, by cultivating more land, was sustainable. On the other hand, the periphery, which was very open to trade, was able to adapt (see section 2.1) to the new conditions and opportunities. This was not a rapid process, but it did allow a recovery of agriculture, export mining, domestic market-oriented manufacturing and services.

On the demographic side we have indications that confirm our suspicions. We know that the population increased significantly from 1787—the best census of the pre-modern era—to 1833. On the first date it amounted to 10.4 million inhabitants and on the second date it reached 12.3 million. There is agreement that almost all of the increase corresponds to the eighteen-year period from 1815 to 1833. The rate of increase, of the order of 0.94%, implies a clear acceleration with respect to the past. We know that the rate remained high (see chapter 1.1) until the 1857 census. On the contrary, we cannot disregard the hypothesis that the demographic impact of the wars against the French armies, which are documented to have caused significant extraordinary mortality and delays in marriage and, therefore, in births, had a positive effect on economic growth. Some authors put the combined effect of more deaths and fewer births at one million. Although it is very unpleasant to see it from this point of view, authors such as N. Voigtländer and H. J. Voth have drawn attention to the positive effect on economic growth that wars had in medieval and modern Europe. They reduced population but left the land intact. The ratio of capital per capita improved, increasing the productivity of labour. This effect must have been intense in the decade and a half immediately following the end of the Napoleonic invasion.

The combination of the loss of foreign markets and the loss of cash strongly encouraged an autarchic withdrawal of the Spanish economy. Indeed, the post-1814 tariff policy can only be described as ultra-protectionist, or simply prohibitionist. The tariff law approved by the liberals themselves in 1820, conceived as a forceful response to the very serious external imbalance caused by the loss of the empire of the American continent, prohibited the import—and in some cases the export—of a very long list of articles; among them were the basic subsistence—cereals in the first place—and manufactured products of mass consumption. The many tariff changes that were subsequently introduced did not significantly alter the extremely protective nature of the legislation adopted in 1820. They did not do so at least in general terms, although some of these tariff rules eliminated bans and substantially lowered tariffs on certain types of goods, including some as strategic as textile machinery.

This autarkic propensity may seem absurd, given that Spain was a poor country with few resources, especially after the loss of the American empire. But the Spanish authorities did not defend a policy that was very different from that practiced by almost all the European governments of the time, which were still imbued with a mercantilist mentality. Spain therefore behaved more or less like most of its neighbours during the first half of the century. Even Great Britain was very closed to foreign trade, as evidenced by the fact that the corn laws, the laws that practically prohibited the import of cereals, were still in force thirty-one years after the end of the Napoleonic wars. The economic circumstances of the time convinced farmers and manufacturers of the mutual desirability of improving the integration of trade flows in the new post-imperial Spain.

5 Spain in the Great Divergence: The Failure of the Prerequisites to Emulate British Industrialization

Better knowledge of the economic trajectory of medieval and modern China and India has led to systematic comparisons of living standards and productivity in the more advanced regions of both economies (Shanghai in China, Mumbai and Calicut in India) with some moments in Europe's pre-industrial past. It has become clear from the many works of R. Allen, S. Broadberry and others that even around 1500 there were no significant differences in prosperity and productivity between Western Europe and East or Indian Asia. By 1800, however, the gap had grown enormously. It seemed insurmountable. In fact, the United Kingdom would go on to gain commercial and then political positions in Asia, just as the Netherlands had previously done. If we go into the Contemporary Age, those differences detectable in 1800 only grew bigger, at least until about 1980, when two great movements took place: the neoliberal turn in the United States and the United Kingdom, which set in motion a second globalizing wave, and the turn towards the market in China, which allowed it to brilliantly take advantage of the opportunities of the second globalization.

By 1800 it was not clear where Spain stood. Having been an undisputed power in the sixteenth and part of the seventeenth centuries, it had been in decline since the mid-seventeenth century. Its good relative positions in 1400 or 1500 were no longer so in 1700. In 1800 it was not easy to decide whether to bet on Spain or China. What was clear was that, from the mid-seventeenth century, one had to bet on Holland and Great Britain. There, following the terminology of D. Acemoglu and J. A. Robinson, inclusive institutions appeared, labour was expensive and capital was cheap. Trade and enterprise flourished. Britain ended up imposing itself economically on the Netherlands because it had cheap energy. This allowed it to explore the path of mechanization and along that path it became the first industrialized power in the world.

R. Allen, in his global perspective on the British industrial revolution, has stressed the importance of having adequate factor endowments to embark on the path of industrialization. He looks at data around 1750 and around 1800. The cost of energy is fundamental, and Spain did not enter the industrialization race with cheap energy, but with expensive energy. It is also fundamental that work is expensive—that there are incentives for mechanization—whereas in Spain work was very cheap. That the population was educated is more important than it used to be, largely because in the initial stages of the industrial revolution—and even more so later—not only factory workers count, but all the types of work involved in the success of industrial companies, from purchasing to sales to product design, administration and finance. Spain, which had not been badly positioned at the beginning of the Modern Age, had lagged behind by 1800. As we will have occasion to see in the next chapters, the problem will become more acute throughout the nineteenth century.

By 1840 Britain had completed its industrial revolution. The railway was spreading rapidly throughout its territory and in the most advanced regions of Europe. Britain's military and economic hegemony was indisputable. The European states had to take a stand on this challenge, either by designing policies to catch up with Britain—catching up policies—or by giving up all manufacturing competitiveness and hoping for new sources of growth. R. Allen synthesizes the pattern of responses from countries seeking to emulate British industrialization as a policy package that typically had four components: formation and integration of a domestic market, including the elimination of internal tariffs and the deployment of tariffs that protect domestic industry from British competition; investment in modern transport technologies, especially railways, to foster domestic market integration; promotion of investment banking that can finance the large investments needed for the deployment of transport technologies and industry; and universal primary education to improve the skills of the workforce. That is what happened in all the countries that aspired to resist the British threat. In the Spain of 1840, traumatized by the loss of the Empire, the integration of the national market was an undisputed objective, as was the use of protective tariffs. But the only railway that existed had just been inaugurated in 1839 in Cuba. There were no plans for the Peninsula. Mass education was directly questioned following the collapse of the local and ecclesiastical estates. The next half century would be clearly defined around these challenges. The political framework that Acemoglu and Robinson valued so much, at the time of 1840, was still to be defined. Spain had repeatedly opted for a very inclusive Constitution, but this had hardly been applied.

The industrial revolution offered a model, a growth path. It also offered opportunities for complementarity. We have detected them when reviewing the readjustment of Spanish foreign trade, which loses some markets but gains others in the United Kingdom itself. The competitiveness of British industrial products was so great that they easily jumped over import bans or tariff barriers. The smuggling of textile products took on great proportions. L. Prados de la Escosura has been able to measure this by comparing British exports and Spanish imports. The new products of the industry were becoming cheaper and more attractive. The real net terms of trade of Spain vis-à-vis Great Britain, calculated by the author himself, leave no room for doubt about the extent of the temptation (see Fig. 2.1).

The level of the last decade of the eighteenth century is around 42. Fifty years later it is between 140 and 150. The import capacity of Spanish exports has increased three to four times. The benefits of free trade and specialization in the export of commodities were in sight. It was worth forgetting the imperial pretensions and concentrating on the opportunities available to an economy that had become peripheral like the Spanish one. The British industrial revolution meant that Spain, without being able to become the equivalent of the United Kingdom—Trafalgar will always be there to remind us of this—could at least aim to escape the fate

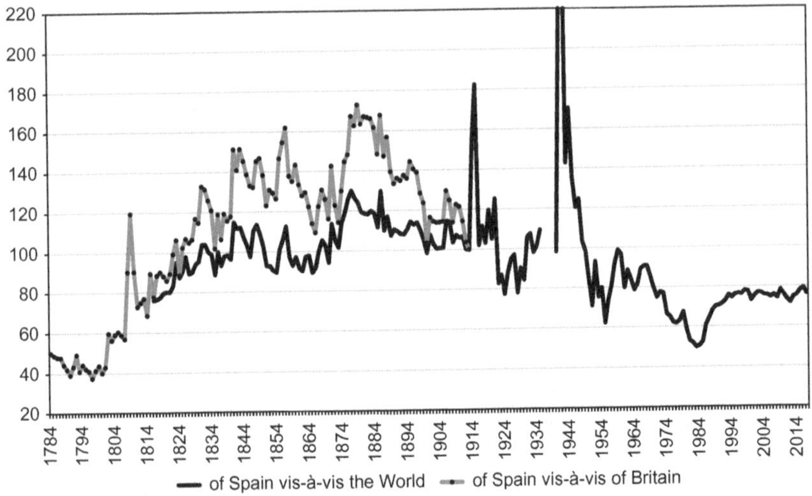

Fig. 2.1 Spain's real terms of trade, 1784–2017 (1913=100). *Sources*: L. Prados de la Escosura (1988): *De imperio a nación. Crecimiento y atraso económico en España (1780–1930)*. Madrid: Alianza; and A. Tena (2005): "Sector exterior", in A. Carreras and X. Tafunell (coords.): *Estadísticas históricas de España. Siglos XIX y XX*. Bilbao: Fundación BBVA, vol.II, table 8.5. The data for 2002 to 2017 come from the Bank of Spain, *Boletín Estadístico*

of China or India. Accepting the "little divergence" but escaping the "great divergence". This will be the subject of the next chapter.

Bibliographic Orientation

A major monograph on the Spanish Empire is A. M. Bernal, (2005): *España, proyecto inacabado. Coste/beneficios del Imperio*, Madrid, Marcial Pons. E. Llopis has published excellent overviews of the period. The last one is E. Llopis (2013): "La crisis del Antiguo Régimen, 1789–1840", in E. Llopis and J. Maluquer de Motes (eds.): *Las grandes depresiones económicas, 1348–2012*, Barcelona, Pasado y Presente. Very recent and suggestive is the interpretative essay by L. Prados de la Escosura and C. Santiago-Caballero (2018): "The Napoleonic Wars: A Watershed in Spanish History?", *EHES working paper*, 130. The collapse of the colonial trade is very well treated, in its link with the bankruptcy of the Treasury and the collapse of the Old Regime, by J. Fontana (1970): *La quiebra de la monarquía absoluta 1814–1820*, Barcelona, Ariel, the classic reference and good reading. Delivering just what the title promises, L. Prados de la Escosura (1993): "La pérdida del Imperio y sus consecuencias económicas", in L. Prados de la Escosura and S. Amaral (eds.) (1993), *La independencia americana: consecuencias económicas*, Madrid. The collapse of the absolutist hacienda is the subject of much of the first volume of F. Comín (1988): *Hacienda y economía en la España contemporánea*, Madrid, Instituto de Estudios Fiscales. The crisis of the Old Regime and the Liberal Revolution has inspired great studies, to which we will not be able to do justice. The classics are J. Fontana (1977): *La Revolución Liberal (Política y Hacienda 1833–45)*, Madrid, Instituto de Estudios Fiscales and F. Tomás y Valiente (1981): "La obra legislativa y el desmantelamiento del Antiguo Régimen", in J.M. Jover (dir.): *Historia de España de Ramón Menéndez Pidal*, vol. XXXIV: *La Era Isabelina y el sexenio democrático*, Madrid, Espasa Calpe. The impact on the agricultural world is the subject of all the papers included in A. García Sanz and R. Garrabou (eds.) (1985): *Historia agraria de la España contemporánea*, vol. 1: *Cambio social y nuevas formas de propiedad (1800–1850)*, Barcelona, Crítica. The impact on the cotton textile industry is explained by J. Martínez-Galarraga and M. Prat (2016), "Wages, prices, and technology in early Catalan industrialization", *The Economic History Review*, 69 (2), and A. Sánchez (2000): "Crisis económica y respuesta empresarial. Los inicios del sistema fabril en la industria algodonera catalana, 1797–1839", *Revista de Historia Económica*, XVIII, 3. Whether or not Spain, at the end of the Old Regime, was too late to jump on the bandwagon of the industrial revolution is the subject of E. Llopis (2004): "España, la 'revolución de los modernistas' y el legado del Antiguo Régimen" in E. Llopis (ed.). R. C. Allen (2009): *The British Industrial Revolution in Global Perspective*, Cambridge, CUP, and (2011): *Global Economic History. A Very Short Introduction*, London, Oxford U.P., chapters 1 and 2, argues that yes. More arguments for a yes in several excerpts from D. Acemoglu and J. A. Robinson (2012): *Why Nations Fail: The Origins of Power, Prosperity and* Poverty, New York: Crown Business. A more refined chronology of the Hispanic divergence in the European context is that of R. Fouquet and S. Broadberry (2015): "Seven Centuries of European Economic Growth and Decline", *The Journal of Economic Perspectives*, 29 (4). A crude but sharp view of the role of war in modern Europe, N. Voigtländer and H.-J. Voth (2013): "Gifts of Mars: Warfare and Europe's Early Rise to Riches", *The Journal of Economic Perspectives*, 27 (4).

CHAPTER 3

The Impact of European Industrialization: The Double Failure of Agrarian and Industrial Strategies (1840–1890)

Between the fourth and ninth decades of the nineteenth century, the Spanish economy tried to grow as quickly as possible within the new institutional framework that it was acquiring. Being already, unequivocally, a small nation instead of the great empire that it was, it adapted to the new circumstances. During the *Bienio Progresista* (1854–1856), it made an enormous effort to modernize the Spanish economy in order to facilitate its fit with the international economy, especially with the United Kingdom, which in 1846, with the abolition of the corn laws, had opened its economy to agricultural and mineral exports from all countries in the world. The task of the *Bienio Progresista* was completed during the *Sexenio Democrático* (1868–1874). In the following years it seemed that all the efforts made had been worthwhile.

The decision to follow the agrarian or the industrial path was not a crossroad that only Spain faced. Immediately after the United Kingdom abolished the corn laws, all European countries and some non-European countries such as the United States of America had to decide whether to imitate the British in order to be in a position to defend themselves from their economic and military hegemony or to adapt to British industrial leadership by becoming their suppliers. The tour of the continent by Richard Cobden, the representative of Manchester industrialism, was a call to follow the second direction by appealing to the advantages of free trade and universal peace. France, with the Cobden-Chevalier Treaty, initially

A. Carreras, X. Tafunell, *Between Empire and Globalization*, Palgrave Studies in Economic History,
https://doi.org/10.1007/978-3-030-60504-9_3

followed this route. Cavour's unified Italy did the same. The small countries of central and northern Europe, too. The most prominent case was that of the Netherlands, a competitor of the British for centuries, which opted for the role of supplier of agricultural products with some degree of processing. Denmark and the Scandinavian countries followed the same course. Not to mention Portugal, the model theorized by David Ricardo when he explained what the theory of comparative advantage consisted of: exchanging wine for fabrics even though the fabric-producing country lacked an advantage in both fabrics and wine.

In this situation, the Spanish economic lobbies were mainly oriented to the agrarian option. It suited the landowners, it suited the bourgeoisie who had acquired land, it suited the peasantry, it suited the urban consumers and it suited the merchants. Who was not interested? Mainly Catalans and Basques, and also some peripheral towns that had successfully adapted to the strategy of manufacturing specialization. Catalan manufacturers, as well as Basque industrialists, had prospered thanks to their protected access to colonial and Spanish markets. They fought hard to preserve that protection. They knew that they could not be competitive with British industry because they lacked market size, but they were convinced that they could reduce costs by embedding the new technologies. The entire nineteenth century after the loss of the American colonies was consumed in endless debates between agrarianists and industrialists, between free traders and protectionists, between Madrid and Barcelona. That harmony obtained in the common fight against the French invader was soured by the confrontation of different economic models. The industrialist option, initially discarded, did not die. It resisted and proved to be resilient. By the end of the period studied, the bulk of the agrarian interests had become protectionist, while the neighbouring countries, such as France and Italy, which at first opted for the agrarian route, gradually switched to the industrialist strategy. Even so, and following J. Nadal's famous characterization, all of them—agrarists and industrialists—failed in their efforts to bring Spain closer to advanced Europe.

1 The Limits of Agricultural Expansion

Liberal land reform and the opening up of the United Kingdom to agricultural exports from the rest of the world seemed to assure Spain an agricultural growth path. However, agriculture expanded at a very moderate pace. According to the information and estimates of J. Simpson, from the decade of 1820–1829 to that of 1880–1889, Spanish agricultural output increased by about 60%, or a modest 0.7% per year, barely more than the 0.6% per year that the population grew. Somewhat more optimistic are the estimates of L. Prados de la Escosura, which raise the agricultural expansion to 1.0% annual cumulative between 1850–1859 and 1880–1889.

The increase in agricultural product was based, fundamentally, on the expansion of the cultivated area. According to R. Garrabou and J. Sanz, between 1800 and 1888 the agricultural area increased from 10.5 to 18.8 million hectares. Other specialists point out that in the forty years following 1815 the area under cultivation was increased by about 50%. Never in the history of the country has as much land been put under cultivation as then. Expressed as an annual rate, the expansion of agricultural land slightly exceeded the rate of increase of the population and equalled that corresponding to the production estimated by J. Simpson. This is a clear indication of the backwardness of the sector. Only by cultivating more land was the marginal production needed to feed the growing population achieved. And let us not forget that this was growing at a moderate rate, clearly below the European population (see chapter 1).

The existing information on agricultural land use confirms the diagnosis of the backwardness of agriculture. Cereals had an overwhelming weight. In 1860, 80% of the agricultural land was dedicated to this type of crop—especially wheat. Given that Spanish soil is, in general, not very suitable for the cultivation of cereals, the overwhelming predominance of cereal cultivation means an inefficient use of resources. This explains why land productivity remained stagnant until 1875, as did labour productivity, which still took four more decades to break out of the traditional low levels, according to M.A. Bringas' calculations. There are basically two ways to increase production: increase the product per hectare or increase the cultivated area. The first implies an intensification of land use, which can be achieved by increasing agricultural yields—improving physical productivity—or, the second, by introducing crops of higher commercial value—improving monetary productivity—. In the second case, agricultural growth is merely extensive. The agricultural growth of the time essentially followed the latter pattern. After all, the easiest way to increase yields is to put more land under cultivation. By 1815, and even in 1830, less than half of the land that could be cultivated with the rudimentary technology and production methods of the time was under cultivation. Traditionally, most of the unploughed land was used for livestock or for very occasional agricultural use. During the first two thirds of the nineteenth century it was possible, for the first time in centuries, to put millions of hectares of grassland and barren land suitable for cultivation to productive use—agricultural. The collapse of the institutions of the Old Regime, from 1808, and the liberal revolution facilitated this sustained increase in agricultural production through a continuous expansion of the area under cultivation, at the expense of the land reserved for grazing.

The question we must now ask ourselves is whether the low output growth and the lack of productivity gains that define the agricultural growth model were inevitable. This is the same as asking about the causes of agricultural backwardness.

The first cause of the delay is environmental factors. The characteristics of the climate and the soil are frankly adverse. As V. Pinilla pointed out, Spain is at the bottom of Europe in terms of agricultural potential. The natural environment imposes moderate or extreme aridity on more than 85% of Spanish territory. The natural fertility of the soil in this dryland Spain is so low that we can speak of an environmental restriction that has become a major obstacle to agricultural development. The technological model that revolutionized agriculture in northern Europe was inapplicable in Spain; neither the climate nor the quality of the soil allowed this model to be implemented. So, did environmental factors condemn Spanish farmers to remain in a backward position? The answer is no. In the first place, because since the middle of the nineteenth century there has been a technology suitable for their natural conditions, that developed by the United States (dry farming). Spain acquired this technology late, and began to import it at the end of the century. Why didn't it do so earlier? Before answering that, let's consider other arguments.

The second, and most important, reason for discarding environmental determinism is that some of the same conditions of the natural environment characteristic of the country lead to the fact that, as soon as the land becomes irrigated, it offers very high yields in Mediterranean crops such as fruit and vegetables, as well as in other crops, such as corn and beets. On this basis, a modern and very competitive agriculture emerged at the end of the nineteenth century. Why did Spanish farmers not abandon the primitive cereal agriculture and specialize in the production and export of the crops in which they had a comparative advantage? Although it is a matter of historiographical debate, most experts are inclined to attribute the fundamental cause of agrarian backwardness to institutional factors; specifically, the distribution of land ownership and the role played by the State.

The distribution of land ownership, tenure and exploitation represented a major stumbling block to agricultural modernization. Farms of an extremely suboptimal size, less than one hectare, were overwhelmingly numerous. Next to them, farms of more than 250 hectares accounted for a substantial part of the total agricultural area, about one third. Such a strong polarization of ownership would be a source of serious social conflict. It permanently fuelled the thorny issue of land reform. Focusing on the purely economic implications, it must be said that the dominant presence of smallholdings (in number) and large holdings (in size) made it very difficult to improve productivity. Smallholder farms did not have the economic capacity to change the production function to improve efficiency. In addition, small non-owner farmers had no incentive to invest or innovate, given the conditions set out in the leases (short duration and crop clauses). As for large owners and tenants, they tended to give up maximizing their income through product maximization. They enjoyed a monopoly position in local markets for land (as providers) and labour (as demanders), which allowed them to earn high incomes by paying miserable wages to day labourers, or by charging rents in line with the "land hunger" of landless peasants. Under such conditions, there was little incentive to make the latifundia more productive.

The landowning class was keen to keep the domestic market safe from foreign competition. Only in this way could they keep their economic power intact without having to invest resources in improving cultivation methods. For a long time (until 1868), the landowners did not have to act as a pressure group: the government maintained the traditional, mercantilist policy of absolute protection for grain. But a decade after the ban on imports was lifted, foreign grain began to enter the country in large numbers. The landowning oligarchy then organized and orchestrated the movement to oppose the entry of grain from the ranks of millions of small farmers, who saw their livelihoods seriously threatened. The governments of the time gave in to a social demand so broad and difficult to resist, especially since the restoration of universal male suffrage in 1890. In return, since the 1870s, trade policy helped export agriculture, by focusing on the negotiation of trade agreements that opened markets for agricultural products.

The government did not make up for the failure of private investment. During the nineteenth century hydraulic policy was conspicuous by its absence. The extension of irrigation required a strong investment commitment from the government, as the history of the twentieth century has shown. The poor state of public finances, combined with the priority given by the authorities to other public investment destinations (mainly railways), left the introduction of irrigation exclusively in the hands of farmers. Only the Mediterranean Levant experienced this transformation, which had already begun in a previous period. In this area, an investment of savings and labour that was socially very widespread, by a large mass of small and medium-sized owners, resulted in a notable increase in production and productivity, based on specialized Mediterranean crops.

The restriction to development imposed by institutional factors is related to the endowment and price of productive factors. The rural world of the time was characterized by a great abundance of land and labour and a scarcity of capital. Relative factor shortages and returns explain the difficulties that agriculture faced in overcoming its initial disadvantage. Why was there little technical change? Spanish farmers were aware of the latest technology. If they did not use it, it was because it was not profitable for them. It saved work but required considerable investment and a greater expenditure of animal energy. In a context like the Spanish countryside, while capital was scarce and expensive, labour and land were abundant and relatively cheap. Farmers would be inclined to use more land and more labour, rather than increasing the return on both factors through more capital-intensive use.

In short, without changing the causes of the agricultural backwardness just mentioned, the only mechanism available to expand high-productivity, more competitive and export-oriented agriculture depended on the evolution of international markets. As long as these markets remained open and growing, a progressive reorientation of the backward cereal agriculture towards the new crops could be expected. The path was followed and all specialists find traces of its impact on the modest rise in (monetary) land productivity and the growing regional specialization of crops. Unfortunately, the pace of change was late and too slow; worse still, there were major setbacks in some export markets, as we shall see in the next chapter.

2 Economic Liberalization and Internationalization

Let us talk about foreign trade policy first. It was the most powerful weapon available to the governments of the time to influence economic activity and one of the pillars of industrialization strategy. It is true that economic agents and historians themselves have exaggerated the capacity for real influence of trade policies. Once we know at least what their nature was, we will examine the trade figures.

Spain, like the other Western European countries, reacted favourably to the liberalizing trend unleashed by the radical change in British trade policy in 1846, which liquidated agricultural protectionism and moved resolutely towards free trade. The Spanish tariff of 1849 timidly reflects the new winds of liberalization that were blowing through Europe in the middle of the century and that would eventually give way to an era of international circulation of goods almost free of obstacles. From the tariff law of 1849 until 1891, Spain followed a very gradual but clear trend towards liberalization. In 1869, all remaining import and export bans were abolished. Tariffs were substantially lowered. In addition, a progressive tariff dismantling horizon was set which foresaw leading, in 1881, to a purely fiscal tariff, lacking a protective function.

The scenario envisaged by the 1869 legislation did not materialize because of political upheavals. However, between 1875 and 1890 customs duties continued to be lowered. The rulers had as a priority objective in the commercial field the promotion of exports. The way to achieve this was the policy of bilateral trade agreements. By signing trade agreements, Spain obtained facilities for the export of its competitive products, while at the same time opening up the Spanish market for the goods that its trading partners were most interested in selling abroad. All European countries did the same at this time. Thanks to the mechanism of reciprocity—the granting of the "most favoured nation clause"—there was a strong liberalization of international trade. In the case of Spain, the degree of trade openness rose from a level of 8% in 1850, typical of an almost autarkic economy, to 19% in 1890 (see Fig. 3.1; data in column 15 of the Appendix).

In comparative terms, there was also an increase. In 1850, Spain's degree of openness to trade was equivalent to 39.4% of that of Western Europe, while in 1890 it was 49.5% of Western Europe (see Fig. 3.2). That said, it should not be overlooked that the Spanish economy remained much more closed to foreign trade than neighbouring economies.

In the first decades of the nineteenth century, Spanish foreign trade was shaken by the loss of the colonies on the American continent, as we have seen in the previous chapter. Although imports and exports had little weight in the national income, the emancipation of the colonies put the Spanish economy in serious trouble. Almost all the captive markets for the export sectors disappeared. The foreign accounts deteriorated alarmingly. With the loss of the continental American empire, Spain had no choice but

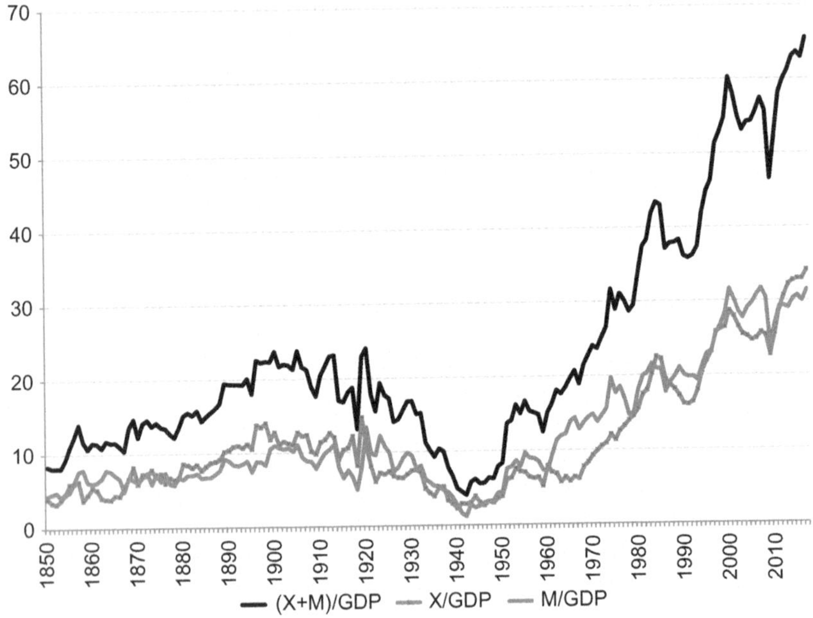

Fig. 3.1 Degree of trade openness of the Spanish economy, 1850–2017 (in %). *Source*: Column 15 of the Appendix and own elaboration from columns 3, 13 and 14

to look for a new model of integration into the international economy. It had to find a niche in the market for agricultural and industrial goods that was taking shape in Western Europe after the end of the Napoleonic wars. The Spanish economy was able to specialize in the production of certain classes of primary goods in which it had a comparative advantage and which were increasingly in demand by the more advanced countries that were industrializing. This productive specialization offered great opportunities for growth as soon as Western Europe and Spain abandoned their mercantilist policies.

Table 3.1 shows the acceleration in the growth of foreign trade since the second third of the century. In the 1820s and 1830s, foreign trade expanded very slowly because of the prevailing ultra-protectionist policy. Sales abroad showed greater dynamism than imports, which expresses the reaction of sectors with export capacity to the pressure of foreign demand. In the half-century between 1835/1839 and 1885/1889 the volumes of

Fig. 3.2 Degree of trade openness of the Spanish economy compared to EU-15, 1850–2016 (in %). *Source*: Appendix, Column 16.

imports and exports grew at the respectable average annual rate of 4.2% and 4.3% respectively. The impetus for imports came from the development of modern industry and the construction of the railway. There was a growing consumption of industrial inputs (raw cotton, coal), capital goods (machinery, wood) and railway material. The strong increase in foreign purchases in the central decades of the century caused a large trade deficit. However, this did not cause tensions in the balance of payments. The excess imports were financed by foreign investment. It is a common phenomenon for a developing economy to incur a trade deficit in order to procure productive equipment and fixed social capital, and to cover that deficit by resorting to foreign capital. But let us not lose sight of the role played by exports. They expanded steadily. In the 1870s and 1880s they intensified their growth rate, thanks to which the trade balance was able to run a surplus. Some specialists have spoken of a golden age by referring to the boost of exports in these decades. Widespread trade liberalization led

Table 3.1 Trade balance, 1821–1889, in million pesetas (decadal averages)

	Exports		*Imports*				
Years	*(1) Values at current prices*	*(2) Values at 1854 prices*	*(3) Values at current prices*	*(4) Values at 1854 prices*	*(5) Trade balance (column 1)–column 3)*	*(6) Real terms of trade (1821–29=100)*	*(7) Exports purchasing power*
1821–1829	105	90	129	113	-25	100	90
1830–1839	122	111	128	127	-6	109.3	121
1840–1849	146	136	153	171	-7	119.9	163
1850–1859	230	224	260	280	-30	109.0	244
1860–1869	320	306	452	463	-131	107.4	329
1870–1879	500	456	490	578	11	128.5	586
1880–1889	784	841	706	987	78	130.4	1096

Source: Cols. 1–5: L. Prados de la Escosura (1988): *De Imperio a nación*. Madrid: Alianza, tables 5-A1 and 5-A3; Col. 6: A. Tena (2005): "Sector exterior", in A. Carreras and X. Tafunell (coords.): *Estadísticas históricas de España. Siglos XIX y XX*, Bilbao: Fundación BBVA, vol.II, table 8.5. *Note*: column 2*column 6=column 7.

to strong growth in global demand. There was also a conjunction of extraordinary events such as the massive exploitation of mineral resources and the fabulous sales of wine caused by phylloxera (a plague that destroyed the vines of France, the world's largest producer and consumer of wine).

The Spanish economy benefited greatly by specializing in the export of these products, along with other primary goods in which it had comparative advantages. Column 7 of Table 3.1 (and Fig. 2.1, with a broader perspective) reveals what it gained by serving foreign demand. The purchasing power of exports increased nine-fold between 1830–1839 and 1880–1889. Spain was able to export a greater volume of products. At the same time, the prices of exported goods increased in relation to the prices of imported goods (see column 6). In other words, the real terms of trade improved significantly, so that Spain was able to buy more products abroad and enjoyed a rise in its national income.

The liberalization and opening up to the outside world went beyond the goods market. It extended to financial flows. Capital imports were of transcendental importance for the modernization of the Spanish economy of the period. The Spanish rulers of the time were aware that without foreign capital they could not carry out strategic economic projects due to the lack of financing, given the low level of technology and national savings. And foreign capital came, attracted by some good business opportunities. This capital inflow helped to finance the acquisition of imported capital goods and industrial inputs. The current account balance was almost always in deficit between 1850 and 1890 (see column 17 in the appendix). If there had not been a net capital inflow to compensate this unfavourable balance, the Spanish economy would necessarily have had to restrict its imports to equilibrate its balance of payments. This would have slowed down its growth. From the perspective of aggregate investment, the contribution of foreign capital was of enormous importance during the period 1850–1876, if not since before. According to the calculations of L. Prados de La Escosura, it represented then 37% of the aggregate investment, reaching half of it in the years 1858–1866, an absolute historical record.

Where did the capitals come from and where did they go? A. Broder's detailed reconstruction allows us to give a clear and direct answer. France provided about 70% of foreign savings; Great Britain provided 20%; from Belgium came almost all the rest. As for the destination of investment, the railway absorbed about two thirds of the total; mining accounted for almost the remaining third.

3 State Reform: Tax Reform

The liberal rulers carried out a profound transformation of the State. The fiscal reform was the most important administrative reform that the liberals undertook from an economic perspective. In the first decades of the nineteenth century, the state of public finances was one of the most serious economic problems. The inability of the Spanish State to meet its debts seriously disrupted the normal development of economic activity. The fiscal crisis could only be resolved by reformulating the foundations of the tax system. It was necessary to do so, moreover, because the taxation of the Old Regime was irreconcilable with the liberal ideology. Moreover, the definitive abolition of the tithe (1841) condemned the Church to ruin. Since the liberal politicians committed themselves before the Vatican to sustain the Church economically, the extinction of the tithe made the reform of the tax system undelayable.

The new tax framework—known as the Mon-Santillan reform—was approved in 1845. The system then established survived the liberal state itself. As F. Comín, the greatest specialist on the subject, made clear, after 1845 in Spain there was no real tax reform until 1977. The countless changes in tax regulations introduced between the two dates did not substantially alter the principles of tax burden sharing.

The tax system to be implemented had to comply with a series of principles, in accordance with the liberal doctrine: universality, equity, legality, sufficiency and systematization; in addition to a precondition: the government had to hold the tax monopoly. Although the 1845 tax reform met some of these conditions, it openly violated the principles of equity and sufficiency. As for the latter, one need only look at Table 3.2 to realize that, from the very beginning, the tax framework established in 1845 did not allow for a sufficient volume of funds to finance public spending. This had serious consequences on the State's ability to provide social capital goods that are essential for economic development, on economic stability and on the allocation of resources (such as spending on education, transport infrastructure, sanitation and water works). These issues will be discussed at length in later chapters.

If liberal politicians departed from some basic principles of their own ideology about the financing of the State, it was for social and political reasons. The modernization of the Spanish Treasury was plagued by difficulties and had to overcome enormous resistance, both from privileged groups and from the popular sectors. The taxation of 1845 lasted because

Table 3.2 Public revenues and expenses, and budget balance, 1850–1879 (million pesetas)

Years	*(1) Revenues*	*(2) Expenses*	*(3) Budget balance*	*(4) Balance/Expenses [(3)/(2)] (in%)*	*(5) Debt service/ Expenses (in%)*
1850–1854	1687	1767	-80	-4.5	14.8
1855–1859	2112	2333	-221	-9.5	20.6
1860–1864	2604	3318	-714	-21.5	22.0
1865–1869	2680	3531	-851	-24.1	37.6
1870–1874	2703	3743	-1040	-27.8	38.3
1875–1879	3696	3944	-248	-6.3	29.7

Source: F. Comín (1985): *Fuentes cuantitativas para el estudio del sector público en España 1801–1980*, Madrid: Instituto de Estudios Fiscales, Tables 3 and 7

it saved everything that could be saved from the previous tax regime and, when it came to introducing new taxes, it was very much aware that the tax authorities had the capacity to manage them and that Spanish society could take them on. The viability of the system was made at the cost of sacrificing some of the equity and collection power. But let's be clear: the new tax framework represented a great leap forward in the history of the Spanish Treasury. It finally emerged from a situation of chaos in which it had been immersed for half a century.

In essence, the tax framework established in 1845 was built with a few direct and indirect taxes, plus customs and some tax monopolies. Direct taxes were levied on income-generating sources—agriculture, industry, professional activities, etc.—rather than on the total income earned by individuals or families and companies. The tax bases of this taxation were therefore quite different in nature from those of modern taxation, which is based on income from labour and capital. Indirect taxes—those which affect the final prices of taxed products—were mainly levied on mass consumption goods with inelastic demand. The system was characterized by its stability. Three decades after the reform, the relative importance of the main tax figures had hardly changed.

A relevant feature of the tax system established in 1845 was the predominance of indirect taxes over direct ones. This made the tax system socially unfair, especially since indirect taxes were concentrated on inferior goods. But the inequity of the system went beyond the preponderance of indirect taxes over direct ones. If the tax burden fell much more heavily on the backs of the lower-income social strata than on those of the higher-income sectors, it was above all because of the way in which it was collected. The tax authorities did not know the income and wealth of each taxpayer. The administration lacked a cadastre of agricultural and real estate wealth, as well as an industrial census. Spain did not have these statistics, for the entire national territory, until the second half of the twentieth century! Instead, the Treasury resorted to the traditional practice in the Crown of Castile of quota and distribution. The Government fixed in the Budget the global figure that would be charged for each direct tax, this being distributed among the municipalities. The quota assigned to each one of them was distributed among the taxpayers.

How was the quota to be paid by each taxpayer fixed? Local bodies, dependent on the municipalities or on trade unions, established the taxpayers' quotas, based on the property declarations submitted by the interested parties themselves. As is easy to imagine, this collection system did not guarantee respect for the basic principles of liberal taxation, such as equity, nor did it guarantee flexibility. The allocation formula led to a tendency to freeze quotas and assessments, as local institutions resisted any increase in the allocated quota. The increase in the amounts collected inevitably lagged behind income growth. The overall tax burden (tax revenues/GDP) remained below 8% throughout the second half of the nineteenth century.

The tax system was, in practice, very inequitable. Tax evasion and concealment reached outrageous levels in the higher categories of direct taxation. The control of the distribution of the quota held by the local elites, in particular the landowners, allowed them to conceal their wealth with impunity and to shift the tax burden onto small owners and producers. The tax evasion of the powerful had as its reverse a relatively strong fiscal pressure on modest farmers, which became a heavy burden in times of economic recession. It is true that liberal taxation was less socially regressive than pre-liberal taxation, but it involved much less modernization than it promised.

Fraud and a lack of flexibility and equity in the tax system led to its inadequacy. The ordinary income of the State was not sufficient to cover current expenses. Here is the most outstanding feature of the Spanish State Budget in the whole second half of the nineteenth century: a persistent, structural deficit. The data in Table 3.2 and Fig. 3.3 are quite eloquent.

Since the first years of the liberal Treasury, public revenues were lower than disbursements. Although revenues have increased spending has always been ahead of the curve. Its dynamism was due, in part, to the new functions assumed by the liberal State: permanent defence, police, justice, public works, maintenance of the clergy. On the other hand, public spending grew steadily due to the very imbalance of public finances. The budget deficit was wiped out by public debt, which, when added to the accumulated debt, generated more interest payments, which meant more deficit. This spiral of indebtedness meant that expenditure tended to expand permanently. As the liberal rulers were unable to provide the Treasury with a sufficient volume of ordinary resources, they condemned it to continued financial deterioration. Debt service was addressed by issuing more debt. As a result, debt burdens increased steadily: in 1850–1854 they absorbed 14.8% of total expenditure; they jumped to 22% in 1860–1864, reaching 38.3% in 1870–1874 (and 53% of budget revenues, see Fig. 3.3). As is easy to imagine, the spiral of indebtedness finally finds an insurmountable limit. It ends up in the suspension of payments and the unilateral

Fig. 3.3 Debt service and State budget balance, 1850–2015 (in %). *Sources*: F. Comín and D. Díaz-Fuentes (2005): "Sector público administrativo y estado del bienestar", in A. Carreras and X. Tafunell (coords.): *Estadísticas históricas de España. Siglos XIX y XX*. Bilbao: Fundación BBVA, vol. II, tables 12.9, 12.13 and 12.24; and Intervención General de la Administración del Estado (IGAE), data on line in: http://www-igae.pap.minhafp.gob.es/sitios/igae/es-ES/EjecucionPresupuestaria/Paginas/ialiquidacionestado.aspx

cancellation (default) by the government of the financial obligations it has assumed. The Spanish Treasury went through the default experience several times (1851, 1864, 1876, 1882, 1899). In the following sections and chapters we will see what the effects of the tax authorities' indebtedness and insolvency were on the Spanish economy.

4 The Great Railways and Banking Business Cycle

The banking system fulfils two essential functions in a modern economy: the mediation between savings and investment and the provision of means of payment. Historically, it has played a third key role for economic progress: the promotion of industrial and service enterprises. In nineteenth century Spain, the banking system was mainly composed of non-corporate banking houses (merchant-banks) and bank stock companies. The first type of entity played a prominent role only in the provision of financial services and means of payment to commerce and industry. These banking establishments did not have the financial capacity to meet large-scale credit demands. Here we will deal only with bank stock corporations. And the first question we must ask ourselves is whether these institutions fulfilled the essential functions that we have just mentioned.

The quantitative indicators developed by P. Martín Aceña provide an unequivocal answer to the question posed. His data reveal a notable level of banking underdevelopment, both if we take into account the very low volume of bank deposits in relation to GDP, and the enormous volume of cash held by the institutions in relation to the deposits they managed (cash ratio), as well as the excessive proportion of the banks' own resources in relation to the total resources they managed, and ending with the disproportionate weight of the Bank of Spain within the banking system. All these indicators show some progress during the second half of the century, but it was clearly insufficient. To understand the level of backwardness of the sector around 1900, it is necessary to know the main milestones in banking history.

The three milestones that define Spain's nineteenth-century banking history are: the banking laws of 1856, the collapse of the system in 1866 and the granting of the Banco de España's banknote issuing monopoly in 1874. In the years prior to 1856, very few trading places had banking companies. Their absence was a drag on economic growth, which required the circulation of a greater volume of banknotes. Moreover, in the absence of banking companies, it was practically impossible to set up very capital-intensive companies and infrastructures like railways.

In 1856, legislation put an end to the extreme shortage of banking companies. The rulers sought to facilitate the creation of a modern banking industry capable of financing the construction of the railway. The laws on banks of issue and credit companies enacted in that year would indeed be the big bang in the Spanish banking system. Under the two banking laws, a large number of banking institutions were founded, more than enough for a developing economy like Spain's. The problem was that, on the one hand, many institutions did not instil enough confidence in savers to attract liquid savings en masse, and on the other hand, the new banks concentrated credit risk extremely on the railway companies, which would soon prove to be a bad business for their investors.

In 1866 the crisis broke out, the worst suffered by the Spanish financial system for more than a century (the other two major systemic banking crises were those initiated in 1977 and 2008). The economic failure of the railway companies pushed the entities that financed them into the abyss. The public sold bank shares and bonds en masse and rushed to bank counters to withdraw deposits and demand the conversion of paper money into cash. Most establishments succumbed to the banking panic (the only one Spain has ever known) and the stock market crash. The dismantling of the banking system must have had a strong negative impact on the Spanish economy. The loss of wealth suffered by the creditors of the bankrupt banks, as well as that suffered by those who had invested in the stock market, was compounded by the monetary contraction and the restriction of sources of financing for productive activities. The reconstruction of the banking system took a long time, hindered by the excessive financial power acquired by the Bank of Spain.

Indeed, in 1874 a new era in Spanish banking history was inaugurated with the decree granting the Bank of Spain the privilege of issuing. The other issuing banks were deprived of their prerogative to create banknotes. The measure taken by the Government was not intended to rationalize the monetary or banking system. It was motivated, purely and simply, by the pressing need of the Treasury to obtain a large volume of additional funds. In 1874, the Treasury was in a critical situation. The government secured an unconditional lender in exchange for granting it a monopoly from which it would extract large revenues. The Bank of Spain would put banknotes into circulation in exchange for the public debt securities that would swell its portfolio. This is known as direct monetization of the debt—direct, since later, in 1917, an indirect procedure was implemented. The monetization was not unlimited in scope, although the issue ceiling was revised upwards by the government on several occasions (1891, 1898, 1920).

The monopoly on issuing paper money strengthened the Bank of Spain enormously. It was not yet properly a central bank. It was a private entity that competed with the rest of the banks and sought to maximize its profits. The issuing monopoly gave it a formidable competitive advantage. Obviously, it is not the same having to raise liquid savings as putting banknotes into circulation in order to be able to grant credits and loans. In the first case, accumulating liabilities has a cost, while in the second case it has virtually no cost. In fact, the Bank of Spain was the first institution to create a national network of branches. With it, it massively drained savings. And it achieved an incontestable power of control over the financial market. A power that he used in favour of the Treasury. Between 1874 and 1900 the credits granted by the Bank of Spain to the public Treasury were five times greater than those contributed to the private sector, which was granted funds on loan exclusively guaranteed by public debt securities. It can be said that the monopoly on issuing banknotes slowed down the development of the banking system and damaged productive activities, which were deprived of sources of funding.

We have stated before that the banks born from the 1856 legislation played a fundamental role in the financing of the railways. We must now get an idea of how important it was for the Spanish economy to have a railway network. In the mid-nineteenth century, the country had a very poor supply of land transport. There were adverse physical conditions, economic backwardness and the poor state of public finances. The relief and climate condemned the country to have no inland waterways. Unlike other countries, Spain could not rely on a network of inland waterways. Moreover, the Spanish road and highway network was seriously deficient. In addition to being insufficient, it was very defective, both in terms of the poor state of repair and the layout of the roads themselves. They crossed great slopes through mountain passes. Transport was generally on horseback. In these circumstances, it was very expensive to move products and people; moreover, the supply of transport services was not able to meet large increases in demand. For an economy like the Spanish one at the time studied, this traditional transport system was a serious bottleneck. The process of economic growth and the articulation of the internal market activated by the liberal revolution could not continue without the modernization of the land transport means. This would come from the hand of the railway.

Although the railways were so necessary for Spain, it took a long time to start building them. Why did it take so long? Because of the lack of means and because the Government did not establish appropriate legislation until 1855. In an activity whose fixed capital is extremely high, with very long term returns on investment and which tends to be a natural monopoly, public regulation is fundamental for private investors to decide to undertake the construction of the lines. The first legislation, passed in 1844, failed because it did not attract foreign investment. A relatively poor economy like the Spanish one at the time had too low a level of savings to be able to finance a national railway network on its own. Foreign capital was essential. But this did not come about because it was not an attractive placement for foreign investors. The country's economic backwardness led them to predict that the concession companies would not obtain acceptable results.

The railway law passed in 1855, combined with the banking laws of 1856, finally attracted foreign investment. The concessionary companies would not only enjoy a number of privileges, including absolute tax exemption and tariff exemption on the import of all railway equipment. They would also benefit from strong financial support from the government. The subsidies received by the companies building the lines were substantial. Until 1867, the railway companies received a sum that represented more than half of the capital paid up by the shareholders and around a fifth of the total financial resources used in the sector. The sale of disentailed lands provided the public coffers for a time with extraordinary income with which the Government granted subsidies to the railway companies, which it would otherwise not have been able to finance.

The 1855 railway law therefore opened the door to large-scale construction. The decade that followed the new legal framework was the period of maximum activity. The network reached a length of more than 5000 km in 1866, which means that an average of 430 km of track was put into service each year. It was the prodigious decade in the formation of the railway infrastructure. In the following half-century the rate of completion fell by half. But the importance of the works carried out between 1855 and 1866 goes beyond the kilometres of track laid. By the end of this great cycle, the fundamental axes of the network had already been built, connecting almost all the regions and the main cities. Spain had managed to provide itself with the basic network in an incredibly short time, given the technical and material means of the time.

The achievement would not have been possible without the massive influx of capital—in every sense of the word: financial, technological, human—from abroad. It is true that with the resources and the local business initiative some strategic lines of the periphery were undertaken and financed: the Mediterranean corridor and that of the Ebro Valley. However, it was railway companies linked to foreign investment banks that built and operated most of the railway lines. Much of the foreign capital came from France, from three credit companies heavily involved in the construction of the railway network in different European nations.

The scheme of participation of French capital gave a strong role to two railway companies, the *Compañía de los Caminos de Hierro del Norte de España* (colloquially, North) and the *Compañía de los Caminos de Hierro de Madrid a Zaragoza y Alicante* (MZA). Its weight would not cease to increase in the following decades, through the absorption of a good number of smaller concession companies. This process of mergers and acquisitions was caused by financial difficulties and the need to reduce unit operating costs. Indeed, the railway companies were faced with a dramatic financial imbalance when the lines were put into service and interconnected. The operating revenues turned out to be much lower than expected. The most serious problem of the Spanish railway was the shortage of demand for transport services. An infrastructure had been created in a hurry to meet the demand. This was, to a certain extent, due to an economic policy strategy pursued by those in power. In the words of A. Hirschman—one of the great scholars of economic development theory—it is the strategy of driving development "by overcapacity" of modern transport infrastructure. Its provision translates into a strong decrease in the costs of productive activities, thus promoting their growth, which in turn results in an increase in the demand for transport services. At the time, both the authorities and the political class as well as business circles in the country were convinced of the merits of this argument. The railways were seen as the lever of economic growth. Historiography has challenged this view, prompting a lively debate about the cost-benefit balance of the model of railway construction that was applied.

The costs of the option taken are, according to some authors, of a dual nature. On the one hand, it had high financial costs, which led to a loss of national wealth and even political disruption (the revolution of 1868). On the other hand, the railway policy developed had high opportunity costs. There is no doubt about the first factor. The trading accounts of the concessionary companies were too meagre. For a long time, shareholders did not receive dividends and bond holders often did not receive interest payments nor the principal of the amortized securities. This situation had very negative effects on the railway companies, their creditors and shareholders and also on the investing public and the Spanish economy as a whole. In 1866, the railway companies suspended payments. It took them some time to be able to lift the suspension. The extension of the line remained almost paralyzed until 1873 and a construction cycle comparable to that of 1856–1866 was never seen again. The low profitability of the lines that were put into service no longer reflected the enthusiasm for investment. Worst of all were the negative externalities of the bankruptcy of the railways. As we saw, the stock market panic dragged down the banking companies, which had their assets concentrated in the sector. The collapse of the banking system had depressive effects on the real economy.

Some authors have defended the thesis that Spanish railway policy had an added social cost, in terms of the opportunity cost. By allowing free imports of railway equipment, the indigenous steel and mechanical construction industry would have been prevented from meeting the extraordinary demand for iron and steel products required for the construction of the network. The incipient modern Spanish steel industry would have been deprived of the great opportunity to develop. Historiography has highlighted the existence of a second opportunity cost, derived from the apparent waste of capital that was consumed by providing railway lines with a low volume of traffic. The execution of a railway route limited to the arteries with high transport demand would have saved many financial resources, which could have been allocated to other jobs of greater private and social utility. However, both reasons have been convincingly refuted by A. Gómez Mendoza, arguing that the alternative scenarios in which these opportunity costs were avoided carried an even greater social cost: the prolongation of a state of the supply of internal transport which, due to its archaism, strangled economic growth. If railway builders had been forced to consume iron produced by the national steel industry, Spain would surely not have had the basic railway network until much later. The same would have happened, obviously, if the government had not promoted a general plan.

The railway network was indeed of enormous social benefit. We said earlier that, for Spain, unlike most European countries, there was no efficient alternative to the railways. There was not until the age of the automobile. Consequently, by having the railway, the Spanish economy saved a great deal of productive resources. A. Gómez Mendoza estimated that this social saving amounted to 7.5% of GDP in 1878. The percentage would not stop growing in the following decades (in 1912 it was close to 20%). A. Herranz, using a different method of calculation, has substantially reduced the percentages, without questioning that the railway made an important contribution to economic growth: between 11% and 13.3% of the increase in per capita income (without considering indirect externalities, which are undoubtedly very relevant and impossible to estimate). The spectacular improvement in efficiency in the transport of goods and people that the railway represented with respect to traditional land transport systems resulted in a strong reduction in freight costs (up to 95% for products with a lower value per unit of weight). Both consumers and producers benefited from this. The price of commodities and intermediate and final goods fell, while their supply became more regular. It was as if the distance between the centres of production and consumption had been greatly reduced, in other words, the market had suddenly widened. From having a regional scale, the market now covers the whole of Spain. The railway was the driving force behind the process of integration of the internal market. Its progressive articulation, measurable in the convergence of prices of agricultural products in local markets, kept pace with the laying of the rails. Moreover, the expansion of the market stimulated the commercialization of production and productive specialization. Through these tracks—externalities—the railway contributed since the 1860s to the dynamism of Spanish agriculture, mining and industry.

5 Problems of the First Industrialization

In the second third of the nineteenth century, modern industry appeared in Spain. By 1830, there were hardly any manufacturing establishments that deserved to be called true industries, that is to say, that employed a considerable mass of workers, employed complex technology and had the manufacturing process mechanized. However, the modern industry that appeared at that time did not come out of nowhere. In Spain, as in the most precociously industrialized nations, the new industry was based on the accumulation of human, technological and financial capital previously generated by traditional manufacturing. At the beginning of the eighteenth century, a powerful textile industry had taken root in Catalonia, which gave rise to modern industry. It initially emerged in the wool sector, taking shape as a rural industry, based on the home work of peasant families and the manufacture of clothing for popular consumption. Medieval Catalan clothmaking had left an essential legacy: the technical and organizational training of guild artisan-entrepreneurs. The development of wool manufacturing paid for the development of the modern cotton industry, which benefited from the external economies of all kinds generated by the former: training of entrepreneurs, technicians and workers; business initiative; commercial infrastructures; a domestic capital market. The Catalan cotton industry took root in the 1730s with the printing of raw cotton fabrics imported from Asia ("indianas"—printed calicos). These modest origins were shared with the soon-to-be all-powerful British cotton industry. In the last third of the eighteenth century, the Catalan cotton industry took off very strongly. The reserve of the Spanish and colonial market and the incorporation of new technology invented by the British industry led to acceleration. The budding industrialization was hampered by the loss of the colonial markets and, during the French invasion, by the loss of the internal market. But, once the War of Independence was over, it continued its trajectory of spinning mechanization, simultaneous to the very active defence of tariff prohibitionism. The increases in income that we mentioned in the previous chapter fed the continuity of industrial growth.

At the height of 1850 Spanish industry still made a reduced contribution to GDP: 13.6%. Industrial employment represented approximately the same proportion of the total (12.1%), according to estimates by L. Prados de la Escosura. By 1890, the relative weight of industrial employment remained unchanged (12.7%), but industrial output had increased by a factor of 3.5. It increased much faster than the production of the other sectors; industrial productivity also grew rapidly. If in 1850 the apparent productivity of labour in the industrial sector was only slightly higher than that of the economy as a whole, in the following three decades it gradually moved away from it until it doubled in 1890.

Industrial development was far from widespread. The transformation only affected a few geographical areas and certain activities. Modern industries were characterized by the use of the steam engine for the mechanization of the manufacturing process. The textile industry and the iron industry (siderometallurgy) emerged as the two leading industries of the first industrial revolution in Spain, as in other countries. However, the country's main industry continued to be, by far, the agro-food industry. The weight of the two leading industries accounted for just over a quarter of manufacturing industry in 1856 and a third in 1900. Moreover, as J. R. Rosés has pointed out, these two sectors made a lesser direct contribution to the growth of the Spanish economy during the period 1850–1892 than the non-leading industries. This fact may seem paradoxical at first glance, but it is similar to what happened in Great Britain during its industrial revolution. The explanation lies, in part, in the reduced size of the leading industries in the first stages of industrialization. In another part, it is due to the fact that modernization spread to many other industrial branches producing consumer and intermediate goods. With delay, they adopted the techniques that had revolutionized the processes of fabric and iron manufacturing and metal processing.

Economic historians have paid much attention to the transformations that have taken place in non-leading industries. The work of a team of researchers led by J. Nadal systematizes the knowledge accumulated in this respect by the historiography. Here we will not outline this complex mosaic of industrial history, but focus the interpretation on the two leading industries, cotton and iron. This conventional approach perhaps simplifies reality, although not too much, since modern technology was not adopted until the end of the period in most of the transformed industries. The narrative scheme we have chosen clearly shows both the achievements of industrial progress in Spain at that time and its limits.

The cotton industry was, in many countries, one of the three pillars of the first industrialization—the other two being coal mining and the iron and steel industry. In Spain, as we have pointed out, the growth and modernization of cotton manufacturing gave rise to the industrialization process. The particularity of the Spanish case lies in the fact that cotton took the leading role in the industrial progress of the period. Suffice it to say that in 1860, 55% of the power developed by the steam engines installed in Spain was employed in the cotton industry.

The most striking feature of the Spanish cotton industry is its extreme concentration in Catalonia. During this period, Catalonia experimented an industrialization process based on the cotton sector. Thanks to it, the Catalan economy—not the Spanish one—was transformed in the course of the nineteenth century into an industrialized economy. What is more, the absolute dominium exhibited by the Catalan cotton industry spread to the other textile branches. What was the key to its success? The answer lies in the competitive advantage gained in the formative years (1770–1830). It turned out to be important enough to ruin almost all the initiatives that had emerged since then in other parts of Spain. The externalities and economies of scale accumulated early on by the Catalan cotton industry made it invincible within the internal market, although it was protected from competition from the most advanced British industry. Taking advantage of these economies and the similarity of technology and manufacturing processes, the cotton industry's dominance was extended to other fibres.

In the period 1830–1860, cotton manufacturing underwent a real revolution. It was not only a sustained increase in production of more than 8% per year. The progression in the volumes of manufactured goods was accompanied by the absorption of modern technology, following the path laid down by the innovative country (Great Britain). Between 1835 and 1861, the spinning industry adopted the steam engine and became fully mechanized while internalizing the different phases of the production process. In the same period, the weaving phase was half-mechanized. So the sector was mechanized at high speed. It did not always incorporate, or employ, the most technologically advanced machinery, although it did adopt the factory organization.

Mechanization resulted in dramatic gains in productivity, which put strong downward pressure on unit costs and final prices. This drop strongly boosted demand, given that, at an income level as low as the Spanish one at the time, the price elasticity of the demand for clothing was usually high. This is one of the sources of the strong expansion experienced by the cotton industry up to 1860: the enlargement of the market due to the displacement of other textile industries. The defeated were the traditional manufactures, such as flax and hemp. We are facing a case of growth by substitution. And we could add: double substitution. Because, in addition to expanding at the expense of other textile industries, the indigenous cotton sector grew by displacing foreign cotton fabrics from the domestic market. If in the 1830s, according to estimates by L. Prados de la Escosura, foreign cotton articles smuggled in supplied around 75% of the Spanish market, by 1890 their share had fallen to virtually zero. The conquest of the internal market reflects the relative modernization of the national cotton industry. Let us clarify: relative modernization, since it was unable to compete in open markets.

By 1860, the Spanish (Catalan) cotton industry occupied a respectable position, in terms of size and technology employed, within Europe. However, it would not manage to maintain this position in the future, nor would it be able to continue growing as it had been doing for three decades. The period 1860–1890 was one of slow growth, an annual increase of 3%. This weak expansion was not due to technological or organizational stagnation, or to the loss of business momentum, as has sometimes been claimed. The national cotton manufacturers did not neglect the technical modernization of their industries, they did not spare any effort to compress unit costs. As J. Nadal and C. Sudrià have shown, the prices of Spanish cotton fabrics fell to the same extent as those in the United Kingdom. So what was the problem facing the cotton industry and, by extension, the whole of the country's industry? The problem was twofold, one on the supply side and the other on the demand side. The first was the lack of cheap energy, i.e. coal. As it is known, the first industrial revolution was based on the exploitation of a fuel—the mineral coal—whose energy feeds an engine—the steam engine—that provides the mechanical force that moves the machines applied to the manufacturing process, as well as some means of transport. Spain has several coal basins, located in various parts of the territory. However, coal is scarce, expensive to extract and of low quality. The importance of this deficit must be stressed. Spain has not been able to count on its own abundant and cheap supply of the main industrial energy source of the nineteenth century. Spanish industry suffered a significant energy cost overrun. In Catalonia, manufacturers paid three to five times more for coal than their British competitors. This cost overrun must be taken into account when explaining the loss of momentum of Catalonia's leading industry and, more generally, Spain's weak industrial growth in the nineteenth century.

The second factor that hindered the growth of the cotton industry and, in general, all modern Spanish industry was the weakness of domestic demand. This was characterized by being quite stagnant and highly unstable. The internal market was small because of the backwardness of agriculture. The poverty of the agricultural sector retained the labour force in an activity of very low productivity, which led to miserable wages for the workers and meagre incomes for most farmers. In addition, their wages and incomes fluctuated widely, depending on crop results. Production tends to be very variable when agriculture is archaic, as it is more exposed to climatic factors. Therefore, the purchasing power of the bulk of consumers for manufactured products was low, virtually non-existent in years of poor harvests. The cotton industry knew how to adapt extraordinarily well to this market, as explained by J. Maluquer de Motes. But it paid a high price for that adaptation: the lack of competitiveness in open markets. The indigenous industrial structure suffered from low business concentration and absence of productive specialization. Both features prevented textile manufacturing from accessing international markets.

Was it therefore inevitable for the Catalan cotton sector to be cut off from foreign markets? This is a question that has been the subject of debate. Some authors have argued that there were possibilities of penetrating the world market and occupying a niche in it through ultra-specialized production or the domination of marginal markets for the largest producers. Industrialists in other countries with similar problems, such as Italy, took advantage of such possibilities. The Catalan cotton manufacturers did not even try, convinced that their competitive disadvantage was insurmountable. Resigned to producing at higher costs, they maintained at all times the strategy of serving the Spanish market and what was left of the Empire. They always demanded tariff protection to keep control of those markets. This was a conservative strategy. They opted for a path of slow growth, given the level of backwardness and lack of dynamism of Spanish agriculture.

If we move from cotton to iron and steel, we discover that the historical development of this industrial sector was subject to the same kind of conditions. The main difference is that the steel industry took off much later than the cotton industry. Until the 1840s, most of the iron produced in Spain corresponded to traditional facilities. The total production levels of this iron and steel industry were as traditional as its melting and forging methods: they would be around 10,000 tons of sweet iron per year. In 1890, production, which had been increasing rapidly since the end of the 1870s, was almost 200,000 tons of iron ingots and 80,000 tons of steel. This may seem like a big leap—it represents an annual growth rate of 7%. But considering the tiny levels from which progress was made, it is disappointing. In 1890, Spanish steel production lagged behind not only the great industrial powers but also the late industrializing European countries.

The fundamental causes of the iron and steel backwardness are familiar to us: the shortage of coal and the limitations of demand. The appropriate fuel for the iron and steel manufacturing process, until the appearance of the electric furnace, has been coal. With it, blast furnaces have been able to benefit from enormous economies of scale. Since coal is a product that becomes very expensive when transported over long distances and the steel industry was extremely intensive in its consumption, it tended to be installed where there were large deposits of the mineral. It was only when a technology—the Bessemer converter—was available that made coal consumption not much more intensive than iron ore, that areas with iron deposits were able to set up steel plants with some chance of success. And this is what happened in Spain.

The modern Spanish steel industry finally took root in Biscay, where the reserves of non-phosphorous iron ore used by the Bessemer process were located. Biscay was privileged to have precisely that kind of iron ore, a rarity on the continent. Biscayan mining supplied it en masse to the British steel industry and, on the rebound, to the indigenous one: the local steel mills prospered because they were able to import at low cost the British coal loaded as return in the ships that transported the iron ore to Great Britain. Obviously, Basque steelmakers paid more for their coal than their main competitors, but they partly compensated for this with the lower cost of iron ore, which was extracted practically at the factory gate. In 1886, the cost of producing steel ingot in Bilbao was only slightly higher than the international price. The large Biscayan plants were in a sufficiently solid position to face up to foreign competition and launch themselves into rapid growth. This did not happen.

Some authors have attributed the insufficient development of the sector at the end of the nineteenth century to technical backwardness and the small size of the facilities. But studies have made it clear that since the middle of the century, steel entrepreneurs have been equipped with the most advanced technology. If they did not use it in the most efficient way it was due to the narrowness of the market. The steel industry and closely related industries—the metal processing and machine building industries—were faced with extremely limited domestic demand. The large potential customers for their products turned their backs on them. Who were these customers? Why did they fail? In the most advanced countries, the main consumers of iron products were agriculture, the textile industry and transport systems, particularly the railways.

In the developed Western world, modernization of agriculture implied a massive demand for iron tools. In an economy that is still essentially agricultural, the main demand for steel products should be agriculture. This is possibly the main reason for the slow expansion of the Spanish steel industry and its technological backwardness during the first half of the nineteenth century. As we know, there was hardly any technical change in the national agriculture of the time.

Clearly, the same cannot be said of the second potential applicant for steel products, the modern textile industry. What happened is that its mechanization did not boost the mechanical construction industry. Tariff policy stifled its development. The sector was punished by negative effective protection: import machinery was hardly subject to any tariffs, while the opposite was true for raw materials. This was in the interests of two powerful economic groups. On the one hand, the traditional steel industry, in defence of which huge barriers to the entry of basic steel products were maintained; on the other hand, as far as machinery was concerned, the interests of textile manufacturers, who were keen to equip themselves with modern capital goods at the lowest possible cost, i.e. by buying them from Great Britain, weighed heavily.

As regards the third major potential customer of modern steel—the railways—it seems unnecessary to repeat the arguments put forward when discussing the construction of the railway network (see above).

In short, the steel industry did not have the demand of the sectors with the greatest theoretical consumption capacity. When the first blast furnaces producing steel in Spain were switched on in the 1880s, it was immediately apparent that their production capacity far exceeded domestic demand. At first, a considerable part of the steel produced was exported, in the line of products in which it was internationally competitive, the steel ingot. However, the Basque steelmakers decided to change their strategy as soon as their main market, Italy, adopted a protectionist tariff in 1887. They then joined forces with the Catalan textile manufacturers and the Castilian wheat producers to demand the lifting of strong tariff barriers in order to reserve the domestic market for themselves.

We will finish the analysis of the diffusion of modern industry with a simple quantitative exercise as a global balance sheet. This exercise aims to answer the following question: how much did industrial development contribute to economic growth? According to the calculations of J. R. Rosés, the expansion of manufacturing industry accounts for 30% of the increase in GDP that took place in 1850–1873 and half of the growth in GDP between 1873 and 1892. This seems to be a decisive contribution if we consider that the calculation only measures the direct contribution and leaves aside the important carry-over effects generated by the rise of modern industrial companies. However, the Spanish economy expanded slowly, as we saw in chapter 1. From this we can conclude that the development of industry, despite its undoubted productive successes, was not a strong enough driving force to transform the Spanish economy. It did, however, transform the regional economies in which it was concentrated: Catalonia and the Basque Country.

If we raise our eyes and, following again R. Allen and his package of policies for catching up from industrial backwardness, and try to place the experience of Spanish nineteenth-century industrialization in a global perspective, we can detect that in the period under consideration a very important effort was made to deploy the railway transport networks that could lower the cost of transporting goods in the domestic market and that the creation of investment banks was facilitated to channel domestic or foreign savings towards the railways and also towards mining operations. The internal market was unified through a combination of tariff protection, border surveillance—one of the missions of the Guardia Civil, created in 1844—and improvements in internal transport. Tariff policies did not provide more protection to domestic industry, but probably protected it more than in other countries, which dismantled more tariffs. This tension between protectionism and free trade consumed infinite political energy. Catalan industry had survived the loss of the Empire, and had been able to be born and grow, like British industry, because of imperial tariff protection. It fought to maintain this strong protection when the Empire was lost and believed that the pact with agrarian interests guaranteed its survival and growth. On the agrarian side, much was expected of the subsequent opening of the British market, which frightened Catalan industrialists so much. However, the result observable at the end of the period under consideration is an industry that has modernized in its modest growth and an agriculture that has lagged behind in its expansion. Disappointing for both interest groups.

There was no progress of any kind with regard to the universalization of education, rather steps backwards derived from the ruin of the providers of educational services—municipalities and parishes—without the State taking over. The absence, during most of the period, of inclusive political institutions hindered the possibilities of devoting greater attention to policies that were more attentive to the demands of the citizenry. The three Carlist wars and the brevity of the episodes of universal suffrage remind us of this.

Spain decided to opt for a growth model based on agriculture and with export ambitions, taking advantage of the market opportunities offered by industrializing Europe. The real terms of trade relations had improved for Spain in the four decades prior to 1840. But then, in the half-century covered in this chapter, they lost their momentum, stagnated and even got slightly worse at some junctures, to decline until 1913 (see Fig. 2.1). Neither the international market offered sufficient incentives for stronger growth, nor did the domestic market succeed in breaking out of an extensive growth pattern. The industrial revolution failed and so did the agricultural export strategy. The result was limited progress that could not prevent divergence from Western Europe from being the dominant trend of the period.

Bibliographic Orientation

The title of the chapter evokes that of J. Nadal (1975): *El fracaso de la revolución industrial en España, 1814–1913*, Barcelona: Ariel. An initial version was first published as "The Failure of the Industrial Revolution in Spain, 1830–1913", a long chapter in C. M. Cipolla (ed.) (1973), *The Fontana Economic History of Europe*, vol.4 (2), *The Emergence of Industrial Societies*, London: Collins. Despite the time that has passed since its publication, N. Sánchez-Albornoz (ed.) (1987): *The Economic Modernization of Spain, 1830–1930*, New York: New York University Press, contains essays that continue to be of great value among the bibliography of economic history of Spain published in English, such as those referring to the population, the railways and the financial system as well as to the diversity of regional experiences.

As a first reading, we recommend P. Pascual and C. Sudrià (2002): "El difícil arranque de la industrialización (1840–1880)", in F. Comín, M. Hernández and E. Llopis (eds.): *Historia económica de España. Siglos X-XX*, Barcelona: Crítica. The chapter by P. Tedde (1994): "Revolución liberal y crecimiento económico en la España del siglo XIX", in A. Bernal *et al. Homenaje a Miguel Artola*, v. 1, Madrid: Alianza, summarily examines the influence of the liberal revolution on economic development. The greatest specialist in public finance is undoubtedly F. Comín. Among his numerous works, the book (1996) *Historia de la Hacienda pública*, II. *España (1808–1995)*, Barcelona: Crítica, stands out for its attractive treatment of the subject and its broad vision of it. On the foreign sector, it is useful the summary provided by its major expert, L. Prados de la Escosura, in "El sector exterior español durante el siglo XIX", in G. Anes (ed.) (1999): *Historia económica de España. Siglos XIX y XX*, Barcelona: Galaxia Gutemberg. The same book contains a valuable reflection on trade policy, opposed to that defended by the previous author: J. Palafox: "Proteccionismo y librecambio ". As for the banking sector, the issuing banks have been the centre of interest for researchers, as C. Sudrià (2016): "La banca emisora provincial y la economía española: dinero y crédito", in C. Sudrià Triay and Y. Blasco-Martel (eds.): *La pluralidad de emisión en España, 1844–1874*, Bilbao: Fundación BBVA. Among the many studies devoted to the Bank of Spain, see P. Martín-Aceña (2017): *The Bank of Spain, 1782–2017. The history of a central bank*, Madrid: Banco de España. On non-corporate banking, M. Titos Martínez: "Banca y banqueros privados", in P. Martín Aceña and M. Titos Martínez (eds.) (1999): *El sistema financiero en España. Una síntesis histórica*, Granada: Universidad de Granada. On the railway the must-read is: F. Comín, P. Martín Aceña, M. Muñoz Rubio and J. Vidal Olivares (1998): *150 años de historia de los ferrocarriles españoles*, Madrid: Fundación de los Ferrocarriles. Regarding the contribution of the railways to economic growth, A. Herranz-Loncán (2006): Railroad Impact in Backward Economies: Spain, 1850–1913, *Journal of Economic History*, 66: 853–881, discusses the previous calculations made on the social savings of the railway and offers a new evaluation. On agriculture, the most clearly formulated classical interpretation is that offered by G. Tortella (2000): *The Development of Modern Spain. An Economic History of the Nineteenth and Twentieth Centuries*, Cambridge (MA): Harvard University Press. After that, it is essential to read J. Simpson

(1995): *Spanish agriculture. The Long Siesta, 1765–1965*, Cambridge: Cambridge University Press, and not only for the period covered in this chapter, but also for subsequent ones, up to chapter 7. A well-balanced survey on the causes of the agricultural backwardness, which reflects the long debate that has arisen around this fundamental issue, in E. Clar and V. Pinilla (2016): "The contribution of agriculture to Spanish economic development, 1870–1973", in P. Lains and V. Pinilla (eds.) (2016): *Agriculture and Economic Development in Europe Since 1870*, New York: Routledge. Regarding industry, a basic reading is J. R. Rosés (2006): "La primera etapa de la industrialización", in A. González Enciso and J. M. Matés Barco (coords.): *Historia económica de España*, Barcelona: Ariel. For a more in-depth knowledge of industrialization, the reference work is J. Nadal (dir.) (2003): *Atlas de la industrialización de España, 1750–2000*, Barcelona: Crítica/Fundación BBVA.

CHAPTER 4

Spain in the First Economic Globalization (1890–1914)

The combination of lower tariffs and, mainly, technological breakthroughs in land and maritime transport made international trade much cheaper. Since the 1870s this was the dominant trend worldwide, strong enough even to increases in tariffs. It was reinforced with the diffusion of the gold standard. For a quarter of a century, the world experienced an unprecedented economic globalization, with massive movements of goods, labour and capital. Spain missed some of the available opportunities.

1 The Transport Revolution and the Great Agrarian Depression

Since the late 1870s, European agriculture has been in a long period of crisis. It originated from the extraordinary expansion of the cultivated area in the "new" countries of recent European colonization (mainly the United States, Canada, Argentina and Australia) plus Russia. On these lands, the production costs of cereals and livestock were much lower than in Western Europe. Agricultural and livestock farming in these territories was made possible by advances in transport technology. To the revolution in land transport represented by the railway was added the extraordinary progress of maritime transport, thanks to the adoption of the steam engine, the use of the steel hull and the invention of the propeller. All

A. Carreras, X. Tafunell, *Between Empire and Globalization*, Palgrave Studies in Economic History,
https://doi.org/10.1007/978-3-030-60504-9_4

these advances matured in the 1860s. By the mid-1870s there were already large overseas areas well connected to Europe by a combination of railways and steamships.

This revolution in transport meant that the agricultural market of the continent was flooded by increasing quantities of foreign agricultural and livestock products. In some crops, like wine, the growing competition derived from the increase of the same European production was added. The agricultural crisis consisted, therefore, of a situation of structural excess supply, which resulted in a sharp fall in prices. The depression affected most of the agricultural and livestock sectors. But it was, above all, a crisis of the cereal system. The emerging agricultural powers were mainly cereal producers.

So from 1878–1879, the coastal regions of the Peninsula began to consume foreign cereals *en masse* because they were cheaper than national ones. With this, the Spanish countryside was facing a deep crisis. Many of the Spanish cereal farms were not in a position to increase production efficiency and reduce production costs. The fall in prices and income would lead to the closure of many farms and a reduction in the demand for work in the countryside.

Before continuing, we must explain that the cereal crisis was tempered, in the first years, by the simultaneous expansion of wine production. Since the 1870's, French vineyards were being devastated by the phylloxera plague. It forced them to be replanted with American vines, which were immune to phylloxera. France, the world's largest exporter of wine, had to resort to importing wine from other countries in order not to lose its markets. The complete opening of the French market for Spanish wines caused a real wine boom. For a few years, a Spain that was suffering from the cereal crisis coexisted with another Spain that was enjoying the expansion of the vineyard. But, by the end of the 1880s, French vineyards had returned to their normal production levels, while the Spanish were being attacked by phylloxera. When wine production entered a crisis, it joined that of the cereal system, forming a very depressing combination.

The transoceanic migration was the most outstanding phenomenon of the great agrarian depression, because of its meaning, its generality and its dimension. The meaning was clear: the European peasants left the European fields to go and cultivate the fields overseas. The massive exploitation of a productive factor—the land—caused a historical alteration in the remuneration of the work factor, to the point of forcing millions of Europeans to take dramatic relocation decisions. The generality of the phenomenon is unquestionable. No European country escapes the expulsive impact of the agricultural depression. In the case of Spain, between 1885 and 1913, in two great waves, more than two and a half million people emigrated. In net terms—permanent migration—they were limited to more than one and a half million, which is already a lot: between 8% and 9% of the Spanish population. Emigration was concentrated in the most cereal regions (the two Castiles) and in those that already had a tradition of emigration (such as Galicia and Asturias). In the half of Spain most affected by emigration, the proportions of emigrants over the total population amounted to 15% or even more. The determinants of Spanish emigration, synthesized by B. Sánchez Alonso, were very sensitive to a few variables. Firstly, the price of cereals. With high prices, less people emigrated. Hence, the protection of Spanish agriculture was the natural reaction of the rulers. Protectionist measures had an undeniable impact on emigration, reducing it. Secondly, the demand for labour in the Americas, which in the Spanish case consisted mainly of Argentina. When Argentina was experiencing an investment boom and the demand for labour was increasing, so was Spanish emigration. In addition, it was important that the population that considered the possibility of emigration had some literacy and mastered a trade. It was more decisive that the potential emigrant had some economic resources to pay for the trip and the installation costs. The illiterate peasants with very low incomes, who were simply surviving, like the Andalusian day labourers, were in a poverty trap: they could not emigrate to America.

In comparative terms, Spanish emigration was not very intense. Many countries experienced higher proportions of emigrants per capita. The lower Spanish propensity to emigrate would be explained, according to some authors, by the strong Spanish protectionist reaction. It cannot be dissociated from the approval of universal male suffrage in 1890. Despite the obstacles posed by *caciquismo*, universal suffrage forced politicians not to disregard the demands of their voters, who did not want to emigrate. The difference with Italy is clear: universal male suffrage was only approved there in 1914, at the end of the period of mass emigration. The Italians emigrated, proportionally, the double than the Spaniards.

The channels open to political participation were an incentive for landowners and farmers to organize as a pressure group. Throughout the 1880s, large masses of cereal farmers were mobilized, in a campaign of growing social unrest. The government soon took up their demands by approving a strongly protectionist tariff in 1891.

2 The Protectionist Shift and the Loss of the Last Overseas Colonies

The Castilian wheat farmers were a very strong lobby in defence of a strongly protectionist tariff. Farmers in other regions did not form a compact mass, as agrarian protectionist interests competed with export interests. The belligerent defence of protectionism by Castilian farmers was enthusiastically received by the Catalan textile industries, which were the group that had traditionally defended the need for more protection. A third powerful economic vector joined the two previous ones: the Basque steelmakers. From 1887 onwards, they lobbied for greater protection of the Spanish market.

What will end up distinguishing Spain is the enormity of the tariff barriers raised. In 1894, no European country had such high levels of protection for cereals as Spain, except Portugal, which prohibited the import of wheat. This explains why the fall in food prices here was lower than in the rest of Europe and why, unlike the latter, prices recovered between 1895 and 1905 to return to pre-crisis levels. In other words, the sharp increase in tariffs allowed farmers to be paid more than the international market had set (see Fig. 4.1).

The adoption of such a protective policy hindered the ongoing process of agricultural transformation, even without blocking it. Covered by the tariff, therefore, without the need for cost adjustment, cereal agriculture postponed the necessary structural transformations. A large part of the small farmers and the mass of day labourers were able to survive, albeit miserably and by producing food at high prices. This hampered the development of the industry, which needed relative food price reductions to boost demand for manufactured goods. Thanks to the tariff, the area dedicated to the cultivation of cereals expanded considerably in the first three decades of the twentieth century.

It is true that modern and dynamic agriculture, that of "new crops", which we can identify with fruits and vegetables, expanded even more, based on its competitiveness in foreign markets. It managed to become part of the diet of the population in the richest countries. The productivity of the land dedicated to these crops increased substantially, thanks to the greater use of chemical fertilizers, the adoption of new technology and the extension of irrigation. The two dynamic components of the Mediterranean triad—wine and oil—did not enjoy the same fate. They suffered major

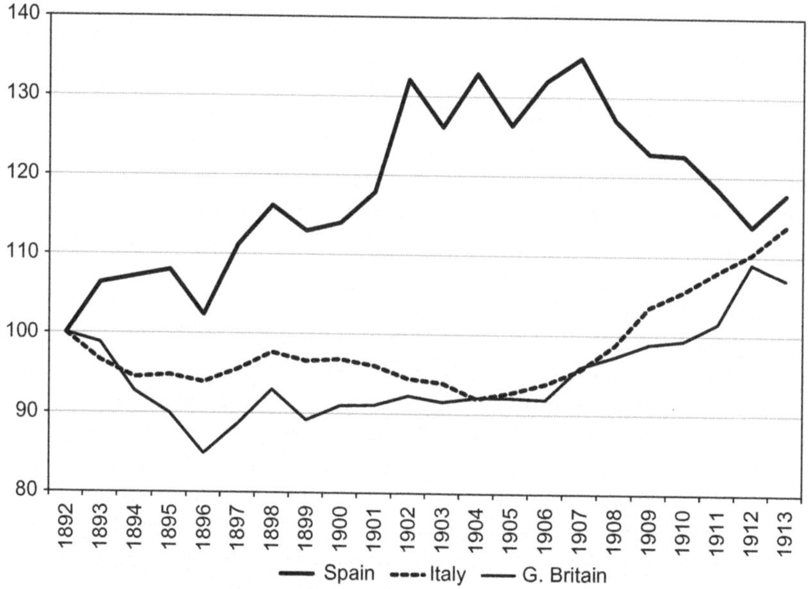

Fig. 4.1 Food prices in Spain, Italy, and Great Britain, 1892–1913 (1892=100). *Source*: J. Palafox (1991): *Atraso económico y democracia. La Segunda República y la economía española*. Barcelona: Crítica.

crises and faced the closure of foreign markets and great difficulties in penetrating new ones.

The 1891 tariff not only protected traditional agriculture, but also the more consolidated industry. This coverage was reinforced by the 1906 tariff. Many more sectors of industry will obtain their protection increased. Emblematic cases will be coal mining, wool industry and mechanical engineering. An increasingly restrictive framework for foreign competition will be established. It was the inevitable consequence of betting on what was called at the time a "comprehensive protectionism", consisting of the defence of all productive sectors against foreign competition. The defensive strategy followed by the industrialists, like most of the agriculturalists, hindered the growth of the economy by preserving inefficient productive activities that had no chance of becoming competitive. Moreover, the protective tariff discouraged innovation and cost reduction by other activities that could become competitive in open markets.

But to what extent was the Spanish economy closed to the outside world? We should not fall into the error of assuming that the rise in the nominal protection levels of the tariff led to an economic retreat of the same intensity. What matters, after all, is the effective degree of trade openness, in its two aspects: considered in itself and in relation to that of the surrounding economies. Well, the data reveal a surprising fact: trade openness was greater around 1913 than in 1890 (see column 15 of the Appendix and Fig. 3.1.). The propensity to import did not decrease; on the contrary, it increased slightly. When putting this evolution into context, it can be seen that Spain behaved in a similar way to Western European countries (see column 16 of the Appendix and Fig. 3.2). Its degree of relative openness in 1913 was exactly the same as in 1890.

How can it be explained that there was no closure of the Spanish economy when economic agents and leaders pursued an anti-globalization strategy to protect the national producer from foreign competition? The key is that the barriers to access to the internal market did not depend only on the tariff but also on the exchange rate of the peseta and on international transport costs. M. Sabaté, C. Fillat and A. B. Gracia have measured what they call the "equivalent tariff". This is the result of combining in an equation the magnitudes of the three trade barriers mentioned, according to the import elasticity of each of them. The equivalent tariff had experienced a significant reduction in the two decades prior to the 1891 tariff. In 1913, the equivalent tariff, as calculated by these authors, was below the level of 1891 after having increased considerably in the 1890s due to the sharp depreciation of the peseta combined with the rise in tariffs. The underlying trend towards a reduction in the equivalent tariff carried over from the sharp fall in international transport costs finally prevailed.

The changes in tariff policy and the ups and downs of the peseta are linked to recent episodes in overseas colonial history. As Spanish domestic demand shrinks, businessmen are attaching more importance to the colonial market. The 1882 Law of Commercial Relations with the Antilles establishes a strong asymmetry between the Peninsula and the island colonies. While the colonial market is, to all intents and purposes, a free and protected market for Spanish producers, colonial producers must pay tariffs to access the Spanish market. The manufacturing industry will make good use of the situation and redirect its surpluses to Cuba, Puerto Rico and, to a much lesser extent, the Philippines. The iniquity of the deal would eventually lead, in 1895, to a new and definitive independence revolt in Cuba.

The war of 1895–1898 was costly. The bill for Spain amounted to about a third of its GDP. How was it financed? By various mechanisms. The tax increase was difficult to propose until the defeat took place. Much more bearable, and quite popular, was the issue of debt. Large debt issues were made. The other financing mechanism was the recourse to the Bank of Spain. Since Spain was not on the gold standard, the temptation to issue more money was irresistible. As we saw (Chap. 1), the exchange rate of the peseta suffered the consequences, more because of public expectations than because of differential inflation. Contrary to popular belief, the Cuban war years were not inflationary (see columns 19 and 20 of the Appendix and Fig. 9.1). The bulk of the increase in the amount of money in circulation was absorbed by economic activity. This is because the war took place during a few years of economic boom. Financing needs are easily met because the public is willing to buy debt and the economy thrives and absorbs the banknotes that are put into circulation. The relaxation of monetary policy probably gave a decisive boost to the growth of an economy constrained by the lack of liquidity. We will return to this issue later. First, we will consider how the defeat was settled.

The government, with Fernández Villaverde in charge of the Treasury portfolio, took advantage of the international abundance of capital, reflected in very low interest rates. Fernández Villaverde made a huge debt issue, at lower rates than those in circulation, and accompanied the issue with a strong patriotic campaign encouraging subscription. It was a success. With this issue he cancelled, without any violence to the economic agents, all the pre-existing debt, contracted at higher rates. The extremely clean conversion made it possible to lower the cost of servicing the debt. However, the volume of the debt had increased. This called for an increase in tax collection or a cut in expenditure. Villaverde attacked from both sides, in what can be described as a real stabilization plan. He proposed a budget with many savings, which would last a decade. On the other hand, he took advantage of the national sensitivity in front of the loss of the last colonies—the humiliation of "the 1898". The fiscal reform he promoted can only be understood in this context. Tax increases require powerful reasons to bear them. Villaverde thoroughly retouched the fiscal system approved in 1845, with new taxes and increases in the tax rates of existing ones. All in all, a significant increase in the tax burden.

3 The Formation of the Modern Business Enterprise and the Start of the Second Industrial Revolution

The so-called "disaster" of 1898 was not a disaster at all, from an economic point of view. The loss of the colonies caused a massive influx of capital that was a powerful aid to the development of the Spanish economy. Spanish businessmen withdrew the many investments they had made in the Americas over the decades. They did so in order to save their patrimonies; also because of the exaggerated depreciation of the peseta, which made it attractive to invest in Spain for all Spaniards living abroad who were waiting for an opportunity to repatriate their capital. The flow of capital was extraordinary: a quarter or more of a year's national income. This influx of private capital had an enormously positive impact. The great investment cycle of 1898–1903, known as the *fin-de-siècle* boom, was caused by the flood of capital from abroad.

It was precisely at this time that the modern business enterprise was formed in Spain (the great railway company and the great mining company already existed). It appears in three fundamental and closely linked areas: the industrial, the electrical and the financial. The most outstanding companies are shown in Table 4.1, although large industrial companies were formed whose shares were not quoted on the stock markets, such as Hispano-Suiza (leading car manufacturer), Sociedad Anónima Cros (second largest chemical company in the country) or Compañía de Hilaturas Fabra y Coats (leading textile industry).

As can be deduced from some of the company names, part of the phenomenon has to do with company mergers. Altos Hornos, Duro-Felguera, Unión Resinera, Unión de Explosivos, Azucarera, Unión Alcoholera and Papelera Española are all mergers. There was, at the heart of the end of the century boom, a component of a wave of mergers, such as the one that took place in the United States in those same years. In part, these were defensive movements, in the face of competitive pressure. On the other hand, they were "offensive" movements, aimed at obtaining economies of scale. As in other countries, mergers and the promotion of new companies were linked to the development of investment banks. And, as elsewhere, new firm promotion and mergers boosted the secondary capital market. The stock markets, which until then had traded almost exclusively in government bonds and railroad securities, began to trade in industrial securities. Share prices rose sharply from 1898 to 1902 (see column 23 of the Appendix), in line with the companies' strong economic performance.

Table 4.1 The 25 largest companies according to their market value in 1913. Million pesetas

N°	*Name of the company*	*Incorporation year*	*Market value*
1	BANCO DE ESPAÑA	1856	676.5
2	CAMINOS DE HIERRO DEL NORTE DE ESPAÑA, CÍA. DE LOS	1858	242.5
3	FERROCARRILES DE MADRID A ZARAGOZA Y ALICANTE, CÍA. DE LOS (MZA)	1856	230.1
4	ARRENDATARIA DE TABACOS, CÍA.	1887	175.8
5	*ALTOS HORNOS DE VIZCAYA*	1902	99.6
6	*GENERAL AZUCARERA DE ESPAÑA, SOCIEDAD*	1903	60.8
7	UNIÓN ESPAÑOLA DE EXPLOSIVOS	1896	60.8
8	*BANCO HISPANO AMERICANO*	1900	53.0
9	BANCO HIPOTECARIO DE ESPAÑA	1872	50.2
10	BANCO DE BILBAO	1857	47.1
11	CATALANA DE GAS Y ELECTRICIDAD	1912	41.2
12	FERROCARRILES ANDALUCES, CÍA. DE LOS	1869	28.9
13	PENINSULAR DE TELÉFONOS, CÍA.	1894	24.4
14	FERROCARRILES DE MADRID A CACERES Y PORTUGAL, SDAD. DE LOS	1880	24.2
15	*BANCO DE VIZCAYA*	1901	22.9
16	*BANCO ESPAÑOL DE CRÉDITO*	1902	22,8
17	*FERROCARRILES VASCONGADOS, CÍA. DE LOS*	1906	20.3
18	*UNIÓN RESINERA*	1898	19.8
19	*METALÚRGICA DURO-FELGUERA, SOCIEDAD*	1900	19.4
20	BANCO HISPANO COLONIAL	1876	19.1
21	*MINERA "EL GUINDO", SOCIEDAD*	1899	17.4
22	*NAVIERA SOTA Y AZNAR, CÍA.*	1906	17.3
23	ESPAÑOLA DE MINAS DEL RIF, CÍA.	1908	16.4
24	FERROCARRILES DE SANTANDER A BILBAO, CÍA. DE LOS	1894	15.3
25	*PAPELERA ESPAÑOLA, LA*	1901	14.6

Source: X. Tafunell (2005): "Empresa y Bolsa", in A. Carreras and X. Tafunell (coords.): *Estadísticas históricas de España. Siglos XIX y XX*. Bilbao, Fundación BBVA, vol.II, Table 10.19, and A.Carreras and X.Tafunell (1993), "La gran empresa en España (1917–1974). Una primera aproximación", *Revista de Historia Industrial*, 3.

These are perhaps the best years for corporate profitability in Spain (see Appendix, column 24).

The constitution and development of this nucleus of large corporations has had a special historical significance. In 1913, the first three places in the classification of Spanish companies by value of stock market capitalization corresponded to two railway companies and a bank, all created in 1856–1858 (see Table 4.1). However, many companies formed during the inter-secular boom follow. They are shown in italics. As the new companies have a very considerable weight in their respective sectors of activity, they tend to hinder the functioning of competitive markets. This does not indicate economic backwardness. One of the distinguishing features of the second industrial revolution is the rise of large industrial enterprises, enjoying huge economies of scale. The rise of big business is often accompanied by the emergence of oligopolies. Perhaps what distinguishes Spain at that time from other more industrially advanced countries is the more pronounced dominance of big business. This is the conclusion that should be drawn from the surprising finding that Spanish industrial companies occupy relevant positions in the world ranking of their respective sectors at the end of the First World War.

The large industrial companies are not the only protagonists of the new path that the Spanish economy is following. The big banks were born and grew up in this period. In Spain, as in other late industrializing countries, the big banks will play a fundamental role. In these years, various entities have emerged which, due to their own resources, are true financial giants. They will be called upon to form the nucleus of the top twentieth century banks. It will not be long before they are so actively involved in promoting and financing industrial and service enterprises that hardly any major one will be created without their financial support.

The set of business initiatives that we have mentioned has another outstanding characteristic: the great majority of them are of Spanish capital. The large railway, banking and mining corporations created in the previous half-century were foreign-owned. The turn-of-the-century boom generates a new Spanish capitalism. In the strong renewal of the leadership of large Spanish companies, there is a component of naturalization of capitalism that must be emphasized. The emergence of new Spanish entrepreneurs and capitalists who are committed to their country's economy in the long term will give impetus to a more nationalist vision of economic policy. This movement coincides with the state of public opinion, which in the face of the colonial disaster, demands that the authorities place greater emphasis on modernizing Spain using Spanish resources. Economic nationalism is one of the deepest legacies of the "1898".

The entrenchment of new activities and the strengthening of basic industrial sectors have much to do with the spread of new technologies, especially the increase and cheapening of the energy supply. Spain will adopt the new electrical technology, developed from 1880 onwards, fairly quickly. A country where coal was so expensive, it had to decisively opt for electric power. The natural conditions favoured this second energy transition: the Spanish rivers contain a great potential for hydroelectric power generation. Once the technical problem of the transport of the electrical fluid to long distance was solved (towards 1905), the electrification advanced with speed. This would imply enormous investments, comparable to those that had been made for the construction of the railroad. The Spanish initiative came punctually to the meeting. The mobilization of Spanish capital is added to the participation of the largest multinational groups in the sector, which are fighting to take control of the Spanish electricity market. This will make it possible to multiply electricity production and make it radically cheaper in the 1910s and 1920s.

The decreasing cost of electricity will greatly benefit Spanish industry in general. And not only because electricity will become a substitute for coal, given the evolution of relative prices. When, at the beginning of the twentieth century, the price of electric motors is reduced and they are miniaturized, the electrification of industry will spread rapidly. The world of small businesses and workshops will have an efficient technology, suitable for their scale of production and relatively cheap. Many manufacturing activities that were still done manually will be mechanized. On the other hand, the availability of abundant and cheap electricity will contribute decisively to the development of heavy, highly energy-intensive industries, such as chemistry, metallurgy and the cement industry.

4 A Slow Divergence

In Europe and the Americas, the years from the beginning of the twentieth century to the outbreak of the European war are years of great prosperity. The international movement of goods, services, capital and people reaches its peak. This results in continuous improvements in the allocation of productive resources and sustained growth of the world economy. It is the golden age of the gold standard, the *belle époque*. Spain, on the other hand, takes relatively little advantage of the boom brought about by the first wave of globalization. Its growth rates are significantly lower than those of all the countries with which it can be compared (see Fig. 1.3).

In 1883, Spain entered into a three-decade trend of divergence. There is a consensus among economic historians on this fact. There is no consensus at all on the causes of this divergence. Throughout this book, we have avoided debates and have sought to build on wide interpretative consensus, as befits a work that aspires to have a formative and introductory component. In this section we must change the register and present one of the great debates of contemporary Spanish economic historiography: to what do we owe this long divergence?

The first diagnosis of the Spanish delay in this period is provided by J. Nadal in *The Failure of the Industrial Revolution in Spain*. In the conclusion of this classic work, he evaluates the failure in terms of W. Hoffmann's typology, which relates the added value of the consumer goods industries to that of the investment goods industries. According to this typology of industrial development, nations go through three stages in their industrialization process. In 1860, Spanish industry had reached the first stage of industrial development, like the other countries of Western Europe, except for Great Britain, Belgium and Switzerland, which were already in the second stage. It reflected the development of a modern textile industry and the first steps of a heavy industry and mechanical constructions. In 1913, when all the European neighbours had already jumped into the second or third stadium, Spain was still stuck in the first one. The whole set of intermediate goods and machinery and transport industries that characterized a mature industrial economy had not been developed. Spain was still in the infancy of its industrialization.

J. Nadal himself put forward some major explanations for this "failure". The main is agricultural backwardness. The liberal agrarian reforms were incapable of increasing agricultural productivity, which did not improve the income of the rural population. In the absence of a growing domestic market, industry was unable to grow rapidly or provide employment for peasants willing to migrate to the urban world. As a result, industry will not be able to transform itself. It will remain anchored in an increasingly backward economic structure. J. Nadal also proposed another explanation, complementary to the previous one: the problems of the public sector had distorted the decisions of governments. They were absorbed by the urgency of public finances and always postponed the deployment of growth-promoting policies. Let us consider the first line of argument.

L. Prados de la Escosura reversed the terms of the debate opened by J. Nadal and stated that the problem was not of agriculture but of the industry itself. It was the only one responsible for not having managed to get into world markets. Spain was the European country with the lowest proportion of GDP originating in industry. Spain's industrial failure stemmed from its inability to specialize. The insistence on the protectionist option caused industry to move away from the path of specialization that would have allowed it to produce internationally competitive manufactures. Prados de la Escosura did not suggest that agriculture was dynamic, but ruled out that industry was held back by the agricultural sector. Against this argument J. Nadal and C. Sudrià defended, as we pointed out, that the leading industry—Catalan textiles—managed to continuously incorporate better technologies and managed to lower its prices to the same extent as the leading industry worldwide. What happened is that the international markets were more closed than they were supposed to be and the available alternatives were very scarce.

The debate on whether it was agriculture or industry that was responsible for Spain's divergence from advanced Europe has dominated the economic historiography of recent decades. The economic historians most sensitive to the agricultural dynamism have highlighted the transformations of the Spanish countryside and its continuous adaptation to the changes in the internal and external demand. The weak point of this view has always been the explanation of why labour productivity remained stagnant. Researchers who reject the idea that agricultural backwardness is the cause of economic backwardness have counter-argumented that if the countryside retained such a high proportion of assets—nearly two thirds of the total working population—it was because industry did not demand labour. J. R. Rosés and B. Sánchez Alonso have supported this idea in their research on internal and external migrations and on wage differentials. According to these authors, the labour market was well integrated. If Spanish peasants did not migrate more to the cities, it was because of the low differential between agricultural and non-agricultural wages. The high proportion of agricultural workforce therefore reflected both the labour-intensive nature of agriculture and the low productivity of industry. The model would only be altered by the economic impacts of the First World War.

A. Carreras insisted on the explanatory importance of losing colonial markets when other countries won them. The process occurred for the first time and on a large scale in the wake of the independence of the continental American colonies. Spain lost its protected colonial markets, which was very negative for the most dynamic sectors and regions, as we have already explained in Chap. 2. But the damage was double, since the lost markets were won mainly by Great Britain, Spain's main enemy and competitor. The divergence between the two countries then suddenly increased. Something similar, although in smaller proportions, occurred in 1898. The loss of the rich Antillean colonies and the Philippines meant the loss of protected markets precisely when the scale of production and commercialization was growing strongly. Moreover, those lost markets were conquered by the United States. And all the European powers were expanding or constituting their colonial empires. Faced with the greater scale of activity of American and European companies, Spanish companies would suffer reductions in the size of their markets.

In a series of papers, K. O'Rourke and J. Williamson have tried to evaluate the participation of the countries of the northern and southern peripheries of Europe in the benefits of the period of international economic integration of 1870–1914. According to their results, Spain hardly participates in the benefits of the first globalization. The failure does not derive, to the surprise of the authors themselves, from the absence of migratory flows, nor from the absence of capital flows, nor from the trade policies adopted, but from the lack of schooling and a residual, ungraspable factor. So the fixation of economic historiography on trade policy—free trade versus protectionism—as responsible for the divergence would be very exaggerated. Nor do the authors find a defect in the mobility of the factors that justify the divergence. In other words, more factor mobility would have helped Spanish convergence, but the existing mobility was sufficient to avoid divergence. In contrast, educational shortcomings prevented Spain from taking advantage of its opportunities in all fields. With a more educated population, farmers and industrialists would have been more competitive, emigration would have been more feasible for everyone, and capital would have come to Spain more intensively and profitably. In fact, the result of O'Rourke and Williamson empirically supports a widely shared assumption: the lack of education has been a drag on Spanish economic growth.

The person who has studied education in contemporary Spain the most has been C.E. Núñez. According to her, the problems of lack of schooling in Spain have various origins. The main one is the low social demand for education, especially among girls and young women (see Table 12.4). Demand was low because of high opportunity costs: poverty encouraged families to put their children to work from a young age. Private returns on education were low because of the limited opportunities to take advantage of it in the rural world. The parents' own ignorance contributed to the lack of value they placed on their children's education. This is a typical vicious circle of educational underdevelopment: the lack of educational opportunities perpetuates poverty and vice versa. To get out of this circle, the action of the institutions is needed. Faced with such a market failure—a social demand for education that is far below the social optimum—the government must ensure that the population receives at least a basic education. However, the Spanish government assumed this function very late. The two institutions that used to provide education—the Church and the municipalities—became poorer with the transition to the liberal regime. They were no longer able to provide adequate care for their schools. In the second half of the nineteenth century, their ruin dealt a severe blow to the stock of Spanish human capital. The new liberal State abandoned school care until 1900, when the government finally created the Ministry of Education and government spending began to cover the main cost of primary education (in the case of secondary education, since 1887). It would be another thirty years before education budgets increased significantly. In fact, the data collected by C.-E. Núñez suggest that between the 1880s and the 1910s there was a real decline in schooling levels (see Fig. 12.3). There is much to suggest that the low level of schooling in Spanish society at the end of the nineteenth century was historically exceptional and exaggerated. The majoritarian illiteracy of the population had very negative consequences for the economic modernization of the country.

The misery of the Spanish public school system was justified, in its time, by public misery. We thus return to J. Nadal's second explanatory argument. A poor State refused to assume new spending obligations. We have already explained in Chap. 3 the moderate liberal tax reform, as well as the difficulties that the new taxation had to provide sufficient funds to the State. As Fig. 3.3 shows, after the fiscal reform was approved, the public deficit did not stop growing during the following quarter of a century. The Restoration regime will manage to contain the deficit. It will rise again from 1909, with the outbreak of the Moroccan war.

The problems of the Treasury were, above all, of indebtedness. As Fig. 4.2 shows, in some stages the public debt, as a proportion of GDP, was extremely high, unsustainable, for public finances. Over-indebtedness led, time and again, to financial insolvency. During the first half of the nineteenth century, a succession of invasions and civil wars left a highly indebted treasury. In 1851, once the tax reform was completed, the government carried out a debt conversion. Converting the debt was a euphemism for the unilateral reduction of the conditions of service and amortization of the debt. The State exchanged ("converted") old debt for

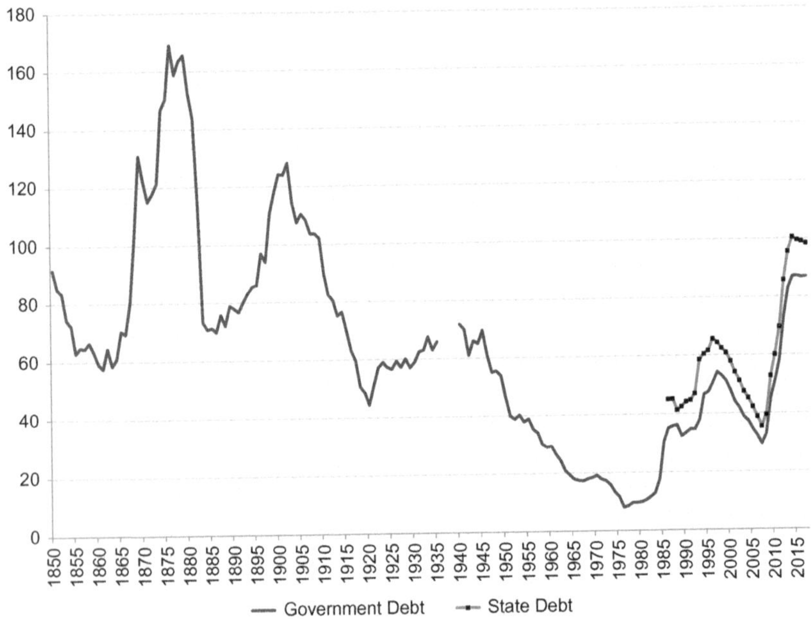

Fig. 4.2 Public debt on GDP (in %), 1850–2017. *Source*: Appendix, column 11

new debt by reducing interest rates, either by reducing the principal (the nominal value of the debt), or by lengthening the repayment terms (the new debt was usually "perpetual" instead of "repayable"). This was a very dangerous operation because, as is still the case today, it made recourse to new debt more expensive not only for the State but for all the citizens of that State. It increased the country risk. The worst thing is that the Treasury fell into financial insolvency on a recurring basis. The vertigo of the increase in indebtedness in the 1860s led once again to fiscally heterodox solutions: the cessation of interest payments, the partial repayment of the debt and, finally (1882), a new conversion. The last "adjustment" of the debt, carried out by Fernández Villaverde, explained in this chapter, was much less harmful for the bondholders. But it was not innocuous: he obliged Spanish investors to collect the interest in pesetas in Spain, eliminating the possibility of collecting the debt in gold abroad. In addition, it imposed a new tax on the yield of the debt.

If the debt was so large and the Treasury did not scrupulously guarantee its service (timely payment of interest and repayment of principal), it should come as no surprise that long-term interest rates reached an all-time high during this period (see column 22 of the Appendix). Not only did they rise sharply, but in international terms they were also well above other Western European countries, as reflected in the rise in the risk premium (see Fig 4.3). It should be noted that since 1899 the risk premium has fallen substantially. The data suggest that investors appreciated the benefits of Fernández Villaverde's fiscal adjustment operation more than the costs. While the public accounts remained balanced (1899–1909), the risk premium remained at historically low levels (see Fig. 4.3).

If we rule out the conversion of Fernandez Villaverde, the preceding ones are preferable candidates to explain the divergence of the Spanish economy from those of its environment. Various works have considered this hypothesis. The research carried out detects the relevance of high

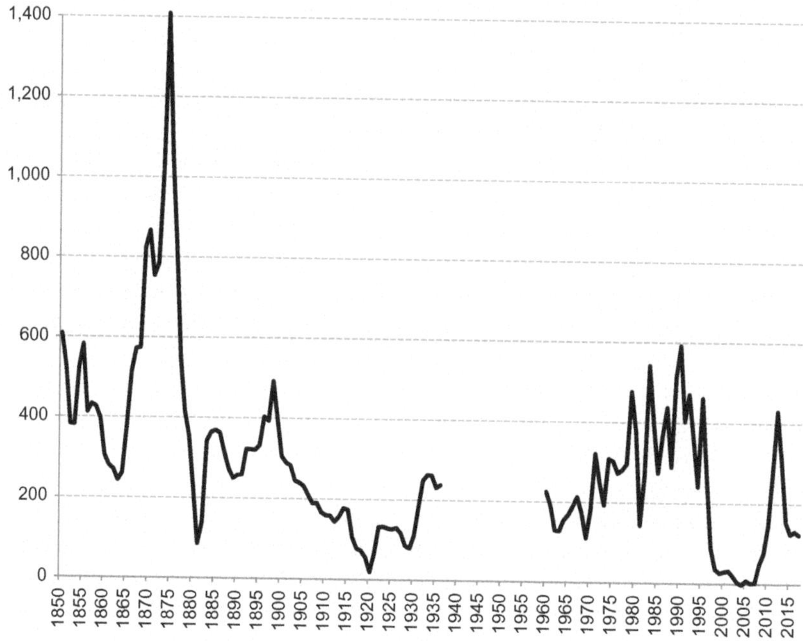

Fig. 4.3 Spanish risk premium (in basis points),1850–2017. *Source*: Appendix, column 22

interest rates, their connection with capital flows, and their direct impact on the exchange rate, but does not reach conclusive results about their effect on growth. Partly because the worst moment of Spanish credibility—the Cuban war—when country risk was sky-high, coincided with a strong convergence of the Spanish economy. Partly also, because when the interest rate differential with the most advanced countries is resolved—after 1901—the Spanish economy maintains its tendency to divergence intact.

If the interest rate differential does not fit in as an explanation of the divergence throughout the thirty pre-war years, the alternative hypothesis that has been considered is Spain's non-participation in the gold standard. Formulated by P. Martín Aceña in a classic article and reformulated and expanded on subsequent occasions, the interpretation underlines the fact that Spain, which remained formally in bimetallism, was, de facto, outside the gold standard. According to P. Martín Aceña, and other authors, non-integration into the gold standard had very negative effects on the Spanish economy by preventing it from sharing in the benefits of international economic integration. The costs of the uncertainty about the evolution of the exchange rate must have been noted in lower investments of foreign capital, higher cost of public debt and private securities, retraction of emigration, higher risk in normal international trade operations, etc. The divergence of the Spanish economy could be explained by these phenomena, all of which derive from non-participation in the gold standard. The explanation is strong, as it allows us to identify a mechanism generally recognized as very powerful and with a chronology that coincides with the phenomenon that we are trying to explain. We should not be surprised that numerous authors have discussed and contrasted their point of view. A. Roldán, reviews the debate, which is still open.

Since the first criticisms by G. Tortella, who held the idea that the gold standard was a luxury that a developing country could not afford, several authors have defended the thesis that, for a peripheral economy, the benefits of a flexible exchange rate were greater than those that the gold standard could provide. It has also been argued that the costs of belonging to the gold standard were excessively high or unsustainable. The latter has to do with the recurrent tensions in the balance of payments and, above all, the large and structural public deficit that characterized the Spanish economy of the period. The former—the benefits of flexible exchange—refers to monetary and fiscal autonomy, which could serve both to avoid deflation and to stabilize the economy in times of crisis or external disturbances. Taking stock, and as A. Roldán concludes, the countless studies devoted to the subject have not provided any certainty about the long-term effects that non-adherence to the gold standard had on the Spanish economy.

L. Prados de la Escosura, in its work of reconstruction of the external position of the Spanish economy, proposes an alternative interpretative line. Before 1885, capital inflows had covered an ever unfavourable balance on the current account and contributed significantly to the capitalization and growth of the Spanish economy. Since that date, the opposite has occurred. In this author's opinion, the reversal in the flow of foreign investment was not so much caused by the country's non-membership of the gold standard as by, on the one hand, its propensity for macroeconomic instability and, on the other, by the loss of interest by foreign investors in Spain in the face of business opportunities arising elsewhere. Emerging economies with enormous growth potential, such as Argentina, Brazil and Russia, offered much more attractive investment opportunities. Spain, like other Southern European countries, had no choice but to contain public spending and capital formation, and therefore growth, in order to balance its balance of payments through a surplus in its current account.

Returning to monetary policy, one possible explanation for the importance of the gold standard and, at the same time, for the efforts made by the government to integrate itself into this metal standard, is to look more closely at the sign of the monetary policies adopted. Spain never joined the gold standard, but the governments of the time multiplied the initiatives to do so. Every time they tried, the authorities did everything possible—monetarily speaking—to raise the price of the peseta and return it to traditional parity. This was confused with the entry into the gold standard. These monetary policies were clearly contractive. They must have had a depressive effect.

A significant contrast to this phenomenon is that Spanish prices, from 1900 to 1913, grew systematically below the prices of Western countries. As stressed by A. Carreras, during this period Spain experienced slight deflation (an annual price decline rate of 0.5%), while all Western European countries experienced moderate inflation rates of between 0.6% and 1.8% per year, reflecting the greater abundance of gold. Logically, the peseta appreciated (see column 18 of the Appendix). Was this—contractive—monetary policy the best for a country impoverished by a military defeat? We do not think so. In our opinion, Spain acted badly not because it was not on the gold standard, but because it tried so hard to join it, to the point of sacrificing national welfare on the altar of the peseta's parity. It could have joined the gold standard at current parity. It would have been good. But forcing appreciation is always a recipe for economic disaster. Years later, in the interwar period, many European countries will follow this temptation, and pay dearly for it.

The harsh adjustment policies implemented in the first decade of the twentieth century, as well as those of the first half of the 1890s, led to economic stagnation and a withdrawal of investment. When, in 1909, "the holy fear of the deficit" was pushed aside to make way for generous financing of the Moroccan war, Spain was freed for a few years from its self-imposed golden fetters. The result was, in economic terms (not in political terms—it should be stressed!), positive. After 1909, foreign capital began to arrive. It does not seem that Spain's absence from the gold standard was a problem there. The opportunities provided by new technologies—electricity in particular—were excellent and were not wasted. Investment increased sharply. Unfortunately, the belle époque was coming to an end.

If the key to relatively poor economic performance lies in institutional factors, we may need to open the analytical focus and go beyond specific economic policies. Recently, D. Acemoglu and J. A. Robinson have proposed a theory of the wealth and poverty of nations based on the character of their economic and political institutions. Under this approach, countries achieve economic development if such institutions are inclusive, while they fail if they are extractive. Interpreting the knowledge accumulated by economic historians in the light of this analytical framework, we can deduce that the economic institutions of liberal Spain were not sufficiently inclusive. Property rights were effectively respected, but the institutional framework only half ensured equality of economic opportunity and clearly failed to give the government the capacity to provide the public goods needed to stimulate growth and foster investment in human capital and the adoption of innovations and new technologies.

The absence of a clear and generally accepted explanation for the progressive divergence of the Spanish economy from that of Europe during the first period of economic globalization remains the main challenge for the economic historiography of contemporary Spain. We have reviewed the existing explanations, but we cannot be unequivocally inclined towards any of them. Other disciplines and other facts could enrich our understanding of the phenomenon. In a very tentative way, taking up again the argumentative thread exposed in the previous paragraph, we can point out that the precocious adoption of the masculine universal suffrage could have strongly conditioned the economic policy in the sense of reinforcing the preference of all the agents (government, companies, workers, families and citizens) for the stability—the known—over the growth—the unknown.

Bibliographic Orientation

The sectoral studies gathered in P. Martín Aceña and J. Simpson (eds.) (1995): *The Economic Development of Spain since 1870*, Aldershot: Edward Elgar, are illuminating of the basic features of the Spanish economy and its trajectory, not only in this period. On certain topics, such as education, public finances or energy, the reader will find sharp interpretations that cover a secular period, extremely useful also for the next chapters. A basic reading on the economy of the period is J. Maluquer de Motes (2002): "Crisis y recuperación económica en la Restauración (1882–1913)", in F. Comín, M. Hernández and E. Llopis (eds.): *Historia económica de España. Siglos X–XX*, Barcelona: Crítica. A. M. Bernal and A. Parejo Barranco (2001): *La España liberal (1868–1913)*, Madrid: Editorial Síntesis, offers a good and detailed overview of the evolution of the two fundamental productive sectors, agriculture and industry. With respect to the agrarian crisis, the first work to be read is R. Garrabou (1988): "La crisis agraria española de finales del siglo XIX: una etapa del desarrollo del capitalismo", in R. Garrabou (ed.): *La crisis agraria de fines del siglo XIX*, Barcelona: Crítica. On foreign emigration B. Sánchez Alonso (2000): European Emigration in the Late Nineteenth-Century: The Paradoxical Case of Spain, *Economic History Review*, 53: 309–330. One of the most controversial issues in economic historiography is the alleged closure of the Spanish economy as a result of the shift towards a protectionist trade policy. For a refutation of this idea, see M. Sabaté, C. Fillat and A. B. Gracia (2011): "The peripheral protectionist backlash in the First Globalization: Spain (1870–1913)", *Revista de Historia Económica-Journal of Iberian and Latin American Economic History*, 29, 1. P. Tedde (ed.) (1999): *Economía y colonias en la España del 98*, Madrid: Síntesis, contains several useful introductory studies on the cost of colonial wars and the impact of the loss of overseas colonies on public finances and the banking system. Regarding the formation of the modern business enterprise, A. Carreras and X. Tafunell (1993): "La gran empresa en España (1917–1974). Una primera aproximación", *Revista de Historia Industrial*, 3. On the causes of Spain's non-integration into the gold standard, see: P. Martín Aceña:

"Spain during the classical gold standard years, 1880–1914", in P. Martín Aceña and J. Simpson (eds.) (1995): *op. cit.* The academic controversy raised by this topic is perfectly displayed by A. Roldán (2017): "Costes y beneficios de la no entrada de España en el patrón oro (1874–1914): una revisión", *Investigaciones de Historia Económica*, 13 (2). The current account foundations of commercial, fiscal and monetary policies is spelled out in L. Prados de la Escosura (2010): "Spain's International Position, 1850-1913", *Revista de Historia Económica-Journal of Iberian and Latin American Economic History*, 28 (1). The terms of the historiographical debate on the causes of economic backwardness have been well surveyed by J.M. Martínez Carrión (2006): "El debate sobre el atraso económico de España", in C. Barciela, G. Chastagnaret and A. Escudero (eds.): *La historia económica en España y Francia (siglos XIX y XX)*, Alicante: Universidad de Alicante/Casa de Velázquez. Within such a debate, one of the most controversial issues has been the responsibility attributable to the supply of entrepreneurs. On this issue, the same book contains a fine essay: J. M. Valdaliso: "El factor empresarial y el desarrollo económico de España en los siglos XIX y XX: Algunas reflexiones derivadas de la producción historiográfica de los últimos veinte años".

CHAPTER 5

The Spanish Economy During Great War and Interwar Years (1914–1936)

Spain escaped the Great War. It was a neutral country. Internal opinion and elites were too much divided between the two blocks to take any decision. This real neutrality, in a very good geostrategic situation, provided many opportunities as well as major losses. The interwar years were quite different to most Western European countries precisely because of a very different—and better—heritage from the Great War. On the contrary, Spain could not enjoy the economic recovery of the late 1930s as it entered into a devastating Civil War.

1 The Impact of War on a Neutral Economy

The Great War profoundly disrupted the world economy. The economies of the neutral nations did not escape the effects of the conflict. For a neighbouring country of the main contenders such as Spain, the economic impact of the war was essentially through foreign trade. The conflict caused great changes in international trade transactions. First, the demand for some manufactured goods increased, both to supply the belligerent nations and to satisfy the demand of third countries that were traditionally supplied by them. Second, the supply of many of the industrial products that were previously purchased abroad decreased, due to the functioning as war economies of the major industrial powers. The latter reduced to a minimum their exports of raw materials, intermediate commodities and

A. Carreras, X. Tafunell, *Between Empire and Globalization*, Palgrave Studies in Economic History,
https://doi.org/10.1007/978-3-030-60504-9_5

capital goods. The exportable supply of manufactured consumer goods from the belligerent countries also contracted drastically, due to the same reconversion of their productive apparatus to serve a full-scale war. Thirdly, foreign demand for two types of goods contracted radically: those that the warring nations would now consider dispensable superior goods and those products that, because of their volume (low value added per unit of weight) were more sensitive to the transport difficulties arising from the naval blockade and the submarine warfare. Freight rates skyrocketed because of the risk of sinking, becoming prohibitive for the most expensive goods to transport.

The combined effect of the above factors can be seen in Fig. 5.1. Until the end of the war, in nominal terms, imports contracted sharply, while exports expanded, except in the first and last year of the conflict. Given that these were years of intense inflation, we must pay more attention to the magnitude of foreign trade in real terms. As the same graph shows, the

Fig. 5.1 Exports and imports of goods and services, 1913–1921 (1913=100). *Sources*: L. Prados de la Escosura (2017): *Spanish Economic Growth, 1850–2015*, London: Palgrave/Macmillan, table S1 and Appendix, columns 13 and 14.

volume of imports fell by 57% between 1913 and 1918. The volume of exports in the latter year was 21.6% lower than in 1913, although between 1915 and 1917 it was at higher levels (see also columns 13 and 14 in the Appendix). The degree of commercial openness of the Spanish economy was significantly reduced (see Fig. 3.1).

The shortage of all kinds of imported goods meant that the Spanish industry enjoyed what J. Nadal and J. Fontana called "automatic spontaneous protection": it had the unique possibility of trying to produce everything that was previously bought from abroad. However, this incentive to import substitution had a limited effect, while the disruption of foreign trade patterns caused considerable damage. The lack of raw materials and intermediate goods disrupted the production process in many sectors. Productive activities in general faced the impossibility of equipping themselves with new machinery because they could not acquire it from abroad. There were, without a doubt, productive branches that grew and diversified taking advantage of the circumstantial disappearance of foreign competition. However, no progress was made in all those fields that were demanding in scientific knowledge and technical competence, as the domestic industry lacked the necessary human capital and know-how. Even the production branches that were long established and benefited from a very atypical and extraordinary foreign demand did not experience great growth. As the shift to the right of the demand curve was much greater than the supply shift for these lucky productive branches, prices and profits increased dramatically. Between 1913 and 1918, the evolution of aggregate industrial output expanded at a mere 1.0% per year.

The foreign trade shocks would not fail to have a powerful transformative effect on the industrial fabric, by an indirect route. The industrial acceleration that occurred in the 1920s was partly caused by radical changes triggered by the war in the relative prices of productive factors and energy resources. There was a notable increase in the price of labour. We will discuss this later. Let us now consider the fundamental change in the second area, the explosive rise in the price of coal. It was caused by the extreme difficulty of importing it. Since coal accounted for more than 90% of modern primary energy and half of the energy consumed came from abroad, the break in external supply caused a real constriction in the energy market. The acute shortage of fuel, which was not remedied by the increase in domestic production, led to a sharp rise in prices. The price of imported coal increased tenfold and that of domestic coal sixfold.

The extraordinary rise in the price of hard coal had a clearly positive consequence, the effects of which would be fully felt after the end of the war. In those years, electricity became a substitute for coal, as it became radically cheaper than coal (electricity prices hardly rose at all). Activities that have the possibility of adopting electrical technology will soon replace coal with electricity. In 1920, basic industry (mining, steel, chemicals, cement and metal processing) already used more electricity than coal. We will discuss the impact of this second energy transition when we analyse the next cycle.

The economic conditions created by the world war had a very unequal impact on the different productive sectors. Some that had significant weight, such as non-energy mining and the building industry, collapsed. Other activities, even more important, such as agriculture and the market services sector, expanded strongly but not in a generalized way. The banking system made an impressive leap forward. The entities that in a few years would form the nucleus of Spanish capitalism launched into a territorial expansion of their network of branches. The banking bonanza was supported by the increasingly abundant business savings.

In view of all this, it is necessary to ask: how did the Spanish economy develop globally during the war cycle? The macroeconomic figures speak for themselves. Its macroeconomic performance was disappointing. The GDP grew at an average rate of 0.8% per year (see column 3 of the Appendix). GDP per capita suffered a slight decline; that is, there was no economic growth. This contradicts the widespread perception among contemporaries that they lived through a period of prosperity, albeit very unevenly distributed. This perception makes sense if one considers the nominal GDP, which increased at a rate of 11% per year. Aggregate production, in quantity, increased very little; in nominal values, it grew rapidly as prices and margins shot up.

The boom was not just a collective mirage, a monetary illusion. The real income of certain economic and social sectors increased greatly. On the other hand, the Spanish economy accumulated a surplus in the balance of payments equivalent, according to calculations by C. Sudrià, to about a third of the national income for one year. The magnitude of the trade surplus was enormous as a result of the brutal contraction of the volume of imports. The balance of services also recorded a large surplus because the Spanish merchant fleet provided extraordinary transport services to other countries. Neutrality provided this kind of dividend. They take on a greater macroeconomic dimension when contrasted with the burdens that the participation in the war imposed on the surrounding economies. The war inflicted a harsh punishment on them, resulting in a significant improvement in Spain's GDP per capita in relation to that of Europe, simply because Spain maintained its position of neutrality (see Fig. 1.3).

2 The Consequences of the War: The Distributive Struggle

The Spain of the first years of the interwar period was dominated by social and political tensions, with a background of economic crisis derived from the problematic international economic environment. The end of the Great War led to an international economic crisis -an inevitable economic adjustment after the many war distortions. It was not long-lasting, but it was very severe. Spanish manufacturing was hit by a sharp deflation and the loss of markets. Indeed, Spanish economy was affected not so much by the seriousness of the economic imbalances as by the virulence of social conflict and the breakdown of the political system. The climate of disorder was such that it facilitated the establishment of a military dictatorship.

As we have just seen, neutrality gave Spain an exceptional surplus in its balance of payments. This was achieved without increasing the aggregate production of goods and services. Business surplus increased dramatically. Inflation made this possible. It was an almost zero-sum game, in which what was gained by the capital factor became equivalent to what was lost by the labour factor. With the Great War, inflation came into play. It was an entirely new phenomenon for contemporary people because of its scope and magnitude. The average annual inflation rate rose to 11.5% between 1914 and 1918 (see column 19 of the Appendix). Because it was unforeseen by economic agents, it resulted in a sharp deterioration in real wages. It is not that nominal wages did not increase. They did, but not as much as prices. Between 1913 and 1918, real wages declined by 17% in both the agricultural and industrial sectors (see Fig. 5.2). Simultaneously, there was a huge rise in corporate profits. The financial rate of return of companies reached a historical high for the twentieth century in 1918 (see column 24 of the Appendix). It is not surprising that personal income inequality reached its pre-Civil War record level in 1918, according to the Gini coefficient calculated by L. Prados de la Escosura (see Fig. 5.3).

The redistribution of national income in favour of company surpluses and against incomes from work unleashed a massive labour movement. Social unrest had been brewing for decades. From the beginning of the Restoration until 1918, private consumption per capita remained almost

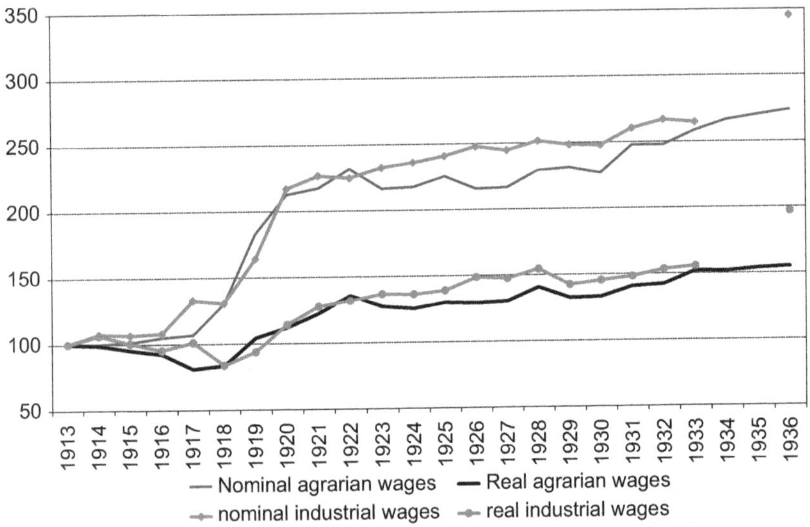

Fig. 5.2 Industrial and agrarian wages, 1913–1936 (1913=100). *Source*: J. Maluquer de Motes and M. Llonch (2005): "Trabajo y relaciones laborales", in A. Carreras and X. Tafunell (coords.): *Estadísticas históricas de España. Siglos XIX y XX*. Bilbao: Fundación BBVA, vol. III, Tables 15.21 and 15.23.

stagnant, even though GDP per capita was slowly but surely increasing (see columns 4 and 8 in the Appendix). The lack of improvement in the living conditions of broad social sectors, in a context of gradual progress in the economy as a whole, had led to a continuous increase in inequality in income distribution, as shown in Fig. 5.3. The long-standing social discontent that had built up in 1917 was triggered by the sudden fall in real wages and the widespread perception of the no less sudden enrichment of businessmen. It is no coincidence that the first general strike in Spain was called in 1917. In the following years, labour conflicts reached the highest levels ever recorded in peacetime (see Fig. 5.4).

Various factors converged to inflame the spirit of protest. Apart from the aforementioned inflation cut in the purchasing power of wages, the success of a supposed proletarian revolution in Russia and the announcement of imminent revolutions of the same kind elsewhere acted as a powerful lever. Throughout the European continent, numerous societies were shaken by revolutionary movements. In Spain, popular discontent and

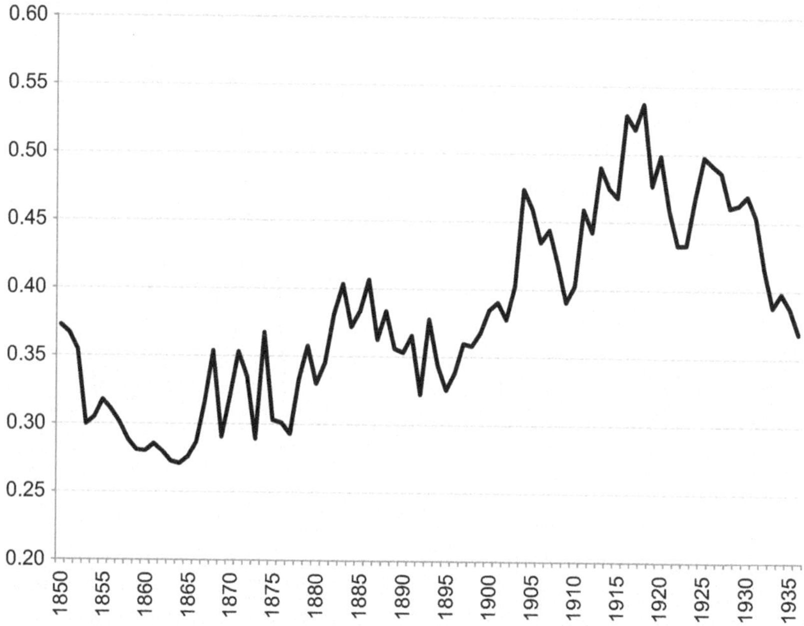

Fig. 5.3 Inequality in income distribution (Gini coefficient), 1850–1936. *Source*: L. Prados de la Escosura (2008): "Inequality, poverty and the Kuznets curve in Spain, 1850–2000", *European Review of Economic History* (12). We thank the author for kindly providing us with the data.

workers' radicalization were also fed by the exasperation of the workers for not participating at all in the wave of prosperity that the conflict had brought to the business world. Finally, when in the immediate post-war period the crisis in certain industrial sectors rapidly increases unemployment, the workers will have an additional reason to persevere in pressure actions, now of a defensive nature.

The outcome of the distributive struggle was relatively favourable to the workers. They achieved intense increases in their wages since 1918, far exceeding pre-war levels (see Fig. 5.2). But the wage increase did not involve a redistribution of income that would restore the pre-war situation. Income inequality remained above pre-war levels throughout the 1920s (see Fig. 5.3). Economic growth made the two compatible. Not without major social tensions. The wage improvements wrenched from

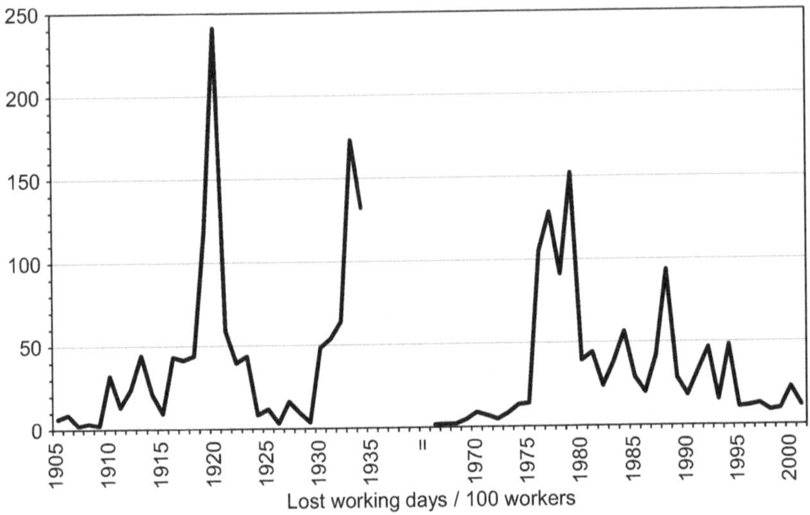

Fig. 5.4 Labour conflicts, 1905–1934 and 1966–2001. *Sources*: Own estimation based in J. Maluquer de Motes and M. Llonch (2005): "Trabajo y relaciones laborales", in A. Carreras and X. Tafunell (coords.): *Estadísticas históricas de España. Siglos XIX y XX*. Bilbao: Fundación BBVA, vol. III, Table 15.42, for lost working days and in column 2 of the Appendix for employment.

the entrepreneurs were made at the cost of pushing the parliamentary regime into the abyss. The employers felt the massive strike movements as a serious threat. The employers' organizations promoted brutal action against the unions and a campaign to pressure the government to crush the workers' mobilization. The escalation of violence so damaged the social climate that it served as a pretext for Primo de Rivera, the captain general of Catalonia, to stage a coup d'état and impose a military dictatorship in September 1923. He had the support of both the business community and the monarch himself.

3 Growth and Structural Changes During the 1920s

From a macroeconomic perspective, there was a basic continuity in the post-war decade, characterized by prosperity and economic welfare. Between 1919 and 1929, GDP grew at an average annual rate of 4.1%. In this expansion of output, investment stood out. Fixed capital formation increased at an annual rate of 10.6%. A process of capitalization of the productive system of such intensity became a powerful driving force of economic growth.

Economic progress was far from balanced. The macro-magnitudes hide disparate developments in the main economic sectors. A distinction must be made between agriculture and industry. On the other hand, export agriculture behaved very differently from traditional agriculture. As far as industry is concerned, there was a very marked contrast between the branches producing capital goods and those manufacturing consumer goods.

The agricultural sector, considered as a whole, grew slowly. Nevertheless, it made an important contribution to economic growth. A large number of agricultural workers left the sector, attracted by the job opportunities that emerged in the main urban centres with the construction boom and the boost to industry. Unemployment and underemployment, which were some of the great traditional ills of Spanish agriculture, were mitigated by the massive rural exodus. At the same time, more competitive agriculture, centred on the cultivation of fruit and garden products and bush crops, made great progress. These crops, mainly oranges, almonds, wine and oil, underwent a remarkable expansion by accessing more consumers and more markets, both inland and abroad. In these years, agricultural products contributed 56% of the total value of Spanish exports. The capacity of the modern agricultural sector to sell abroad increasing quantities of products served to finance the purchases, also increasing, of energy and capital goods necessary for the development of the industry.

Industry was the main actor of the economic boom of the 1920s. Not all industry, but the so-called basic industry, that is, the production of intermediate goods and production goods, plus the generation of electricity. Industrial production, in global terms, grew at the very remarkable annual rate of 5.8% between 1919 and 1929. But the industrial sectors advanced at very different speeds. The fastest was in the capital goods industries. The mining and consumer goods industries progressed much more slowly. The different pace of development of the two branches of production altered the industrial structure.

The change in the industrial structure was important enough for us to say that Spain has entered a new stage in the industrialization process. The step forward is clearly reflected in Hoffmann's index, which we have already referred to in the chapter before. In 1920, Spain had not yet passed the first stage of industrialization that it had entered in 1860. In the course of the 1920s, it would unequivocally and irreversibly enter the second stage.

To what can this historic leap in industrialization be attributed? The driving forces were essentially five. Two of them had to do with the disruptive effect of the war on economic activity. As many authors have argued for other nations, the expansion of the 1920s was, in large part, a movement of recovery generated by the conflict itself. This also applies to a neutral country like Spain. The first explanatory factor of the economic boom of the period is the equipment of the industry once normality in international trade was restored. The investment in new machinery and facilities was enormous because companies had had to postpone it for years.

The second factor causing the expansion was the construction boom. This was partly due to the weak production rate during the conflict years. The main driving force behind the construction boom was the rapid urbanization of the Spanish population during those years. The large industrial cities, such as Barcelona and Bilbao, grew rapidly. Also Madrid. In general, urbanization progressed rapidly from the European war until 1930. Some major sanitation and urban transport programmes helped to improve the general tone of urban life. The push of the construction industry had important dragging effects, in the short term. Housing construction is one of the activities that generates the greatest demand for employment and the greatest and widest demand for other industries.

The third engine of industrial expansion was even more important than the two previous ones. It is none other than electrification, deployed in two parallel directions: the creation of large-scale electricity generation capacity and the adoption of the new technology by the whole of industry and part of the transport sector. From 1919 until the Civil War, the country was immersed in a wave of construction of large hydroelectric power plants. The rapid expansion of electricity production and installed power required a colossal investment effort in civil works and capital goods. At the same time as the electricity companies were mobilizing enormous resources to increase their production capacity, industrial companies of all kinds were making the transition to the new technology. This led to a massive renewal of machinery and facilities.

The fourth factor, which has been highlighted by C. Betrán and other authors, concerns the thrust of industrial districts. The industrial growth that had been taking place throughout the second half of the nineteenth century in some industrial districts was able to take full advantage of the opportunities for import substitution provided by the 1906 tariff and the world war. These developments generated a level of industrial specialization and a level of agglomeration in some localities or districts sufficient to fuel the growth of industry. Intra-industrial trade developed, but even more so inter-industrial trade. Once a certain critical level was reached, the process accelerated to the point of breaking the vicious circle of backwardness: lack of demand. So much so that industry became the main demand for itself. The main players in the sector were the industries producing intermediate goods, which, by incorporating new technology, transferred important productivity gains to the rest of the industry. The process also had a component of growing territorial specialization that especially benefited Catalonia, Madrid and the Basque Country, and to a lesser extent some other historical communities.

The last factor that fostered industrial growth, in chronological order and perhaps also in order of importance, was the public works programme of the Primo de Rivera dictatorship. For the rulers, the government had to assume as a priority task the modernization and expansion of transport and communication infrastructures. Government investment activism concentrated on four components of fixed social capital: railways, roads, dams and ports. The largest sums were invested in the railways, mainly to solve the situation of decapitalization of the sector, which was reverting to a bad transport service. The plan for the building and renovation of roads proved to be more spectacular. Spain went from having a very deficient road network to having an extensive and high quality one. This new infrastructure had far-reaching economic effects by stimulating the spread of the car. Not only did cars become popular, but also trucks and buses, which revolutionized the market for transporting goods and people. Finally, and as we have mentioned, a fairly large public investment was made in the construction of reservoirs to produce electrical energy.

The implementation of such an ambitious public works programme benefited the industries that supplied the required goods. Traditionally, economic historiography has interpreted this policy of public investment as the driving force behind the strong industrial growth registered during the period. This thesis is hardly sustainable, as F. Comín has shown. Public investment had a very small weight in domestic demand. There was no close connection between spending on public works and the growth of industry. This does not deny that public investment had a strong influence on some specific sectors, such as the production of railway material. In short, public sector investment activism contributed to the acceleration of industrial growth driven by more powerful forces.

4 The Depression of the 1930s in Spain

The economic growth model of the 1920s was exhausted by the end of the decade. Several elements converged in that exhaustion. One of them, decisive, was the dramatic change in the international context. The world economy was shaken in 1929 by an extremely serious crisis—the Great Depression—which spread through the collapse of demand and prices. However, endogenous factors weighed more heavily in the breakdown of economic progress. The very long investment cycle was exhausted simply because technological renewal and modernization had been completed, thus extinguishing one of the primary sources of industrial acceleration. It was not only the industrialists who broke their investment plans. The government also abruptly cancelled its investment programme, which had a considerable negative impact on the expectations of industrialists. An even more unfavourable effect on the continuity of economic growth was the breakdown of the political regime itself—in January 1930 Primo de Rivera resigned as head of government.

The breakdown was caused by the discredit of the economic policy of the Dictatorship. The expansive policy of public spending carried out through the extraordinary programme of public works was incompatible with the tax and monetary policies defended by the regime. The two essential objectives in these areas were a balanced budget and the stability of the peseta‘s exchange rate around the theoretical parity with gold. Meeting these two objectives required a restrictive policy, which was totally contradictory to the expansionary nature of the public works programme. The authorities concealed the public deficit by means of countable tricks. Despite the fact that the financing scheme of the public investment programme worked well until 1929, the Government had to cancel it when public opinion discovered the deception and was scandalized by the massive indebtedness incurred by the government to finance the public works plan. The drastic cutback in public orders came at the worst time, when capital goods industries were facing an imminent and severe recession.

The discrediting of the dictatorship's economic policy was also caused by the exchange rate policy. The underlying problem was the current account deficit, which pushed the exchange rate of the peseta down. The government was opposed to the devaluation of the peseta as an external balance adjustment mechanism. Consequently, it could only be balanced by net inflows of foreign capital. But speculative foreign capital was withdrawn, as the authorities did not decide to incorporate the peseta into the gold standard, against what their promised. Its depreciation from 1928 onwards irremediably discredited Primo de Rivera's government. Before, when the peseta was rising, he had deployed a propaganda campaign that identified the strength of the peseta with the strength of the economy. A crisis of confidence was generated in the economic solvency of the regime, at the same time that the loss of political support was evident. The dictator's resignation gave way to a period of uncertainty in the political system at the same time that the Spanish economy was being hit by the Great Depression. The proclamation of the Second Republic in April 1931 did not put an end to the political and economic misfortunes. The new democratic regime would, throughout its existence, be strongly conditioned by the economic crisis.

When the series of the most significant economic variables are reviewed, it can be seen that the economic crisis of 1929 manifested itself in Spain fundamentally through the collapse of exports and investment. Both macromagnitudes contracted by approximately half between 1929–1930 and 1932–1933. The spectacular collapse of foreign demand plunged the sectors that served it into an acute recession. The difficulties of these sectors were in turn extended to the rest of the economy through the channels of consumption and investment. The decline in capital formation was no less violent. It must be made clear that it is limited to the private sector. Public investment, after the great step backwards of 1930, not only did not decline, but recovered the high levels of the years of the dictatorship's public works programme.

Logically, in the evolution of many other macro-magnitudes, the mark of the recession can be seen. Among these, industrial production stands out. In 1933 it was 12.6% lower than in 1929. In contrast, the decline in GDP was relatively mild. When it stopped, in 1933, the product was 94.2% of that of 1929. Two years later the ongoing recovery led to a return to the peak level of 1929. In view of this behaviour, some authors have maintained that Spain did not suffer a real economic depression comparable to that experienced by most industrialized countries and those specialized in exports of commodities. The thesis is debatable, but it has an empirical basis.

As is well known, the national and per capita income of many economies suffered a huge setback in the early years of the decade. In Table 5.1 we summarize the experience of all European countries that experienced some decline in GDP after 1929. We begin with the United States, the country where the crisis originated and where its impact was greatest. The economic crisis in Spain, seen in this comparative perspective, was one of the least intense. The severity of the impact of a six-point drop in GDP should not be underestimated, but relatively to the other European countries there is no doubt that Spain did not suffer anything comparable to what the Central European countries experienced. Even France, the paradigm of a country that endured the crisis well, suffered a drop of almost fifteen points in its GDP. Spain's trajectory is more similar to that of Greece, Italy and Britain.

For a long time, historians have discussed whether the Second Republic failed because of the international economic crisis or whether, on the

Table 5.1 The impact of the crisis in Europe (GDP 1929 = 100)

Country	*Minimum*		*Year of recovery of 1929 level*
	Year	*GDP*	
United States	1933	71.5	1939
Germany	1932	74.8	1935
Austria	1933	77.5	1939
Poland	1933	79.3	1937
Czechoslovakia	1935	81.8	*Post* 1937
France	1932	85.3	1939
Yugoslavia	1932	86.3	1936
Netherlands	1934	90.5	1937
Hungary	1932	90.6	1935
Switzerland	1932	92.0	1937
Belgium	1932	92.9	1936
Greece	1931	93.5	1932
Spain	1931	93.4	1935
United Kingdom	1931	94.2	1934
Italy	1931	94.5	1935
Finland	1932	96.0	1933
Norway	1931	99.1	1932
Sweden	1932	99.9	1933

Source: A. Maddison (2010): "Statistics on World Population, GDP and Per Capita GDP", in: http://www.ggdc.net/maddison, and A. Carreras and X. Tafunell (2005): "El crecimiento económico en la Unión Europea, 1830–2000", *Cuadernos de ICE*, 70, 2

contrary, the crisis did not affect the Spanish economy. The data force a nuanced response. It will help us to clarify what happened to analyse the channels of diffusion of the crisis. There were mainly two.

Firstly, there was a financial channel. The Great Depression began with the collapse of the New York Stock Exchange. The stock market collapse forced American banks to recover their loans. They had granted a large volume of loans to European companies, banks and public administrations. When the American banks reclaimed the loans they had granted, the Central European financial network collapsed. This happened in the spring of 1931 and affected many countries. The banking crisis dragged the industry—the ultimate recipient of loans—down in many cases. Spain was not at all affected by this crisis spreading mechanism. Spain came out of the world war not only debt-free, but with a solid position vis-à-vis the rest of the world. It had the world's fourth largest gold reserves. Its banking system was not tied to the web of financial reconstruction in Central Europe. Nor did the gold standard, which turned out to be the most effective propagator of the crisis by inducing contractive policies, directly affect Spain, since it was not part of it.

The second channel for spreading the crisis was foreign trade. The stock market crisis led to a general feeling of impoverishment in the United States. Companies that were not in a position to repay their bank loans were closed down and jobs were massively destroyed. All this led to a drop in demand for US imports. In addition, at the same time as the stock market crisis, the United States had approved a strongly protectionist tariff. The hardening of trade by the world's leading power led to a chain of commercial reprisals in an environment of reduced international trade. For four years in a row, international trade declined month by month, until it was reduced to a third of what it was in 1929. Spain did not escape this contractionary spiral. It is not surprising that exports first and imports later were strongly reduced. Through this mechanism, the international crisis did indeed affect the Spanish economy, in particular its export sectors.

Spain suffered somewhat less from the crisis than the other European countries because it was more economically backward—more dependent on an agricultural sector geared to the internal market—and less open to international trade. Other European countries similar in economic development to Spain suffered more from the crisis because they were exposed to the financial contagion that we have described above. But others more advanced than Spain and equally immune to financial contagion suffered less because they managed to avoid the other element of instability that affected the Spanish economy.

Indeed, in Spain there were specific causes generating a deep economic crisis. The change of political regime was viewed with great apprehension by the business community, which had been more closely linked to the prosperity of the Primo de Rivera dictatorship. Manufacturers of intermediate goods and capital goods were very unhappy with the new republican regime. Sectors of the landowning aristocracy feared expropriation. The bankers felt threatened by the risk of nationalization. Just in case, many fortunes decided to put the part they had for the better outside Spain. In addition to the clandestine evasion of capital by wealthy Spaniards, there was the flight of foreign investors. To all this was added the shift in budgetary policy from expansive to contractive.

Against these depressive tendencies born of the Spanish political cycle itself, there were some expansive factors that had the same origin. Salaries had, for political reasons, a totally counter-cyclical behaviour. During the whole recessionary phase, wage payments registered continuous and very strong increases (see Fig. 5.2), both in the industrial and agricultural sectors. This remarkable rise in employee remuneration had a positive macroeconomic effect, as it increased the propensity of the economy as a whole to consume at a time when the economy was in danger of falling into a depression due to the collapse in demand. The rise in wages boosted the consumer goods industry, whose modest prosperity offset the fall in the capital goods industry.

The relative boom in private consumption of manufactured goods naturally also extended to food. Agriculture and livestock that were oriented to the domestic market enjoyed an increase in demand for the same reason outlined in the previous paragraph. In addition, the increased demand for agricultural products was accompanied by a succession of good harvests that boosted production.

Having said all this, the question inevitably arises: why then did Spain have such a parsimonious recovery? Note that per capita income in relation to the group of reference countries fell by 8 percentage points between 1932 and 1935 (see Fig. 1.3 and column 5 of the Appendix). The anaemic economic recovery can only be explained by socio-political reasons. Throughout the short life of the Republic, there was a climate of perpetual and growing conflict. It easily led to a confrontation between various sectors of society—workers against manufacturers, labourers against landowners, Catalan and Basque nationalists against centralists, defenders of the Catholic tradition against supporters of a secular State, etc. This atmosphere of confrontation gave rise to an absolute lack of confidence among businessmen and investors. They themselves showed open hostility to public policies undertaken or planned by left-wing political forces.

So, was the economic stagnation caused by the economic policy measures taken by the Republican governments? The answer to the question is complex, since while some sectoral policies did not cushion the impact of the crisis, or even aggravated it, others were correct. Among the former are exchange rate, monetary and labour policies. Among the latter, budgetary policy stood out.

The exchange rate and monetary policies are the best example of subordination to an economic ideology, that of scrupulous respect for the rules of the gold standard. In Spain, as everywhere else, this approach has proved to be clearly counterproductive in confronting the crisis. With the advent of the Republic, the depreciation of the peseta that had been taking place since 1928 intensified. The Republican economic authorities were as obsessed with the stability of the peseta's external value as those of the Dictatorship. They made the mistake of fighting depreciation with a policy of expensive money, in order to attract foreign capital. It was an illusion to expect that it would come when the international financial system was literally disintegrating. When the policy of monetary tightening proved ineffective in curbing the devaluation of the peseta, the government resorted to exchange control, that is, the imposition of import quotas and a public monopoly on foreign currency. In 1933, the peseta was de facto stabilized by joining the so-called gold bloc. This was as surprising as Spain becoming part of the last stronghold of countries faithful to the gold standard without having adopted, then or ever, this monetary regime. This fierce defence of monetary orthodoxy had significant economic costs. Interest rate cuts were ruled out, thus losing the possibility of stimulating investment. The overvaluation of the peseta did not cease to penalise the exporting sectors.

The labour policy implemented by the centre-left government shows us a different side of the economic policy, with similar negative results on economic activity. In this case, the measures were innovative, or rather breakthrough. They were intended to create a regulatory framework for labour relations that would greatly strengthen the bargaining power of the unions. All these measures dictated by the Ministry of Labour accentuated the climate of mistrust and opposition of employers and large agricultural owners and tenants towards the new political regime. The economic crisis could only be exacerbated by a policy that directly induced a sharp increase in labour costs, at a time when companies were facing a drop in sales and profits. The positive side of the significant increase in labour costs was a significant reduction in economic inequalities (see Fig. 5.3). Paradoxically, this aggravated rather than alleviated social tensions.

In the opposite sense, fiscal policy proves that the macroeconomic management of the Republican governments was, in some areas, well oriented to alleviate the effects of the crisis. In this area, the authorities followed a policy that was consistent with that of the Dictatorship. That is, they opted for an expansive policy. Total public spending increased sharply in the same years that national income tended to decline. As the fiscal pressure hardly changed, a large budget deficit was produced, which was wiped out with large debt issues. Public investment grew significantly, offsetting in some measure the collapse of private investment. So, as F. Comín has made clear, the fiscal action of Republican governments was countercyclical, compensating for demand. If it did not bear more fruit, it is because at that time the public sector—in Spain, as elsewhere—had a reduced weight in the economy.

The economic policies implemented by the Republican governments did not succeed in freeing the country from living permanently in an oppressive environment of economic crisis. This happened not because of the greater or lesser skill of the policy-makers in macroeconomic management, but because of the expectations and social reactions to the structural reform projects aimed at promoting a more equitable distribution of income and wealth.

Since the proclamation of the Republic, governments formed by representatives of progressive liberalism and socialism had attempted to carry out reform policies to modernize Spanish society. These policies were not limited to the economic sphere, but affected a wide range of areas (religion, the army, the education system, etc.). In all of them, society was polarized into irreconcilable camps. The reformist will of the Government was put to a critical test in an economic-social reform, the agrarian reform. It raised the most acrimonious positions and struggles between the social sectors in favour and against the policies of modernization. The reactions to the agrarian reform were so virulent that, when combined with other sources of intense political and social conflict, they led the country to Civil War and the shipwreck of democracy.

The agrarian reform had to consist on the expropriation of land from the latifundia and its subsequent distribution, in small lots, to the landless farmers, who were the same workers who cultivated the large properties to be expropriated. The reform immediately became a political and social problem of the utmost importance, even though it was not really implemented until the electoral victory of the Popular Front in February 1936.

The agrarian reform raised the highest expectations. Broad layers of the rural population aspired to a redistribution of land ownership. The enormous social pressure for reform, which had been more or less well-contained for a century, was unleashed with the establishment of the Republic. The hopes placed in it by the day labourers were soon dashed by the land reform law passed in 1932. Among its many limitations, two stood out. The law did not provide for any system of financing the reform. Nor did it correctly define the expropriable lands, leaving a large number of small plots of land surrounding the villages affected. This had the disastrous effect of turning a considerable number of farmers against the reform. Without mobilizing financial resources to carry out the expropriations, the republican regime gained a whole army of enemies without managing to win the support of those who were to be the beneficiaries of the reform. Thus, the army that took up arms against the Republic was able to count on a broad social base.

Bibliographic Orientation

The classic reference is J. Fontana and J. Nadal (1976): "Spain 1914–1970" in C. M. Cipolla (ed.): *The Fontana Economic History of Europe*, vol. 6 (2), *Contemporary Economies*, London: Collins. A. Parejo Barranco and A. Sánchez Picón (2007): *La modernización de España (1914–1939)*, Madrid: Síntesis, stands out for its rigour and depth. On the First World War C. Sudrià (1990), "Los beneficios de España durante la gran guerra. Una aproximación a la balanza de pagos española, 1914–1920", *Revista de Historia Económica*, VIII, 2. On technological change it is still very useful to read J. Nadal *et al.* (1988): *España. 200 años de tecnología*, Madrid: Instituto Nacional de Industria. As for the impact of electricity, a rigorous study both from a quantitative and qualitative point of view of the diffusion of the electrification process in I. Bartolomé (2007): *La industria eléctrica en España, 1890–1936*, Madrid: Banco de España. Attention should be paid to internal migratory flows, as they were both cause and effect of significant structural changes. On the importance of internal migratory movements, see J. Silvestre (2005): "Las migraciones internas durante la modernización económica de España, 1860–1930", *Cuadernos Económicos de ICE*, 70. An enlightening reading, despite its brevity, of the monetary and exchange policy of the period is P. Martín

Aceña (2000): "La Peseta entre dos guerras y una crisis, 1919–1936", in J. L. García Delgado and J. M. Serrano Sanz (dirs.): *Del real al euro. Una historia de la peseta*, Barcelona: La Caixa. The impact of the Great Depression of 1929 on the Spanish economy and the influence that the establishment of the Second Republic had on its development has given rise to an abundant historiography. From this, we have selected the following two essays. One is a stimulating comparison between the crisis of the 1930s and that which began in 2008, J. Palafox (2011): "España y la crisis internacional de 1929: el papel de los desequilibrios internos" in P. Martín Aceña (ed.): *Pasado y presente. De la Gran Depresión del siglo XX a la Gran Recesión del siglo XXI*, Bilbao: Fundación BBVA. The other essay reviews the evidence to reassess the fluctuations of the Spanish economy during the years 1930–1936, as well as the role played by the Republican economic policy, F. Comín (2013): "La gran depresión internacional y la Segunda República", in E. Llopis and J. Maluquer de Motes (eds.): *España en crisis. Las grandes depresiones económicas, 1348–2012*, Barcelona: Pasado y Presente.

CHAPTER 6

The Isolation from the International Economy: Civil War and Autarky (1936–1951)

Spain was a closed economy during fifteen years. Initially it was so because of the exceptional Civil War situation. Closing was not complete, but quite general as foreign currency was scarce for both contending blocks. During Second World War closing was more radical as foreign currency was even scarcer and military alliances very risky. Franco was politically and ideologically supportive of the Axis powers but without extensive military involvement. The new regime deployed a completely closed economy—an autarky—that was defined as a permanent and strategic choice for Spain. Once the War was over, Spain retained its autarky as any opening had heavy political penalties for Franco's regime. Consequently, Spain did not enjoy most benefits of post-war reconstruction, contrary to most Western European countries. This long autarky made a strong imprint in Spanish economy, difficult to overcome.

1 War Economy, Social Revolution and War Financing

On July 18th, 1936, there was a military insurrection that immediately turned into a long and bloody civil war. Why did the Spanish fight a new civil war? From what we have explained in the previous topic, the causes were not so much economic as social. With the electoral victory of the

A. Carreras, X. Tafunell, *Between Empire and Globalization*, Palgrave Studies in Economic History,
https://doi.org/10.1007/978-3-030-60504-9_6

Popular Front in February 1936, the social sectors that supported the winning left-wing coalition felt that the time had come for a strongly redistributive policy. On the other hand, some social strata were totally hostile to the Popular Front because they saw their property rights and economic interests as being threatened as well as its religious and social ideology. These sectors, determined to overthrow the government by force, gave their support to the military insurgents.

How did the economy behave during the war? Statistical information does not allow us to know with any degree of accuracy. However, the work of numerous specialists gathered in two works edited by P. Martín Aceña and E. Martínez Ruiz and by E. Fuentes Quintana and F. Comín, offers an overall view that can be summarized as follows. Agriculture and industry suffered a fall of nearly a third in the first months of the war. They would not recover at all during the course of the war. The decline of agriculture was decisively influenced by the lack of manpower, as well as by organizational problems. The decline of the industry was caused by difficulties in the supply of raw materials and access to markets, in addition to organizational failures. The transport of goods and people—apart from the military personnel—had to decrease even more sharply. Exports were reduced by half. Imports, according to official statistics, fell somewhat less. However, if arms purchases—not recorded in the statistics—are taken into account, imports actually increased, according to E. Martínez. The resulting trade deficit, much larger than before the conflict, forced recourse to external sources of financing. This gave certain countries the power to tilt the balance of strategic resources (economic and military) in favour of one of the warring sides. Public finances also faced a critical situation, due to the collapse of direct tax collection. The authorities in both sides had to resort to extraordinary sources of internal financing and make massive appeals for credit from the Bank of Spain (in each zone). As for the financial system, it functioned in a totally abnormal way during the war. At the beginning, a blockade of accounts was decreed. Financial operations collapsed due to the combined effect of the absence of investment, the decline in productive activity, the dismantling of domestic trade and monetary disruption.

Having said this, we must point out that it is not possible to analyse the evolution of the Spanish economy during the conflict with the same approach as in the other historical periods, for two reasons. One is that the Spanish economy ceased to exist as a unitary reality when the peninsular territory was divided into two parts, the one controlled by the Francoist side and the one controlled by the Republic, which in turn was divided into two parts. The immediate consequence of this partition was the breakdown of the unity of the market. The forceful division of the integrated internal market caused enormous disruption to the functioning of economic activity.

The second reason is that Republican Spain and Franco's Spain were two completely different economic models. The latter became an economy subject to extreme intervention and with militarized resources, while the former ceased to be a capitalist economy and faced serious problems of organization and resource allocation. We therefore need to examine both economic models separately. Following E. Malefakis, the most important thing is to understand how a war economy was organized and how it worked on both sides. A war economy essentially means the mobilization of productive resources to meet two objectives: the provision of essential goods for the population and the production or acquisition of war material on the scale necessary to win the war. A key element for the achievement of both objectives is financing.

The insurgents managed to develop an efficient war economy. They had at least four major advantages. First, the military organization was predominantly on their side. We are referring to the hierarchy of command. The army faithful to the Republic had practically no officers and fell into a situation of disorganization. The militias, which had to perform the functions of the regular army of the Republic, never had a well-trained or well-armed force. Second, Franco's troops always controlled the main agricultural regions. This meant that in Franco's Spain the problem of feeding the civilian population and the troops was easily solved from the beginning. The third economic advantage of the "national zone" was that it had the support of most of the country's businessmen and managers. They passed *en masse* to the territory occupied by Franco's armies. They had a very relevant participation in the financing of the war.

The last, decisive advantage of Franco's Spain was the support of the fascist powers. Nazi Germany and Fascist Italy offered invaluable material and military aid to the rebels. The Axis powers were willing to buy the products that Franco's Spain could export. They also generously granted him credits for the acquisition of armaments. In addition, they sent large contingents of soldiers and airplanes to fight in Spain. Thanks to such formidable financial and military assistance, Franco's government was able to equip itself with the military machinery it initially lacked and which it needed to defeat the enemy. The aid was not disinterested. As soon as the war was over, the Axis powers passed the bill and claimed that Spain align with their side.

To the above advantages was added an economic policy that managed to make the most of the resources available to cover the fundamental objectives of the war economy. The new Francoist State was established as an absolutely interventionist power. The direction of economic activity was carried out with an implacable iron hand. From the first moment, it decreed the forced mobilization of the civilian population for the agricultural campaign and other productive tasks. A centralized control of all production, distribution and foreign trade was introduced; combined with a fierce repression of any attitude of non-cooperation, it allowed for an increase in the productive levels of strategic goods.

The economy of Republican Spain evolved in a diametrically opposed way. Its initial resource endowment was good. If victory had depended on the economic resources that each side had in July 1936, the Republic would have won. It gathered the majority of the population; it had almost all the industry and agriculture for export, the ports and most of the merchant fleet; it had in its possession the immense gold reserves of the Bank of Spain and had a large part of the national savings. But the Civil War is a magnificent example of how more important it is to be able to mobilize resources and factors of production effectively than to have them at one's disposal. The Republic failed miserably in this task.

Various factors prevented the Republican zone from functioning as an efficient war economy. First, the loss or annulment of the entrepreneurial sector. The management of many enterprises and farms deteriorated seriously by falling back on inexperienced workers. The lack of management capacity was compounded by a shortage of capital, which dragged many enterprises into a situation of collapse. Second, the Republican economy faced difficulties in supplying industrial raw materials, weapons and food to a population that was mainly urban. The progressive suffocation in the supply of inputs, together with the loss of markets, paralyzed the Republican economy. The airplanes and warships that fought on Franco's side made communications increasingly difficult, progressively strangling the Republic's agriculture and industry. A third factor that weakened its economy was the geographical partitioning into two unconnected and distant areas. This disconnection frustrated the possibility that Asturian and Basque heavy industry could supply the armaments needed by the other Republican zone.

An external condition was probably the most important. It was the unfriendly attitude of the main Western democracies towards the republican regime. Possibly, the war would have had another outcome if the governments of France, the United Kingdom and the United States had not maintained an attitude of apparent neutrality. This position favoured Franco's side by denying the supply of war material and the concession of credits to the Republican government. The position was in line with the policy of appeasement advocated by the British and French to contain Nazi Germany. It also responded to the fear that if Republican Spain won the war, a Communist regime would be established. In view of the revolution taking place in the republican zone, these fears seemed to be well founded. Britain and France dragged the international community into a commitment not to sell weapons to Spain, which the Axis powers did not respect. The Republic was harshly discriminated. It had to resort to buying arms from the Soviet Union under unfavourable conditions. When the gold reserves of the Bank of Spain were exhausted, the Republican government could not continue to acquire arms.

Since external contributions of arms and other strategic goods clearly favoured Franco's side, the Republicans could only have won if they had managed to organize a highly efficient war economy. It is here that the aforementioned social and economic revolution in the Republican zone takes on its full importance. The workers took control of the factories and the farms; they were "collectivized", usually by using violence and coercion. The social experiment had high costs. The companies produced far below their potential. In Republican Spain, something atypical happened in the context of a modern conflict. In the World Wars, the governments of the belligerent countries established massive intervention and planning over the industrial sectors to promote the manufacture of armaments and other goods necessary for war. Thanks to this total mobilization of resources, they managed to increase industrial production, especially the manufacture of armaments. What happened in Republican Spain? Well, that industrial production, instead of increasing, did not cease to decrease throughout the war. Under these circumstances it cannot surprise anyone that the defenders of the Republican regime lost the war.

2 The Macroeconomic and Distributional Impact of Autarkic Francoism

The war and the establishment of the Franco regime were enormously traumatic for Spanish society; they fractured the dynamic of slow but uninterrupted economic growth that Spain had known for more than a century. During the first decade of Francoism, Spain lived in a situation of deep depression and misery. As Spain was emerging from a war that had caused a major contraction in GDP, stagnation meant the failure of the process of economic reconstruction. It took the country an extraordinarily long time to complete the reconstruction, to recover its pre-war productive level.

The rate of increase of the Spanish GDP throughout the 1940s was so mediocre that the level of 1935 was not reached again until 1951. To recover the pre-war (1929) maximum per capita income level had to wait until 1954. Fifteen years—or twelve, depending on how you measure it—is too long to recover from the ravages of war. We are facing an unmitigated and unparalleled economic failure in post-war Western Europe. By 1950, all the Western European countries that had participated in the Second World War had managed to exceed the pre-conflict maximum per capita output levels. A conflict—let us not forget—that was longer and more destructive than the one suffered by Spain and that ended six years later than this one. The European economies that did not participate in the world war performed much better than the belligerent ones: all of them, except Spain, had in 1945 production levels higher than in 1939.

Spain's macroeconomic performance thus stands in stark contrast to that of neighbouring economies. In view of the figures, the autarkic Francoism must be described as an economic disaster. In Spain, the Great Depression of the 20th century did not occur as in other capitalist countries between 1929 and the mid-1930s, but between 1936 and 1950. The decline in the welfare levels of the population is historically exceptional. Throughout contemporary history, the Spanish have not endured such a prolonged and dramatic impoverishment as that suffered between 1936 and 1950. The gap, in terms of levels of economic development, that separated the Spanish economy from the other economies of Western Europe widened dramatically. A gap that in this period is greater than at any other time in recent centuries (see Fig. 1.3).

What can explain a failure of such proportions? The first thing to think about is the impact of the very war that Spain had just emerged from. This had a high economic cost, both in terms of military expenditure and lost production. The former can be estimated to have represented, according to official calculations, more than 70% of the national income in 1935. The second consisted of a lower production of goods and services during the war, the accumulated volume of which exceeded 80% of the 1935 GDP. However, neither one nor the other explains the weak post-war reactivation. Francoist leaders repeatedly invoked the material destruction caused by the armed conflict as a justification for the extraordinary persistence of the economic depression. But there is no basis for this. The losses of physical capital caused by the Civil War were inferior to those inflicted by the Second World War on the countries of southern Europe that were the scene of military operations, as J. Catalan has shown. The capital assets that suffered the greatest damage were easily repaired: three years after the end of the war their stock returned to pre-war levels, according to the calculations of L. Prados de la Escosura and J. R. Rosés.

The rulers attributed the failure of the reconstruction to a second factor, exogenous: the policy of economic isolation to which Spain was subjected by the allied powers. Franco's regime politically exploited this myth. It is an evident exaggeration. After the war, the United States and the United Kingdom marked to the western community a non-aggressive strategy towards Franco's regime. It is true that in December 1946 the United Nations approved a resolution imposing economic sanctions on Spain, which was lifted after three years. But that resolution did not lead to the paralysis of Spanish foreign trade, although it did hinder it. During those years, some European countries practically interrupted their commercial relations with Spain, but others did the opposite, considering Spanish products useful for their economic reconstruction, as F. Guirao had argued. There was no international blockade or economic boycott. Another thing, as we will see, is that Spain's economic reconstruction was hindered by its political segregation from the Western European community. For political reasons, it was unable to join the institutions of international economic cooperation that would play an essential role in the reconstruction and relaunching of the post-war European economy.

It should not be overlooked that there was one productive factor that suffered serious losses: labour. The Civil War had a high cost in human lives. However, the percentage of those who died as a result of the conflict, and even the total excess mortality rate, is too low to have been an obstacle to economic reconstruction. Thus, the Spanish post-war stagnation cannot be attributed to the human destruction caused by the Civil War either.

That said, we must stress that the post-war repression amplified the loss of labour and decimated human capital. Franco's triumphant regime was so bloodthirsty and cruel that it tripled the number of deaths and incapacitated people for economic activities. Adding up the executed, exiled and retaliated against, the labour losses most likely surpassed 10% of the active population. As J. Catalan states, these casualties seriously damaged the stock of human capital by concentrating on a few highly qualified, highly educated socio-professional groups. The new regime purged the entire teaching profession and the secondary and university teaching staff, all of whom were suspected of being sympathetic to the Republican regime. Prevention against teachers and teaching was also reflected in the contraction of educational expenditure and schooling levels. In part, these fell for other reasons that were just as or more sad: with the fall in the real income of wage earners, there was a legion of children who could not attend school in the early post-war years. The education statistics compiled by C.-E. Núñez reflect that the level of primary schooling that children had achieved during the Second Republic collapsed and took twenty-five years to recover. The collapse of primary school enrolment rates delayed the take-off of secondary schooling. Spain broke away from the post-compulsory education universalization pattern of Western Europe. The accumulated delay has not yet been overcome.

Indeed, the main problem facing the Spanish economy in 1939 was not the destruction of the factors of production. The real problem consisted in getting the production system to function normally. We have just seen that the very political action of the new State missed opportunities for economic recovery by imposing harsh punishments on all opponents to the regime, removing them from participation in the productive activity. The regime's labour and income policies had an even greater impact on post-war macroeconomic developments by delaying recovery.

One of the main objectives of the insurrection of July 1936 was to reverse the trends in the distribution of national income and wealth that had been dominant during the Republic. The victory of the Francoist army was the victory of the landowners and businessmen and the defeat of the workers and day labourers. Wages were drastically reduced in real terms. In the case of the industrial workers, as calculated by M. Vilar, applying the official price index (AEE -Spanish Statistical Yearbook), the real wage fell throughout the 1940s to about half the 1936 level. That level would not be recovered until 1956–1957 (see Fig. 6.1). But, considering the prices of goods purchased on the black market

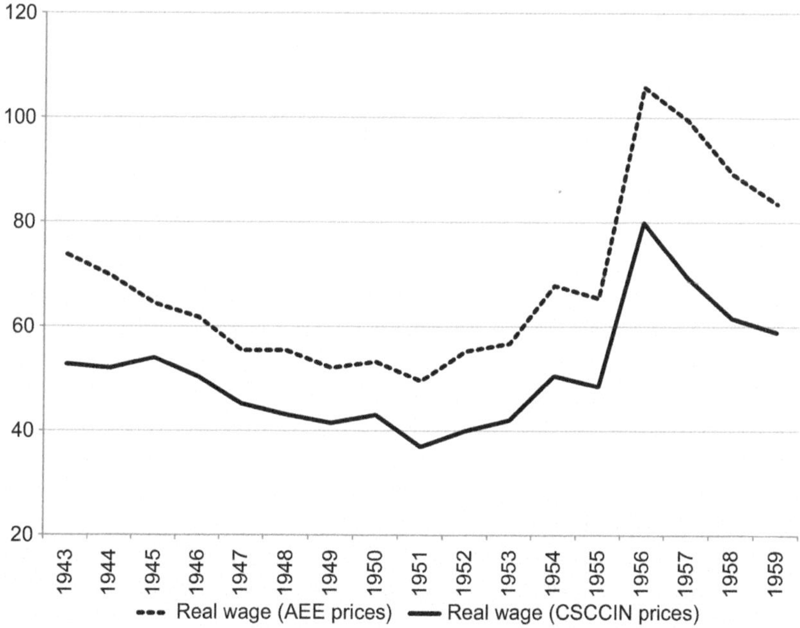

Fig. 6.1 Wages of male industrial workers, 1943–1959 (1936=100). *Source*: M.Vilar (2009): *Los salarios del miedo. Mercado de trabajo y crecimiento económico en España durante el franquismo*. Santiago de Compostela: Fundación 10 de Marzo. Table III-5.

(CSCCIN -Chambers of Commerce- index), the fall in the real wage was even more dramatic. In the late 1940s and early 1950s it was about 40% of the 1936 level. Throughout the 1950s it was far from recovering to that level.

The regime established an authoritarian model of labour relations, inspired by fascist legislation, which prohibited free trade unions and strikes. Wages were set administratively, by decree of the Ministry of Labour. This labour policy scheme was aimed at containing and reducing wages. In view of Fig. 6.1, we must conclude that such a policy was completely successful. The fall in real income of the employees led to a dramatic worsening of their living conditions. This was the time of hunger.

It is important to understand that the collapse of wages had a powerful depressive macroeconomic effect, as C. Sudrià has argued. Private consumption suffered a great compression. The structure of demand changed radically. The relative scarcities and relative prices of productive factors were also altered. As wages collapsed, the demand for manufactured products of mass consumption decreased radically. Demand for luxury goods and services for the beneficiaries of the new order increased. This transformation in the structure of demand reduced industrial productivity and aggregate productivity. The goods and services most in demand were now of low productivity, while the activities most negatively affected by the loss of purchasing power of employees were those with a higher degree of mechanization. Overall productivity also declined as the composition of the production function changed. Entrepreneurs replaced capital with labour as this became cheaper. Difficulties in importing machinery reinforced this substitution.

The fall in real wages caused another effect of maximum importance: the reagrarization of the Spanish economy. With lower incomes many workers could not survive in the urban world. They had to return to the countryside to concentrate their efforts on feeding themselves. The active agricultural population increased, while the industrial one contracted. However, the agricultural sector, with more people but less capital, did not manage to produce more. Faced with the impossibility of having tractors or fertilizers, it was necessary to return to the mule economy and to handwork. The levels of productivity of the land and of labour went back decades. The concentration of demand on inferior goods—those whose demand increases when income is reduced—rendered useless much of the investment that had been made in the first third of the century to adapt the Spanish countryside to more advanced demand patterns. The same happened in industry and transport. The retreat towards more archaic technical and productive solutions, in parallel with the intensification of the use of the labour factor, occurred in all areas of economic life.

Beyond labour and income policy, the regime's key economic policies condemned Spain to a veritable economic blockage. The interventionism and dirigisme that characterized all the economic policy of the early Franco regime had profoundly disruptive effects on economic organization. They prevented the rational allocation of resources. The extreme intervention of the Administration in all spheres of economic activity plunged the national economy into an almost cataleptic state, into a permanent depression. In the following two sections we will analyse this policy, which had such disastrous effects on post-war reconstruction.

First we will recall that the interventionism of the early Francoism did not imply public expenditure. On the contrary, it multiplied regulations to save on expenditure. The priority of the regime was clear: a strong concentration of expenditure on defence and police. These activities consumed almost all public resources. Everything else was secondary. On the income side, the political balances of the new regime excluded any increase in taxation on the wealthy classes. The reform of taxation consisted in re-implanting anachronistic taxes on consumption and raising the rates of all taxes, aggravating the fall in private consumption. The budgetary imbalances resulting from excess spending on defence and public order were covered by resorting to the Bank of Spain and to the issuing of pledgeable public debt. Inflation would be in charge of reducing the weight of the debt.

3 Market Intervention: Black Market and Rationing

Autarky and interventionism are the two basic orientations of the economic policy of early Francoism. The economy was subordinated to the supreme objectives of political and military independence. The leaders of the regime pursued economic self-sufficiency and interventionism at all costs. In the following we will see how the unbridled intervention of the authorities in economic life was the cause, together with the autarkic dream, of the calamitous evolution of the Spanish economy. The interventionist action caused a shortage of essential goods that would be added to the one caused by the brutal restriction of imports. Producers and consumers suffered a great shortage of essential goods. This resulted in losses of income, both from the surcharges paid for the few products on offer and from the income not received for everything that was not produced despite having the capacity to do so.

Interventionism was deployed in two directions: price formation and resource allocation. It led to the creation of a very heavy bureaucratic machinery, composed of multiple regulatory bodies, inspectors and sanctioning. Underlying the gigantic interventionist machinery was a military conception of the functioning of the economy, according to which markets, agents and prices could be "disciplined".

The application of a mentality as alien to economics as this one inevitably had dire consequences for the functioning of the productive system. We know well what happened in agriculture and in the energy sector. Farmers were forced to sell the production of staple crops to the intervention agency at a price fixed by the agency itself. The same was true for many strategic industrial products (coal, steel, cement, etc.). The administrative setting of prices seriously distorted the functioning of the market, since the regulators set prices at a deliberately low level in order to benefit consumers.

This policy had effects diametrically opposed to those pursued by the authorities, as demonstrated by C. Barciela for cereal agriculture and C. Sudrià for electricity. The immediate effect of setting a price below the equilibrium price is a reduction in production on the official market. The supply of the intervened good will be diverted, whenever possible, to a parallel underground market. In this black market, operations will be carried out at prices well above the official price and also above the equilibrium price. This was precisely the result of the mistaken policy of intervention in prices: the flourishing of an illegal market—known at the time as "estraperlo"—in which products were sold at prices that were a multiple (from 2 to 10) of the official ones. Half, or even more, of the production was placed on this black market.

Moreover, as economic analysis predicts, the overall production marketed—sales on the official market plus sales on the black market—will be lower than that of the non-intervened market. Hence the shortage of supply, and hence the authorities complemented price intervention with consumer intervention to ration it. The rationing of food and some other basic goods—the infamous "ration books"—was in place for thirteen years. A much wider range of goods was rationed to the public because shortages were as pervasive as taxed prices and because nothing could be imported without a specific import license. The rationing of foreign products was a simple variant of the same shortage phenomenon and had the same cause. The government rationed imports severely because the country was suffering from an acute shortage of foreign currency. This was the result of the administrative fixing of a price for the peseta that was very far from the one that would mark the market without exchange control.

The complete survival of the rationing mechanisms throughout the early Francoist period is an expression of the complete failure of the regime's intervention policy. A policy that, apart from being ineffective, had perverse economic and social effects. The families and the industrialists faced strong economic losses. They had to resort to the black market to provide themselves with essential goods not assigned by the ration books and quotas, paying astronomical prices for such goods. The small producers also lost out, as they received low remuneration for the fruits of their labour and for their fixed capital.

The policy of price intervention and consumption of rationed goods promoted what some authors have called "speculative capitalism". In the Spain of the time, the best business was not done by genuine businessmen but by the black marketers, who quickly amassed large fortunes. The large agricultural and industrial producers and the intermediaries could avoid the compulsory delivery quotas, and could also assume the risks of selling to the black market. They could do so through their political contacts or because they corrupted the officials in charge of market surveillance. A very lucrative operation was to buy supplies at the official price and resell them to an industrialist at suitably inflated prices on the black market. In a dictatorial system that was strongly interventionist, political connections encouraged the speculative orientation of entrepreneurs, who became rent seekers. On the political connections depended the allocation of scarce resources, be it quotas of industrial raw materials or import licenses. Among the great beneficiaries of autarkic Francoism were those who made scarcity the basis of their businesses.

Price intervention also had devastating effects in the field of energy. The insufficient energy supply represented an insurmountable obstacle to industrial recovery. The shortage was twofold: oil and electricity. The shortage of electricity was particularly long-lasting and distressing. The problems of electricity supply were caused by the decision of the authorities to freeze electricity tariffs at the 1936 level. They did the same with the prices of other products and with the salaries, looking for the impossible objective of returning the nominal variables to the point where they were before the beginning of the Civil War. They applied the absurd procedure of administratively abolishing accumulated inflation while leaving the money supply intact. Real electricity prices fell by about 70% between 1939 and 1951. Logically, the producers—the electricity companies—had no incentive to invest in expanding supply. They did not build new plants. Soon, the installed capacity was not sufficient to meet the demand, which increased accordingly. Consumers were demanding more of a commodity whose relative price was falling rapidly, and they were forced to do so by the scarcity of coal and oil. The same policy of the new State aggravated the problem by promoting a type of industry that was highly intensive in energy consumption

The imbalance between supply and demand caused a persistent strangling of the electricity market. From 1944 onwards and for a whole decade, there was indiscriminate rationing in the form of cuts in the electricity supply. The electrical restrictions implied continuous paralysis of industrial activity. Consequently, production and productivity decreased.

We have stated before that during the autarkic Franco regime, the State applied a policy of extremist intervention in price formation and in resource allocation. On the latter, interventionism took place in three ways. We have already talked about one: the allocation of all kinds of inputs, including capital goods, through quotas and import licenses. The production possibilities of industrial companies were greatly conditioned by the authorities' decisions on the amounts of inputs they were entitled to receive, that is, to buy.

The other two channels of intervention were the regulation of private investment and the creation of a public business sector. The declared objective of these policies was self-sufficiency. The absolute priority of the rulers was to promote those sectors and industries that they considered of high strategic interest for the economy and national defence, always from the logic of self-sufficiency. This would justify that all private investment in directly productive activities be subject to prior administrative authorization. It was not permitted to create a company, open a new plant or even expand production capacity without government permission. The government granted itself total discretion in the control of investment initiatives. It was not guided by criteria of economic rationality. Some geographical areas were discriminated, either positively or negatively, and some productive sectors were penalized or rewarded in the granting of investment permits. The political contacts of the entrepreneurs were decisive in the decision-making process. This led to a very poor allocation of available resources. While accumulated human and physical capital was being wasted, uneconomic activities were being developed in inappropriate places.

But it was in the field of the creation of public companies where the interventionism of the Franco regime is shown in a more diaphanous way and where the profoundly negative consequences of the policy of replacing the market by the State in the economic reconstruction are more clearly appreciated. Franco's close collaborators boasted of having an industrialization strategy that broke radically with the past and would give a strong impulse to economic development. The diagnosis of these new rulers was that private entrepreneurs had failed in the task of industrializing the country. The government would have to assume the role of development engine that they had been unable to play. With this in mind, the

National Institute of Industry (INI) was created in 1941. This was a holding of State-owned companies, either created on the initiative of INI itself or incorporated through nationalization of existing companies. For the first time, the Spanish State took on the role of entrepreneur. But not just any entrepreneur, but one who received preferential treatment in the supply of the most scarce productive resources and who, in the productive activities he entered, could relegate private companies or abort private business projects.

The initiatives that INI launched in this first formative stage were aimed at covering, above all, two characteristically autarkic objectives: to manufacture military equipment and to reduce foreign dependence on energy products. Some of the companies founded by INI were electricity companies that would contribute to solve the energy deficit in the 1950s. But during its first stage of development, INI devoted most of its resources to promote a type of industrial activity with low social profitability. So INI's action hampered economic recovery. A substantial part of the country's scarce resources—raw materials, foreign exchange, etc.—were wasted by INI promoting activities and companies that did not solve any of the problems that prevented the Spanish economy from returning to the path of long-term growth.

4 Autarkic Policies

For an economy as dependent on the outside world for the supply of energy, raw materials and capital goods as Spain was, the success of reconstruction would depend on a policy that guaranteed the supply of these inputs, as J. Catalan has argued. The autarkic policy did not in any way guarantee the supply of these strategic goods. The regime's trade policy was in no way geared to recovering the normal level of imports.

The evolution of foreign trade during the 1940s must be described as catastrophic. Trade exchanges (arms excluded) had collapsed during the war. After the end of the war, trade remained at exceptionally low levels throughout the decade (see Fig. 6.2). By 1940, foreign trade, in volume terms, had fallen to 40% of the level reached in 1935. It would remain below half that year's level until 1948. Note that the quantities of products exported and imported in 1935 were already abnormally low due to the impact of the Great Depression. Comparing this with 1929 (Fig. 6.2), we see that during the first half of the 1940s imports were at one-third and

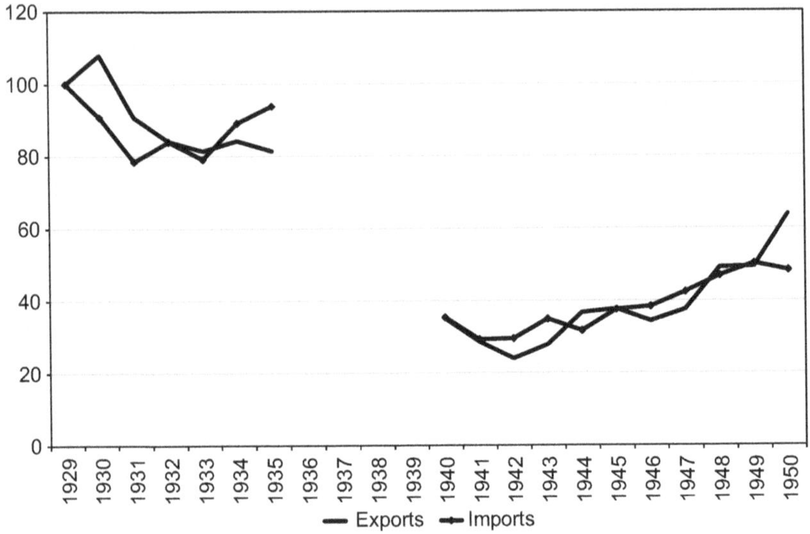

Fig. 6.2 Quantum indices of Spanish foreign trade, 1929–1950 (1929=100). *Source*: A. Tena (2005): "Sector exterior", in A. Carreras and X. Tafunell (coords.): *Estadísticas históricas de España. Siglos XIX y XX*. Bilbao: Fundación BBVA, vol. II, table 8.5.

during the second half at 45% of that level. The evolution of exports was even slightly worse than that of imports until 1949.

The degree of trade openness of the Spanish economy even fell below 5%. In no year of the decade did it reach 8% (on average, it was 5.8%). Figure 3.1 shows that what happened during this period was a completely abnormal phenomenon in historical terms. To find such a meagre share of foreign trade in the national economy, we would have to go back to the worst years of the first decades of the nineteenth century. It does not seem exaggerated to talk about the collapse of foreign trade.

Figure 3.2 illustrates the uniqueness of the Spanish pattern in these years. The brutal contraction of Spanish foreign trade contrasts sharply with the evolution followed by other European countries, even during the world conflagration. Before the Civil War, foreign trade flows had a weight in the Spanish economy that was about half of that in Western Europe (EU-15). During the Second World War, the relative weight of Spanish foreign trade fell much more than that of the foreign trade of European countries. Spain's degree of relative trade openness was reduced to 22%. In the rest of the 1940s it did not improve at all. While Spain's foreign trade was barely reviving, the countries of Western Europe were experiencing a vibrant revitalization of their foreign trade.

What repercussions did the stagnation of foreign trade have on the Spanish economy? Importing much less than before the war would mean an acute shortage of energy, industrial raw materials, machinery and even spare parts. In short, there was a shortage of all those goods that are essential for economic recovery. To make matters worse, the quantities of these inputs that could be imported were cut back by the pressing need to import more food and by the priority given by the regime to the purchase of arms. Spain was a country technically in state of war until 1948.

The main problem in buying products abroad was how to finance the purchases. The country had spent all its gold and currency reserves during the Civil War. The possibilities of importing would depend on foreign financing and export capacity.

Spain received practically no capital from abroad during the whole decade. It was a desired option before it was imposed for political-ideological reasons. Franco rejected the financial aid offered by the US government in the midst of the world war. Following the autarchic ideology, he immediately enacted legislation that almost vetoed foreign investment. In the early years, Spain was even a net exporter of capital. The Franco regime scrupulously repaid the foreign debt it had contracted with the Axis powers during the Civil War for the provision of arms. From 1945 onwards, the autarchic will of the Francoist State mattered less than the international diplomatic isolation dictated by the UN. Unlike the other countries in its environment, Spain did not participate in the new international cooperation schemes (OEEC, IMF, WB, GATT). Therefore, it was deprived of credits and foreign aid, such as the Marshall Plan. This must be underlined because it was external financing that allowed many European countries to immediately recover their pre-conflict import capacity, and thus to quickly carry out reconstruction.

So, in the case of Spain, the recovery of imports fell back on the improvement of its export capacity. And since sales to the exterior did not pick up, Spain was doomed to import less than it needed. Why did exports remain so depressed?

The causes of the poor export performance are varied. Three were particularly relevant. First, the pattern of specialization in agricultural products. The lack of fertilizers, livestock and agricultural machinery significantly reduced the supply of exportable products. The main export sector was trapped in a vicious circle: the very insufficiency of imports mortgaged the capacity to export, which, in turn, did not allow for the import of capital goods indispensable for increasing production. Second, exports were not revived because of a trade policy that was dominated by an obsession to save foreign currency and that favoured trade relations with Germany (until 1945). Rigid bilateralism and the forced reorientation of trade relations towards the German economy constrained exchanges.

The third and main factor explaining the stagnation of exports is the exchange rate policy. The authorities opted for an exchange rate that overvalued the peseta, and increasingly so. Franco, like other dictators, was imbued with the absurd idea that the country's prestige was associated with a high exchange rate. Until December 1948, the Caudillo was determined to keep the official exchange rate established in 1940 unchanged. His government then authorized an extremely complicated system of multiple exchange rates, in which the peseta had a different value depending on what type of article was being imported or exported or what balance of payments item the operation corresponded to. This mechanism was used to surreptitiously devalue the peseta. The operation was repeated in 1949, in the wake of the devaluations of European currencies. These late devaluations did not correct, by any means, the appreciation of the real exchange rate generated by the intense inflationary process that Spain suffered during the 1940s.

The anomaly of the Spanish exchange rate during the early Franco regime can be seen in all its exceptionality thanks to the estimated real effective exchange rate (REER). The relationship with the United States, France and Great Britain, which were Spain's main long-term trading partners, has been considered. As Fig. 6.3 shows, the early Francoism is the great exception in this more than secular series. While the Spanish REER has tended to remain at long-term purchasing power parity with the dollar, franc and pound, with its fluctuations and deviations, from 1936 to 1948 the dictator's preference for a stable currency completely distorted the price of the Spanish currency. Meanwhile, during the years of reconstruction almost all the Western European countries devalued their currencies, in order to recover export capacity and to slow down the import momentum. Spain did not.

The excessive official exchange rate of the peseta could only be sustained through strict—suffocating—control of imports by the

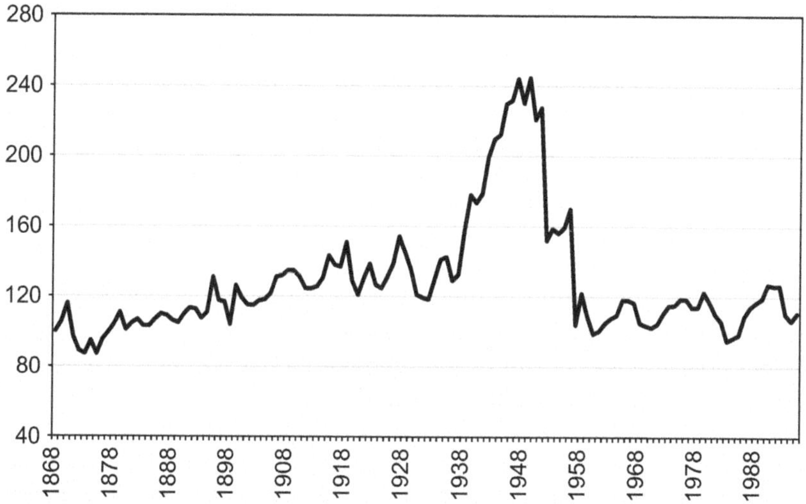

Fig. 6.3 Peseta real effective exchange rate, 1868–1995 (1868=100). *Source*: J. Aixalá (1999): *La peseta y los precios. Un análisis de largo plazo (1868-1995)*, Zaragoza: Prensas Universitarias de Zaragoza.

government, which had a monopoly on foreign exchange. The government had to ration imports, whose demand far exceeded the availability of foreign currency, precisely because the excessive exchange rate of the peseta severely penalized Spanish products on the international market. As a result, foreign sales did not reach pre-war levels for any of the main export products and all of them lost ground on the world market.

Bibliographical Orientation

The two essential reference works on the Spanish economy during the Civil War are P. Martín Aceña and E. Martínez Ruiz (eds.)(2006): *La economía de la guerra civil*, Madrid: Marcial Pons; and E. Fuentes Quintana (dir.) and F. Comín (ed.)(2008): *Economía y economistas españoles en la Guerra Civil*, Barcelona: Galaxia Gutenberg. The essays included in the second part and some of the fourth part are of great value. J. Fontana and J. Nadal (1976): "Spain 1914–1970" in C. M. Cipolla (ed.): *The Fontana Economic History of Europe*, vol. 6 (2), *Contemporary Economies*, London: Collins, still are a valuable reference for 1936–1951 and beyond. The book by C. Barciela *et al.* (2001): *La España de Franco (1939–1975)*, Madrid: Síntesis, which covers the economy during the Franco regime, deals in some detail with all the relevant aspects of the autarkic economy. A sharp analytical perspective on the Spanish post-war economy in L. Prados de la Escosura and J. C. Sanz (1996): 'Growth and macroeconomic performance in Spain, 1939-93', in N. Crafts and Toniolo (eds.) (1996): *Economic Growth in Europe since 1945*, Cambridge: Cambridge University Press. This essay is equally valuable for subsequent historical periods (Chaps. 7–10 of this work).

An excellent analysis of the economic impact of the autarkic and interventionist policy of the first years of the Franco regime in J. Catalan (1995): *La economía española y la segunda guerra mundial*, Barcelona: Ariel. C. Barciela (ed.)(2003): *Autarquía y mercado negro. El fracaso económico del primer franquismo*, 1939–1959, Barcelona: Crítica, is useful for several important topics of the economy of this period, such as the educational, agrarian, industrial and labour policies. The public regulation of initiatives to establish and expand industrial companies is dealt with by L. E. Pires (2005): "Los empresarios y el Estado en torno a las intervenciones del régimen de Franco: la regulación de la inversión industrial (1938-1963)", *Investigaciones de Historia Económica*, 2. M. Vilar Rodríguez (2009): *Los salarios del miedo. Mercado de trabajo y crecimiento económico en España durante el franquismo.* Santiago de Compostela: Fundación 10 de Marzo, provides a valuable quantitative elaboration on salaries and factorial distribution of income, making the point that labour market and income policy were key factors in the Francoist economic model. On public intervention in the electricity sector and its effects, C. Sudrià (2007): "El Estado y el sector eléctrico español bajo el franquismo: regulación y empresa pública", in A. Gómez Mendoza, C. Sudrià and J. Pueyo: *Electra y el Estado. La intervención pública en la industria eléctrica bajo el franquismo*, Madrid: Thomson-Cívitas. The exchange rate policy is briefly but surely addressed by J. M. Serrano Sanz (2000): "Veinte años de soledad. La autarquía de la peseta, 1939-1959", in J. L. García Delgado and J. M. Serrano Sanz (dirs.): *Del real al euro. Una historia de peseta*, Barcelona: La Caixa.

CHAPTER 7

Import Substitution Industrialization (1951–1959)

In the 1940s Spain went through an autarkic industrialization. As it was politically and economically unsustainable, especially in front of Western Europe's successful post-war reconstruction, it had to move to a less rigid scheme: import substitution industrialization (ISI). It happened at the same time than in many other countries, notably in Latin America and the Middle East. But there, ISI was a reaction against the closing of world markets. In Spain it was a flexibilization of autarky, a voluntary closing of its own economy.

1 Cold War, American Aid and Tempering of Interventionism

The political isolation suffered by Spain was dissolved from 1950 onwards. The new international context was increasingly dominated by the Cold War. This scenario was instrumental in the rehabilitation of General Franco's regime within the international community. Many Western countries, led by the United States, no longer considered the Spanish State as a former ally of the fascist front. They have come to see it as a reliable member of the anti-communist bloc, although not comparable to the bloc of democratic nations. Spain would be incorporated into the Western defence system. In November 1950 the UN revoked Spain's

A. Carreras, X. Tafunell, *Between Empire and Globalization*, Palgrave Studies in Economic History,
https://doi.org/10.1007/978-3-030-60504-9_7

diplomatic isolation. Thus began a very gradual process of normalization of relations between Spain and the international community. In the same year, the US Congress granted the first official loans to Spain. Subsequently, the U.S. Administration addressed the negotiation of economic aid to Franco's Spain in exchange for having several military bases in Spanish territory. In 1953, an agreement was reached, known as the Madrid Pact.

Was American aid to Spain similar to the Marshall Plan? On a fundamental level the answer is no. The aid did not have effects comparable to those resulting from the European Recovery Program (known as the Marshall Plan) for Western European countries. Spain did not join the multilateral institutions that managed and optimized aid. These institutions played a decisive role in the post-war European model. It was not until very late that Spain joined the main international economic organizations. Entry into the International Monetary Fund, the World Bank and the OECD would not take place until 1958–1959.

How crucial was the economic aid that Spain received, and was it decisive for its economic reactivation? The total amount received (donations and loans) amounted to the equivalent of 1% of GDP. But its impact was diluted when it was spread over more than a decade. In fact, Spain only began to receive significant amounts from 1955 onwards. As F. Guirao argues, American aid did not play a major role in the Spanish economy's take-off from 1951 onwards. Between 1955 and 1958 the flow of aid did increase considerably the import capacity. This facilitated the normalization of the supply of raw materials, capital goods and even food. However, US dollars and loans would not be enough to prevent the trade deficit from overflowing, as we shall see. American aid made another valuable contribution. As O. Calvo has stressed, perhaps the most important thing was not the aid itself, but its impact on the expectations of economic agents. Businessmen and investors understood that the bilateral agreement with the United States definitively consolidated the Franco regime.

If the accelerated growth of the Spanish economy in the first 1950s cannot be explained by American aid, what were its causes? Basically, there were two. First, the intensification of trade between Spain and the Western European countries. The economic boom caused by the Korean War (1950–1953) and the very intense growth of some large European economies boosted Spanish exports. In 1949–1953, exports (of goods and services) multiplied by 2.3, that is, they increased at a rate of 22.5% per year (see column 13 of Appendix). The Spanish economy then had more foreign currency to finance imports of the goods needed to make better use of its installed productive capacity; it also had to expand it. It was especially important to begin equipping industry with new machinery. It should be borne in mind that the country's productive apparatus was using tremendously aged and obsolete machinery, which had not been renewed for twenty years. The acquisition of machinery that incorporated the technological progress accumulated during that period resulted in a great increase in industrial productivity. Agriculture also made significant productivity gains, thanks to the importation of fertilizers. As soon as exports stopped expanding, US aid took over as a source of foreign exchange to finance rising imports.

A second force for economic recovery was the relaxation of economic interventionism. In 1951 Franco formed a new government that rectified the economic strategy followed until then and which had given such poor results. The miserable living conditions of the population became less and less bearable in view of the rapid reconstruction and subsequent prosperity of the neighbouring countries. The cautious approach to the United States and the community of Western nations also led to a policy that was not so self-sufficient and interventionist.

The reader should note that we are talking about relaxation and rectification. The fact is that there was no radical shift. So much so that many historians are now discussing the period 1950–1959 together with the previous decade in a single stage: autarky. The liberalization of the 1950s was extremely limited. Private investment will continue to be subject to administrative authorization; the foreign exchange market severely controlled; foreign investment strictly restricted. So what was the change in economic policy?

The more extreme interventionist measures on product markets were relaxed and corrected. Ration books were abolished in 1952. Gradually, the centralized allocation of scarce inputs, i.e. quotas for raw materials and energy products, was abolished. Most agricultural products became freely priced and production of all crops was deregulated.

The supply response to the liberalization policy was immediate and spectacular: a sudden increase in production, stabilization of prices after an initial rise and the disappearance of shortages. The black market disappeared as if by magic.

The energy sector, which had hampered economic recovery so much in the previous decade, also reemerged strongly as a result of an adequate industrial policy and the availability of more foreign currency to import oil. Large power plants built by public companies came into operation.

The government established a new regulatory framework for the electricity sector. The various regional networks were interconnected to compensate for deficits in some areas with surpluses in others. Once the interconnection was completed, tariffs were unified and electricity prices were raised. This gave the private electricity companies the stimulus they needed to encourage them to invest in new plants. In a short time, the electricity supply cuts disappeared, despite the accelerated pace of demand growth.

Another measure to make the schemes applied during the first post-war decade more flexible was the management of the multiple exchange rate mechanism. As we said, the complexity and opacity of this system made it easy for the authorities to surreptitiously devalue the peseta. Between 1948 and 1951 they proceeded to devaluations that accumulated a depreciation of the peseta of 225%, from 13 to 29 pesetas per dollar. This drastic reduction in the peseta's value, which went unnoticed by public opinion, boosted exports and played an important role in the recovery of the foreign sector in the early 1950s. The devaluations then lost importance, which slowed down the expansion of exports from 1954 onwards.

2 From Autarky to Import Substitution Industrialization

The entry into the new decade marks an unequivocal change in the evolution of the Spanish economy. While the 1940s had been slow in progress after the disruption caused by the war, the 1950s were to be a time of strong expansion. Between 1939 and 1949 the GDP had grown at an annual rate of 2.1% (1.4, the GDP per inhabitant). Between 1950 and 1959, it increased at a rate of 5.2% per year (4.3%, the per capita GDP).

We must put this growth in context, to assess it in its fair measure. In the 1950s, the Spanish economy did not manage to advance faster than the EU-15 economies as a whole. At this point, it is necessary to refer to Fig. 1.3 (and column 5 of the Appendix). Spain's per capita income relative to that of the reference group of countries barely improved, despite being at an extremely low level in 1950. So the huge gap that had opened up between Western Europe and Spain in the years of the Civil War was by no means bridged during the second decade of Francoism. It could have happened. If the Spanish economy had behaved in this decade as the norm for Western European economies it would have grown more than it actually did. Franco's industrializing model led to the economy growing below its potential in the 1950s.

Could it not be that the intense growth of the 1950s was the post-war recovery that did not occur during the 1940s? It seems that it did, indeed. If GDP had continued to grow as it had in the years between 1900 and 1935, it would have reached a somewhat higher level in 1958 than it actually did.

All this does not deny that during the period studied the productive system underwent great changes. In the intense economic expansion of these years, investment played a very important role. Between 1950 and 1958, gross fixed capital formation grew at an annual rate of 8.3%. The share of investment in GDP rose sharply to around 25% by the middle of the decade, a record that left far behind the levels reached previously. The Spanish economy was making a major capitalization effort to be able to industrialize rapidly. If the propensity to invest increased in such an unprecedented way, it was due to the combination of a radical change in business expectations and a more gradual but substantial improvement in the possibilities of renewing and expanding the productive apparatus. As we pointed out, national entrepreneurs gained confidence in the survival of the regime, which encouraged them to undertake new investment plans and to take up again those that had been forced to be paralyzed for a long time. If they were able to execute them—not all of them—it was thanks to the greater facilities granted by the Administration to import industrial inputs as foreign reserves increased.

Industry, which had become the engine of economic growth, progressed as never before: at a rate of 8.0% per year. The dynamism of the industrial sector led to more than an unprecedented rise in the production of manufactured goods. A profound, structural transformation of the economy took place. The contribution of industry to GDP rose from 21.4% (1949) to 31.2% (1958), displacing agriculture as the main productive sector. The turnaround expresses a leap forward in the industrialization process. A closer look at the industrial sector provides several quantitative indications that confirm the diagnosis. The most significant of all is the measure of industrial progress proposed by Hoffmann, which we have referred to in previous parts of the work when analysing the stages of strong modernization. During this decade, an accelerated intra-industrial change took place which led to Spain being on the verge of reaching full industrial maturity in 1958, according to the typology of industrialization formulated by Hoffmann.

The industrializing achievements were the natural consequence of applying an import substitution strategy (ISI) that made the rigid autarkic and interventionist schemes established at the end of the war more flexible. In the previous chapter we have seen that in the period 1939–1949 Franco collaborators had the dream that autarky was viable and would lead to industrialization. Far from fulfilling their predictions, the autarkic policy blocked reconstruction and plunged the economy into permanent stagnation. The brutal restriction of imports of energy products, raw materials and capital goods jammed the bomb that was to set the productive system in motion. The autarkic dream of building a broad industrial base using national resources proved unattainable, precisely because, paradoxical as it may seem, in order to forge it, indispensable inputs had to be imported in large quantities.

The relaxation of the autarkic scheme from 1951 onwards opened the door to the effective development of an inward industrialization strategy (ISI). Its essential components would be: insurmountable barriers to the entry of foreign products, combined with a certain flexibility in the importation of raw materials and capital goods; rigid currency exchange controls; and direct and very active intervention of the State in the production of basic goods. The essential objective of this policy was to build up a powerful and diversified industry of its own, from which economic development would automatically follow. The means of achieving the objective was simply to substitute imports, i.e., to promote industries oriented to serve the domestic market. By following such a strategy, Spain was moving away from Western Europe but was in tune with many peripheral economies. At the time, a large number of nations seeking to industrialize on all continents, particularly in Latin America and Asia, embraced the ISI strategy.

Spain managed to grow vigorously for a few years on the basis of producing internally the industrial goods demanded by consumers and by the producers themselves. Donges' estimates make this abundantly clear. Spanish industry took over virtually all domestic demand for consumer goods and a large part for intermediate goods; in particular, the share of domestic demand covered by domestic producers in 1958 reached 94.4% and 82.4%, respectively. Only in the area of capital goods supply was the presence of domestic producers not overwhelming, which is typical of the ISI models. The limited capacity to produce machinery with medium or high technological requirements forced to continue depending on the more developed countries.

In order to allow the creation of companies dedicated to the production of goods that were previously imported, it was necessary to equip these companies with machinery and inputs that often had to be imported. If the import substitution process failed in the first decade of the post-war period, it was due to the inflexible application of autarkic schemes by the rulers. When they abandoned the idea of restricting imports as much as possible and were inclined to authorize the purchase of equipment and commodities from abroad, the ISI model could be developed. With great success, from the point of view of productive capacities. Not from the point of view of efficiency. It was impossible to have an efficient industry with a market that was not subject to cost discipline, because foreign competition was excluded and because public enterprises did not seek to produce at the lowest cost. Moreover, the small size of the domestic market did not allow for the exploitation of large economies of scale.

The success of the import substitution industrialization model was, in fact, short-lived. Contrary to the prognosis and expectations of self-reliance, it did not lay the foundations for long-term economic growth. As it deepened, import-substitution industrialization became increasingly unfeasible. It created a serious macroeconomic imbalance: the trade deficit. Within a few years, it would lead to the definitive collapse of that model of economic growth. We will analyse this in the last section of the chapter, after examining the business model championed by the ISI.

3 The Structuring of a National Capitalism

The autarky in the 1940s and import-substitution industrialization in the 1950s ended up forming a completely different business system to the existing before the Civil War. The latter was dominated by large public service companies, especially railway and electricity companies. The large companies were all private and foreign capital held a dominant or significant position in them (see Table 7.1).

The autarkic project was totally opposed to the presence of foreign capital in Spanish companies. After the Civil War, the new regime nationalized some large companies. RENFE was born in 1942 from the nationalization of the broad gauge railway companies; Telefónica was bought by the government from ITT in 1944; of similar origin was Tabacalera (established in 1945), although in its case the government bought it from the nationally owned Compañía Arrendataria de Tabacos; ENASA was born in 1946 from the purchase of Hispano-Suiza; etc.

Table 7.1 The 12 largest non-financial Spanish companies ranked by assets, 1930 and 1960

1930		*1960*	
Ferrocarriles MZA	4	RENFE	1
Caminos de Hierro del Norte E.	4	Empresa Nac. Siderúrgica, ENSIDESA	1
CHADE	4	Cía. Telefónica Nacional de España	2
Barcelona Traction, Light and Power	5	Empresa Nac. Calvo Sotelo, ENCASO	1
Riegos y Fuerzas del Ebro	5	Hidroeléctrica Española, HIDROLA	3
R. Cía. Asturiana de Minas	5	Hidroeléctrica Ibérica, IBERDUERO	3
Cía. Minera y Siderúrgica Peñarroya	5	CAMPSA	2
Cía. Telefónica Nacional de España	5	Empresa Nac. Const. Naval, BAZÁN	1
Cía. F.E. del Ferrocarril de Tánger	4	Altos Hornos de Vizcaya	3
Cía. de los Ferrocarriles Andaluces	4	Empresa Nac. de Electricidad ENDESA	1
S. Española de Construcción Naval	5	Empresa Nac. Hidr.Ribagorz., ENHER	1
Rio Tinto Co. Ltd.	5	Cía. Española de Petróleos, CEPSA	3

Sources: A. Carreras and X. Tafunell: "La gran empresa en España (1917–1974). Una primera aproximación", *Revista de Historia Industrial* (1993), 3; and "La gran empresa en la España contemporánea: entre el mercado y el Estado", in F. Comín and P. Martín Aceña, eds. (1996) *La empresa en la historia de España*. Madrid: Cívitas

Codes: 1, public (State-owned); 2, mixed national; 3, private national; 4, private mixed (national-foreign); 5, foreign

The formation of INI meant the creation of a large number of new companies. Most of them were born in the 1940s, but they would make the bulk of the investments during the 1950s. The last of INI's great creations was ENSIDESA, in 1950. SEAT, also born in 1950, was the first of the large industrial companies in which INI had a minority stake, together with Spanish companies and banks, and associating the Italian FIAT.

The companies wholly owned by INI were all called "national". This designation condensed the essence of the autarkic programme: comprehensive economic and business nationalism. Not only was it necessary production to be Spanish, but it was also desirable for the company to be Spanish owned. And the most Spanish of all capitals was the capital of the Spanish State. In the future we will see many companies that call themselves "Spanish" or whose company name refers to Spain. These will be foreign capital companies. The "national companies" will be the bulwark of nationalist industrialization, in its autarkic form or in the gentler form of the ISI.

Large private companies lost much of their foreign ownership. In addition to those that were nationalized, there were others that suffered strong pressure to sell their shares to Spanish suitors. This course of action was characteristic of the 1950s. Some companies, such as Rio Tinto and Ford, resisted "naturalization". This followed constant pressure from the authorities, who blocked all the owners' business projects if they did not comply with their (the authorities) conditions. Eventually, they accepted the offers of Spanish business groups and sold—both in 1954. By 1960, at the end of the long period of self-sufficiency, the apex of Spanish big business had changed considerably (see Table 7.1).

All the large companies were Spanish. Most of the main companies were public. The corporate names that had risen to corporate hegemony dominated the system for decades.

Historiography has always stressed the centrality of banking in this business system. The dominant hypothesis has been that banking controlled the industry. But the vision of "banking power" has been disputed. In general terms, we can say that the control of industry by the banking sector is a feature common to all economies in which the capital market has not been sufficiently developed. These are usually economies in which the Government has played an important role in the economic take-off. This is the case in Germany, Japan and Italy. This is also the case in Spain. The large Spanish private banks received a strong injection of liquidity thanks to the large compensation obtained by the nationalization of the railway companies. Autarky and the ISI were the golden age of banking control of the industry. In a framework of scarce competition in the capital market thanks to the banking status quo and with foreign banks out of the picture, the credit oligopoly gradually handed over all private industrial initiatives to the control of the banks. The need for financing to meet a rapidly growing demand led many industrialists to seek the help of private banks. In addition, the centralization of the industrial business due to the strong politicization of the administrative authorization process gave wings to the banking entrepreneurship. Banks were more likely to succeed in this tangle than individual entrepreneurs. The 1950s thus saw an increase in the importance of banking, which played a major role in business decision-making.

4 The Unsustainability of the Growth Model. The Stabilization Plan

The import-substitution industrialization model generated two serious macroeconomic imbalances: inflation and current account deficit. The former disrupted the allocation of resources and caused a number of problems, including the deterioration of the external competitive position, i.e. the worsening of the trade deficit. This second imbalance made the economic model unsustainable.

Inflation was very high in 1950–1951 and from 1956 onwards (see columns 19 and 20 in the Appendix). The rise in the early years was due to the removal of much of the price controls, before an expansion of the productive supply stabilized prices. This upsurge in inflation caused serious problems. It caused the first major strike movement after the Civil War. The regime took this into account and learned to combine price increases with wage increases. From 1956 onwards prices rose again sharply. The immediate cause of the resurgence of inflation was an excessive increase in the amount of money. There were two causes: the deficit of the public sector and the demand for credit from private companies, which was met almost without restriction by the private banks. The public deficit—made compatible with the budget balance of the Public Treasury (see column 10 of the Appendix)—was caused by the investment programme developed by INI. Instead of financing it through a tax increase, it was done through the issuance of public debt that banks and savings banks were obliged to buy, as well as through loans from the Bank of Spain. The escalation in bank credit was motivated by cost inflation caused by wage increases and the financing of a rapid expansion of production capacity.

The large differential between domestic and international inflation can easily become a powerful constraint on growth. This is what happened in the second half of the 1950s, when the real exchange rate of the peseta appreciated strongly. As a result, the external imbalance rapidly worsened. According to the calculations of E. Martínez, the loss of competitiveness caused by the overvaluation of the peseta largely cancelled out the export-led increase in foreign demand.

Two features stand out in the evolution of trade (goods and services) with the outside world in the period 1950–1959. First, imports are growing strongly, at a slightly higher rate than GDP, while exports are stagnating after the great boom of the period 1950–1953 (see columns 13 and

14 of the Appendix). Second, the value of purchases is increasingly higher than that of sales, so that the trade deficit is steadily increasing. All the efforts made in import substitution policy did not serve to reduce the propensity to import: as production expanded, a more than proportional amount of capital goods was purchased abroad. In contrast, the propensity to export tended to decline continuously, given the lack of competitive capacity of the ISI-powered productive sectors in open markets. The combination of an upward import propensity and a downward export propensity resulted in a trade balance deficit that would end up being unsustainable because unfinanceable.

The deficit in the trade balance could only be covered by capital inflows. But foreign investment continued to be severely limited. For a while, the surplus in the balance of transfers compensated for the deficit in the balance of goods. While the Americans transferred dollars *en masse* in exchange for the installation of the military bases, it was possible to finance the external imbalance. When the volume of funds provided by the United States was reduced, Spain's foreign accounts deteriorated very quickly up to foreign reserves exhaustion. The foreign sector thus caused the collapse of the flexible autarkic model that we know as the ISI model.

At the end of the first half of 1959, a balance of payments crisis emerged. Spain was virtually in default due to lack of foreign currency. The public entity that held the monopoly of foreign exchange and managed its assignment had a negative net position, after having suffered an uncontrollable decline since 1956. So Spain was faced with a dilemma: either the government drastically cut the volume of imports, with the aim of preserving, at any price, the autarkic principles; or else external balance was restored and economic growth was boosted through the liberalization of foreign trade, the attraction of foreign capital and foreign aid.

The first option was hardly practicable for political reasons. Franco did not feel capable of imposing on the population a return to the situation of deprivation and restrictions of the first post-war period. Even a dictatorship needs to have a certain social legitimacy. It could have lost that legitimacy if the leaders had resorted to the heroic slogans of the 1940s. So, as much as the Francoist leaders disliked it, they had no choice but to reintegrate Spain into the international capitalist economic order.

In fact, from 1957 onwards, influential sectors of the Government and Administration argued that the orientation of economic policy had to be drastically changed. The actions taken by the Government in 1957 and 1958 to break the economic isolation and correct the main internal and external imbalances paved the way for the implementation of the Stabilization Plan. This period is known as "the pre-stabilizing biennium". This adjustment policy failed because it was not sufficiently vigorous. Moreover, the measures taken were not effective because they were implemented in an uncoordinated manner. Much more important would be to approach international economic bodies. In 1958, the Spanish Government requested Spain's membership to the International Monetary Fund (IMF) and the World Bank, which became effective the same year. It also requested membership to the Organisation for European Economic Co-operation (OEEC; since 1961, OECD). These organizations were willing to provide technical and financial assistance to Spain, so that it could dismantle the autarkic system in a non-traumatic way and open it up to the outside world.

In July 1959 the government approved the main measures of a stabilization and liberalization programme negotiated with the IMF. This programme was to have the greatest importance for the future of the Spanish economy. Economic historians unanimously maintain that the so-called Stabilization Plan was one of the most important economic policy decisions and one of the most important economic events in the history of the country in the twentieth century. Why should a set of actions aimed at correcting some macroeconomic imbalances be so important? The Spanish government itself offers the answer in the memorandum it sent in June 1959 for approval to the IMF and the OEEC. In this document, which contained all the lines of action of the Stabilization Plan, it was stated that "the time had come to give a new direction to economic policy, in order to align the Spanish economy with the countries of the Western world and free it from interventions inherited from the past".

The Plan represented, in effect, a radical reorientation of economic policy. Radical in two ways. First, because it was a shock treatment—using the terminology used by the Fund—of an economy afflicted by serious internal and external imbalances. Second, because it implied the unreserved acceptance by the Spanish economic leaders of the principles of liberal capitalism; that is, the renunciation of a closed economy intervened by the State and the acceptance of an economy regulated by the market and open to the outside world.

The international context made it easier a change in policy. In Western Europe, a new era was opening with the signing of the Treaty of Rome in March 1957, which gave birth to the European Economic Community (EEC). The customs union—the "Common Market"—was to lead to the creation and diversion of trade in the world's fastest growing area at the time. By 1958, the European Payments Union (EPU) had achieved free convertibility of European currencies and of all of them with the dollar at a fixed exchange rate. The basic objective of the Bretton Woods agreement regarding the international monetary system had finally been achieved. Monetary stability guaranteed a much more stable framework for trade and international capital and labour movements. The autarkic Spanish scheme, even in its flexible version of import-substitution industrialization, was aging by the moment. All the Western European countries were forced to open up to the outside world to take advantage of the powerful tailwind that was driving the European economy.

The central objective of the Stabilization Plan was to correct the external balance deficit. This would require a package of monetary, fiscal and exchange rate measures. But, in addition, the stabilization programme sought to create the right conditions so that the payments crisis would not recur. To achieve this second, long-term objective, very deep and varied structural reforms would be required, consisting essentially of deregulation and internal and external liberalization of the economy. In short, the programme adopted in 1959 was a typical stabilization and liberalization plan at the same time. In the rest of this section, we will deal only with the characteristics of the former. The measures designed to open up the economy to the outside world, introduce competition and replace the State with the market will be examined in the following chapter, since they would mark the path followed by the Spanish economy during the period considered there.

Given that, in order to cut the external deficit, it was necessary to curb domestic demand and divert productive supply abroad, the Stabilization Plan consisted of a combination of restrictive monetary, credit and fiscal policies. Also in the establishment of a new exchange rate that allowed maintaining the external balance without the government controlling commercial transactions.

Specifically, the stabilizing operation consisted of the following: (1) the recovery of control by the authorities of the monetary policy and its tightening. The former was achieved by definitively eliminating the issuance of automatically pledged public debt. The automatic pledge gave private banks the right to obtain credit from the Bank of Spain at preferential rates in exchange for the assignment of the securities as collateral. As a result, private banks had until then had the capacity to neutralize the monetary policy designed by the authorities. The latter, in addition to taking control of monetary policy, raised interest rates; (2) credit restriction to the private sector by decreeing a ceiling on the increase in bank credit; (3) this quantitative rationing mechanism was extended to public spending; (4) fiscal consolidation was also to be achieved by increasing public revenues and the tax burden. This, of course, would have the effect of reducing the purchasing power of households and businesses. To this end, tariffs and prices of public services and goods with administratively fixed prices were raised; (5) the imposition of a mandatory and unremunerated prior deposit equal to the value of imports. This measure was intended to prevent an avalanche of imports following the repeal of the legal requirement to obtain an import license; and (6) the establishment of a new exchange rate, unique for all types of transactions, which represented a substantial devaluation. The exchange rate was set at a value which proved to be around the market price. The decree establishing the new parity with the dollar declared the external convertibility of the peseta and the liberalization of the foreign exchange market. It therefore led to Spain's entry into the Bretton Woods monetary system.

The results of the Stabilization Plan were spectacular. So much so that the IMF would later consider it a model. The depressive effects on consumption and investment were immediately and strongly felt but were not lasting (see Appendix series). In the second half of 1959, GDP fell by 2.5%. For the year as a whole, investment in fixed capital fell by 6.5% and imports by 15.5%. The contraction of economic activity obviously had significant social costs. Labour market rigidities prevented an increase in unemployment but not a sharp fall in household disposable income. However, the recession was short lived. Within a year of the plan's adoption, signs of recovery were multiplying. The consolidation achieved by the stabilization operation, added to the dynamic effects of the liberalization measures that accompanied it, propelled the country's economy into extraordinary growth.

The success of the Stabilization Plan was immediate in the core of its action: the external accounts. Reserves began to increase immediately, thanks to the repatriation of capital and the expansion of exports of goods and services. The initial contraction in imports also helped a lot. Shortly afterwards, foreign capital investments were added. After only four or five months, the danger of financial insolvency had evaporated. The most critical economic policy operation of Franco's regime was coming to a more successful conclusion than anyone could have foreseen for an economy as closed and as strongly distorted as the Spanish one at the end of the 1950s.

Bibliographic Orientation

A general view of the Spanish economy of the period can be found in C. Barciela *et al.* (2001): *La España de Franco (1939–1975)*, Madrid: Síntesis. On the economic effects of the aid provided by the United States, see O. Calvo (2001): "¡Bienvenido Míster Marshall! La ayuda económica americana y la economía española en la década de 1950", *Revista de Historia Económica-Journal of Iberian and Latin American Economic History*, 19, 1. The importance of European reconstruction and foreign demand for the economic take-off of the 1950s has been carefully displayed by F. Guirao (1998): *Spain and the Reconstruction of Western Europe 1945–1957. Challenge and Response*, London: Macmillan. On how foreign trade affected the economic growth of the period and the limited significance of capital inflows, see E. Martínez Ruiz (2003): *El sector exterior durante la autarquía. Una reconstrucción de las balanzas de pagos de España (1940–1958)*, Madrid: Banco de España. On trade and industrial policy and the model of import-substitution industrialization, and given the soundness of his empirical and conceptual foundations, J. B. Donges (1976) still remains a must read: *La industrialización en España*, Vilassar de Mar: Oikos-tau. An assessment of the power of banks and the contribution of the banking system to post-war economic growth in M.A. Pons (2001): "Banca e industria en España, 1939–1985: la influencia de la banca universal en el crecimiento económico", *Revista de Historia Industrial*, 19–20. Regarding the business side of the economy during the autarkic Franco regime, including public enterprise and such fundamental sectors as the banking sector, see G. Sánchez Recio and J. Tascón Fernández (eds.)(2003): *Los empresarios de Franco. Política y economía en España, 1936–1957*, Barcelona: Crítica. Since the role played by INI has proved controversial, it is instructive to complement the above reading with the alternative view offered by A. Gómez Mendoza (ed.)(2000): *De mitos y milagros. El Instituto Nacional de Autarquía (1941–1963)*, Barcelona: Edicions Universitat de Barcelona. An econometric assessment of the cost in terms of economic growth that would have been incurred had the Stabilization Plan not been implemented and the anti-market policies of the first twenty years of Franco's regime been maintained, in L. Prados de la Escosura, J.R. Rosés and I. Sanz-Villarroya (2012): "Economic Reforms and Growth in Franco's Spain", *Revista de Historia Económica-Journal of Iberian and Latin American Economic History*, 30, 1. A succinct but insightful analysis of the content and economic effects of the Stabilization and Liberalisation Plan in E. Fuentes Quintana (1993): "Tres decenios largos de la economía española en perspectiva", in J. L. García Delgado (dir.): *España, economía*, Madrid: Espasa Calpe.

CHAPTER 8

Spain in the Golden Age: Reintegration into the International Economy (1960–1973)

After the Second World War, Western Europe experienced a rapid and successful economic reconstruction. Once completed, the era of the greatest economic prosperity in history, the Golden Age, was inaugurated. Virtually every economy in the world, capitalist and communist, developed and developing, enjoyed this extraordinary expansion, although it was more successful in Western Europe than almost anywhere else. However, the Spain of the 1950s did not fully participate in the wave of general welfare, because of the survival of its autarkic scheme. In Spain, the Golden Age would not truly arrive until after the implementation of the Stabilization Plan. With the opening to the world, the Spanish economy took advantage, at last, of the growth opportunities provided by the dynamism of the international economy to give a definitive push to industrialization.

1 Liberalization, Opening Up to the Outside World and Economic Integration

If the Stabilization Plan was transcendental, it is not so much because it allowed the reestablishment of basic macroeconomic balances but because it laid the foundations for a new model of economic growth. Its essence was the integration—or, rather, the reintegration—of the Spanish

A. Carreras, X. Tafunell, *Between Empire and Globalization*, Palgrave Studies in Economic History,
https://doi.org/10.1007/978-3-030-60504-9_8

economy into the international economy. The reincorporation was based on a strategy of double opening towards the outside: commercial and financial. Let us start with the first one.

In 1959, the Spanish authorities assumed that they should liberalize foreign trade. Until then, the Administration had rationed imports by means of direct control. From now on, it would regulate the volume of imported products by imposing tariffs and other taxes. In other words, it would replace a scheme restricting purchases abroad by means of quantities with another operating by means of prices. The new trade policy would be much less disruptive of resource allocation. Rulers tended to leave it to the market to decide what was imported and in what quantities.

Liberalization would be gradual and relative. The government took two types of measures: (1) the establishment of various import trade regimes; (2) the introduction of a new tariff. The first line of action was aimed at phasing out state-intervened trade. Imported goods were classified into different trade regimes. One of them was "liberalized trade". The others were regimes of intervened trade, in different degrees of intensity. Trade liberalization consisted of the transfer of goods covered by the various trade regimes to the liberalized trade regime. When the Stabilization Plan was approved, the liberalized trade regime was extended to 33% of imports, including most raw materials, capital goods and spare parts. The Government gradually expanded the liberalized trade. In 1965 it covered more than 2/3 of the total value of imports; from 1967 it was definitely above 3/4.

The liberalization movement described above was countered by the establishment in 1960 of a new tariff. It formed a very protective framework. According to J.B. Donges, the average tariff was 24.9%. And if the average nominal protection was high, the effective protection—that referring to the added value of the goods produced by each branch—of the manufactures was much higher. According to the same author's estimate, by 1962, effective protection amounted to 68%. The tariff provided extremely high protection for consumer durables and more sophisticated intermediate products, while it provided relatively moderate protection for machinery, less sophisticated intermediate products and transport equipment. Overall, Spain remained one of the most closed Western economies.

Within the cautious movement of trade liberalization and consequent integration of the Spanish economy with the neighbouring economies, the Preferential Trade Agreement signed by Spain and the European

Economic Community in 1970 was of particular significance. Thanks to this agreement, the Community—not Spain, which was in breach of the agreement—completely abolished the remaining quantum restrictions on the import of industrial products. The agreement also led to a sharp reduction in tariff barriers in non-agricultural trade between Spain and the EEC. A very asymmetrical reduction in favour of Spain: the Community granted an average reduction of 60%, in steps, in the tariffs it applied to almost all Spanish industrial products, while Spain applied a final reduction of 25%.

The Spanish economy benefited twice as much from this treaty. Firstly, the removal of the barriers to access of Spanish manufacturers to the Community space boosted the country's industry by giving it new possibilities for growth through greater specialization and better use of comparative advantages. The sales of Spanish industrial products to the Community increased in the seventies at a very strong rate, clearly higher than the purchases from the Community countries. Second, the Spanish economy enjoyed a significant increase in productivity as a result of greater consumption of more efficient industrial goods from the EEC, particularly intermediate and capital goods.

Financial openness went hand in hand with trade openness. Until 1959, one of the axes of the economic policy of the Franco regime had been to establish an economy free from foreign capital dependence. With the Stabilization Plan, the legislation was completely overturned. The new legal framework established absolute freedom of investment and repatriation of the capital invested and the income generated. Foreign investors would receive equal treatment with domestic investors in terms of access to bank credit and payment of taxes. The new regulatory framework thus provided the necessary legal guarantees and economic incentives to encourage foreign capitalists to invest in the country.

This policy of financial liberalization must be described as very liberal, given the economic and political context in which it was implemented. The change was more radical in this area than in that of foreign trade. Franco's collaborators embraced the old liberal paradigm that saw foreign capital as a key lever for national economic development. The authorities' interest in attracting foreign capital was motivated by their conviction that capital inflows would bring in foreign currency that was essential for external balance. They were also aware that it was necessary to attract foreign investment in order to solve the technological gap and the low level of productivity of national companies. They also recognized that domestic savings were certainly insufficient to finance the country's definitive industrialization.

Trade and financial openness had extremely favourable effects on economic growth. Trade exchanges multiplied, as did financial flows. As several authors have argued, trade and financial openness generated an extraordinary virtuous circle of growth.

Why do we speak of a "virtuous circle"? Because the same opening to the outside world provided the sources of income that played the role of balancing items in the balance of payments. Opening up triggered a sharp increase in imports, which became the engine of growth; at the same time, it facilitated the arrival of the foreign currencies needed to finance these steadily increasing imports. The virtuous circle would not be broken until the oil shock brought an abrupt end to the era of prosperity in the industrialized countries.

Before referring to these components, it should be noted that, between 1960 and 1973, imports of goods, in real terms, expanded at an annual rate of 14.6%, while exports of goods expanded at 11.1%. These records express the unprecedented dynamism of foreign trade. They also express the worsening of the trade deficit. Exports barely financed half of imports. The compensatory contribution of some components of the balance of payments would be indispensable to sustain the growing trade imbalance. As shown in Table 8.1, three were the sources of large volumes of foreign exchange: migrant remittances, tourism and foreign capital investment.

Table 8.1 Main components of the balance of payments, 1961 and 1973 (in million dollars)

	1961	*1973*	*Annual average, 1961–1973*
Imports	1038	8948	3591
Exports	759	5402	1956
Trade balance	-279	-3546	-1635
Tourism	330	2878	1265
Emigrant remittances	116	916	377
Current account balance[a]	221	557	10
Long term capital	215	765	458

Source: J.A. Biescas (1980): "Estructura y coyuntura económicas", in M. Tuñón de Lara (dir.): *Historia de España*. Vol. X: *España bajo la dictadura franquista (1939–1975)*, Barcelona: Labor

[a]The current account balance is not the algebraic sum of the previous items, since some of the service and transfer balances are not included

Remittances from migrants were the counterpart of the wave of migration that took place from the 1950s to 1973. Approximately one and a half million Spaniards emigrated abroad, preferably to France, Germany and Switzerland. The Spanish economy benefited doubly from this export of labour. First, by placing about 10% of the working population abroad, it saved itself the problem of unemployment. Before the oil crisis it was a full employment economy. It would hardly have been so without emigration abroad. Second, Spain received a considerable amount of foreign currencies from the savings that migrants sent home to their families. Remittances from migrants covered about a quarter of the trade deficit.

Tourism was much more important, both in the equilibrium of the external balance and in the transformations it triggered in the productive system and even in Spanish society. Tourism symbolizes a real revolution in consumption that Western Europe experienced at the time. The middle classes of developed European countries were able to travel abroad on holiday. Spain had particularly favourable conditions for meeting this demand. Its greatest advantage was, and still is, its exceptionally favourable natural conditions for developing the type of tourist offer (sun and beach) most desired by the citizens of neighbouring countries. Together with other competitive advantages, they would make Spain unbeatable as a provider of mass tourism. During these years, the growth of tourism was explosive: the number of visitors increased tenfold and Spain became one of the major powers in the world tourism market. Tourism became, as is often said, "the country's leading industry". But let's look at the balancing role of tourism income in the balance of payments. Tourism came to represent 40% of exports of goods and services. The foreign exchange provided by tourism, in net terms, financed 35% of total imports and covered more than 3/4 of the trade deficit.

The third external source of financial resources that contributed to the capitalization of the Spanish economy was long-term foreign investment. Since legislation allowed it, massive inflows of foreign capital have taken place. The incentives were diverse and powerful. First, the country's economic growth potential. Given its level of backwardness, it was very large. Second, trade barriers remained high, which induced foreign companies to settle in the domestic market to benefit from its dynamism. Thirdly, the Preferential Agreement with the EEC encouraged non-EU multinational companies to create subsidiaries in Spanish territory to take advantage of the facilities for entering the Community market. The latter makes more sense when considering the lower labour costs and the low tax burden.

Between 1959 and 1973 Spain was among the economies that received the greatest volume of foreign capital. It was almost entirely private. Direct investment prevailed over credit and loans. The United States ranked first as investor, followed by other neighbouring developed economies (Switzerland, Germany, the United Kingdom, France, the Netherlands, in that order). Manufacturing industry was the main recipient of foreign direct investment. It absorbed 3/4 of the capital. Globally, more than 20% of gross industrial investment came from abroad. A similar proportion of industrial employment depended on external financing. Undoubtedly, foreign investment made an important contribution to the capitalization process experienced during the period. It was also an essential compensatory item for the trade imbalance. In the absence of long-term net capital inflows, the Spanish economy would have faced, in some years, serious difficulties in balancing its external accounts. It would have been forced into short-term debt. In contrast, Spain accumulated a large stock of foreign reserves. With this financial solvency mattress, the country was able to pay for some time the heavy bill of the 1973–1974 oil crisis, thus postponing the inevitable application of an adjustment policy.

2 The Transition from a Semi-Industrial to an Industrialized Economy

From 1960 onwards, the Spanish economy progressed faster than ever before. At the time, the expression "the Spanish economic miracle" became popular to refer to what was happening. This is debatable. It occurred in a context characterized by the existence of numerous countries in the Western world that were growing at explosive rates. However, Spain—with an average growth rate of 7.3% of GDP and 6.1% of GDP per capita in the period 1960–1974—ranks at the top of the OECD economies, only behind Japan. Such hyper-growth was obviously not a supernatural phenomenon—a "miracle"—, but it is originated by perfectly recognizable and explainable economic forces. The intensification of economic relations with the outside world was an absolutely decisive factor in achieving the acceleration. Thanks to the opening up of trade, increasing quantities of energy products, raw materials, intermediate goods and equipment could be imported at competitive prices; in other words, everything that Spanish industry needed to be equipped with in order to expand and modernize.

Manufacturing industry was, in fact, the driving force behind the formidable economic progress. It grew faster than other sectors—at 10.3% per year between 1960 and 1973—and played a leading role in the structural change that occurred in the Spanish economy. Its transformation was so profound that it opened the doors to the restricted club of developed economies. In this section we will see what kind of transformations in the industrial sector led Spain to complete the industrialization that began more than a century ago.

Industrial activities increased their share of GDP continuously and significantly throughout the period. This is what the fundamental structural change consisted of: a strong increase in the relative weight of manufacturing industry in total employment and production simultaneous to the loss of relative importance of agriculture. In 1960, the production of the industrial sector was already 30% higher than that of the agricultural sector, but the latter still employed twice as many workers as the former. Agriculture still retained almost 40% of the labour force. Between 1960 and 1973 the situation changed radically. The industrial workforce expanded by one million, from 2.6 to 3.6 million. Active population in the agricultural sector fell from 4.9 to 3 million. In percentage terms, they were almost halved. But if industry played a crucial role in the growth and modernization of the Spanish economy, it was not through the creation of a large number of jobs, but through its capacity to substantially and cumulatively increase the productivity of the resources employed.

Industrial growth was driven by large changes in demand. These stimulated profound transformations in the productive supply, which, in turn, pushed up demand. Let us consider, first, the forces that acted on the demand side. According to their origin, we must distinguish between final demand, external demand and demand generated within the sector itself (intra-industry).

The final demand, which is what consumers do, underwent enormous changes. We know this from household budget surveys. In addition to expanding at a very fast rate (7.7% per year), its composition was also significantly altered. Nothing could be more logical. As Engel's law postulates, consumer goods have different income elasticities. As the level of household income rises, increases will tend to be allocated to the acquisition of higher goods. Lower goods, whose consumption will increase less than proportionally to the increase in income, will lose relative importance. In household budget surveys we can identify lower goods such as food, beverages, tobacco, clothing and footwear groups. In 1958, they absorbed 70% of household expenditure. By 1973–1974 their share had fallen to 47.2%. The remaining groups of goods and services account for a larger share of household income. Among the goods with high income elasticity, the transport and communications group stands out very significantly. From representing an insignificant 1% of household expenditure in 1958, it rose to nearly 10% in 1973–1974. Precisely, transport and communications symbolize those durable goods that have a very high income elasticity.

At this point, we can ask ourselves: why did a greater demand for this kind of goods act as a driving force for industrial growth? The answer is that in the manufacture of durable consumer goods such as automobiles or household appliances there are increasing returns to scale. Above a certain minimum production volume, the industries that manufacture these goods are able to offer them at a decreasing price. Cheaper prices have an additional stimulating effect on demand, amplifying the market in such a way that there is a cumulative process of increasing demand and, therefore, an accelerated expansion of the industrial sectors involved in the manufacture of these types of goods.

International trade could be a second lever for industrialization and economic growth. During the period it expanded at a very strong pace, providing opportunities for the expansion of foreign markets both to industry in the most developed countries and to that of the follower countries. Did Spanish industry take advantage of these opportunities? The answer is neither categorically yes nor no. The arguments in the first sense are forceful. As we have seen, exports have grown at an extraordinary rate, almost double the already very high level of world exports. The vast majority of the country's industrial sectors gained share in the international market, as J.B. Donges has shown. Even more spectacular was the change in the pattern of specialization as expressed in the structure of exports. At the beginning of the 1960s, about half were agricultural products. Adding other non-manufactured goods, primary products accounted for almost 70% of total foreign sales. By 1972–1974, the relative weight of primary products had been reduced to 35.2%. So in just one decade the positions were reversed. The significance of this phenomenon must be emphasized. We are facing a historical structural change, in the sense that it is indicative of a process of economic modernization and development. Like the structural change that took place in the areas of production and employment, it involved the rise and dominance of the manufacturing sector to the detriment of the agricultural sector. If at the beginning of the period Spain was still mainly an exporter of commodities, a decade later it had become an exporter of industrial products.

Nevertheless, Spanish industry continued to have a low export propensity. Foreign markets were undoubtedly important for some branches of production. But, according to J.B. Donges' calculations, exports contributed only 22% to the growth of overall manufacturing output. As J. Maluquer de Motes has pointed out, multiple factors stifled the export vocation of firms: their small size, the lack of marketing networks and export support institutions, the lack of proprietary technology and the export restrictions that used to be imposed by the patents with which domestic industries worked.

Let us look at domestic demand, the fundamental driver of the accelerated industrialization process. It fulfilled this function, in part, because of the pressure of final demand (from consumers), as we have seen. But certainly more important was the pressure of demand generated within the industry itself, from some sectors with respect to others. How was it possible for the relations between industrial sectors to give rise to a dynamic of endogenous and self-sustained growth? Intra-industrial demand increased incessantly because some branches were able to exploit large economies of scale in production by incorporating modern technology and achieving adequate productive specialization. The productivity gains they achieved were passed on to the industrial sectors that consumed their products, either as capital goods or as inputs, through lower prices. As this process of diffusion tended to be cumulative in nature, all industrial sectors enjoyed a continuous expansion of the market. The issue is so important that it is worthwhile to look a little more closely at the explanation, paying attention to the transformations that have taken place in the productive supply.

Industrial production accelerated in a very different way from one sector to another. Between the growth rate of the least dynamic industry—6.8% of the food, beverage and tobacco group—and that of the industry that progressed the most—16.2% of the chemical group—there was a remarkable gap. The production of the former increased by a factor of 2.4, while that of the latter increased by a factor of 7. The activities that stood out the most, with annual growth rates of 13% or more, were those that concentrated technical change, through the import of technology and the manufacture of goods with foreign patents, often accompanied by the entry of foreign capital. In the chemical industry, all the driving forces were combined. As a producer par excellence of intermediate goods, its productive efficiency improvements brought tangible benefits to many industries in the form of declining prices for the chemicals they used as inputs, which in turn boosted the growth of the chemical industry by constantly widening its market. The mechanical and metalworking industries expanded almost as much as the chemical industry. The producers of capital goods, as soon as they incorporated the new techniques by means of foreign patents, were able to supply modern and increasingly cheap machinery to the rest of the industrial sectors. The transport equipment manufacturing sector expanded even faster, under the leadership of the automotive industry. The era of motorization had finally arrived. The production of vehicles grew vertiginously, dragging along an enormous amount of activities that were directly or indirectly dependent.

3 The "Industrialization" of Agriculture

Agriculture underwent a very profound structural transformation in an incredibly short time, which contributed to the acceleration of industrialization. By 1960, the sector remained in a state of great backwardness. Its labour reserves were so abundant that by mobilizing them it was able to help industrialize the country, and also trigger effects that were fundamental for the productive modernization of agriculture itself.

The Spain of the 1960s fits the growth model formulated by W. A. Lewis. In this model, the virtually unlimited labour supply resulting from a massive reallocation of labour plays the role of an engine of economic growth. In a backward industrializing economy, two sectors coexist, the traditional and the modern. In the traditional sector—agriculture—average productivity is very low and marginal productivity tends to be zero. Therefore, there is open unemployment and wages are very low. In the modern sector—industry—wages are significantly higher, corresponding to their higher productivity. The overabundance of workers in agriculture determines that for the industry the supply of labour can be perfectly elastic to the prevailing wage in the sector. The wage differential between the two sectors gives agricultural workers a powerful incentive to leave agriculture and seek employment in industry. So, as soon as there are no obstacles to the development of the industry there will be a massive transfer of labour from the traditional to the modern sector. This shift will lead to a strong increase in the overall productivity of the economic system—total factor productivity—as a result of a more efficient allocation of resources. The available labour force is now used much more productively. The income generated will increase dramatically, both national income and the income received by workers. The process will be sustained because industrial investment will remain high, fuelling the rise in production, productivity and employment demand. The high level of investment is due to the fact that the profits of companies in the modern sector will also be high, as a consequence of the containment of salaries and the continuous increase in consumption resulting from the higher income of the new industrial workers. The process of active population transfer will continue until it leads to a depletion of the reserves of the traditional sector's workforce. As this situation approaches, agricultural labour will become more expensive, which will trigger a process of replacement of labour by capital and other productive factors that will lead to the modernization of the backward sector.

In short, the model of W. A. Lewis teaches us that, given a state of economic dualism and given conditions that make possible the expansion of the modern sector, economic growth will take place through a massive exodus of rural labour that will be directed towards that sector. These circumstances took place in the Spain of the time. Another fundamental lesson that can be drawn from this interpretative scheme is that growth will be all the more intense the greater the scale of the exodus, since productivity gains depend on the magnitude of the exodus. This also helps us to understand the Spanish "economic miracle".

The reserves of labour in the countryside, as we indicated earlier, were still enormous in 1960. The mass emigration of the rural population actually began in the early 1950s. In this decade the migration balance amounted to 1.1 million people of working age. From 1960 onwards, the exodus took on greater proportions. Until 1973, 2 million agricultural workers emigrated. At that time, population mobility took place on a scale unknown in the past. The migratory flows covered the whole territory. They led to extremely rapid urbanization of the population, one of the fastest in the Western world. This process of urbanization gave a strong impetus to the building industry and the service sector, in addition to the manufacturing industry. It should be noted that not all the labour that left the countryside was absorbed by the non-agricultural sectors. Half of those who left their homelands migrated abroad.

The mass abandonment of the rural population caused what experts have called the "crisis of traditional agriculture". This is a productive system whose main pillar was the existence of a very abundant and cheap labour force. In addition, traditional agriculture was based on the use of backward technology.

The decisive trigger for agricultural modernization was the decline in the workforce. Emigration was massive and intense enough to cause a sharp rise in agricultural wages. The increase in the cost of labour and the shortage of agricultural labourers itself triggered far-reaching changes in the production function of agriculture. Work was massively replaced by all kinds of productive factors, from selected seeds to fertilizers to tractors. It was during these years that cultivation techniques were revolutionized almost overnight. The Spanish countryside was populated with diverse machinery that did the work that until then was done by men and animals. From an almost null mechanization of the agricultural work in 1960, it passed to a practically complete mechanization in 1973. The farms made an enormous effort of capitalization, which resulted in a great improvement in productivity. It should be pointed out that the process of modernizing agriculture was far from complete at the end of the period. The forces of modernization continued to develop in the following decades.

The profound transformation of agriculture resulted in a sharp and sustained rise in productivity, through a very intense contraction in the number of workers combined with an increasing use of intermediate and capital goods. It was, without a doubt, the greatest structural change experienced by agriculture since its birth. Paradoxically, such modernization did not prevent, very much the contrary, the loss of relative weight of the sector in global economic activity.

4 Franco's Neo-Interventionism

In the previous sections of this chapter we have examined the growth factors. The time has come to talk about the factors that distorted growth and reduced the capacity of the Spanish economy to react when, after 1973, the situation of the industrialized economies was dramatically altered by the energy shock and the instability of the international monetary system. The distortions were mainly due to the slowdown in the policy of economic liberalization and the introduction of a new type of interventionism, deployed through the so-called "development plans". In addition, the banking system was at the service of the Government's priorities, through the financing mechanisms of public enterprises and those of "preferential interest". There were, therefore, three types of forces that distorted the allocation of resources and prevented the efficient functioning of the economy: restrictions on foreign and domestic competition, the planning policy of the Administration and its capacity to condition the credit activity of the banking institutions.

The policy of opening up to the outside world undertaken since the Stabilization Plan was extinguished in 1964. Spain surreptitiously failed to comply with the liberalization commitments acquired through its membership to the GATT. The reductions in tariffs that the Government approved by bowing to international pressure were neutralized by the imposition of quantitative restrictions on the import of certain goods, applied at the discretion of the authorities. Also, by the establishment of a new tax on all imports that acted as a para-tariff barrier. Three factors converged in this orientation towards a less open policy. Firstly, the favourable evolution of the external accounts: as reserves were built up, the reformist impulse weakened. Second, the less competitive industrial and agricultural sectors acted as powerful pressure groups. Thirdly, the interests of these groups were carefully considered by the leadership because their economic ideology was pro-intervention and anti-liberalization. For this reason, domestic liberalization was also slowed down. Private investment, which had been declared free, became subject to the fulfilment of certain conditions regarding minimum plant and capital size, supposedly to avoid corporate small-holding.

The second force we have enunciated is of greater complexity. From 1964 until the dictator's death, economic policy revolved around the "Development Plans". This was indicative planning, in line with the mixed economic policies developed after the Second World War in some Western European countries, particularly France. The goals set in the plan were not compulsory for private agents, although on paper they were of a similar nature for public administrations and companies. The planning aimed at maximizing growth and promoting regional development, which the market was supposed to be unable to achieve on its own.

The Franco regime was under the illusion that it was leading and sustaining the process of economic growth. However, it is doubtful that the action of the State was effective in stimulating and sustaining growth. Public investment programmes were far from being fulfilled. Both the Administrations and the private entrepreneurs made their decisions without regard to the plan. This does not mean that the planning did not affect economic activity. Even if it did not have an appreciable impact in macroeconomic terms, it could have had a significant impact on some productive branches and on certain industrial districts promoted by the territorial rebalancing policy.

Some economic historians have maintained that thanks to the regional development policy, the map of the location of Spanish industry was altered and its limited spatial deconcentration was produced. The Administration intended to carry out a policy of territorial rebalancing by promoting industrialization in the most backward regions. Very varied and generous incentives were granted to companies that decided to set up in these promotion poles. This policy did not produce any tangible results in areas where there was no previous industrial presence. The location of these industrial estates designed by the economic leaders was inadequate—far from the large markets of consumption, qualified labour, entrepreneurs, and even far from the main communication routes. In the balance, the existing externalities in consolidated industrial areas weighed more heavily on companies than the incentives offered by the Government in exchange for their presence in the so-called "industrial promotion poles". But a large volume of public funds was invested in providing them with the necessary infrastructure; that is, resources were wasted that could have had an alternative use of much greater social profitability. On the contrary, public intervention yielded positive results in the case of the "development poles", which were areas with some industrial tradition. At least this was the case in areas such as Valladolid, Vigo and Zaragoza, which had adequate preconditions to become powerful industrial districts.

It cannot be said, therefore, that the policy of territorial rebalancing had a distorting effect on economic growth, although it was costly and partly ineffective. Very different was the case of the aid system that the State mobilized through the so-called "concerted actions", within the framework of the "development plans". A concerted action was a kind of contract between the government and the companies in a certain sector. The companies committed themselves to achieving certain levels of investment and production, in line with the objectives of the development plan. In return, the Government provided generous aid of various kinds: tax benefits, subsidies and, above all, privileged financing. The concerted actions were applied to a number of sectors—steel, shipbuilding, coal mining, etc.—which were characterized by a markedly oligopolistic structure and by a significant presence of public companies. These policies, instead of improving economic efficiency and raising the productivity of the beneficiary companies and sectors, served to encourage their disproportionate growth. This was a very expensive and bad intervention from the point of view of economic efficiency. The substantial privileges that could be obtained through concertation encouraged the rent seeking by entrepreneurs. The interventionist model promoted the figure of the "concerted" entrepreneur, a type of businessman unconcerned with innovation and competitiveness, busy making a profit from his political contacts. This basic line of intervention in Franco's planning policy had extremely harmful consequences in the medium and long term. To understand this, it is necessary to examine the mechanism of privileged financing.

The banking system of the time was widely mediated by the government, to the point that the provision of credit was folded into their designs. Private banks and savings banks had to allocate a substantial part of the resources they managed to investments dictated by the authorities. The privileged credit circuit captured between 35% and 45% of the resources managed by the banking system. Financial institutions had to apply such a high proportion of their assets to cover a double coefficient: the so-called cash ratio and the compulsory investment ratio. The former involved the immobilization of a certain percentage of their computable liabilities (demand deposits) in public funds. Through this mechanism, the State assured itself of low-cost financing.

The compulsory investment ratio was that financial institutions had to allocate a certain percentage of their liabilities to granting loans and credits to those companies designated by the government as receiving preferential treatment. Financially privileged companies launched large bond issues, which banks and savings banks bought without taking into account the profitability prospects or the viability of the strategic plans of the companies receiving the loans. As the latter had a captive capital market, they were able to obtain them almost without restriction at a price that was significantly lower than that for non-privileged creditors. Worse still, the manipulation of the financial system, for the sake of achieving the developmental goals—more production, more investment, more income—pursued by Franco's planners, had a serious perverse effect. Huge amounts of economic resources were allocated to activities with low marginal productivity and with a problematic future as they were mature industries. The sectors privileged by the Government became over-sized sectors. The dire consequences of the supposedly growth-planning interventionism would become evident when the oil crisis broke out. From that moment on and for two decades, there was no choice but to apply the exact opposite policy: the thinning out of the over-dimensioned sectors through successive reconversion plans. As we will see in the next chapter, the legacy of the developmentalist policy of the Franco regime was very heavy. The reconversion policy had enormous social and economic costs. It hindered a prompt and solid recovery of the Spanish economy.

The strong economic growth of the period 1960–1973 did not lead to a substantial increase in public expenditure and income. This was prevented by the regime's allergy to any tax reform that involved the obligation to contribute according to the income received. The government did not collect the resources necessary to provide the public goods that were indispensable for promoting long-term economic development. It increased the provision of such goods, but not to a sufficient degree. Only to the extent that the increases in collection of a system based on indirect taxes allowed it, did technocratic governments propose the expansion of some social expenditures. During the period of greatest splendour of the Welfare State in Western Europe, the Franco regime deployed only a modest version of it. It erected the Social Security, a system of universal coverage based on the pay-as-you-go financing method. The social contributions paid by active workers—in reality, mostly by the companies that employed them—covered the pension expenses of retired people and also the disability leave of active people. The introduction of social security in 1963 (in the collection of contributions) and 1967 (in the payment of pensions and sick leave) represented a significant advance in the provision of one of the fundamental social expenses. The significance of this progress is recorded in our series on public social spending, which made an extraordinary leap forward starting in 1967 (see column 12 of the Appendix and Fig. 9.3). Social Security itself was used by the government to extend the benefits in kind of another preferential public good, health. In the final decade of the Franco regime, health infrastructures began to be developed, especially a network of large hospitals. At the same time, and in this case at the expense of the State budget, educational expenditure, which had recovered pre-war levels, in real terms, in the 1950s, grew intensely in the 1960s. As a result, education spending, as a proportion of GDP, recovered the levels reached in the Second Republic, which, logically, cannot be considered an extraordinary achievement. The dearth of State expenditure did not allow for more. The other functions of the Welfare State, the redistributive fiscal policies, would be ignored by Franco's rulers. With the advent of democracy, the new policy-makers would have to respond urgently to the social demand for the government to provide the social functions that Franco's developmentalism neglected.

Bibliographical Orientation

An overall view on the evolution of the Spanish economy during the period and its determining factors is J.M. Serrano Sanz and E. Pardos (2002): "Los años de crecimiento del franquismo (1959–1975)", in F. Comín, M. Hernández and E. Llopis (eds.): *Historia económica de España. Siglos X–XX*, Barcelona: Crítica. An interpretation on causes and retardation factors of economic development in E. Fuentes Quintana (1993): "Tres decenios largos de la economía española en perspectiva", in J.L. García Delgado (dir.): *España, economía*, Madrid: Espasa Calpe. This encyclopaedic book contains numerous sectorial and thematic studies carried out by specialists on the changes registered during the period 1960–1973, as well as in the two following decades, in major productive sectors (agriculture, industry, energy, trade, finance, public administration) and economic policies (commercial, monetary, labour, fiscal). A cliometric reassessment of the 1959–1960 turning point in L. Prados de la Escosura, J. R. Rosés and I. Sanz-Villaroya (2012): "Economic Reforms and Growth in Franco's Spain", *Revista de Historia Económica—Journal of Iberian and Latin American Economic History*, 30 (1). A detailed account on macroeconomic evolution and contemporary economic policy in S. Lieberman (1995): *Growth and Crisis in the Spanish Economy: 1940–93*, London–New York: Routledge. Regarding the industrialization process, the structural approach of M. Buesa and J. Molero (2000) is useful: "La industrialización en la segunda mitad del siglo XX", in J. Velarde (coord.): *1900–2000 Historia de un esfuerzo colectivo. Cómo España superó el pesimismo y la pobreza*, Barcelona: Planeta. Regarding the industrial policy of late Francoism, the essays compiled by J. de la Torre y M. García-Zúñiga (2009): *Entre el Mercado y el Estado. Los planes de desarrollo durante el franquismo*, Pamplona: Universidad Pública de Navarra, offer a nuanced view of the effects that the "poles of development" had. On public finances, see R. Vallejo (2002): "Economía y Hacienda Pública durante los años del desarrollismo, 1959–1975", *Hacienda Pública Española*. Monograph 2002. The huge investment effort of those years is perfectly documented, in a long-term perspective also useful for other chapters, in L. Prados de la Escosura and J. R. Rosés (2010): "Capital Accumulation in the Long-Run: The Case of Spain, 1850–2000", *Research in Economic History*, 27.

CHAPTER 9

Economic Crisis and Political Transition (1973–1985)

The 1973–1974 oil crisis exploded against a background of inflationary trends across developed economies and a growth deceleration after many years of exceptional growth rates. It put an abrupt end to the Golden Age. In Spain this happened simultaneously with the end of the Franco era and the transition to a new democratic regime. Weak political foundations explained weak economic policy reactions for a number of years, until the new regime was well established.

1 The Macroeconomic Impact of the Double Oil Shock and the Transition to Democracy

In 1974, the explosive growth in economic activity enjoyed by Spain since 1960 slowed down sharply. In the decade 1975–1984 as a whole, GDP increased at an annual rate of 2.1%. The material well-being of the population almost stagnated; measured by private consumption per inhabitant, the advance was reduced to 0.5% per year, twelve times less than during the previous period (see Appendix, column 9).

The deceleration of GDP occurred in two steps: 1975 and 1979. Each of these is associated with an oil shock. Oil prices multiplied—by 4 in the last quarter of 1973 and, again, by almost 3 between 1979 and 1980. Such an explosion in the price of the commodity that was the fuel *par*

A. Carreras, X. Tafunell, *Between Empire and Globalization*, Palgrave Studies in Economic History,
https://doi.org/10.1007/978-3-030-60504-9_9

excellence of transport, the main source of energy and the basic raw material of a wide variety of industrial goods, would inevitably cause great economic disturbances; especially in a country like Spain, so dependent on oil and completely lacking of it. It was an extraordinary supply shock. The rise in the price of crude oil caused a radical worsening of the real terms of trade (see Fig. 2.1). It increased the external deficit and meant a loss of national income of 3 or 4 points per year. It fuelled inflation. Rising production costs reduced business margins and overshadowed entrepreneurs' expectations. Investment contracted and unemployment increased. Private consumption suffered from the erosion of purchasing power caused by inflation and the contraction of employment.

The series in the Appendix show the deterioration of the macroeconomic picture. We will draw some figures from it. First, inflation. It had already been growing at high rates since the beginning of the decade (see Fig. 9.1). It shot up in 1974 to an all-time high of 24.5% in 1977 and then declined very gradually in the following years. Average inflation in this

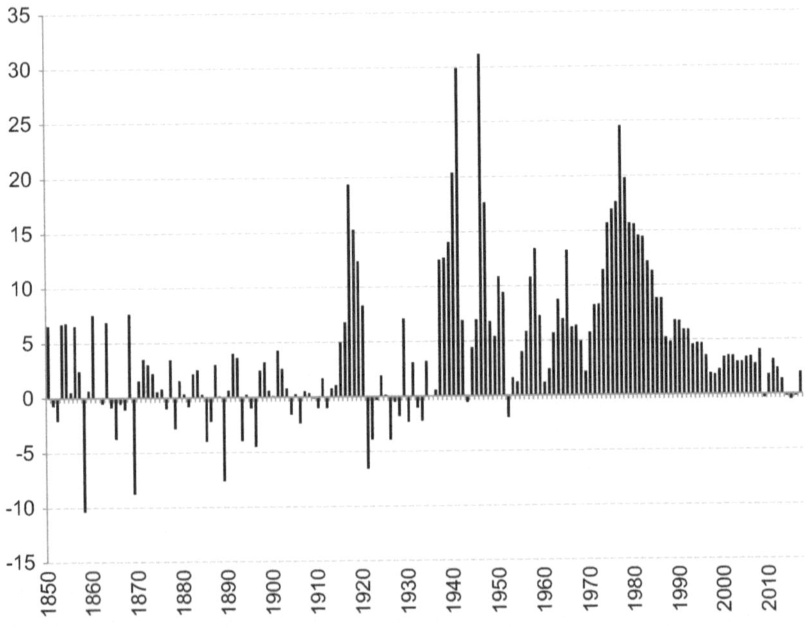

Fig. 9.1 Inflation rate (%), 1850–2017. *Source*: Appendix, column 19

period—15.7% per year—was higher than in any other historical period. It was also higher than in the neighbouring economies, despite the fact that they suffered from high inflationary pressures. Spanish inflation was, on average, 7 percentage points higher than in OECD countries.

Second, the working population decreased from 13.2 million in 1974 to 11.2 million in 1985. The unemployment rate followed the opposite path. At the initial point, Spain was a full employment economy. At the end of the period, 20.7% of the labour force was in a situation of forced unemployment. A third indicator of the deteriorating economic situation is found in investment. It declined very sharply until 1984, which led to a marked process of decapitalization. Fourthly, the Spanish economy faced a large current account deficit after each oil price explosion. These negative balances in the external accounts put downward pressure on reserves and forced the country to incur into considerable foreign debt. Finally, public expenditure increased disproportionately. This resulted in a large budget deficit. As in the case of inflation and unemployment, Spain had to face a new problem—the overflow of the public deficit—which would be very serious.

When comparing the macroeconomic trajectory with that of other neighbouring countries, it can be seen that Spain suffered the crisis with greater intensity. We have pointed out that its inflation was much higher. So was its unemployment rate. Spain became the OECD economy with the highest unemployment rate, doubling the EU average (see Fig. 9.2). In terms of the relative income of the Spanish people, 1975 saw the end of the impetuous process of real convergence that had taken place since 1960 (see column 5 of the Appendix). From 1975 to 1985, Spain diverged, despite the fact that the European economy advanced parsimoniously. The crisis meant for Spain more than a decade lost of convergence to the level of per capita income of the European Union.

Why was the Spanish economy hit harder than other economies by the international crisis, and why did it have greater difficulty in overcoming it? The answer is twofold: because of the legacy of the Franco regime and because of the challenges posed by the transition to democracy. G. Tortella's statement that Spaniards have paid for Franco's regime twice is very accurate: once at the entrance—during the post-war period—and once at the exit—precisely in the period we are studying now. The mortgage was of an institutional and economic nature. Late Francoism bequeathed to democracy an institutional structure regulating the organization and functioning of the economic system that largely conditioned

Fig. 9.2 Unemployment rate (%) in Spain and in the European Union, 1974–2017. *Sources*: A. de la Fuente: "Series enlazadas de los principales agregados de la EPA (1964–2014)", in http://www.fedea.net/datos/; INE, http://www.ine.es/; and, for the European Union, AMECO database, https://ec.europa/info/business-economy-euro/indicators-statistics/economic-databases/macro-economic-database-ameco_en

the actions of the agents. Goods and factor markets were extensively regulated. Economic regulation, which was either due to the interventionist nature of the regime or was aimed at restricting competition, distorted relative prices and made productive goods and resources more expensive. Worse still, it made the economic system extremely rigid at a time when the course of the international economy demanded maximum adaptive flexibility, in order to transfer resources from sectors that had become obsolete due to the rise in oil prices to sectors with growth potential.

The production system set up by Franco's developmentalism made the Spanish economy particularly vulnerable to the oil shock. It specialized in the production of goods that required high energy consumption. Energy consumption per unit of GDP (the "energy intensity") was very high. Spain was extremely dependent on oil, because the Francoist State had promoted basic industries that consumed a lot of hydrocarbons, such as the steel, chemical and shipbuilding industries.

The Spanish economy was also burdened, as we said, with the mortgage of the political transition from Franco's dictatorship to a democratic regime. This really started with the assassination of Carrero Blanco, President of the government and Franco's successor in pectore. The assassination occurred in December 1973, that is, simultaneously with the first oil shock. After Franco's death in November 1975, the country began a political process of building a democratic system. The process of political transition was fraught with difficulties. As it unfolded simultaneously with the international economic crisis, the government applied with delay the adjustment and reform measures needed to adapt to the new situation. The transition was not definitively closed until December 1982, when the PSOE, led by Felipe González, came to power thanks to a resounding electoral victory. It took nine years from the outbreak of the economic crisis for the government to achieve a stable political environment conducive to the successful adoption of an economic recovery strategy. Hence, for Spain, the crisis was more intense, complex and prolonged.

The way it unfolded, the transition to democracy greatly conditioned the government's economic strategy. It reacted very slowly and wrongly to the first explosion in oil prices. The authorities, because of their lack of social legitimacy, were unable to impose socially harsh measures, as always are those to share the costs of a serious economic crisis. The citizens, who had been kept out of public management by the dictatorship, did not even understand the nature and gravity of the crisis. All the economic and social agents fought to prevent the burden of adjustment from falling on them. The government was unable to persuade the population to accept a reduction in their income in line with the contraction of national income. They chose to accommodate the excess demand with a lax monetary policy, low interest rates and abundant financing for all. The gap between final expenditure and national production triggered inflation. Rising prices would be the mechanism by which the real income of agents would be reduced in a socially unequal way. Another very painful mechanism was unemployment.

The most obvious and illustrative example of the lack of decision in the formulation and application of an adjustment strategy is found in the compensating policy for fuel prices. This policy was intended to avoid drastic internal adjustment. This was a vain objective. Spain finally had to make the adjustment, as the irreversible nature of the oil price hike made it inevitable. And it paid a high price for the delay, which was expressed, among other things, in a sharp deterioration in public and external accounts. Spain's behaviour in terms of oil consumption was completely anomalous. Instead of decreasing consumption per unit of product (energy intensity), as happened in all Western countries, in Spain it increased between 1973 and 1979. During these years the national industry did not undertake any serious investment to save energy. The reason is that the government decided to subsidize oil consumption. Most of the increase in the oil bill was borne by the public treasury itself. When such an erroneous energy policy was rectified, Spanish industry was forced to make a much harder adjustment. It had to do so twice over as it happened during the second oil shock.

So between 1974 and mid-1977 the authorities were unable to share the costs of the crisis by imposing sacrifices among social and economic sectors. Consumption, public and private, fattened by the emission of money, barely budged. Meanwhile, with the developed economies plunged into recession, all the components of the "virtuous circle" of growth ceased to function: foreign direct investment came to a standstill, migrants' remittances collapsed with their return, and the foreign currencies contributed by foreign tourists diminished. All of which resulted in a combination of accelerating inflation and growing deficits in the external balance. Naturally, there was a limit to the external imbalance. An attempt was made to remedy it with the devaluation of the peseta. It was not enough. Without internal adjustment, devaluation never fixes anything. Prices continued to rise, faster and faster. They quickly absorbed the devaluation. The macroeconomic situation deteriorated so seriously that by July 1977, when the first democratic government took office, a situation similar to that of 1959 was being experienced. Certain imbalances were threatening the collapse of the economy. Inflation had been unleashed. There was a danger that the price spiral would get out of control. The problems in the balance of payments were serious enough to leave the country without foreign reserves in a very short time.

2 Adjustment Policies and Social Pacts

In 1977, the circumstances required a new economic policy, in order to cut the most destabilizing imbalances. If it could be implemented then, it was not only because it was necessary to do so, but also because the new government had the political legitimacy that the previous ones lacked. The economic programme of the first democratic cabinet materialized in the so-called Moncloa Pacts'. This was a social pact signed in October 1977 by all the political parties with parliamentary representation. The pact consisted of an agreement aimed at fairly distributing the sacrifices required by the economic situation.

What exactly did the "Moncloa Pacts" consist of? Above all, they were an adjustment policy aimed at halting the rise in prices. As agreed, the anti-inflationary policy would be an income policy accompanied by a restrictive budgetary and monetary policy. But, in practice, this was not the case: the last two were expansive, although not as much as in previous years. The fight against inflation was based on the containment of nominal wage increases. This would be done by changing the method of indexing wages in labour agreements. Wage increases would no longer be set according to previous inflation, but according to the inflation forecast by the government. As for the other imbalance, the external one, it would be fought with a more conventional measure: a strong devaluation, which would be followed for a time by the floating of the exchange rate.

But the Moncloa Pacts were more than just an adjustment and stabilization policy. They also had the character of a reform policy. Their fundamental axis was fiscal reform, in coherence with the pact sealed between the political forces in favour of an equitable distribution of the costs of the crisis.

The fiscal system in place in the mid-seventies was extremely obsolete and inadequate for the needs and demands for public goods put forward by Spanish society at the time. The current tax system did not allow for the sharp increases in public social spending that citizens were insisting on in the emerging democracy.

Social pressure and the political pact gave rise to a new tax system. It would be based on three pillars, in line with EEC taxation: personal income tax (IRPF), corporate income tax and value added tax (VAT). The latter, which was to become the main indirect tax, was finally introduced in 1986 when Spain joined the EEC. The tax reform—known as the Fernández Ordóñez reform—focused on income and wealth tax. It radically altered the distribution of the tax burden. Personal income tax became a powerful instrument of income redistribution. It provided more resources to the public coffers. The tax reform also led to an increase in the tax burden by one percentage point (of GDP) per year.

The modernization of the tax system was not the only policy reform promoted by the Moncloa Pacts. It was agreed to undertake structural policies in other areas, without major practical results, except in one: the liberalization of the financial system. As we saw, this sector was extremely regulated during the Franco era. Under the new legal framework, banks and savings banks were no longer subject to restrictions on their business; they were free to expand territorially and could freely set interest rates.

What was the result of the Moncloa Pacts? As a stabilizing policy, they were discreetly effective. They stopped the upward spiral of prices by breaking the feedback mechanism between prices and wages. A process of disinflation began. But it advanced slowly because of the lack of moderation in wage increases (see Fig. 9.4). On the external accounts, by contrast, the imbalance was quickly corrected, thanks to a combination of devaluation and export-enhancing trade liberalization. Unfortunately, the second oil shock completely reversed the progress made between 1977 and 1979 in resolving the macroeconomic imbalances. To make matters worse, when the Spanish economy was hit by the new escalation in the price of crude oil, those in power did not immediately take strong measures to stop the resurgence of the imbalances. Once again, the economic policy agenda was relegated to the political agenda in the face of the problems and difficulties of the political transition. When the PSOE came to power in late 1982, it had to use the same adjustment recipes applied in 1977 to correct macroeconomic imbalances: devaluation, anti-inflationary policy based on wage restraint and the strengthening of restrictive monetary policy. Likewise, the first socialist cabinet had to face the deepening and broadening of the reform policies, a matter that we will analyse in the following sections.

3 The Emergence of the Welfare State

One of the most outstanding features of the Spanish economy in this period is the extraordinary growth of public finances. As F. Comín has stated, if until 1975 public intervention in the economy had been carried out through regulation, from that moment on public intervention would increasingly use the budget. In fact, there was an unprecedented increase in public administration spending. It was mainly motivated by the accelerated formation of the Welfare State. The demand for social benefits by the citizens became very strong. They expected the new democratic State to help alleviate the crisis, to compensate for the deterioration of household incomes and also to provide public goods that the Francoist State had been meaning to supply. So the first democratic governments had to build a Welfare State quickly and in the worst financial situation.

The total expenditure of the public administrations shot up, indeed. If in 1973 it represented 22.7% of the GDP in 1985 it rose to 42.5%. The gap between Spain and the EEC countries in terms of the size of public administrations was reduced from 40% to 15%. Such an impressive increase in public spending could not be fully financed by taxes, even though the tax burden rose from 23.8% to 35.5% of the GDP. Hence the deterioration of the public sector's financial position: from a fiscal surplus in 1973 to a deficit equivalent to 7 percent of GDP in 1985 (see column 10 of the Appendix).

If we look at the distribution of public expenditure by functional categories (see Table 9.1), we can see that there have been significant changes in spending priorities. The large expansion of spending is essentially explained by three components: social expenditures; capital transfers to enterprises, both public and private; and financial charges. Let us stop for a moment and look at social expenditure. As Table 9.1 shows, between 1970 and 1985 it practically doubled in terms of GDP. Within the group of preferential goods, the greatest increase corresponded to education, both because of the expansion of the coverage rate and because of the improvement of benefits and skills in non-compulsory education. Spending on health did not grow as much, because the deficits that existed in 1975 in health seemed less lacerating than in education. Within maintenance or income replacement spending, the main focus was on pension payments and, secondarily, unemployment benefits. Pensions doubled their share of GDP, reaching 10%, as a result of a substantial increase in coverage, a rise in average pensions in real terms and demographic factors. As for economic services, the absorption of an additional 7.5 points of GDP between 1975 and 1985 was not due to an increase in public investment, which hardly took place, but rather to capital transfers to companies in financial difficulty or under restructuring plans. Finally, the financial burdens resulting from the State's own borrowing process also played a role in the accelerated increase in public spending. In a very short time, these burdens went from not being too significant to consuming a greater volume of funds than those allocated to such emblematic areas as defence or public investment. Returning to public social spending, which is the

Table 9.1 Public administrations expenditure functional structure, 1970–1985 (GDP percentage)

	1970	*1975*	*1980*	*1982*	*1985*
I. Public goods	4.3	4.6	5.3	5.6	6.1
1. Defence	1.7	1.7	2.0	2.0	2.0
2. General public services	2.6	2.9	3.3	3.6	4.1
II. Welfare State	13.0	16.2	21.6	22.8	24.8
3. Preferential goods	5.6	6.9	8.9	8.7	9.9
3.a Education	1.9	2.1	3.3	3.0	3.6
3.b Health	2.8	3.8	4.5	4.3	4.5
3.c Housing and collective services	0.9	1.0	1.1	1.4	1.8
4. Income maintenance	7.4	9.3	12.7	14.0	14.9
4.a Pensions	4.0	5.6	8.6	9.2	10.0
4.b Unemployment benefits	0.2	0.5	2.2	2.6	2.9
4.c Other	3.2	3.2	1.9	2.2	2.0
III. Mixed economy	4.8	4.2	6.2	9.3	11.6
5. Economic services	4.2	3.7	5.5	8.3	8.4
5.a Investment	2.3	2.1	1.6	2.8	2.9
5.b Grants and transfers	1.9	1.6	3.9	5.5	5.5
6. Interests on public debt	0.6	0.5	0.7	1.0	3.2
Total expenditure	22.1	24.9	33.1	37.7	42.5

Source: J. M. González-Páramo (1990): "Tres lustros de cambios estructurales en el sector público", in J. L. García Delgado (dir.): *Economía española de la transición y la democracia, 1973–1986*, Madrid: CIS

dominant component of the new role assumed by the public administrations, the series shown in the Appendix (see Fig. 9.3) indicates that the growth recorded between 1975 and 1985 was not matched again in any ten-year period after the latter year, which defines the stage as one of emergence of the Welfare State.

Spain made an enormous effort to converge towards the EEC model of the Welfare State. This is proven by the battery of data contained in the table above. The specialists affirm that Spain has tended to converge towards the "community norm". Certainly, the budgetary efforts of a decade—of a decade of economic crisis—were not enough to achieve full convergence. Nevertheless, there had been a very notable advance. The effort made had a liability, in the form of a new economic imbalance that was burdensome and difficult to resolve: the public deficit. But it served to gain an important asset: a great inequality decrease in the social distribution of income. It was reduced, both because of the strongly redistributive effects of the new direct taxation scheme—income tax had a markedly progressive character—and because of the income received by low-income

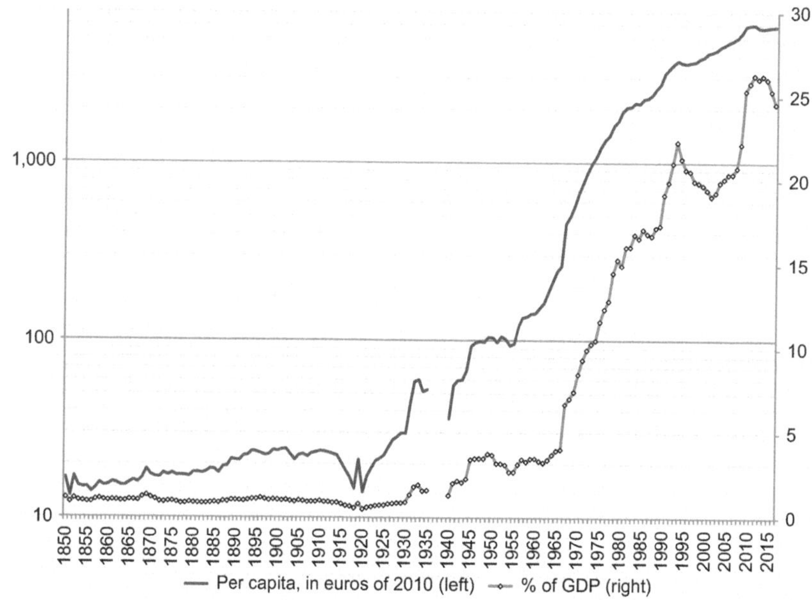

Fig. 9.3 Public social expenditure, 1850–2016. *Sources*: Appendix, column 12 and own elaboration on the same sources used to build the appendix series

families in the form of social benefits. If around 1974 Spain was characterized as one of the societies with the highest levels of inequality within the OECD, throughout the period studied there was a change that can be described as truly revolutionary. Inequality, measured as the relationship between the two extreme deciles in terms of income, was reduced in 1990 to a third of that existing in 1970. In the same period, the Gini index fell by 4 points (11%), which, in comparative perspective, is an exceptional phenomenon. The bulk of this income equalization took place between 1975 and 1980, when business profits went down and real wages went up.

4 Industrial and Banking Crisis and Mass Unemployment

The crisis that the international economy went through between 1973 and 1983 was basically industrial in nature. The explosion in oil prices affected industry more acutely than any other economic activity except transport. An additional factor was the increasing competition from newly industrialized countries. The industries in developed countries that would be most affected were those, such as Spain, whose comparative advantage was concentrated in the most energy and labour-intensive branches and which had the lowest content of technology and human capital.

Spanish industry was not really suffering from a brutal supply shock, but from three. The energy shock was compounded by two others, driving up production costs: the rise in the prices of labour and of capital. Under these circumstances it is understandable that Spanish industry suffered a very severe crisis. During these years it went through the worst depression of the twentieth century.

Wages rose sharply since the dictatorship's authoritarian model of industrial relations began to break down. This occurred before the political transition, specifically at the beginning of the 1970s (see Fig. 9.4). At the beginning of the transition (1974–1978) there was a gigantic wave of

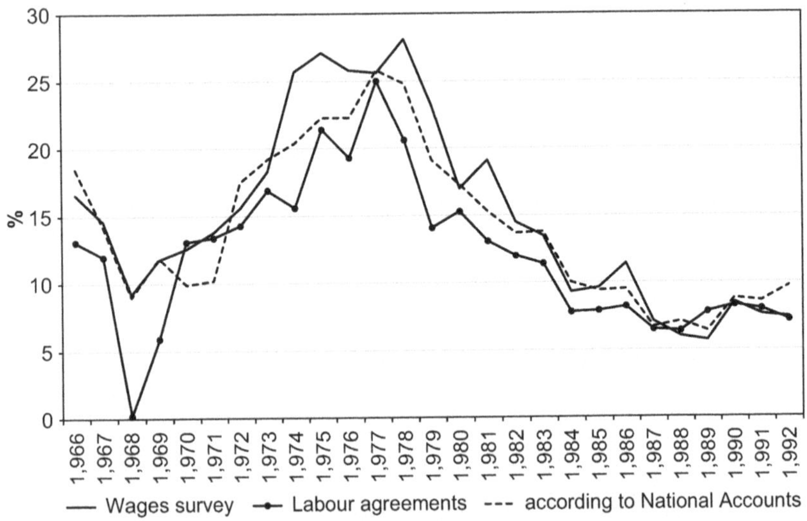

Fig. 9.4 Yearly wage increases, 1966–1992. *Source:* J. L. Malo de Molina (1993): "Mercado de trabajo: empleo y salarios", in J. L. García Delgado (dir.): *España. Economía*. Madrid: Espasa-Calpe

demands, the largest in Western Europe (regarding the extent of the strikes, see Fig. 5.4). The workers aimed to an improvement in their living conditions; they felt that their demands had been long suppressed and neglected during the dictatorship. The workers' mobilization triggered a real wage explosion. Annual increases in total labour costs far exceeded 20%, especially since working hours were reduced. This happened precisely when business margins were drastically cut by the retraction of demand and cost inflation caused by the growth of energy products and raw materials (on the evolution of profitability, see column 24 of the Appendix). These increases in labour costs bore no relation to productivity gains, nor to the wage improvements achieved by workers in the surrounding countries. Obviously, such exorbitant increases had devastating effects on the competitiveness and financial equilibrium of companies. Particularly when, from 1978 onwards, a third shock, the financial one, fell on them.

If until 1977 the industrial companies were able to absorb, more bad than good, the impact of the increase of the production costs was thanks to indebtedness. They had a powerful incentive to get into debt, in addition to the sheer necessity of doing so: real interest rates were negative. This is a unique phenomenon because of its magnitude (see Fig. 9.5). It was the result of a combination of runaway inflation and controlled nominal interest rates. Until 1977, banks could not freely set interest rates, they were managed prices. When the sector was liberalized, interest rates shot up. They would remain at very high levels for the rest of the period (see Fig. 9.5). The spectacular rise in the cost of capital aggravated the industrial crisis, given the volume of debt incurred by companies in previous years. These will now face heavy financial burdens. A large number of firms will simply not be able to bear the extra financial cost and will close their doors.

The combination of the three above-mentioned shocks pushed the industry into a drastic downward adjustment of jobs and productive capacity. Hence, from 1978 onwards, mass unemployment appeared. The manufacturing industry would lose 1 out of every 4 jobs. In the construction industry, the loss will exceed 40%. The rise in the unemployment rate is far greater than in other developed economies (see Fig. 9.2). The extraordinary scale of unemployment is the clearest evidence of a massive devastation of the productive fabric, of a real process of deindustrialization. To make the problem even more dramatic, the unemployment generated by

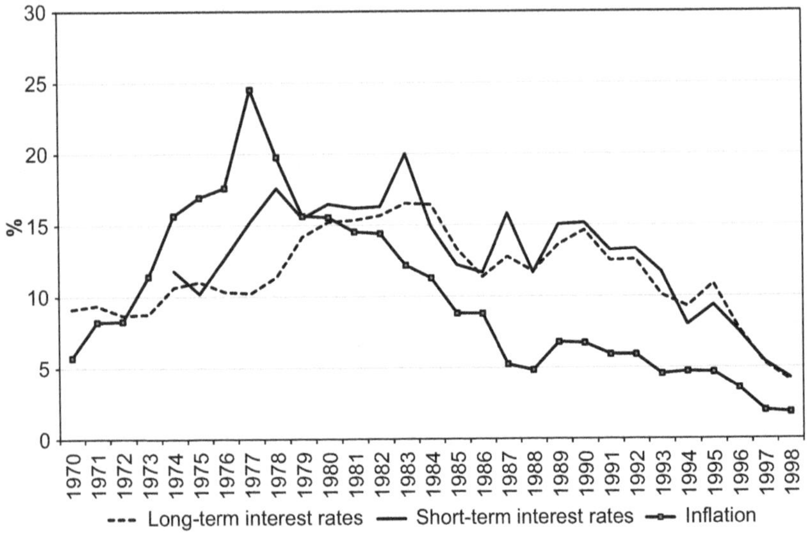

Fig. 9.5 Nominal interest rates and inflation (%), 1970–1998. *Sources*: Appendix, columns 20 and 22; for the short-term interest rate (interbank lending market at 3 months): Banco de España, *Informe anual*

the industrial depression was compounded by other destabilizing forces in the labour market.

We can distinguish, at least, three other factors that aggravated the level of unemployment in Spain. First, the coincidence of the industrial crisis with the arrival on the labour market of the most abundant generations in the history of Spain. The baby boomers entered the labour market in 1973. Bad time. For more than twenty years, this strictly demographic factor has weighed heavily.

The second factor was the sudden interruption of foreign emigration and its reversal. In European economies, the cessation of immigration flows was immediate after the outbreak of the first oil crisis. The closure of the "escape valve" that emigration represented during the previous expansion cycle weighed heavily on the Spanish labour market. The migration flow even changed the sign: many Spanish emigrants returned to Spain.

Thirdly, we must add the unemployment caused by the culmination of the process of modernization of agriculture that began in the 1950s. The improvements in the productivity of Spanish agriculture were such that, like any highly mechanized industry, it could continue to increase its production with a decreasing number of employed people. Between 1973 and 1985, agriculture lost more full-time jobs than manufacturing and construction combined. R. Marimón and F. Zilibotti have argued that this phenomenon would be sufficient to explain the unemployment differential between Spain and Western European countries during these years.

Let's turn to banking. The banking crisis is less well known than the industrial one, no doubt because it was less visible. Thousands and thousands of salaried workers did not lose their jobs, nor were entire towns and regions productively deserted. But this does not mean that the sector did not suffer a profound crisis. And very costly. In this period many nations had to face bank failures. But in none of the developed economies did the problem become as serious as in Spain. The crisis caused great havoc, as A. Cuervo's definitive study has revealed. Between 1977 and 1985, more than half of all Spanish banks were affected! It should be clarified that the crisis punished small and some medium-sized institutions. It did not hit the institutions that formed the core of the big banks, nor did the whole banking system stagger. The banks that had to be saved or liquidated or received some relevant aid represented between 25% and 30% of the system.

The banking crisis had its origin in the industrial crisis. Industrial companies were the most important customers for the banks. In Spain, the links between banking and industry were very close. Each large bank had a kind of industrial group. The banks' portfolios were full of shareholdings and loans to group companies. Bank assets would deteriorate irrevocably when industrial companies lost their financial solvency and stopped repaying loans and credits. Moreover, the banks were concentrating their risk on companies in the sectors that would suffer most from the depression. Two additional factors led to the banking crisis. First, the effects of financial liberalization. Banks and savings banks were in a race to open branches, competing to capture liabilities and gain market share. This, of course, meant a significant increase in investment and operating costs. Just at a time when there was a loss of asset quality. Secondly, the poor capacity of the monetary authorities to supervise and monitor the financial system allowed the crisis to unfold. The Bank of Spain had very few mechanisms for supervising the sector. As a result, it was unable to prevent insolvencies caused by overly risky or unprofessional management by bank managers. As the crisis unfolded, it gradually equipped itself with such mechanisms.

5 Industrial Restructuring, Bank Rescue and Other Structural Policies

The industrial crisis was so intense and affected public enterprises so devastatingly that governments came under pressure to implement a policy of aid and restructuring of the sector, at least for its most affected branches. This policy is usually called industrial restructuring. The neighbouring countries did the same. One of the peculiarities of the Spanish industrial restructuring ("reconversion") is its great delay. It was only in 1984 that the PSOE government passed the second reconversion law. Before the first law (1981), the government, unable to deal with socially harsh measures that were highly contested by the workers affected, opted for the so-called socialization of losses policy. This consisted on the nationalization of the companies in the most fragile situation, provided that they were large and emblematic, typically companies that had taken part in the "concerted action" of the developmentalist era. INI became a business hospital, financed in an inflationary manner.

The ultimate aim of the restructuring was to enable the chosen industries to cope with the new conditions of international competition. Before that, companies had to be financially rehabilitated, wiping out the losses—which were extremely high—with transfers of public capital. At the same time, adjustment and restructuring had to be carried out to drastically reduce capacity and staff, including plant closures. Afterwards, abundant public resources would have to be invested in new technological equipment to make the restructured industries competitive. Or, alternatively, to boost dynamic activities in the areas where companies in the more mature industrial sectors were concentrated, those that were simply about to liquidate.

This policy was not indiscriminate. It consisted of sectoral actions, even though they were guided by common principles and procedures. Conversion was applied only to specific sectors, such as the steel industry, shipyards, the fertilizer industry, the household appliances industry and the manufacturing of large capital goods. All of them suffered very sharp falls in demand, were faced with large overcapacities and incurred very large losses. They were also characterized by a strong presence of state-owned companies. Overall, the sectors subject to restructuring plans accounted for less than 10% of industrial employment.

How successful was this policy? The assessment is, in our opinion, quite negative. It did not produce any results in terms of the objective of reindustrialization. The regions where the steel industry, mining and shipyards played a predominant role in the productive fabric did not escape an unstoppable decline at all. Apparently, the reconversion gave an acceptable result as a strategy of withdrawal and liquidation. The instrumental objectives of job reduction and plant closure were more than covered. Indeed, most of the companies affected by the restructuring could not face the new conditions of the economy that emerged from the oil crisis. Their unavoidable final destination was the closing. After all, the main virtue of the reconversion policy was that it allowed for an orderly dismantling of sectors without a future. Huge public resources were mobilized to suffocate the enormous social conflict that would be caused by the closure of large plants. It could be argued that such a policy was socially inevitable. But it is less defensible from an economic point of view. It was a strongly discriminatory policy in the provision of social protection. Workers laid off from the converted industries received clearly privileged treatment over the rest. Most districts and industrial sectors in crisis had to endure it with their own means and sacrifice. In any case, and in conclusion, this policy had a high effective cost—leaving aside the opportunity cost—in terms of public expenditure. The budgetary funds devoted to it amounted to the equivalent of approximately 3.5% of GDP.

Surprisingly, the bill for the clean-up of the banking sector was considerably higher than that of the industrial sector. It has been estimated that the bank rescue was equivalent to between 6% and 16% of GDP (the discrepancy is large because there are different ways of assessing that cost). But the cost of the bailout was not borne by public finances alone. A substantial part of it was assumed by the sector itself; that is, healthy entities were forced to contribute to the financial salvation of insolvent entities. Private banks also provided resources for a new institution—the Deposit Guarantee Fund—which had the essential mission of providing absolute guarantees to depositors. This was critically important to maintain public confidence and prevent a systemic crisis from materializing through a massive withdrawal of deposits.

The policies for industrial restructuring and the reorganization of the banking industry were markedly defensive in nature. The first democratic governments sought to promote structural reform policies aimed at improving the working of the markets. In this chapter, when dealing with the Moncloa Pacts, we have reviewed fiscal reform and the liberalization of the financial system. In order to have a complete view of the reform agenda carried out during the transition period, three more issues need to be examined: the reform of the framework of industrial relations, trade liberalization and financial openness to the outside world.

The Franco regime had compensated to some extent for the lack of trade union freedoms with a system that was highly job protective. The economic crisis forced to redefine the regulation of the labour market. The democratic regime would allow it to be reformed, channelling the interests of the various social agents. Before the establishment of the constitutional regime (1978), the government simply recognized the freedom of association, legalized the right to strike and preserved in its entirety the rigidly interventionist nature of Franco's labour legislation.

The Moncloa Pacts inaugurated the "era" of social pacts. Between 1980 and 1985, four different social pacts were signed by three sides: by the majority unions, the employers' organizations and the government. In exchange for containing wage increases, the government made certain commitments to social spending. What did this social agreement achieve? The greatest achievement was that it forged a framework of recognition and negotiation between the main social actors. This was undoubtedly valuable for a society that had just emerged from a dictatorship and was suffering the effects of an extraordinarily harsh economic crisis. The main beneficiaries of the pacts were the trade unions. They gained much more power of representation and pressure than they would have had if the negotiation had been carried out in a decentralized manner. But the centralized negotiation model had considerable economic and social costs. Setting wage increases in a completely centralized way led to differences in the level and variation of productivity between different sectors and companies being ignored. Moreover, this model of social concertation did not serve in any way to reduce the rigidities of the regulatory framework for labour contracts.

The explosive growth in unemployment convinced both major political parties that these rigidities needed to be reduced. They opted for a flexible exit from the labour market in order to avoid companies' bankruptcy. A large number of them were caught between, on the one hand, the unbearable rise in production costs and the fall in demand and, on the other hand, the legal impossibility of making workforce adjustments. However, fierce resistance from the trade unions and the government's interest in sponsoring social pacts led to the failure of liberalization. The Workers' Statute adopted in 1980 reaffirmed the strong barriers to market exit. The reform drive would have to come from the other route, the reduction of barriers to entry into the labour market. The establishment in 1984 of the temporary contract would play a decisive role in the re-launch of employment from the following year. The new legal hiring framework stimulated the massive creation of—temporary—jobs as soon as companies had cleaned up their financial situation and the economy returned to the path of recovery and expansion.

Let us see what progress was made in the area of trade liberalization. The Spanish economy took an important step forward in opening up foreign trade. Foreign trade in goods and services rose from 26.5% of GDP in 1973 to 43% in 1985 (see Appendix, column 15). This was due much more to the growth of exports (11.3 percentage points) than to that of imports (5.2 points). The reduction of trade barriers played an important role in the dynamism of trade flows. Trade liberalization resumed in 1977 after the paralysis caused by the first energy crisis. The will of the Spanish authorities was to move forward in the liberalization process with a view to join the EEC. The Preferential Agreement signed with the Community was bearing all its fruits for the exporting sectors, which encouraged the government to assume new international liberalization commitments. In 1979, Spain signed an agreement with the EFTA by which it extended to the countries of this commercial area the tariff rates applied to those of the EEC by virtue of the Preferential Agreement. The following year, Spain accepted the tariff reductions approved in the Tokyo Round of the GATT, which affected a large number of items. These liberalizing impulses paved the way for the definitive leap forward in the reduction of trade barriers, which would take place upon entry into the EEC.

The desire for liberalization and opening up to the outside world extended to the financial system and to capital movements abroad. Everything had to be done in this area, which was one of the most strictly regulated. In the banking industry, self-sufficiency still prevailed, while financial relations with the outside world were subject to stifling restrictions, with the exception of foreign investment. Most foreign currency transactions were still prohibited and criminalized or subject to prior administrative authorization. This is known as exchange control. It was the historical result of the chronic shortage of foreign means of payment and the Spanish economy's propensity to incur current account imbalances, combined with a strategy of self-sufficiency or strong nationalism.

From 1978 onwards, foreign banks were able to establish themselves in the country, although with certain limitations that conditioned their establishment as retail banks. The foreign banks only managed to take a small market share from the national banks, as they were unable to compete with them on an equal footing. However, this does not mean that the sector was not liberalized in a very cautious way. Foreign institutions played a major role in the emergence of new financial products and markets in the 1980s.

With respect to financial transactions abroad, the desire for greater internationalization of the Spanish economy led to the liberalization of capital movements and foreign payments. In 1979 the legal regime of exchange control was thoroughly modified, repealing the stale law of monetary crimes of 1938. Under the new legal framework, Spaniards were free to make direct investments abroad. The law immediately opened the door to a complete liberalization of most invisible current account operations. The deregulation of short-term capital movements will come a few years after integration into the EEC.

Finally, we should not forget the package of domestic liberalizing measures adopted on the initiative of the Minister of Economy of the first socialist government, Miguel Boyer, which included the liberalization of rents (practically frozen since the end of the Civil War) and the liberalization of shopping hours. Both would allow for greater flexibility and modernization of habits and customs.

Bibliographic Orientation

An excellent overall approach to the economic dynamics of the period can be found in C. Betrán, A. Cubel, M. A. Pons and M. T. Sanchís (2010): *La España democrática (1975–2000). Economía*, Madrid: Síntesis. Also Chapter 7 of the book by J. Maluquer de Motes (2014): *La economía española en perspectiva histórica*, Barcelona: Pasado y Presente, offers a more synthetic vision, very convenient as a first reading. It is also highly recommended, because it combines a stylized story with a sharp interpretation, J. M. Serrano Sanz (1994): "Crisis económica y transición política", *Ayer*, 15. The reader interested in a detailed knowledge of macroeconomic dynamics and structural changes underwent by the Spanish economy during those years may check S. Lieberman (1995): *Growth and Crisis in the Spanish Economy: 1940–93*, London–New York: Routledge. The book edited by J. L. García Delgado (dir.) (1990): *Economía española de la transición y la democracia*, Madrid: Centro de Investigaciones Sociológicas, contains a large number of essays carried out by specialists on many relevant aspects, such as, on the one hand, the detailed examination of the different historical periods (first energy crisis, Moncloa Pacts, second energy crisis, first socialist government and integration into the EEC); and on the other hand, the institutional transformations and reforms registered in fundamental areas, such as the foreign, financial and public sectors, among others, without forgetting the very instructive analysis of the reform of the general institutional framework. An overall view of the macroeconomic policies of the Transition year governments, in E. Fuentes Quintana (1993): "Tres decenios largos de la economía española en perspectiva", in J. L. García Delgado (dir.): *España, economía*, Madrid: Espasa Calpe. On the economic policy of the "Pactos de la Moncloa" we have a study, which, due to its length and level of detail, is only advisable for readers who have a special interest in the subject: J. Trullén i Thomàs (1993): *Fundamentos económicos de la transición política española. La política económica de los Acuerdos de la Moncloa*, Madrid: Ministerio de Trabajo y Seguridad Social. An analysis of the economic policy of the first socialist government by his main person in charge, M. Boyer Salvador (2004): "El segundo ajuste económico de la democracia española (diciembre de 1982–julio de 1985)", in E. Fuentes Quintana (dir.): *Economía y economistas españoles*. Vol. 8, Barcelona: Galaxia Gutenberg. The reference book on the reorganization and restructuring of the banking system is: A. Cuervo (1988): *La crisis bancaria en España, 1977–1985. Causas, sistemas de tratamiento y coste*, Barcelona: Ariel. A major monograph on the industrial crisis with a wealth of data, in J. Segura *et al.* (1989): *La industria española en la crisis (1978–1984)*, Madrid: Alianza. Social spending now has an excellent monograph by S. Espuelas (2013): *La evolución del gasto social público en España, 1850–2005*. Madrid: Banco de España.

CHAPTER 10

Integration into the European Economy (1986–1998)

Spain's entry into the European Union (then the EEC) has undoubtedly been one of the most important events in the history of modern Spain. The negotiating process for Spain's incorporation into the European Communities, initiated in 1977, was finally closed in 1985. In accordance with the accession treaty signed in June of this year, Spain and Portugal became members of the EEC on January, 1st, 1986. Right after the entry of the Iberian States, the Community countries set themselves more ambitious goals for economic integration. The first was the Single European Market, an economic area in which goods, services, people and capital would circulate freely. Before reaching this goal—planned for 1993—the Community took on an even greater integration challenge: the so-called Economic and Monetary Union (EMU). According to this plan, which was approved in 1989, the Community States would create a common and single currency within ten years, as well as a European Central Bank that would manage monetary policy autonomously. So in a few years the Spanish economy had to face the enormous challenges posed by such a deep interdependence with more developed, open and flexible economies.

A. Carreras, X. Tafunell, *Between Empire and Globalization*, Palgrave Studies in Economic History,
https://doi.org/10.1007/978-3-030-60504-9_10

1 The Business Cycle of Joining the European Union

The evolution of the Spanish economy describes a complete cycle between 1985 and 1993—the cycle of integration—, the profile of which is shown in Fig. 10.1. Two aspects stand out in this graph. The first is the total synchronization between the Spanish and Community cycles. This is conclusive proof that since 1986 the Spanish economy has been fully integrated into the European economy and is highly dependent on it. That link is qualitatively different from the one that existed before, that being more distant made possible mismatches and discordances between the cycles of the Spanish and the European economy.

The second aspect to be highlighted is the more pronounced profile of the Spanish economic cycle. During its upward phase it experienced the strongest expansion, in production and employment, among the OECD countries. Similarly, when the European economies fell into a recession in

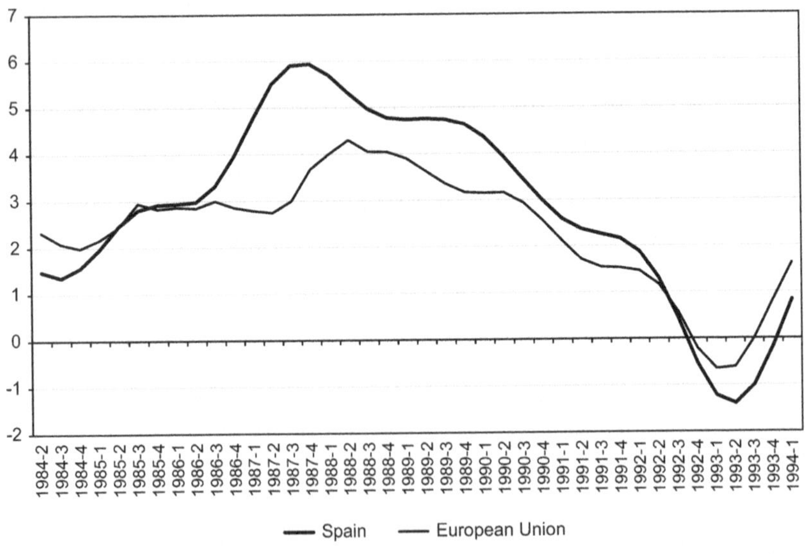

Fig. 10.1 Spain and European Union economic cycles, 1984–1994 (GDP quarterly growth moving average). *Source*: E. Fuentes Quintana (1995): “El modelo de economía abierta y el modelo castizo en el desarrollo económico de la España de los años 90”, in J. Alcaide *et al.*: *Problemas económicos españoles en la década de los 90*. Barcelona: Galaxia Gutenberg

the early 1990s, Spain suffered more severely. In two years of contraction it destroyed almost half of the jobs generated during the boom. The figure clearly shows that Spanish GDP rose and fell more sharply than the EU's GDP between 1985 and 1993. The former has to do with its relative backwardness, while the latter is due to the fact that it incurred greater macroeconomic imbalances.

A review of the series included in the Appendix allows us to characterize the most salient features of that cycle. In its expansionary phase, GDP grew at an annual rate of 5.7%. Employment increased during its expansionary phase more than it did between 1960 and 1973. On the demand side, the main driver of expansion was investment. It increased even more explosively than in the Golden Age, at an annual rate of 13.3%. Public consumption also expanded vigorously, due to expenditures related to the Welfare State, which the PSOE governments continued to promote. The dynamism of private consumption was in line with that of aggregate demand, driven by the increase in employment and wages and by the wealth effect generated by the formidable revaluation of financial and real assets (real estate). All of the above components combined resulted in domestic demand growth in the order of 7–8% per year. These levels were difficult to sustain, as they coexisted with a huge and growing current account deficit. The contrasting behaviour of imports and exports sheds light on this situation. While the rise in imports was measured in annual rates of two digits (17.4%), the rise in exports was quite discreet (5.5%).

The year 1990 represented the turning point between the expansionary and contractionary phases. From then on, the Spanish economy reacted to the change in the international panorama by sliding downwards. The industrialized economies turned towards recession due to the great uncertainties generated by the collapse of the communist regimes, the German reunification and the preparation of the Gulf War (the first war between the United States and Iraq). The strong slowdown suffered by the Spanish economy in 1991 was transformed into a severe recession in the second half of 1992 and throughout 1993. Investment, again, led the way with a very intense drop. Private consumption was also sensitive to the change in the economy. Public consumption, on the other hand, maintained its expansive tone, due both to the counter-cyclical mechanisms of the Welfare State and to the extraordinary expenses caused by the great celebrations of 1992 (the Olympics in Barcelona, the Expo in Seville and the cultural capital of Madrid). The combination of rising public expenditure and falling productive activity led to a rapid worsening of the public deficit, which became a destabilizing imbalance. Another was added: the current account balance, which was also in deficit and highly destabilizing. It had to be finally corrected by a contraction of domestic demand and a deviation of national production towards foreign markets, both forced by a fall in the value of the peseta. Thanks to these, a great improvement was achieved in the external accounts from 1993 onwards. There was, however, no improvement in the area of inflation, which was very inflexible to the fall in production and the increase in unemployment. And it is in this last variable that the crisis of the early nineties displays its worst side. The unemployment rate undoes the downward trend of the prosperity period at such a speed that in a couple of years it reached the highest level ever recorded (see Fig. 9.1).

2 The Real Effects of Integration

The first and fundamental impact of the accession to the EEC was on foreign trade. It is logical that this was the case, with Spain in 1985 having levels of trade protection that were three times higher than those of the Community. Integration into the Community would therefore entail radical trade liberalization. As a result, Spain eventually became an open economy (see Figs. 3.1 and 3.2). The liberalization of external trade does not happen overnight because the Accession Treaty sets out a timetable for tariff dismantling. In any case, absolute market liberalization with regard to the Community area will eventually have a powerful trade creation effect. The proportion of internal demand which is covered by Community imports increases considerably, replacing national production which is not as efficient or competitive. Community imports of manufactured goods rose from less than 9% of domestic demand in 1985 to 26% in 1995. This will not be done at the expense of reducing the relative weight of extra-EU imports (trade diversion effect); on the contrary, it will also increase. Since Spain is no longer a closed economy, Community producers, and to a lesser extent those of other countries, are now supplying a greater part of domestic demand.

Naturally, the increase in EU manufacturing imports has led to a significant change in the geographical structure of foreign trade. The weight, already dominant in 1985, that the EEC had for Spain was greatly reinforced. In imports, products from the area went from representing 36.8% in 1985 to almost 60% in 1990. The percentage continued to rise in the following years until stabilizing at around 65%. On the export side, there was also a geographical concentration, although not of the same proportions. While on the eve of accession the EEC absorbed just over half of Spanish exports, since 1990 the percentage has been around 70%.

Trade liberalization led to a very uneven expansion of imports and exports, as we have pointed out. During the boom, the former increased at a rate almost three times that of world trade; in contrast, the latter grew less than world exports, for the first time since 1960. Two factors interplay here. One, industrial exporters did not benefit from Spain's membership of the Community club because before it, they already had easy access to the Community market thanks to the Preferential Agreement, and because they would now be deprived of the subsidies that had been disguised. Two, the appreciation of the peseta and higher inflation made Spanish products less competitive. Obviously, the latter factor played in the opposite direction for imports, although their strong expansion was due more to trade liberalization and the great dynamism of internal demand.

The result was a huge trade deficit, which, as J. Viñals states, represented the most visible impact of Spain's integration into the EEC. In 1985, the unfavourable balance of trade was equivalent to 2.5% of GDP; from 1989 to 1991 the percentage was over 6%. A large deficit in the current account emerged, which was necessarily financed by foreign savings. Indeed, Spain received a large inflow of foreign capital. Here we find the second fundamental impact that the incorporation to the EEC had on the Spanish economy.

In the first years of integration, there was an investment boom in Spain. It was of such magnitude that, according to the OECD, it must be qualified as a powerful (positive) demand shock. Investors, mainly European companies, wanted to be present in the peninsular market because they anticipated that it would expand greatly as a result of integration. There was then a large-scale acquisition of Spanish companies, which was followed by massive investment in capital goods aimed at providing them with new technology. Investment in machinery and equipment increased every year at rates of the order of 15% to 20%. Foreign capital played a very active role in this investment boom. It contributed almost half of the investment in the manufacturing industry. In the case of industries with strong demand, foreign capital amounted to 97%, according to the OECD. In moderate-demand industries it also accounted for the majority, although not as overwhelmingly. Thus, foreign capital turned to the sectors with the highest growth potential; they were the most technologically advanced and could exploit the most economies of scale. As has so often happened in the past, foreign investment contributed to improving the efficiency of Spanish industry. It will provide it with new competitive capabilities, which will involve new specializations.

These new capacities will not be shown immediately but once the adverse effect of the overvaluation of the peseta and the international recession of the early 1990s has been overcome. Spain will be oriented towards the export of products from advanced and intermediate industrial sectors—motor vehicles and machinery and electrical and electronic material, in particular, breaking with the pattern of specialization prior to 1986. The branches of the traditional sectors—such as basic metal industries, textiles and clothing, or footwear—will no longer provide the majority of the value of foreign sales and will lose relative weight fairly quickly in those years.

The entry into the EEC had a third significant effect on the Spanish economy, resulting from Community aid. For three decades, Spain has been a net recipient of Community funds as it is an economy with a per capita income level below the European Union average. The volume of net financial transfer has been very relevant in macroeconomic terms: in the first two decades, it was equivalent to 0.7% of GDP per year. The total amount received since 1986 amounts to nearly half of that year's GDP. The largest economic aid in history, far greater than the Marshall Plan! What did Spain do with the funds it received? A significant part of these went to the agricultural sector. The Community's agricultural policy (CAP) became a fundamental pillar of farmers' income. The rest was used mainly to co-finance infrastructures and other components of fixed social capital and, to a lesser extent, programmes to strengthen the skills of the labour force. The greatest economic benefit that Spain derived from the aid was that it was able to provide itself with a dense network of modern infrastructure, even if it ended up carrying out public works of doubtful social profitability.

3 The Nominal Effects of Integration

We have seen in the previous section that Spain's entry into the EEC had an immediate and intense impact on its real economy. In the area of nominal variables, the effects were, in the short term, less perceptible. But they ended up coming to the fore strongly as a result of the failure of the socialist government's policy of competitive disinflation, combined with the worsening of the international economic environment and the crisis of confidence in the European project of monetary union. In these circumstances, the monetary and financial ties that had closely linked the Spanish economy to the European one acted as a powerful depressive force.

The key nominal variables would be inflation and the exchange rate. Both had a major impact since the incorporation of the peseta into the European Monetary System (EMS) in 1989. The government took this decision to signal Spain's commitment to participate in the European monetary union project that was being launched at that time. However, it also took this step to try to force the convergence of the inflation rate by imposing the corset of a quasi-fixed exchange rate. Since the Spanish leaders were unable to create effective stabilizing institutions, they tied the country to an external commitment to achieve the desired nominal convergence. However, Spanish society was not aware that membership to the EMS posed the famous trilemma of foreign financial relations. It is not possible to have at the same time an (almost) fixed exchange rate, freedom of capital movements and an autonomous monetary policy in correspondence with a differential inflation. If the first two options are chosen, as was the case, the third must be abandoned; in other words, monetary policy must be aligned with that of the country acting as the anchor of the system, and inflation cannot deviate significantly from that registered in that country. Otherwise, there will be a continuous appreciation of the real exchange rate that will end up making the fixed (nominal) exchange rate unsustainable.

Spain did not meet this condition of monetary discipline, nor the condition of fiscal discipline that is closely linked to it. As Fig. 10.2 shows, it maintained a persistently higher inflation rate than the EU average and, even more so, than the German average. Let us note that Germany was the leading, anchor economy of the EMS. The socialist government's disinflationary strategy clearly failed. For many reasons. The three listed below were decisive. One, the government was unable to persuade social partners to moderate their demands for higher incomes in order to curb price increases. Inflation was too entrenched in the behaviour of workers and employers to be easily driven out. It has taken a long time to achieve this; it has only been possible after going through a deep depression from 2008 onwards.

Two, the persistently higher inflation was caused by the low level of competition and the low dynamism of some markets, typically from sectors not exposed to external competition. The activities that produce non-tradable goods internationally—concentrated in the services sector and in

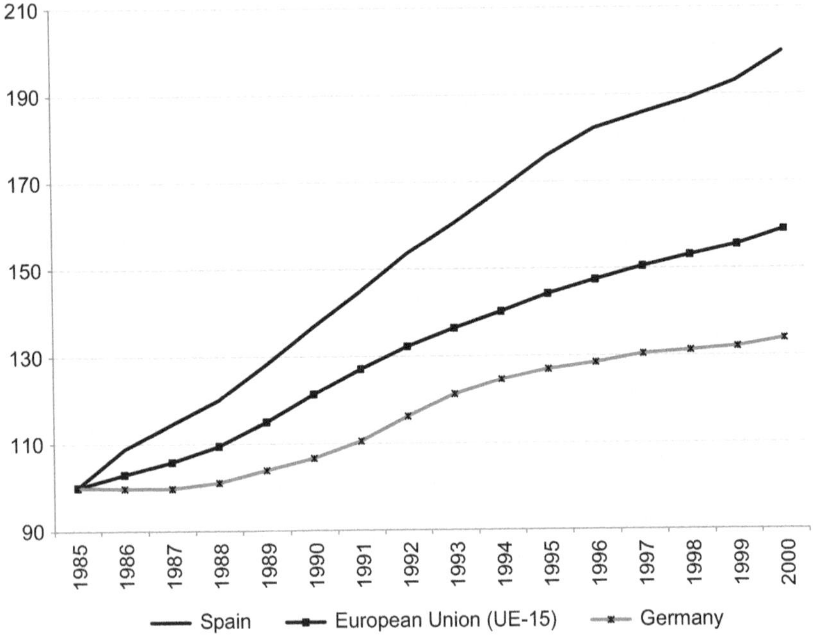

Fig. 10.2 Consumer price indices (CPI), 1985–2000 (1985=100). *Sources*: Appendix, column 20; A. Carreras and X. Tafunell (2004): "The European Union economic growth experience, 1830-2000", in S. Heikkinen and J. L. Van Zanden (eds.): *The experience of Economic Growth*. Amsterdam: Aksant

the public administration—had a strong inflationary path. The government is responsible for not having carried out the necessary institutional reforms to introduce greater competition in these sectors.

Last but not least, fiscal policy encouraged inflation rather than curbing it. Spending policy was very expansionary. It resulted in a high public deficit, which was basically structural. Both of these things generated strong inflationary pressures. The accelerated growth of public spending ignited the rise in prices because of the pressure it exerted on aggregate demand. And the deficit became inflationary because of the way it was financed, with liquid assets that increased the amount of money.

In short, Spain's membership of the EMS meant that its currency had an almost fixed exchange rate while its prices rose faster than those of the other countries that were part of the monetary system. As a result, the real exchange rate of the peseta was appreciating. This led to a continuous deterioration in the competitiveness of Spanish companies. As they were now fully exposed to external competition, not only in European markets but also in the domestic market itself, such an erosion of their competitive capacity would eventually become unsustainable.

That imbalance led to an economic recession after a short time. It exploded when external financing of the public deficit failed. The entry of the peseta into the EMS had made it easier for the Spanish State to make a continuous and massive appeal to foreign savings to finance its overspending. Spain's membership of the EMS meant a powerful element in attracting savings from the rest of the world. Firstly, because it was part of a system of quasi-fixed exchange rates, the exchange rate risk was minimized. Second, because Spanish government debt offered much higher yields than French or German debt (see Fig. 10.3). In a context of absolute liberalization of capital movements, the above factors explain why there was a lot of foreign capital interested in acquiring Spanish government debt.

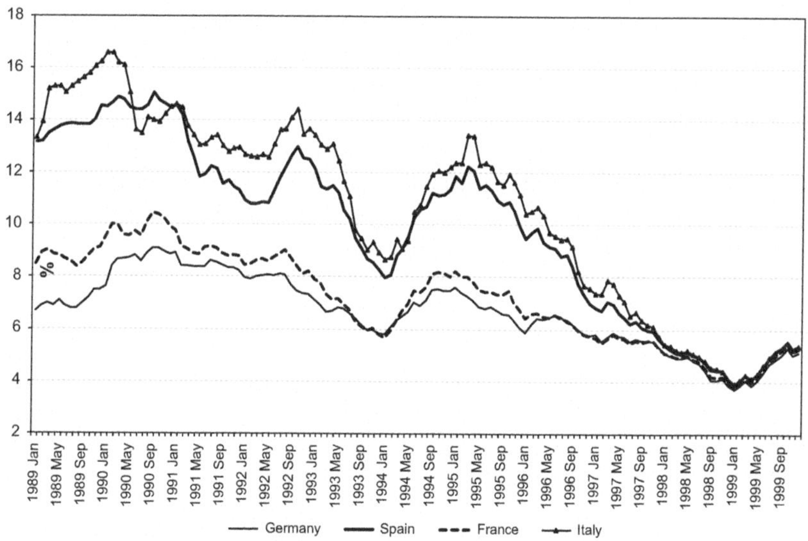

Fig. 10.3 Long-term interest rates in some European countries, 1989–1999 (monthly averages). *Source*: Banco de España: *Boletín Estadístico*

The problem laid in the sustainability of this situation. There was a risk that Spanish debt would lose the confidence of foreign investors. This is what happened when the European financial crisis broke out in 1992. The referendums on the Maastricht Treaty held in Denmark and France in the summer of that year raised great doubts about Europe's willingness to create a single currency. The political uncertainties aroused investors' fears, leading them to change their expectations completely. Confidence in the viability of the monetary union plan was shaken in the financial markets. Suddenly, investors realized that European countries, instead of converging, were diverging and moving away from the criteria established in Maastricht. The current parities in the European Monetary System no longer seemed credible. Investors quickly disposed of assets denominated in overvalued currencies such as the peseta. The brutal withdrawal of foreign investors forced a succession of devaluations of the peseta. There were three between September 1992 and March 1993, plus a fourth in 1995.

The fall in the peseta's value restored external balance by boosting exports and inhibiting imports. But the lesson from the experience of the 1992–1993 monetary and economic crisis was clear: maintaining large public and current-account deficits was not compatible with belonging to a system of exchange-rate stability. Unfortunately, the Spanish authorities forgot the lessons of that balance-of-payments crisis once Spain joined the single currency. For its part, Spanish public opinion, dazzled by the immediate benefits of the euro, also forgot the lessons of the 1992–1993 crisis. Everyone in Spain turned a deaf ear to the critical—Eurosceptic—views that emerged in the Anglo-Saxon world, which warned of the dangers that the single currency posed in the long term to economies prone to current account deficits. Ignoring the past often leads to the same mistakes, which in this case would be very painful (see Chap. 11).

4 Institutional Reform Policies

Since joining the EEC, Spain's economic policy has been guided by the reduction of State intervention in economic activity. The objective has been to improve the efficiency of the productive sectors, for which it has been deemed necessary to promote the functioning of competitive markets. It should be stressed that Spanish governments have almost always applied these policies constrained by the liberalization agreements (directives) adopted by the European Union. The pro-market strategy has consisted of the following: privatization of state-owned companies, liberalization and "re-regulation", that is, the creation of a regulatory framework that precisely defends competition.

However, the authorities applied these three policies with very different intensities and doses: extreme, in the case of the privatization of state-owned companies; decisive but very unequal, in the field of market liberalization; timid and ineffective, with regard to policies aimed at effectively guaranteeing free competition in markets where it was threatened by the action of the already established companies. We will now deal with these three issues, in the reverse order in which they have been set out.

Competition policies continued to be in their infancy in Spain. They were taken in tow from the Community competition policy agenda. In 1989, the first legal framework prohibiting restrictive practices of competition, such as collusion and abuse of dominant position, was approved. Then the Court of Competition Defence was created, an institution in charge of ensuring that there is as much competition as possible in the markets and empowered to prosecute and sanction conducts that restrict competition. How effective has this policy been? The results have been poor. The lack of appreciation for competition in Spanish society has been a major factor. The government has always made sense of and even facilitated economic concentration. It has not opposed the formation of monopolies if they would serve to have large Spanish companies capable of competing abroad and at home with those of other countries. The government has bowed to pressure from the very powerful interest groups formed by oligopolistic industries such as the electricity and telecommunications sectors.

Fortunately, further progress was made in the field of liberalization policies. The first liberalization was that of the external sector, which had tremendously important and irreversible consequences for domestic industry. This is an issue which we have already discussed. We will now add that, in the 1990s, the policy of liberalization was concentrated on the services sector. It was less forceful than the policy applied previously in the field of goods. Some of the tertiary activities that are key to economic growth, such as telecommunications, transport or the supply of electricity, were subject to the liberalization programmes and timetables agreed by the European Union's decision-making bodies. They advanced, and are still advancing, very slowly, due to insufficient reform momentum from Community leaders and strong resistance from the companies concerned.

In the area of production factors, the most radical and far-reaching changes occurred in the financial system, as a result of complete outward liberalization and very extensive deregulation. It is in this period that the financial system undergoes enormous transformations and accelerated development. Such modernization has been caused, fundamentally, by the internationalization of the sector, resulting both from the European integration process and from the globalization of financial markets. The institutional reform measure that had a great transcendence was the absolute liberalization of capital movements in February 1992, dictated by the Economic and Monetary Union programme.

The Community's single market project, which involved the removal of all barriers to the mobility of capital, led to profound changes in the regulation of banking, the securities markets and insurance. These institutions had to be adapted to basic rules common to the entire European economic area. The deregulation of the banking system meant the elimination of all administrative intervention on the amounts managed by the banks. The institutional reforms of the securities market brought the functioning of the stock markets up to date, which favoured their dizzying growth. A final institutional development contributed to the stock market's flourishing: the legal creation of collective investment institutions, investment funds and pension plans.

The changes in the institutional environment described above and the challenges of European integration led the large Spanish banks to embark on a process of major mergers and takeovers. In 1988, Banco de Bilbao and Banco de Vizcaya merged to form BBV. In 1991, the Banco Central and Banco Hispano Americano carried out a similar operation, forming the BCH. In 1999, the latter merged with Banco de Santander to form BSCH, in an operation that was in fact a true takeover by the Cantabrian entity. In 1991, the Corporación Bancaria de España (Argentaria) was set up, which would eventually absorb almost all the Spanish state-owned banks. Almost simultaneously with the creation of the BSCH, the Argentaria Corporation and the BBV also merged, giving rise to the BBVA. Meanwhile, Banesto was bought by BSCH. In short, from the former seven entities that for decades constituted Spanish big banking, the duopoly BBVA—BSCH (today, Banco de Santander) was created.

In the field of the labour market, liberalization was very limited, as it faced strong social resistance. We should describe it as the relaxation of an extremely rigid framework of administrative and judicial intervention, rather than a genuine liberalization policy. The most important legal measure to make employment more flexible was taken before this period, in 1984. In the previous chapter we referred to this reform, through which various types of temporary contracts were created. Almost all of the employment generated in the years of economic boom was in the form of temporary contracts. This labour market reform had two very important and persistent perverse effects. One, a dual market was formed: permanent workers (with indefinite contracts) and temporary workers. The excessive volume of the second segment had long-term negative effects on economic growth. Companies had no incentive to invest in human capital. Today's Spanish economy is paying for it and will continue to do so in the near future. The second perverse effect is that it increased the bargaining power of the permanent worker segment. Their position was strengthened by the fact that companies now use the hiring and firing of temporary workers as a workforce adjustment tool.

The destruction of (temporary) jobs in the downturns was so brutal that it encouraged further labour reforms. The first one, approved in 1994, established the freedom to create temporary employment companies—the much-criticized ETTs—and introduced some facilities for dismissal. The social agents soon assumed that this labour reform was insufficient. In 1997, under the first Popular Party government, they sealed an agreement for a new labour reform, with the aim of reducing the high rate of temporary work that has characterized the Spanish labour market since the end of the 1980s. To this end, a new type of contract of indefinite duration was created, which is less difficult to terminate and with not so high dismissal costs.

The results of both reforms were ambivalent. Their implementation was made difficult by the existing judicialization of the functioning of the labour market. However, the simple approval of the first reform seems to have helped greatly in the area of wage moderation. Some experts argue that the unions bought the non-implementation of the reform with extremely discrete wage claims. Eventually, these reforms seem to have stimulated intense temporary job creation.

Finally, let us look at what happened in the third vector of institutional reform policies: the privatization of state-owned enterprises. The Spanish public sector was basically composed of the "national companies" created during the autarky, the ruinous companies nationalized during the 1970s and the group that formed the holding company Rumasa, nationalized in 1983 by the first socialist cabinet. From 1986 until the early years of the twenty-first century, the public business sector continued to shrink as a result of the privatization process. Something similar happened everywhere because of economic globalization. In the face of it, public enterprises had little capacity to adapt to the rapid changes and continuous innovations required to compete in international markets.

The privatization carried out by the PSOE governments was, as A. Cuervo argues, shameful and silent. For ideological and political reasons, the socialist leaders tried to hide the privatization process from public scrutiny. In doing so, they renounced the design of a global and explicit privatization plan. Despite this, it was far-reaching. Many companies were sold directly, generally to multinationals in their respective sectors, after having been financially cleaned up. Among the most emblematic cases are SEAT, awarded to Volkswagen, and ENASA, awarded to FIAT. The privatization of the largest state-owned companies considered strategic—Telefónica, Repsol, ENDESA, etc.—was carried out through public offerings of shares (IPO).

When the Popular Party came to power in 1996, it gave a new impetus to the privatization process. Conservative leaders explicitly proposed privatization as the central strategy to increase competition in the markets and to improve the efficiency of the business sector. Privatization was guided by a comprehensive plan, with defined objectives and timetables. It was far-reaching. Between 1996 and 1998 alone, the government sold—or completed the sale of—large companies for some 25 billion euros, equivalent to 5% of GDP in one of these years. This is twice the figure for the whole of the previous decade. In a favourable stock market climate (see column 23 of the Appendix), the IPO operations were a resounding success with the public of small investors, many of whom were attracted to the stock market for the first time by these share offerings. As had happened in Thatcher's Britain in the early 1980s, privatizations gave wings to popular capitalism. By the end of the decade, the State had divested itself of all the jewels in the crown. There was practically nothing left to sell; to be precise, nothing that could be sold. The Conservative government desisted from privatizing a not very large number of public companies in non-competitive sectors without any future. If, on balance, the privatization operation deserves a critical evaluation, it is not because of that—the survival of a nucleus of highly loss-making residual state-owned companies. The serious failure is that the belief in the improvement of market efficiency that would be achieved by transferring state-owned companies into private hands has proved to be unfounded. In the absence of a truly effective antitrust policy, the replacement of public monopolies by private monopolies (or oligopolies) has brought little economic benefit to consumers.

5 The Transition to the Single Currency

The Maastricht Treaty of 1992 established the conditions for the introduction of the common and single European currency, the euro. It set out a timetable for the transition phase which was to run from January 1994 to December 1998. During this phase, countries wishing to join the monetary union should aim at nominal convergence with the more stable countries. The Treaty defined five convergence criteria that countries should meet in order to qualify for the euro. In the spring of 1998, an assessment would be made of which countries met these criteria, and this group of countries would proceed at the end of 1998 to launch the new currency (for three years, 1999–2001, it would coexist with the national currencies).

What were these convergence criteria? First, inflation. It should not exceed by more than 1.5 percentage points the average of the three countries with the lowest inflation. Second, public deficit. It did not have to exceed 3% of GDP. Third, public debt, which should not exceed 60% of GDP. Fourth, nominal long-term interest rates, which should not exceed by more than 2 percentage points the average of the three countries with the lowest inflation. Fifth, exchange rate. The currency should not have devalued or overstepped the EMS fluctuation band in the two previous years.

The fulfilment of these conditions has been the guiding principle for the policies of all EU governments since 1995, after the worst effects of the 1992–1993 recession were over. Spain, like the rest of the EU countries, embarked on a determined policy of fiscal consolidation. The governments convinced public opinion of the sacrifices that had to be made to achieve the goal of monetary integration. The finance ministers of the last PSOE government and the first PP government imposed, with a broad social consensus, a strict policy of containing public spending and deficits. Budgetary discipline bore the desired fruit: in 1998 Spain met the basic convergence criterion of fiscal consolidation, that of the public deficit.

It should be made clear that it met the objective thanks to a number of favourable factors, apart from the strong policy of budgetary rigour. Firstly, Germany's willingness—never openly admitted—to apply the convergence criteria flexibly. Germany—the leading economy in the area and champion of nominal stability—allowed its partners to use accounting tricks to balance their public accounts. The German government's predisposition to benevolence was due, firstly, to the acceptance by its partners of its proposal for a Stability Pact, which made the requirement to control the public deficit a permanent requirement; and secondly, to its conviction that it would be very difficult for Germany itself to comply fully with the Maastricht criteria, due to the enormous financial costs of German reunification.

Secondly, fiscal consolidation achieved its goal partly thanks to economic recovery. From 1995 onwards, economic activity maintained a high rate of growth, driven by the drastic reduction in interest rates and by the climate of "euro-euphoria" that engulfed agents as it became credible that Spain would join the euro on schedule. The spectacular fall in interest rates was caused by the financial markets' own expectations, which discounted the fact that monetary union would actually be achieved in 1998. This self-fulfilling prophecy had the virtue of resolving the condition concerning convergence in long-term nominal interest rates without any major problems (see Fig. 10.3). The collapse of interest rates drastically reduced the burden of financing the deficit, facilitating fiscal adjustment. It also had very positive macroeconomic effects. A powerful virtuous circle was generated. The fall in rates reduced public expenditure and the deficit while promoting economic growth by reducing the costs of financing private sector investment. Economic growth implied a substantial increase in tax revenues and a decrease in income maintenance costs (unemployment benefits, transfers, etc.). This generated further deficit reductions that allowed the circle to be re-fed.

Inflation, like the public deficit, could be mastered sufficiently to meet the Maastricht criteria in extremis. Several factors combined to achieve this historic achievement. First, the excellent management of monetary control by the Bank of Spain, that enjoyed independence from the government since 1994. Second, the extraordinary wage moderation and the environment of virtual absence of social conflict (see Fig. 5.3). Trade unions and employers' organizations assumed that it was essential for Spain to be able to participate in the launch of the single currency. In addition, the impact of the severe crisis of 1992–1993 and the labour reforms of 1994 and 1997 had an influence on the containment of wage claims. Finally, it should not be overlooked that inflation was subdued at the right time by pure chance. In 1997 and 1998, European countries enjoyed a very favourable situation in terms of the evolution of oil, commodities and food prices. This had a probably decisive disinflationary influence right at the last stage of the phase when countries had to meet convergence criteria.

Bibliographic Orientation

A work that provides an accurate overview of the Spanish economy in this period is that of C. Betrán, A. Cubel, M. A. Pons and M. T. Sanchís (2010): *La España democrática (1975–2000). Economía*, Madrid: Síntesis. A global approach that deals with all the fundamental aspects in a short space can be found in chapter 8 of the book by J. Maluquer de Motes (2014): *La economía española en perspectiva histórica*, Barcelona: Pasado y Presente. For an approach to the structural transformations induced by the incorporation to the European Union, the studies edited by J. L. García Delgado and R. Myro (dirs.) (2014): *The Spanish Economy: An introduction*, Thomson Reuters/Cívitas are useful. The reader interested in a more detailed knowledge of the evolution of the main economic sectors will benefit from J. Harrison and D. Corkill (2004): *Spain: A Modern European Economy*, Ashgate: Aldershot. In the same line, it is also useful K. Salmon (1991): *The Modern Spanish Economy. Transformation and Integration into Europe*, London–New York: Pinter; and, by the same author, 'The Spanish Economy: From the Single Market to EMU', in R. Gillespie and R. Youngs (eds.) (2001): *Spain: The European and International Challenges*, London: Frank Cass. About the Hispanic Welfare State, G. Rodríguez Cabero (2011): 'The Consolidation of the Spanish Welfare State (1975–2010)', in A.M. Guillén and M. León (eds.): *The Spanish Welfare State in European Context*, Farnham: Ashgate. On the economic policy applied during the period, it is instructive to read the book by the man who was primarily responsible for this policy, C. Solchaga (1997): *El final de la edad dorada*, Madrid: Taurus. It serves to understand the limited capacity of the government to set the macroeconomic policy in front of social actors behaviour. A very enlightening study, both from a theoretical and descriptive perspective, on the privatization of public enterprise is found in G. Bel and A. Costas (2001): "La privatización y sus motivaciones en España: de instrumento a política", *Revista de Historia Industrial*, 19–20. A critical assessment on liberalization and competition regulation policies in M. A. Fernández Ordóñez (2004): "La liberalización y la competencia en los mercados de bienes y servicios", in E. Fuentes Quintana (dir.): *Economía y economistas españoles.* Vol. 8, Barcelona: Galaxia Gutenberg. On the negotiation process for Spain's entry into the EEC, C. Powell (2011): 'The Long Road to Europe: Spain and the European Community, 1957–1986', in J. Roy and M. Lorca-Susino (eds.): *Spain in the European Union: the First Twenty-Five Years (1986–2011)*, Miami: Miami-Florida European Union Center. A work that rigorously and systematically evaluates the degree of Europeanization of the Spanish economy and the impact that its integration into the European Union has had on it is M. Farrell (2001): *Spain in the EU. The Road to Economic Convergence*, Basingstoke: Palgrave. This same subject is dealt with in even greater depth by C. Martín (2000): *The Spanish Economy in the New Europe*, Basingstoke: Macmillan.

CHAPTER 11

Spain in the Euro Area (1999–2017)

The path of the Spanish economy over the last twenty years has been marked by two complex historical processes: economic globalization and the European Monetary Union (officially, the Economic and Monetary Union, EMU). Globalization has profoundly altered the productive systems and macro-financial balances of all economies. The developed economies have been affected by multiple channels, among which we will highlight two. One is the flood of cheap manufactured goods of all kinds, manufactured by the emerging Asian economies, with China at the forefront. It has helped greatly to keep inflation rates low. But it has destroyed millions of industrial jobs in the former industrial economies. The second channel of impact has to do with the surpluses in the current account balances of these emerging economies. They materialized into a gigantic supply of liquidity available to the advanced economies. The new economic context was described, at the beginning of the twenty-first century, as the "Great Moderation". Economic leaders thought that the developed economies had entered into a regime of endlessly predictable macroeconomic stability. They believed that the global economy was progressing strongly and steadily because markets were functioning efficiently after being deregulated. What actually happened was large-scale indebtedness in advanced economies, fuelled by excess liquidity resulting from high global savings and low interest rate policy by central banks. The deregulation of financial markets and the careless supervision of financial institutions made

A. Carreras, X. Tafunell, *Between Empire and Globalization*, Palgrave Studies in Economic History,
https://doi.org/10.1007/978-3-030-60504-9_11

massive indebtedness as easy as possible. Financial institutions granted too much credit and took too many risks. The outcome was a debt crisis. In some countries, mostly in the periphery of the EMU, it triggered dramatic sovereign debt crisis that shook the very existence of the Euro. Overcoming a debt crisis is quite a difficult challenge that requires a set of financial, institutional and governance treatments. It became a long story.

1 The Economic Cycle of Joining the Euro and Unbridled Indebtedness

For the Spanish economy, accession to EMU meant following with greater impetus the path opened up by a financially deregulated globalization. It is impossible to exaggerate the significance of Spain's entry into the euro area. In the eyes of Spanish society, the country entered a new economic era. The citizens were unanimous in thinking that sharing the same currency with Germany would bring great benefits to the Spanish economy. The country would abandon its traditional macroeconomic regime. The governments and the elites in general, as A. Costas has pointed out, abounded in this optimistic vision, trusting that the euro would act, on its own, as an anchor of internal stability. It would prevent the Spanish economy from falling back into its long-standing macroeconomic imbalances. The new environment would supposedly be characterized by a great and permanent stability of the nominal variables (inflation, interest rates, exchange rate).

There was little discussion on what monetary policy in the hands of the European Central Bank (ECB) would mean. Logically, the ECB would pay more attention to the large economies of the Eurozone than to the medium and small ones. The setting of interest rates, as M. Sebastián explains, followed a pattern (the "Taylor rule" in economic jargon) that was suitable for Germany but not for Spain. These interest rates that suited Germany were a powerful incentive for Spain to get into much more debt than it could already afford simply by joining the single currency, with a zero risk premium and maximum reputation.

The benefits that simple membership to the euro zone promised dazzled economic agents and politicians. A climate of "Euro-ecstasy" was created, leading to overspending and overindebtedness. Optimism also overwhelmed foreign lenders and investors, who set out to finance the demand for funds from Spanish companies, banks and public administrations. So the expansion experienced by the Spanish economy until 2007 was based on indebtedness. Consequently, the crisis that broke out in 2008 was a debt crisis. This makes the economic cycle experienced by Spain in the last two decades different from all previous history. Let us look at it.

Table 11.1 compares the evolution of some economic magnitudes during this cycle and the major cycles of the twentieth century. If we accept that the upward phase began in 1996, when the horizon for the implementation of the euro was clear, this expansionary cycle exceeded the others of the last century, except for the golden age (1960–1974). This is if we take the accumulated growth of GDP as a yardstick for measuring expansion. But if the metric of the boom is the improvement of the population's welfare, approximated by the GDP per inhabitant, the 1996–2007 boom does not stand out at all. Nor does it stand out if we look at the growth of domestic demand. The reason is that investment, more specifically investment in equipment goods, was less dynamic. So was the progress of the manufacturing industry.

The three most relevant aspects in which the expansion of 1996–2007 differs from the previous ones are the following. The most outstanding is the capacity to generate employment: 6.4 million full-time equivalent (FTE) jobs were created, representing an increase in the workforce of almost 50%. The number of employed people in 1996 was 13.5 million, approximately the same as in 1974! In 2007, it reached 19.8 million (see column 2 of the Appendix). These figures are far higher than those recorded at any other time.

The other side of this labour-intensive expansion was the stagnation of productivity. Here we find a second key difference with the other great expansion cycles of the twentieth century, which have had as one of their fundamental pillars the improvement of labour and total factor productivities. Finally, the figures in the table show that the expansion of 1996–2007 was based on bank credit, the volume of which increased much more than in the past, except for the 1960–1974 period, when accelerated industrialization made it possible to beat historical records on all fronts except for employment. In short, the economic boom of 1996–2007 has only been extraordinary, in historical perspective, because of the massive mobilization of labour and credit.

The same cannot be said of the crisis of 2007–2013. The data in the table reveal that it has been exceptionally severe, whatever the indicator used. While GDP and private consumption stagnated or even grew slightly

Table 11.1 Increase/reduction of some economic indices during expansive/contractive periods, Spain, 1919–2013 (in %)[a]

	1996–2013 cycle		*1985–1993 cycle*		*1960–1984 cycle*		*1919–1939 cycle*	
	1995/2007	*2007/2013*	*1984/1991*	*1991/1993*	*1959/1974*	*1974/1984*	*1918/1929*	*1929/1939*
GDP	57.4	-8.1	40.6	-0.1	186.2	25.2	53.9	-23.0
GDP per capita	38.2	-10.7	38.4	-1.1	143.6	15.5	40.1	-30.9
Private consumption	53.2	-12.5	35.9	0.4	161.4	18.1	55.6	-30.9
Gross Fixed Capital Formation	109.8	-37.6	97.9	-12.4	395.1	-9.5	234.7	-64.2
Dwelling investment	145.1	-54.3	68.1	0.6	209.6	-21.1	286.7	-82.2
Equipment investment	135.7	-14.1	106.7	-19.6	619.7	3.0	204.2	-55.6
Domestic demand	67.8	-17.0	51.0	-2.0	191.3	15.5	69.0	-17.9
Industrial GVA, excluding construction	46.5	-15.6	22.1	-4.3	303.6	30.1	63.6	-31.7
Employment (full-time equivalent)	49.1	-18.1	20.4	-4.0	19.1	-15.3	11.0	9.6
Unemployment rate[b]	8.2	26.1	13.1	18.3	2.4	16.7	n.d	n.d
Labour productivity	3.4	13.8	12.1	4.5	163.5	47.9	34.6	-28.9
Total factor productivity (TFP)	0.3	0.0	8.1	0.0	88.8	10.7	n.d	n.d
Real bank credit	306.1	-20.3	56.2	-3.5	524.3	75.4	160.8	16.9[c]

Sources: Appendix, L. Prados de la Escosura (2017): ***Spanish Economic Growth, 1850–2015***, London: Palgrave Macmillan, https://www.palgrave.com/la/book/9783319580418; Banco de España, ***Boletín Estadístico***; and, for bank credit deflated in 1919–1939, P. Martín Aceña and M. A. Pons (2005): "Sistema monetario y financiero", in A. Carreras and X. Tafunell (coords.): ***Estadísticas Históricas de España***. ***Siglos XIX y XX***, Bilbao, Fundación BBVA, vol. II.

[a]The percentage of change has been calculated taking as a reference for the starting level of the expansion the year prior to the growth phase and as a reference for the starting level of the contraction the year of the cyclical peak. Both years are those indicated in the headings of the two phases of each cycle, for example, 1984 and 1991

[b]Annual minimum and maximum of the cycle

[c]1929–1942

in the contractionary phases of the cycles of the second half of the twentieth century, between 2007 and 2013 they suffered a sharp fall. Investment fell much further, dragged down by the collapse of the real estate sector. It is true that all these indicators, and others, fell even more sharply between 1929 and 1939. It could hardly be otherwise, given the brutal impact of the Civil War. But, in this sense, it is very striking that the fall in domestic demand between 2007 and 2013 is analogous to that which took place in 1929–1939. That is, without the positive contribution of foreign trade, productive activity would have gone through a crisis as acute in 2007–2013 as in 1929–1939! In terms of jobs destroyed, no previous downturn has been as severe as the one suffered in 2007–2013. Nor was there any other crisis in the twentieth century in which credit was significantly reduced. This denotes precisely that the crisis of 2007–2013 has been, unlike the others, a debt crisis. Its resolution has required a long and painful process of debt reduction.

Economists call the recent crisis the "Great Recession". The term is certainly appropriate to refer to large developed economies such as the United States or Germany that had an intense, but short, crisis. It is not appropriate if we are talking about Spain. What it experienced in the years after 2007 was a full-blown economic depression, a Great Depression. The unprecedented level of unemployment is proof of this (see Fig. 9.1). We do not know of any previous recession in which nearly one in five jobs were destroyed. Another very expressive indicator of the singular depth of the crisis is the drop in GDP per capita. Since 1850, only the crisis of 1929–1939 was worse than the latter in terms of intensity and duration.

2 The Credit, Real Estate and Immigration Boom. The Internationalization of Spanish Business

During the first decade of the euro's existence, Spain's economic model was based on private sector indebtedness. The accumulation of debt reached levels unknown in the past; it surpassed those reached by other countries in those years characterized by a superabundance of credit. As D. Taguas has pointed out, in no country in the euro area did credit increase as much as in Spain.

The statistical data on bank credit leave no room for doubt. Until 1996, the stock of bank credit grew at the same rate as nominal GDP. From 1997 onwards, in anticipation of Spain's entry into the euro, the volume of bank loans increased at rates double those of nominal GDP. Since 2004, they have picked up even more rapidly. The stock of bank credit expanded at a rate of between 20% and 25% per year, tripling that of nominal GDP. This crazy debt race came to an abrupt halt in 2008. In the following years, until 2012, the variations in the credit stock were in line with those of the economy. Since 2013, credit has been decreasing every year, moving away from the pulse of nominal GDP, reflecting an intense process of debt reduction.

Why was there such an unbridled acceleration in credit? How could the banks finance it? What use did the borrowers make of this mountain of money? To find the answer to these questions, it is necessary to examine this extraordinary private indebtedness from the supply and demand side. Let us start with the first approach, since banks fed the demand for credit.

The business model of the Spanish banking system is that of retail banking with an extensive network of branches. This model has very high fixed costs, challenging profitability when interest rates are low. The problem is solved with a large volume of operations. As commercial banks went multinational, the savings banks launched a large expansion of their branch network in Spain outside their traditional territories. As they increased the network they did everything possible to grant loans and credits. They relaxed the criteria for granting them and paid little attention to the ability of debtors to pay. They offered them extremely cheap credit on very advantageous terms, overvaluing the assets that served as collateral (housing). The households did not resist these siren songs. In Spain, everyone thought they had an extremely abundant and cheap credit supply at their disposal. The appetite for credit became insatiable for both households and businesses. In the years leading up to EMU, the volume of credit contracted by both represented, respectively 31% and 43% of GDP. From there it climbed to over 80% and 110% of GDP.

The question that arises next is: how did Spanish banks manage to finance such a volume of credit? Commercial banks usually finance their credit activity with bank deposits. Historically, the relationship between the size of those assets and liabilities has been very stable. From 1998 to 2008 this was not the case, credit grew faster than deposits. This happened because savings banks and banks found the wholesale capital markets in the euro area to be a seemingly inexhaustible source of funds. Financial institutions in Germany, France and other countries in the area with foreign financing capacity were happy to buy as many fixed-income securities as Spanish banks issued. These loans were denominated in euros and backed by real assets, and were guaranteed by mortgages granted by Spanish banks. Spanish bank indebtedness rose from 2% of GDP to over 60% at the peak.

As has happened so many times in the past, when credit is very abundant and cheap, it often generates an asset bubble that attracts the interest of investors. In this case, the plethora of credit inflated a real estate bubble. It pleased a large part of Spanish society. Families would be able to access a home of their own. The banking institutions would expand their business unrestrainedly by granting mortgage loans. Those who lived from the promotion and building of houses would enjoy a golden age. The public administrations themselves would fill their coffers with extraordinary income linked to the real estate boom. The credit explosion and the real estate bubble fed back. As debt rose, house prices went up. This redoubled the supply and demand for credit, in anticipation that property values would continue to rise. But this was not just a sustained wave of debt speculation. Real factors pulled the demand for housing. The influx of migration and the creation of new jobs formed millions of new households in a few years.

The housing bubble triggered a boom in housing construction of enormous dimensions, which in turn fed the bubble. Previously, some 230,000 homes were built each year. From 1996 to 2007 the figure increased by 10% a year, to 700,000. A very flexible supply of land for development triggered the construction boom. A judgement of the Constitutional Court and the Land Law approved in 1998 declared almost the entire national territory suitable for development. The municipalities had a strong incentive to facilitate the production of urban land and housing, as it would become a juicy source of funding for local authorities. The regional and state governments also had an interest in sustaining the real estate bubble. The various taxes that fall on the building activity and real estate transactions fattened the collection.

The boom in housing construction was joined by the boom in infrastructure. These were years of great investment in public works. They were partly financed by the generous contribution of funds from the European Union. On the other hand, the financing was, of course, provided by the public budgets of the State and the Autonomous Communities. But there was a large remaining part of investments structured under imaginative and dark accounting and financial schemes that will weigh on the public budgets of the coming decades. Curiously, they have not been detected as public deficit or debt by the European authorities. This fiscal overload will be very burdensome because, as M. Sebastián has stated, many excesses were committed and there was a lot of waste. The political profitability that the governments could extract from such investments weighed more than their social and financial profitability. In many cases the latter are simply nil or negative. The revenues will never cover the investment made; often they do not even cover the variable costs. Spain has become the European country with the most extensive network of high-speed railways and motorways at the expense of trains, roads and airports empty or with few passengers.

The explosive increase in housing construction and public works led to the building sector acting as an engine for economic growth. Employment in the sector doubled, with new workers taking up about a quarter of the jobs created by the economy as a whole. It contributed directly in equal proportion to GDP growth. We must add the indirect contribution, the induced demand effects. The construction boom pulled strongly not only from the auxiliary and building materials industries—cement production surpassed that of Germany, France, the United Kingdom and Italy combined—but from a wide variety of manufacturing and service industries.

The leadership of the construction sector explains the extremely labour-intensive growth pattern of the period. Immigration facilitated this. There was a supply shock of enormous power. Spain, which for centuries was a land of emigrants, suddenly became a country of destination for large masses of migrants.

Indeed, the flow of immigrants was of great dimensions, causing an unprecedented demographic acceleration (see Table 1.1). In 1998, 0.6 million foreign nationals were resident in Spain, equivalent to 1.6% of the total population; in 2007, they amounted to 5.3 million, representing 11.4% of the population resident in the country. These figures indicate that Spain has converged with the European migration pattern in a very short period of time.

Such a massive influx of immigrants is explained by the labour mobilization caused by economic globalization. It is also due to the greater opportunities for low-skilled jobs offered by the Spanish economy compared to other European economies. The authorities facilitated this human influx, responding to social demand, both from employers and from families. The law on foreigners (2000) meant a policy of open doors to immigration. It regularized virtually all foreign residents and established a procedure for regularization and family reunification for those who arrived next. While they had the condition of illegal immigrants, public administrations would grant them access to public goods (health, education, etc.).

The influx of immigrants had a great impact on the labour market. It increased the available labour supply and made the market more flexible. Huge numbers of cheap labour occupied low-skilled jobs. First, in the building industry, feeding back the sector boom: immigrants found themselves working in the productive activity that they were promoting as final housing consumers. The arrival of millions of foreign workers also quietly revolutionized the labour markets for various service activities, agricultural work and other tasks that Spanish workers were reluctant to perform. Domestic and elderly care services expanded enormously. The wide range of foreign workers available to perform these family support tasks contributed to the entry of many Spanish women into the labour market. The female participation rate rose from 47% in 1996 to 61.4% in 2007, almost matching the EU-15 average.

The factors discussed so far were responsible for the economic boom. Below this vibrant but ultimately fragile economic reality there was a major transformation in business organization that strengthened the productive system: the internationalization of Spanish business. In those years, many domestic companies assumed that their business should be developed in the global economy. Within the manufacturing industry, many Spanish companies were integrated into global value chains, although never in a position of leadership, as J. Palafox warns us. Participation in international production chains boosted exports and sheltered these companies from the vagaries of domestic demand. The most striking change was the multinationalization of the Spanish company. Until the mid-1990s, the Spanish company had had an extremely limited presence abroad. In just a few years, a good number of companies became multinational. An extraordinary process of change and modernization took place in this area, which should be highlighted.

As we have seen in previous chapters, Spain used to be a recipient of foreign investment. Around 1992, Spain was at the bottom of the list of European Union countries in terms of the accumulated volume of direct investment abroad (in relation to GDP). The internationalization of Spanish companies was almost non-existent. Well, according to M. Guillén, the Spanish company came of age then. In the first half of the 1990s, a few of the Spanish company's flagships, such as Iberia and Telefónica, undertook their international expansion. The situation changed radically during the transition to the euro. The landing in other countries became very visible to public opinion with the high-flying purchase operations carried out by Repsol, BBVA and Banco Santander, among others. The latter two entities became the two main banks in Latin America, and Telefónica the first telephone operator in the region. Glittering investment operations coexisted with the investment initiatives taken by nearly a thousand Spanish companies. Direct investment abroad took on great macroeconomic significance. While until the mid-1990s it accounted for less than 1% of Spanish GDP, from 1996 to 2007 annual flows of productive investment abroad rose to 10% of GDP. Accumulated investment in 2007 represented 4.1% of the world stock of direct investment abroad, i.e. more than double the share of Spanish exports in the world market. The boom in Spanish investment abroad was so strong that it equalled, in less than a decade, foreign investment in Spain and almost reached the same relative importance as foreign direct investment from the euro area. Since 2008, the foreign projection of Spanish companies has grown with less impetus. After 2012, it has tended to stagnate.

Three aspects of this accelerated process of multinationalization of Spanish companies should be highlighted. The first refers to the sectorial pattern. The competitive strength of Spanish multinationals lies clearly in the utilities, financial and construction companies. Two activities stand out in particular: banking and telecommunications. Energy occupies a less preeminent but relevant position, while manufacturing carries little weight.

The second remarkable feature of the multinationalization process is its territorial scope. It is often wrongly argued that direct investment by Spanish companies abroad has had no other destination than Latin America. That is where it began, taking advantage of the opportunities offered by the massive privatization programmes of public companies in the region. Also, of course, the advantages of sharing the same language and certain cultural patterns. But in the first decade of the twenty-first century, Spanish multinationals have diversified their assets considerably by directing investments towards European Union countries and other developed economies.

The third aspect to consider concerns the causes of internationalization. The reason that impelled many companies—including medium-sized family businesses—to invest abroad was the search for new markets to be able to compete in the context created by economic globalization. The saturation of the Spanish market required entering new markets. Globalization and the formation of the Single European Market—globalization at a regional level—drove companies to grow in size to avoid the threat of being swallowed up by competing companies. A decisive factor in the internationalization of large Spanish companies was the ease of financing. The country's firms with a vocation for global business enjoyed many opportunities to obtain abundant funds through the issuance of shares and bonds at low interest rates in the capital markets of the euro zone. They also had a tax incentive to do so by leveraging themselves.

It is possible to discuss, as M. Sebastián does, the massive internationalization strategy followed by large Spanish companies based on high indebtedness. According to this author, the operations of the internationalization wave that occurred between 2004 and 2008 were carried out by paying very high prices, financing investments with too much corporate debt and entering markets that did not give the expected profitability. In spite of these erroneous decisions and excesses in investment strategy, the balance of the internationalization and multinationalization of Spanish companies is clearly positive. The national companies converted into global companies have managed to weather the crisis without major shocks. The income and profits of their subsidiaries in dynamic economic areas have compensated for the fall in their business in Spain. In macroeconomic terms, internationalization and multinationalization have also given unquestionable returns; thanks to them, during the crisis the production system escaped the catastrophic collapse to which domestic demand was dragging it. Multinationalization ensures, through income from investment abroad, that the country's national income is higher and more stable than GDP.

3 Macroeconomic Imbalances and the Bursting of the Bubble: The Banking and Fiscal Crises

The growth pattern of the Spanish economy was good for a decade, but it was not sustainable. It was based on pillars that generated imbalances that would eventually undermine the expansionary momentum and lead to economic collapse. The two most destabilizing imbalances were private sector indebtedness and the current account deficit. Both were closely related because they had the same origin: the boom in the construction sector. The foreign deficit had another cause: the loss of competitiveness of the Spanish economy, a key structural problem that compromised its growth in the medium and long term.

The ills of the Spanish economy were the ills of the peripheral European economies that took advantage of their entry into the euro area to grow by resorting massively to foreign debt. These economies followed a somewhat similar but differentiated path to that taken by the economies of the core Eurozone. Figure 11.1 illustrates the disparity in the paths of the two groups and illuminates the unique journey of the Spanish economy.

Figure shows that up to 2007 Spain's economic growth exceeded that of the rest of the economies, including the group of southern peripheral economies. Spain's highest growth is attributable to the real estate boom and the flood of immigrants. The better economic performance of the countries of the South, with lower per capita income, suggest a process of economic convergence. But it was a false convergence. False because it was based on foreign indebtedness, rather than on improved productivity. Since the crisis broke out, the trajectory of the groups in the core and the

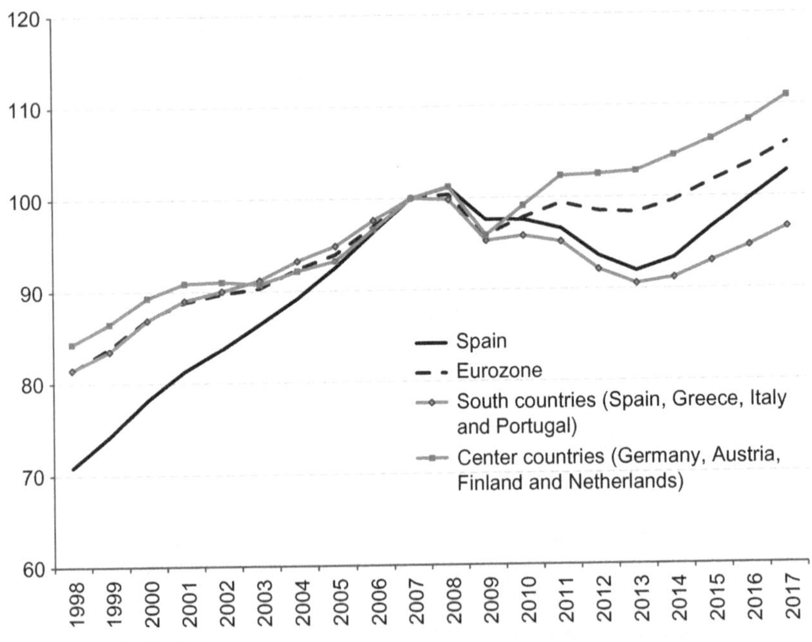

Fig. 11.1 GDP of eurozone economies, 1998–2017 (2007=100). *Source:* Prepared by the authors, based on EUROSTAT online database: http://ec.europa.eu/eurostat/data/database

periphery of the eurozone has been the opposite. It took the creditor and more developed economies only three years to recover to their pre-crisis level. By 2017, their GDP was already 11% above that level. By contrast, the peripheral economies had been in a depression since 2009, and in 2017 their end was not yet in sight. In this sense, the performance of the Spanish economy has been more encouraging since the recovery began in 2013.

The different fortunes of the peripheral economies and the central economies can be explained, fundamentally, by the indebtedness of the former. In the national accounts, it is expressed in a current account deficit. Figure 11.2 shows that, in the Spanish case, the deficit rose steadily during this period to almost 10% of GDP in 2007. On the same date, Greece reached 15%, Cyprus 12%, and Portugal the same percentage as Spain. All of them would end up receiving financial aid—a bailout—from the Eurogroup. Returning to Spain, the graph highlights two relevant aspects. The first is that, historically, the Spanish economy has been prone to resort to foreign savings to finance its aggregate level of expenditure. The second notable feature is that, since statistical records exist, the

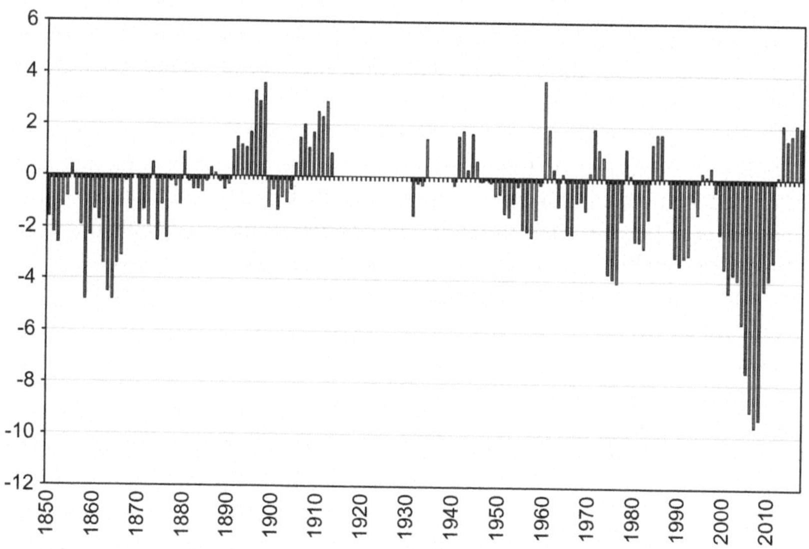

Fig. 11.2 Current account balance, as percentage of GDP (1850–2017). *Source*: Appendix, column 17

external accounts have never experienced such a large external imbalance. Traditionally, the external financial constraint acted as a brake on the deficit in the current balance. When the deficit exceeded the threshold of 2–3%, foreign investors withdrew in anticipation of a depreciation of the peseta, which either actually occurred or was avoided by restraining domestic demand. Either alternative tended to correct the current account deficit. Once inside the EMU, the exchange rate risk disappears, and the external financial constraint is altered to such an extent that it seems to have ceased to exist for Spanish society and governments. And foreign investors are willing to lend much more money in the belief that they will not suffer a capital loss from a currency devaluation.

A persistent and large current account deficit indicates that the country is living beyond its means: it spends more than it earns. Less colloquially put, it consumes and invests in excess of the income it is able to generate from what it produces. Now, an economy, like a household or a business, cannot permanently spend more than it earns. It can do so for a certain period of time by borrowing money. But it is not possible to accumulate a growing volume of debt indefinitely. Foreign investors will be willing to provide it with financing as long as they have reasonable security about the return on their investments and the repayment of their loans. If the foreign financing is used for sufficiently productive investments, the income will increase. Thus, the country will close the gap between expenditure and production, paying off the debt incurred. But if it uses foreign savings to finance consumption or unproductive investments, such as the construction of housing or infrastructures with low social profitability, the foreign deficit will end up becoming unsustainable. At some point, foreign investors will perceive that the indebtedness has gone so far that the economy will probably be unable to pay its creditors. At that point, investors will not grant it any more financing. This is exactly what happened between 2008 and 2012.

Spain did not take advantage of the injection of foreign savings to provide itself with the capital that would make it a more competitive economy, on the contrary. The seemingly unlimited access to foreign financing made it possible to cover without sacrifice a trade deficit that was steadily growing as a result of the progressive loss of competitiveness.

Why did competitiveness deteriorate? First, because Spain's inflation rate was higher than that of the other advanced economies. It is telling that the same thing happened in the other peripheral economies of the EMU. The inflation differential emanated from sectors not exposed to foreign competition. The strong pressure of domestic demand drove prices higher than in neighbouring economies. Spain's inflation rate also tended to be higher because of wage adjustment to it.

The evolution of unit labour costs (ULCs are the ratio between labour remuneration and output per hour worked) is the best indicator of the loss of competitiveness of the Spanish economy. As shown in Fig. 11.3, its trajectory openly diverges from that of the euro zone. From 1999 to 2008, ULCs in Spain increased by 22% more than in EMU. Only Ireland and Greece performed worse. Both had to be bailed out financially. In Spain, as the figure shows, ULCs increased more than in other countries because nominal wages grew more (13% more). But also because labour productivity decreased relatively (by 11%). In absolute terms, labour productivity remained almost stagnant, while multifactorial productivity

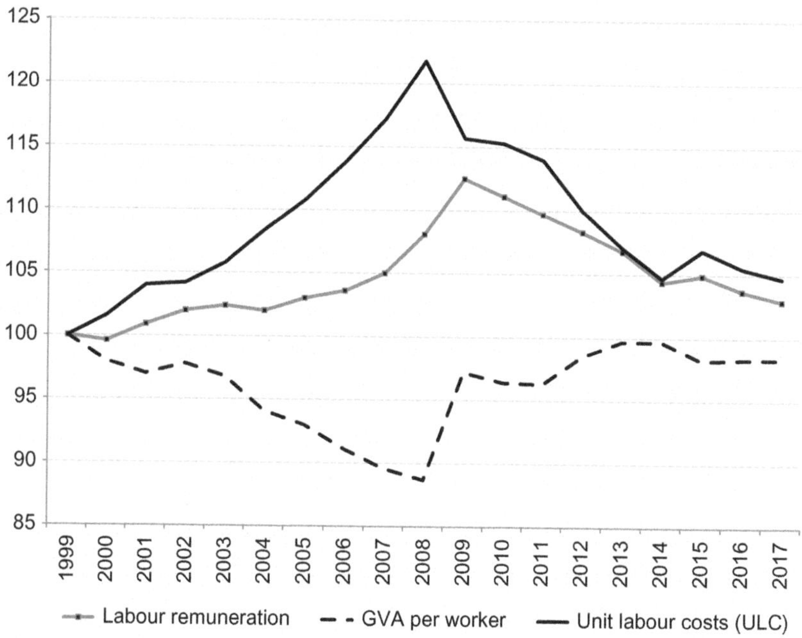

Fig. 11.3 Labour remuneration, labour productivity, and unit labour costs, compared to euro area (euro area=100), 1998–2017. *Source*: Bank of Spain (2018): *Annual Report 2017*

(TFP) declined slightly (see Table 11.1). All European economies achieved better productivity records than Spain.

The stagnation of productivity has to do with the provision of productive factors and their use. During the period 1999–2007, Spain expanded its factors at a much faster rate than the rest of the EMU and OECD nations. The most impressive difference was in the labour factor. In Spain it expanded at such a pace that it alone contributed to an annual increase in GDP of 2.1 percentage points (in the EMU, around 0.5 points). The contribution to growth of the capital factor was no less strong: 2.2 points of GDP per year. It also exceeded by far that enjoyed by the other advanced economies, except Ireland. However, the massive incorporation of productive factors did not make the Spanish economy the most competitive, but rather the least. This was due to the inefficient use of such factors. New employment was concentrated in activities that were very labour-intensive but low in value added, such as building. And a clearly excessive portion of the stock of new capital consisted of housing and other types of construction that did not contribute to improving the productivity of the productive system. The very abundance of labour seems to have induced companies not to use the most modern, labour-saving technology.

The economic boom depended on credit and the price of housing not stopping increasing. The real estate bubble would burst when prices started to decline, dragging the institutions that financed the real estate-builder sector into bankruptcy. The international financial crisis erupted in August 2007 in the United States, when low-income U.S. home buyers stopped paying their mortgage loans. The financial institutions most committed to financing the sector went bankrupt. The problem was that the banks that had granted massive credit to easily insolvent people—the famous "subprime mortgages"—had transferred the risk to other entities, national and foreign, by issuing structured debt packages in which mortgages of different quality were mixed. When the crisis broke out, nobody knew who had bought this structured debt. As banks were suspicious of each other because they did not know how many poor-quality assets each had in its portfolio, the wholesale capital markets dried up. The Spanish banks ran out of foreign financing. In this way, the international financial crisis would hit Spanish banks, although it would be after a long period of incubation.

The Spanish banks apparently resisted the first effects of the global financial crisis well. The Bank of Spain had prevented the institutions from buying the toxic securities. But if the portfolios of Spanish banks were empty of foreign "garbage mortgages", they were instead full of domestic mortgages that would soon deteriorate, making many of them insolvent.

In 2008 the real estate bubble burst in Spain. At the beginning of this year, the demand for housing came to a halt. A few months earlier, prices had begun to fall, denying the long-held notion that property prices would never fall. They would not stop doing so until 2013, accumulating a drop of 37%. The imbalance between supply and demand led the construction sector to a dramatic productive and capacity adjustment. Housing construction decreased, between 2008 and 2013, by 95%! In the construction sector, 65% of jobs were destroyed. Aggregate investment was halved. The knock-on effects, downwards, on the manufacturing industry and the various service branches were very strong. Banks were among the main victims. It could not be otherwise when at least two thirds of banking assets consisted of loans linked to the real estate sector.

The 2008–2012 banking crisis was one of the sector's great systemic crises, which, as P. Martín Aceña, E. Martínez Ruiz and M. A. Pons remind us, are those characterized by a combination of external contagion, internal economic recession and serious management failures. It is probably the biggest systemic banking crisis suffered by Spain. It led to the disappearance of the savings banks, which controlled more than half of the market share. The direct losses caused by the crisis have been, in absolute terms and as a proportion of GDP, much higher than those caused by any of the previous crises: some 400 billion euros, close to 40% of GDP. A part of this heavy burden ended up falling on public finances (we will give some details later).

Let us focus precisely on public finances. When the economic crisis broke out there was no doubt about its origin and nature: it was a debt crisis caused by an enormous leverage of the private sector. During the boom, the public sector did not get indebted; on the contrary, it did reduce its indebtedness: public debt, which accounted for 64.4% of GDP in 1997, fell to 35.6% in 2007 (see column 11 of the Appendix). However, once the economy entered into recession, a very acute fiscal crisis was unleashed. From a surplus of 2% of GDP in 2007, it went into a deficit of no less than 11% of GDP in 2009, the absolute historical record. Until 2012 the fiscal hole was practically not plugged. Never has the public deficit been of such macroeconomic significance as in those years (see Fig. 11.4). Since 2013, the imbalance has been corrected parsimoniously. So much so that, until 2018, Spain remained under the European Union's Excessive Deficit Procedure, which it entered in 2009. It has been the

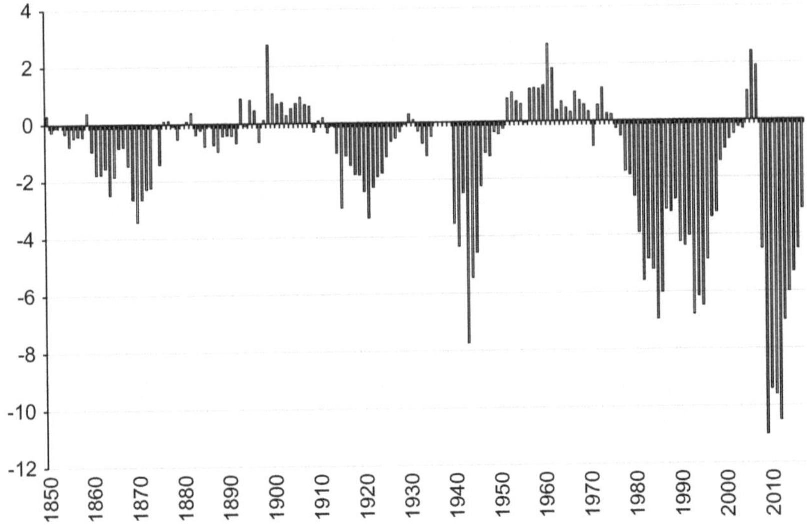

Fig. 11.4 Public deficit, in GDP percentage, 1850–2017. *Source*: Appendix, column 10

European country that has remained in it the longest and the last to leave it. In no other European country, except Greece, has public debt grown as much as in Spain in the decade after 2007.

The huge budget hole was created by a scissor-like movement in public revenue and expenditure between 2007 and 2009. While the former decreased by 15%, the latter increased by 17%. After that, and despite the much-vaunted fiscal consolidation measures, there has been no major change. Public revenues rose so slowly that in 2017 they were still below 2007 in nominal terms. And public spending, contrary to public opinion, has remained above that of 2007. This does not mean, of course, that the composition of public revenues and expenditures has not changed.

Why did the revenue collapse? The obvious answer is because of the economic recession. But it's an insufficient explanation. In the euro area, public revenues did not fall in relation to GDP between 2007 and 2011, and then rose. In Spain, despite having the lowest tax burden, they fell from 41% to 34.8% of GDP between 2007 and 2009. The fiscal consolidation undertaken in 2010 raised revenue only modestly. During the prosperous period, public finances were doped by the real estate boom. The bursting of the housing bubble would lead to tax breakdown. The collapse of tax revenues had two other causes. One is the inefficiency of the tax system. It gives little return, despite high tax rates, because it offers great tax benefits and because it is unable to combat extensive tax fraud, which intensified with the crisis. The other cause is the fiscal stimulus policy implemented by Rodríguez Zapatero's government in the first two years of the crisis.

From the beginning of 2008, the government reacted to the crisis that was about to hit Spain with a Keynesian, counter-cyclical policy. It decreed tax cuts. But they did not serve to sustain consumption, as the government had intended. In fact, the discretional fiscal policy of stimulating the economy was turned over to public spending. It received much criticism, especially for the programme to finance municipal public works, which absorbed 2.3% of GDP in useless investments. But it was not at odds with the G-20 countries, which, in the autumn of 2008, advocated expansionary fiscal and monetary policies to prevent the world economy from slipping into a depression. The European Union took up this strategy, despite the misgivings of Germany and other financial-stability-loving countries. The Spanish government anticipated such plans and adopted the counter-cyclical policy with more enthusiasm. The euro and sovereign debt crises put an abrupt end to the Keynesianism practiced by the Spanish government. It opened a new, dramatic chapter in the fiscal crisis.

In the first months of 2010, the sovereign debt crisis broke out in the Eurozone. The financial markets understood that the debt path of Greece and other heavily indebted economies was explosive, leading to sovereign debt default. Market pressure was felt in the risk premiums of these countries. The mirage that, with access to the euro, country risk had ceased to exist—a mirage that lasted throughout the boom period, as shown in Fig. 11.5, facilitating the great credit "party"—was shattered. Spain was among the nations that were now on the target of the financial markets. It would not cease to be so until the summer of 2012. The Spanish governments would live these two long years permanently on the edge because of the risk premium. The European authorities would also be living on the edge. Each sharp rise in the risk premium forced the Spanish government, under strong pressure from the Eurogroup and the European Commission, to take urgent measures to stabilize the economy and correct macroeconomic imbalances. The rise in the premium above an indeterminate level—400 basis points, 500, 600?—was perceived by all economic leaders as a sign of the imminent expulsion from the markets. It

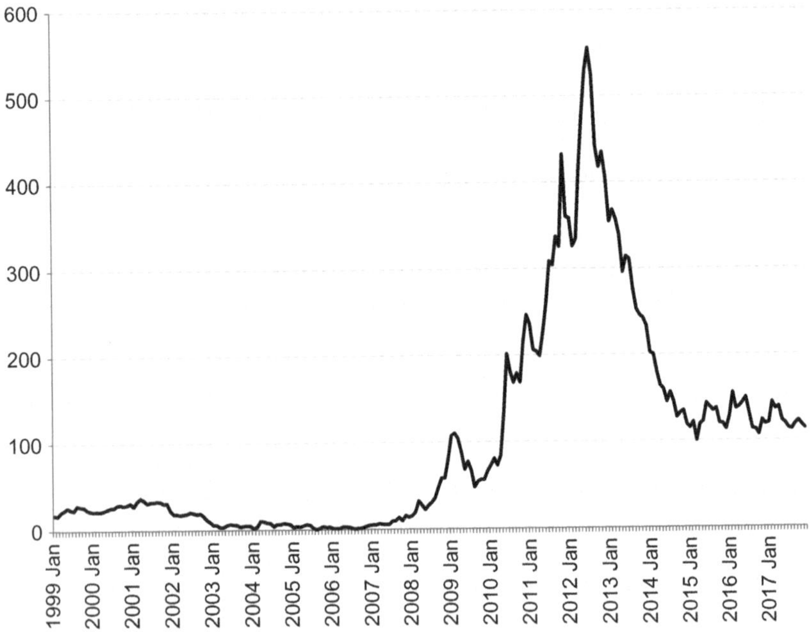

Fig. 11.5 Risk premium. Monthly average, in basis points, 1999–2017. *Source*: Bank of Spain: *Statistical Bulletin*

would precipitate the financial bailouts of several debtor nations. But the EMU had not been designed to deal with a situation where a government could not finance itself in the markets, which complicated and delayed the exit from the European economic crisis. The creditor countries, led by Germany, were reluctant to help debtors. Germany wanted to prevent some peripheral economies from acting as free riders by taking on too much debt and discounting the fact that they would be saved by the others. Creditors nations only granted aid on the condition that debtors nations would implement tough fiscal austerity and reform policies. Countries that, like Spain, were at risk of having to apply for aid would be given a milder dose of the same medicine, under the prescription of the (mandatory) "recommendations" of the European authorities in the framework of the excessive deficit procedure.

In May 2010, the Rodríguez Zapatero government was forced to implement the first adjustment plan, inaugurating a phase of fiscal consolidation that would last until 2014. The package of measures included a reduction in public employees' salaries and a one-off freeze on pensions. Other measures would be added between 2010 and 2011, both in terms of spending cuts and tax increases. The Socialist government put the finishing touches to its novel policy of fiscal rigour by agreeing with the Popular Party on a reform of the Constitution that enshrined the budgetary stability of the public administrations—zero structural deficit—and made it an absolute priority to service the debt. All of this was done with the aim of reassuring foreign creditors, who feared a "haircut" on their investments if Spain was to be rescued as Greece. The radical shift in the Socialist government's fiscal policy facilitated the electoral victory by an absolute majority of the conservative Popular Party in November 2011.

Rajoy's government went deeper into the policy of fiscal consolidation. It immediately approved a major tax increase and supplemented it with a further reduction in the salaries of public employees. From then on, the entire battle to rebalance public accounts would take place in the context of the reduction of public spending. Part of the adjustment fell on public investment, which was reduced so much that it compromised the maintenance of infrastructures. But the government unloaded on the Autonomous Communities the axe on public spending. It imposed on them a reduction in their budgetary deficit that was much greater than that which corresponded to them due to the relative weight of their spending. As the provision of the essential public goods—education and health—is in charge of the Communities, the cuts of the autonomic expenditure undermined the Welfare State. Until 2014, according to the calculations of J. I. Conde Ruiz, social spending without pensions and unemployment benefits was reduced in Spain by about 14%, compared to a decrease of 2–3% in the European Union. If the aggregate public social expenditure, in relation to GDP, increased until 2013 it was because unemployment benefits and pensions gained much importance (see column 12 of the Appendix). The increase in these social transfers, together with debt service, explains why total public expenditure has not fallen. This raises questions about the extent of the much-denounced austerity policy.

There has been an intense debate in academic and political circles on the dilemma between austerity and growth. For some authors, such as A. Costas, the austerity policy imposed on debtor nations by European authorities and creditor nations was counterproductive; it pushed those economies into a deeper and more protracted depression. In the case of Spain, it is undeniable that fiscal policy was pro-cyclical between 2010 and

2014. Not before or after. Since 2015 the fiscal impulse applied by the government has contributed significantly to the reactivation of the Spanish economy at the cost of delaying the rebalancing of public accounts. The Government has made the minimum adjustments demanded by European authorities and markets. Spain has repeatedly failed to meet the deficit targets committed to Brussels. It is difficult to imagine how a more lax fiscal policy could have fostered sustained economic growth when the one that has actually been applied has led Spain to such a threatening level of debt.

4 The Rescue of the Banking, and Labour and Pension System Reforms

The banking crisis that began in 2008 has been so serious and profound for three reasons. The first is that for a long time there was no accounting recognition of the deterioration of banking assets, or, what was the same, of the economic insolvency of many banks. The managers of the entities affected by the real estate disaster, which were mainly savings banks, were responsible for the concealment. The corporate governance model of these entities led to a politicized and unprofessional management, characterized by an excessive concentration of credit risk in the real estate sector and a high financial dependence on the wholesale capital markets. The closure of these markets pushed them into illiquidity. No such thing happened for too long. Here we find the second reason for the depth of the crisis.

The banks (savings banks) were able to survive for a long time because they had the ECB's rescue package. Since 2008, the European Central Bank has injected almost unlimited and indiscriminate liquidity into the institutions of the Eurosystem in order to avoid systemic crises, trusting that the national authorities would face up to the problems of insolvency. Spanish banks came to absorb a disproportionate share of these resources. The ECB's premise was not fulfilled: the Spanish authorities did not detect the solvency problems, or did not react until they became extraordinarily serious. This leads us to the third cause of the intensity of the crisis.

The Spanish government and the Bank of Spain intervened very late and with the wrong strategy. They committed the typical diagnostic error of a financial crisis: confusing a solvency problem with a lack of liquidity. The supervisor of the system, the Bank of Spain, took the wrong way. For various reasons, as A. de Juan, F. Uría and I. de Barrón point out. The Government pressured the Bank of Spain not to reveal a systemic problem. The supervisor could have been held captive by its own inaction after failing to take action when the first insolvent institutions were discovered. The supervisor probably relaxed the criteria on non-performing loans to prevent institutions from declaring losses. There was another reason: the authorities secretly hoped in vain that real estate prices would soon recover, just as the managers of the credit institutions whose balance sheets were bricked up were hoping.

The initial misdiagnosis of the sector's problems was followed by a misguided restructuring strategy. The authorities promoted the merger between savings banks, supporting it with public funds. The idea was that the insolvency problems of some savings banks would be diluted by merging them with other banks with healthier balance sheets. What actually happened was quite the opposite. Real monsters were born of the mergers, like Bankia, which delayed the resolution of the crisis and made it much more costly. The mergers of the savings banks also failed to produce the results expected by the authorities because, at a critical time for the survival of the institutions, costs increased instead of decreasing. The employees who were dismissed received generous compensation, in the interests of union peace, and the managers granted themselves multi-million dollar pensions as a reward for their incompetent, if not corrupt, management. The new institutions did not generate synergies. For all these reasons, the mistrust of foreign investors was accentuated. They refused to refinance the debt contracted by Spanish financial institutions because they suspected that their portfolios were full of damaged assets.

The process of sector restructuring and consolidation was turned upside down in June 2012, when the IMF warned that Bankia was masking large latent losses, spreading suspicion to the entire financial sector. The revelation precipitated the nationalization of the entity and the recognition of an equity gap of 24 billion euros. The mistrust of foreign investors increased. Spain was suffering a balance-of-payments crisis due to a sudden flood of capital flowing out of the country (a volume equivalent to 29% of GDP, according to the Bank of Spain). Only a huge injection of capital by the ECB saved Spain from having to decree a banking "corralito", according to the Minister of Economy L. de Guindos. The Rajoy government, fearing the complete closure of the international financial markets, decided to request financial aid from the EMU to recapitalize the banking sector. The European aid in the form of a loan—of 100 billion, of which 41.3 billion was used—was granted under strict conditions. The Memorandum of Understanding signed by the Spanish government and the European Financial Stabilisation Facility (EFSF) in July 2012 stipulated very precisely the measures that the Spanish government was obliged to take on the banking sector. From that moment on, its consolidation would be carried out under the dictates and rigorous scrutiny of the troika (the European Commission, the European Central Bank and the IMF). The Spanish financial system was left entirely to Brussels.

The troika's bank rescue programme consisted essentially on the following. First, an in-depth examination of the capitalization needs of all banks, commissioned not from the Bank of Spain but from independent experts. Second, once the additional capital requirements had been determined, they were partly financed by shareholders and holders of preference shares and subordinated debt, who were stripped of some of their investments. Thirdly, a "bad bank" (Sareb) was created, to which the institutions recapitalized with public funds transferred their real estate assets, so that their balance sheets would be free of bad assets. Fourth, the savings banks lost their status as credit institutions. They became foundations without the capacity for political control over the banks set up with their assets.

The programme was a success. The financial system stabilized after a few months and did not suffer any further turbulence, except for the episodic resurgence of the Banco Popular bankruptcy in 2017. But what is the price paid for the restructuring and reorganization of the banking sector? The question admits several answers. From the perspective of the functioning of the market, the price has been paid for an extreme decrease in the number of players. After the rescue, banking concentration has reached levels not known throughout Europe. But the price that matters most in macroeconomic terms—and politically, since it encouraged popular indignation and institutional crisis—is the very monetary cost of the rescue operation. The Bank of Spain, in a recent report, has done the math (until the end of 2015). It is provisional, but useful to roughly quantify the amount of the bill. We indicate before its astronomical figure. Here we break it down minimally. The financial effort made by the sector itself has been enormous, amounting to a total of 370 billion. As far as the bill for the taxpayer is concerned, the net public aid amounts to 39.5 billion. To this figure must be added a still undetermined one of the 50.8 billion delivered by the assets transferred to Sareb. In conclusion, the aid granted by the Spanish State to the sector, in terms of GDP, is more than double that the one provided by the EMU countries.

From banking reform to labour reform. It was motivated, naturally, by mass unemployment. Since the beginning of 2008, unemployment had risen sharply. The unemployment rate, which stood at 8.5% at the end of 2007, rose to 13.8% a year later and exceeded the 20% mark by the end of 2010. It amounted to 26.9% by early 2013. At the same time as this labour hecatomb was occurring, wages were increasing by 6.1 and 4.4% in 2008 and 2009, respectively. All of the—brutal—adjustment of the labour market was carried out via quantities (jobs) rather than prices (wages). The Spanish labour market operated very differently from neighbouring countries, where redundancies were avoided through agreements to reduce working time and wages. The numerous labour reforms approved in Spain since the establishment of democracy had not solved the endemic problem of structural unemployment at a very high level—14%—nor did they serve to save the country from having an unemployment rate twice as high as the European average in each recession (see Fig. 9.1). The only truly relevant innovation in the labour market occurred, as we said, in 1984, with the introduction of the temporary contract. In practice, compensation for dismissal of temporary workers was zero, while that of permanent workers was one of the highest in the developed world. The collective agreements were of a higher level than the company's, unlike in the rest of Europe, and represented the interests of both employers and permanent workers in large companies.

Faced with the dramatic drift of the labour market, in 2010 the socialist government of Rodríguez Zapatero decided to reform its regulation. The new labour legislation reduced the cost of dismissal for new, permanent contracts and made collective bargaining more flexible by authorizing the opting out of companies under certain conditions. It did not work, because the flexibilization was too cautious to be effective.

The Popular Party government undertook a much more forceful labour reform. The law passed in February 2012, according to experts, has changed the framework for regulating the labour market more profoundly than any other enacted over the past three decades. It has made it cheaper and easier to fire people, both individually and collectively. It has given employers capabilities they did not previously have to change the conditions of work in their companies, including altering wages. It has established the prevalence of the company collective agreement over the higher-level agreement. But what have been the real results of this labour reform?

In the area of employment protection, its impact has been less destructive than expected because of the judicialization of labour layoffs. The courts have accentuated their traditional bias against companies, especially in the processing of collective dismissals (ERE). Nor has the reform succeeded in changing collective bargaining, simply because the company agreement is not within the reach of small companies, which have so much weight in employment. It is true that internal flexibility in companies has increased significantly because the law has strengthened the bargaining power of employers. They have used it to reduce wages, not of the workers on the payroll, but of the new employees. Their salaries are much lower than those of the old employees. This has been the main effect of labour reform, and the one that has drawn the most criticism. The new legal framework has led to the formation of a class of poor workers, that is, those with jobs but with very low wages. In the opinion of analysts critical of the reform, this would be the cause of the increase in economic inequality that has occurred in recent years. Three points need to be made here. One is that the wage devaluation was caused both by the labour reform and by the centralized agreements signed between the unions and the employers for collective bargaining from 2012 to 2017. The unions, frightened by the brutal rise in unemployment, accepted minimal wage increases that were unrelated to the rate of inflation, breaking with an iron law that had been in place for four decades. The second point is that the wage moderation induced by the reform has had positive effects on employment, as soon as the economy has been revived. The last point concerns the worsening of the personal income distribution. Economists insist that the main cause of inequality in income distribution is not the wage cut for new workers but the massive unemployment caused by the crisis.

There is one point of consensus among economic analysts: the 2012 labour reform has by no means solved the biggest flaw in the labour market, its dualism. The market is segmented into two groups. One is made up of workers on permanent contracts, whose redundancy costs remain the highest in the European Union. The other group consists of workers on temporary contracts, who are unprotected, exposed to high turnover and much lower wages. This duality has major perverse economic effects, the greatest of which is that it slows down the improvement in productivity. Temporary workers have no incentive to get trained on the job. Nor do the employers who hire them have any incentive to provide them with such training. The duality of the labour market also has devastating social effects. Workers on temporary contracts, who are generally young, are unable to escape their precarious situation and are paid such low wages that they see jeopardized such basic life goals as economic independence and raising a family. The precariousness of the new workers has undoubtedly become one of the worst consequences of the economic crisis.

The last structural reform policy carried out by Spanish governments during this period was the reform of the pension system. As with the bank bailout and labour reform, the force of circumstances pushed the authorities to take action. In this case, they reacted to the threats to the financial sustainability of the public pension system and to the deterioration of public accounts.

In 2011, the government of Rodríguez Zapatero approved a law to reform public pensions, after an arduous process of negotiation with the unions. Broad layers of the public did not see the need to reform the system. In the decade preceding the crisis, the huge increase in employment had generated a large surplus in Social Security, which fed the pension reserve fund (to over 6% of GDP). However, international economic organizations and European authorities kept insisting that it was essential for Spain to carry out a thorough reform of the public pension scheme. The unstoppable ageing process of the Spanish population would lead to a serious structural financial imbalance in the system when, from 2020 onwards, the most numerous generations, the baby boomers of the golden age, would begin to retire.

The reform law approved in 2011 consisted of a gradual modification of key parameters of the system aimed at ensuring its long-term financial sustainability. It raised the retirement age, extended the period for calculating the pension and increased the number of years of contribution to qualify for full retirement. This was in line with reforms recently adopted by many European countries. For Spain, it was the most important change in the system since the mid-1980s. And yet, events led to it being amended very soon.

Since 2010, Spanish governments, finding themselves unable to control the public deficit as required by the excessive deficit procedure, have been under pressure from the European authorities and under constant threat from the financial markets. The financial imbalance of the Social Security system has become a major obstacle to the consolidation of public finances. The massive destruction of jobs has led to a collapse in social security contributions, and hence a Social Security deficit that has entirely exhausted the accumulated reserve fund. The Social Security deficit requires public borrowing and forces the restraint of the remaining public administrations' expenditure. When the conservative Popular Party came to power it did not take long to heed the positions defended by experts and the European authorities who considered the 2011 reform to be insufficient and urged additional measures to be taken.

The new law reforming the public pension system was passed in 2013 without any political consensus. The Rajoy government added two key mechanisms to the previous scheme: the sustainability factor and the annual pension revaluation index. The first, which was to be applied from 2019, reduces the initial pension in line with the increase in life expectancy. The second established a revaluation formula whose objective is the medium-term budgetary balance of the system. It abolished the revaluation method based on the inflation rate, which had been used since the establishment of democracy. The new revaluation mechanism was to have a very significant economic effect over time. As the system is not expected to return to financial equilibrium for decades to come, the application of the revaluation index would lead to a continuous erosion of the purchasing power of public pensions. However, such gloomy predictions are unlikely to be fulfilled. A slight rise in inflation in 2017 and a few protests from pensioners were enough to cancel the reform passed in 2013. The Rajoy government gave it up in exchange for securing the necessary parliamentary support to approve the 2018 State budget. This break in the structural reform policy reveals something important. In the current historical cycle, the Spanish government's will to reform is fading as soon as it is no longer under pressure from the European authorities, the financial markets and an economic emergency.

5 The Economic Recovery

In the second half of 2013 the economic depression ended. A new economic cycle started before the end of the year. Since 2015, it has shown surprising and unexpected vigour for all economic analysts. Annual growth rates of GDP and employment of over 3% made it possible in 2017 to return to the pre-crisis level of GDP, to increase the number of jobs by 2 million and to reduce the unemployment rate by 10 percentage points.

The factors that have driven the economy from 2014 to 2018 are both external and internal. The former have weighed more heavily. These are the so-called tailwinds that have carried the Spanish economy on its back. The first, chronologically, is the new architecture of the EMU, the changes in the governance model of the eurozone. The second is the ECB's ultra-expansive monetary policy. The third, purely cyclical, growth lever has been the radical lowering of the price of oil and other commodities. We will not pay attention to this last factor, given its temporary nature. We will only recall that the price of hydrocarbons is very volatile and that the Spanish economy is very dependent on them. Therefore, the nearly 50% decrease in their price between mid-2014 and the end of 2016 was a blessing for the Spanish economy, in the form of lower inflation, increased disposable income for consumers and a reduction in the foreign trade deficit.

The changes in the governance of the euro area were of decisive importance for the financial stabilization of Spain and the other peripheral economies in the focus of the financial markets. They restored the confidence of foreign and domestic investors in the Spanish economy. The redefinition of the governance of the EMU began in 2011 with the creation of a permanent fund (ESM) to help countries in difficulty. In return, the creditor nations, led by Germany, imposed the new rules of the game: in exchange for receiving aid, the debtor economies would have to carry out the necessary reforms to converge in real and financial terms with the economies of the centre. This would take the form of the institutionalization of various instruments for their supervision and control of the financial systems, public finances and macroeconomic fundamentals of the countries in the euro area. The commitment to balance public budgets was reinforced. It was agreed to give the European Commission greater powers to supervise countries' public accounts, particularly those countries that have requested financial assistance.

The reform of the governance of the euro that contributed most to the Spanish economy returning to the path of growth was the project for a banking union, approved in June 2012. As J. Andrés and R. Doménech, among others, have pointed out, this was the greatest institutional advance achieved after the launch of the euro. It stabilized the most damaged financial systems, such as the Spanish one. The first objective pursued with the banking union was to break the vicious circle between sovereign risk and banking risk in which Spain and other countries were caught. The State and the national banks seemed to be bound by a mutually destructive relationship: the sovereign debt crisis turned the banks into financiers of the deficit of a treasury at risk of default, while, in turn, the solvency problems of the banks threatened to drag the public treasury into an uncontrollable deficit when it had to save them from bankruptcy. The banking union cut this evil link.

Progress towards a single banking market has been based on two pillars. The first is the Single Supervisory Mechanism. It assigns the ECB the task of supervising the large banks of the eurozone. This ensures that institutions are subject to adequate supervision, the same for all. The second pillar is the Single Resolution Mechanism. This is an institution that centralizes decision-making when managing a non-viable bank and guarantees that the resolution (liquidation) processes follow the same rules. The third pillar of the banking union, the creation of a common fund to guarantee bank deposits, has yet to be established. Germany and other stable nations are reluctant to mutualize guarantee funds, due to fears of massive insolvency of banks in certain countries, particularly Italy.

Undoubtedly, the main responsible for the strong Spanish economic recovery in 2014–2017 has been the European Central Bank. The ECB played a decisive role in ending the sovereign debt crisis. In July 2012, ECB Governor Mario Draghi announced that "within our mandate, the ECB will do everything possible to protect the euro. And believe me, that will be enough". These words had a thaumaturgical effect: for months, the simple statement that the ECB was prepared to intervene without limit as a lender of last resort was enough to restore calm to the financial markets. In the autumn of the same year, the ECB set up a programme of unlimited purchase of government debt (OMT). Under this programme, the ECB purchased Spanish government debt, and that of other countries, in sufficiently significant amounts to radically lower the risk premium (see Fig. 11.5). From 2014 onwards, the ECB redoubled its expansionary policy. The Bank feared that the sluggishness and deflationary pressures would push the eurozone economy into persistent stagnation and lead to "Japanese disease". The ECB launched a package of measures, maintained until now (2020), consisting firstly of an aggressive cut in interest rates until they reach zero. Second, new programmes of massive long-term financing (the TLTROs). With the funds received—at zero cost—the banks were to grant new credit to the private sector. Third, the ECB launched a large-scale, unconditional purchase programme of public debt and private corporate bonds (PPPs). This was the most innovative and probably the most impactful. The European Central Bank was five years late in adopting the quantitative easing monetary policy applied by the US Federal Reserve and other major central banks as shock therapy for the recession. The scale of this programme was such that, with regard to

Spain, the ECB bought volumes of government debt that exceeded net issuance, and by the end of 2017 it had accumulated a quarter of the government debt in circulation in its portfolio.

This extraordinary injection of liquidity has had very powerful revitalizing effects on the Spanish economy. It has facilitated the consolidation of public finances, thanks to the containment of the debt interest burden. Interest rates, in nominal terms, have never been so low. Long-term debt rates have recently reached 1.5% (see column 21 in the Appendix), while short-term debt is now bearing a negative return (the government is charging for debt!). The private sector has also benefited from the ECB's ultra-expansionary policy. The drastic reduction in interest rates has accelerated the painful process of deleveraging of households and companies. The provision of credit to large companies has returned to pre-crisis levels, thanks to the ECB's purchases of corporate debt. Spanish banks have focused their large volumes of liquid funds on financing SMEs. Although the total stock of bank credit continued to decline until 2017 because the deleveraging process had not yet been completed, the flow of new credit has allowed for a sustained increase in investment, particularly in capital goods.

The roots of the expansion begun in 2014 are also internal. They are condensed in the process of internal devaluation and its greatest achievement, the strengthening of the export sectors. Internal devaluation was inevitable. As we saw, during the period of prosperity the Spanish economy became less and less competitive and accumulated a large foreign deficit. To correct this imbalance and regain competitiveness, it inevitably had to reduce its costs and relative prices. The single currency prevented this by means of a currency devaluation, the path followed by Spain during the half-century before the creation of the euro. However, the internal devaluation has been nothing more than a wage devaluation. The business surplus has not been significantly compressed, unlike in previous crises (see column 24 of the Appendix). Factors that have a relevant impact on final prices, such as energy supply or the degree of competition in the markets for non-tradable goods, have not contributed in any way to the internal devaluation. The entire burden of adjustment has fallen on wages. Between 2010 and 2013, real wages fell by 6%. From this year to 2017, they have remained unchanged, even though GDP has accumulated 12% growth. The wage devaluation has translated into a spectacular improvement in the price competitiveness of the Spanish economy. As shown in Fig. 11.3, between 2009 and 2017, labour costs per unit of product

(ULC) redid the path set out during the first decade of the euro. Spain has managed to fully recover the competitive position it lost during the economic boom. And this has been mainly due to the effect of wage cuts. The figure shows that productivity gains have helped little. The increase in productivity has been due to the destruction of less productive companies and jobs.

What has been the price paid by society for the internal devaluation, limited to wage devaluation? The price has certainly been elevated. Large academic and political sectors attribute the increase in economic inequality to wage deflation. Spain has become the Eurozone country where inequality has increased the most between 2007 and 2016. It holds, along with Greece, the sad record of having the highest levels of inequality. The lowest paid workers have had to endure further wage cuts. However, we must not overlook the fact that unemployment has been by far the biggest culprit in the increase in inequality.

The favourable side of improving competitive capacity is the unusual dynamism of export activities (see Fig. 11.2). Fifteen years of current account deficits have given way to an unusual surplus in 2013–2017 (still maintained in 2019). Exports have grown strongly since 2010, while imports were still below the level of a decade ago in 2017. The latter is partly explained by the very strength of domestic companies, which are capable of substituting imports just as much as they are capable of conquering foreign markets. The adaptation of Spanish companies to the new economic environment has yielded promising results. The export base, the proportion of companies selling in international markets, has been significantly expanded. Target markets have also been expanded: companies have penetrated markets with high growth potential. The fruits of this effort are surprising. For the first time since Spain became an industrialized economy, its export share in world markets clearly exceeds that which would correspond to it due to the relative weight of the Spanish economy in world GDP. Moreover, among the large European economies—including Germany—Spain is the one that has best defended its export share in world markets against the overwhelming push of the emerging economies. If this encouraging performance were to continue, we might well be able to say in the future that a more mature and competitive economy emerged from the euro's founding economic cycle.

The original text was completed early 2018. Nothing special was to be changed even early 2020, but the coronavirus pandemics has put a sudden stop to the undergoing growth trends. The Spanish economy, as many others around the world, has been obliged to interrupt or reduce its activity for an unknown period of time. The losses in GDP have been estimated in ranges that will be, for sure, the biggest fall in GDP since the one that happened at the start of the Civil War, in 1936 (see Appendix, column 4). We stop here, aware that our book displays economic history up to the very recent present, but that we are entering into a completely different epoch. At the very least, a new chapter.

Bibliographical Orientation

The transformations experienced by the productive sectors and the most relevant macroeconomic aspects during the first decade of the euro are briefly and didactically dealt with in J.L. García Delgado and R.Myro (dirs.) (2014): *The Spanish Economy: An introduction*, Pamplona: Thomson Reuters/Cívitas. Economic historians have shed light on the nature and characteristics of the recent economic crisis by examining it from a very long-term perspective. Among the essays that globally compare the 2008 crisis with previous major economic crises, E. Llopis and J. Maluquer de Motes (eds.) (2013): *España en crisis. Las grandes depresiones económicas, 1348–2012*, Barcelona: Pasado y Presente. With a comparative approach but from a sectorial perspective, see F. Comín and M. Hernández (eds.) (2013): *Crisis económicas en España, 1300–2012. Lecciones de la historia*, Madrid: Alianza. In the specific case of the financial sector, it is advisable to read P. Martín Aceña, E. Martínez Ruiz and M.A. Pons (eds.) (2013): *Las crisis financieras en la España contemporánea, 1850–2012*, Barcelona: Crítica. A large number of essays written by economists on the recent development of the Spanish economy have been published. Regarding the period of prosperity, Jorge Juan's books (2011) are enlightening: *Nada es gratis. Cómo evitar la década perdida tras la década prodigiosa*, Madrid: Destino; L. Garicano (2014): *El dilema de España. Ser más productivos para vivir mejor*, Barcelona: Península; and M. Sebastián (2015): *La falsa bonanza. Cómo hemos llegado hasta aquí y cómo intentar que no se repita*, Barcelona: Península. A penetrating analysis of the causes of the crisis in D. Taguas (2014): *Cuatro bodas y un funeral. Cómo salir de la crisis sin salir del euro*, Barcelona: Deusto, as well as the one by J. Oliver (2017): *La crisis económica en España*, Barcelona: Deusto, which has the added virtue of extending the analysis to the post-crisis economic recovery. Economic inequality and the competitive strengths and weaknesses of companies and the Spanish productive system are dealt with critically by J. Palafox (2017): *Cuatro vientos en contra. El porvenir económico en España*, Barcelona: Pasado y Presente; and A. Costas (2017):

El final del desconcierto. Un nuevo contrato social para que España funcione, Barcelona: Península. On public finances, see FEDEA working papers written by J.I. Conde Ruiz et al. (2016): *Evolución del gasto público por funciones durante la crisis (2007–2014): España vs UE*, and (2017): *Los ingresos públicos en España*. A very complete, deep and accurate diagnosis of why the Spanish economy has not converged with the more developed economies is found in J. Andrés and R. Doménech (2015): *En busca de la prosperidad. Los retos de la sociedad española en la economía global del siglo XXI*, Barcelona: Deusto. Among the works published in English, a highly recommended reading for anyone interested in knowing the impact that the 2008 crisis has had on the Spanish economy is S. Royo's (2013): *Lessons from the Economic Crisis in Spain*, New York: Palgrave Macmillan, which, in addition to deepening the lines of argument of our work, includes others not dealt with here, typical of an institutionalist and political sociology approach. For an alternative approach to that of this book, with a Marxist interpretation of the euro cycle of the Spanish economy, L. Buendía and R. Molero-Simarro (eds.) (2018): *The Political Economy of Contemporary Spain*, London–New York: Routledge. On the internationalization of Spanish business, see M.F. Guillén (2005): *The Rise of Spanish Multinationals. European Business in the Global Economy*, New York: Cambridge University Press. Our personal experience of the years 2011–2015 is explained in A. Carreras, A. Mas-Colell and I. Planas (2018): *Turbulències i tribulacions. Els anys de les retallades*, Barcelona, Edicions 62.

CHAPTER 12

Balance of Two Centuries: Growth Engines and Economic Policies

In this last chapter we will return to the whole story we have explained, with a long-term perspective and with the concern of reviewing the behaviour of those factors that are usually considered to be mainly responsible for the improvement of material well-being. First, we will look at the factors driving economic growth in order to better understand the underlying trends of the Spanish economy in the long term, especially the brakes on its growth. All this will allow us to better understand the most characteristic features of the different periods we have studied. Second, we will briefly focus on the two main economic issues affecting growth stability: the foreign trade balance and the public sector balance. Both may build up major challenges to stability and growth when they become "twin deficits". Monetary policy has the responsibility to respond to these challenges achieving monetary stability. Growth and stability are the main argument of the book, and they use to be quantifiable. We then review the impact of both on income distribution, the major issue in collective action. We wrap up this two centuries balance with some final comments on institutional change.

A. Carreras, X. Tafunell, *Between Empire and Globalization*, Palgrave Studies in Economic History, https://doi.org/10.1007/978-3-030-60504-9_12

1 Growth Engines: The Sources of Productivity Growth

1.1 *Structural Change*

We refer to structural change to describe the transformations in the composition of GDP. We deal with the sectors of activity that contribute value added to the gross domestic product and the population dedicated to each sector. We also refer to changes in the composition of expenditure, i.e., of aggregate demand. In this case we distinguish between consumption and investment, and within consumption between the private and public sectors. On the income side—national income—we will be interested in distinguishing between wages and benefits. We will briefly discuss this later (Sect. 3) when we will study distribution and inequality.

The simplest and most powerful structural change is to shift economic activity from the primary to the secondary sector. This is the process of industrialization. It can be measured by various parameters, but only from the second half of the nineteenth century onwards. The available data for the eighteenth century suffer from a well-studied underestimation of female activity. The bias is important because it underestimates the participation rate, especially manufacturing activity, which in pre-industrial Spain was very female.

If we look at the labour force data, we must conclude (see Table 12.1) that the primary sector maintained its very high share until 1913. It declined sharply between 1913 and 1935, to the benefit of the secondary and tertiary sectors. In an important historical anomaly, this process was reversed after the Civil War, giving rise to a period of remarkable ruralisation that reached its peak around 1950, and lasted until beyond 1960. From then until now, the path of labour displacement from the countryside to the city has come back. Industry and services benefited from this process between 1950 and 1973, while after 1973 only services have benefited.

The absolute figures give us some additional indication. We will only use the number of employed people, measured in full time equivalents (FTE), following the strategy followed by Prados de la Escosura to solve the traditional under-registration of employment of non-agricultural activities. The stability of the population dedicated to the agricultural sector is remarkable. Between 1850 and 1973, the Spanish countryside always had more than three million people working in agriculture. Certainly, it is

Table 12.1 Employed population by sectors, in full time equivalents (FTE) (1850–2017)

	Employed population (FTE), in %					*Employed population (FTE), in 000 s*				
	Agrarian (1)	*Manufacturing*	*Construction*	*Services*	*Total*	*Agrarian (1)*	*Manufacturing*	*Construction*	*Services*	*Total*
1850	63.3	12.1	4.3	20.2	100	3317	636	225	1061	5239
1890	62.4	12.7	4.5	20.5	100	3879	787	278	1272	6216
1913	57.1	14.5	4.4	24.0	100	4119	1044	318	1726	7207
1935	41.2	19.3	6.3	33.2	100	3854	1807	594	3106	9360
1950	47.7	17.4	7.3	27.7	100	4972	1810	758	2884	10,424
1960	39.0	20.7	8.2	32.1	100	4313	2295	905	3547	11,059
1973	23.1	23.8	10.3	42.8	100	3073	3164	1367	5681	13,286
1985	15.2	22.2	7.5	55.0	100	1701	2486	840	6148	11,175
1998	6.8	19.5	9.9	63.8	100	982	2833	1441	9261	14,517
2017	4.2	12.8	5.9	77.0	100	754	2299	1065	13,789	17,908

Note: (1) includes agricultural, livestock, forest and fishing activities

Source: L.Prados de la Escosura (2017): *Spanish Economic Growth 1850–2015*, London: Palgrave/Macmillan. Tables S18 and S19. We have used his last updating to 2017, available at: https://espacioinvestiga.org/bbdd-chne/

possible to distinguish trends: the figures increase slightly from 1850 to 1913, exceeding four million. They decrease significantly from 1913 to 1935, until they fall below four million. They rise dramatically until 1950 (one million more agrarian occupied than in 1935). The 1950 census records the highest number of employed persons in the agricultural sector in the whole history of Spain: almost five million (FTE). This is the point from which the emptying of the Spanish countryside begins. But in 1960 there was still more agricultural occupation than at any time before the war. The most intense emigration took place between 1960 and 1985, when the countryside lost 2.6 million occupied people (FTE).

The population employed in industry and construction grew slowly from 1850 to 1913, but it will almost double in the next two decades-to 1935. The importance of this spectacular increase cannot be ignored. It will not be repeated with such intensity in the rest of the twentieth century. In fact, it constitutes the period of formation of a population of salaried manufacturing workers in Spain—the working class. The Civil War will reduce the size of the manufacturing occupation. Starting from the minimum of 1940, each of the three successive decades will see significant increases in this population. With annual data, it can be seen that the maximum will be reached in 1977. It will fall in the following years and will recover in two successive cycles, with relative highs in 1990 and 2001. However, the years of the housing and financial bubble and the following crisis have reduced it to levels of sixty years before. Employment in construction followed industry patterns, but with a more pronounced cyclical profile, as can be seen from the peaks of 1973 and 1998. In its case, the great expansion of the first decade of the twenty-first century has been completely decoupled from the industrial cycle. Its historical peak was reached in 2007, with 84% more employment than in 1998. The fall from 2007 to 2014 has meant a loss of almost two thirds of its employed people (FTE).

Services will initially follow a path very similar to that of industry, which reminds us that, until very recently, they were only an indispensable support—in trade, finance, transport, etc.—for manufacturing activity. Only in the last quarter of the twentieth century has the growth of services become completely dissociated from that of industry. The extension of the Welfare State—and of all public administrations, which is explained in Chap. 9, has implied the massive hiring of workers for services of a social, educational, health and administrative nature. It should be noted that the expansion of employment in services between 1985 and 1998 has been the most important in relative terms (50%), but not in absolute terms. Even more so was the expansion of employment in 1998–2017 (4.5

million employed persons, full-time equivalents). It is worth noting that the trend in services appears to be permanently expansive, but the annual data show that it has also suffered from crises and depressions, but proportionally less than industry.

The data on the working population only tells us part of the story. The breakdown of GDP by sector (Table 12.2, panel A), allows us to nuance the explanation. For example, between 1850 and 1913, the growth of industrial output is significantly faster than that of the agricultural sector. The resistance of the agricultural sector to reduce its weight has given rise to the most lively debates in Spanish economic historiography (see Chap. 4). The interwar years were clearly characterised by an increase in the share of output devoted to services. On the other hand, the Civil War and autarchy years were of authentic "agrarianization" at the expense of industry and services. Revenge came in the 1950s, but was limited to the shift from agriculture to industry. After 1960, on the other hand, the emptying of the primary sector has been carried out almost exclusively for the benefit of the service sector, and some of the construction, which has doubled its weight in the GDP. Since 1985 the share of industry has also been continuously reduced in favour of services only.

If we evaluate the changes in the composition of demand, which can be followed in the same Table 12.2 (Panel B), we will see how the weight of consumption has been reduced over time. By decomposing private and public consumption we can better understand that the role of the State as provider of public goods and services (excluding capital goods, which are included in gross capital formation) has been very passive before the advent of the democratic regime of 1978. It is then that the weight of public consumption rises rapidly. In the percentage terms that we present the data, the recent crisis does not interrupt it, quite the contrary. Private consumption is behaving as predicted in all economic and statistical textbooks: it is decreasing proportionally as per capita GDP rises. But the interaction with the other components of demand produce significant effects, which can be seen in the annual series. For example, the war years from 1936 to 1945 (the Civil War and the military mobilization that continued throughout World War II) led to such a large increase in public spending—precisely in years of impoverishment—that private consumption fell proportionally by between ten and fifteen points, depending on the year. It fell due to the drop in GDP and fell even more due to the increase in military spending. On the contrary, during the years of maximum GDP growth, from 1960 to 1973, the overcoming of the Spanish economy's external constraint (see Chap. 8), which allowed much more to

Table 12.2 Distribution of GDP by activity sector and by demand components, 1850–2017 (in %)

	Panel A. GDP distribution by activity sector					*Panel B. Demand composition*				
	Agrarian (1)	*Manufacturing*	*Construction*	*Services*	*Total*	*Private consumption*	*Public consumption*	*Gross Capital Formation*	*Foreign goods and services balance*	*Total*
1850	37.4	13.6	3.6	45.4	100	85.3	9.6	5.5	-0.4	100
1890	33.6	25.5	2.5	38.4	100	84.9	8.1	5.5	1.4	100
1913	29.1	27.1	3.4	40.4	100	77.2	9.7	12.2	0.9	100
1935	23.0	24.3	3.2	49.5	100	78.6	11.3	11.4	-1.4	100
1950	28.7	23.0	4.1	44.3	100	71.7	11.2	17.7	-0.6	100
1960	23.5	30.8	3.9	41.7	100	72.3	8.4	18.7	0.6	100
1973	10.8	30.9	7.7	50.6	100	69.8	9.0	25.8	-4.7	100
1985	5.7	29.7	7.8	56.8	100	64.9	14.5	19.2	1.4	100
1998	4.6	21.3	9.2	64.9	100	59.8	16.9	23.8	-0.5	100
2017	2.9	18.1	5.8	73.3	100	57.7	18.5	21.1	2.7	100

Note: (1) includes agricultural, livestock, forest and fishing activities

Source: L.Prados de la Escosura (2017): *Spanish Economic Growth 1850–2015*, London: Palgrave/Macmillan. Tables S5 and S15. We have used his last updating to 2017, available at: https://espacioinvestiga.org/bbdd-chne/

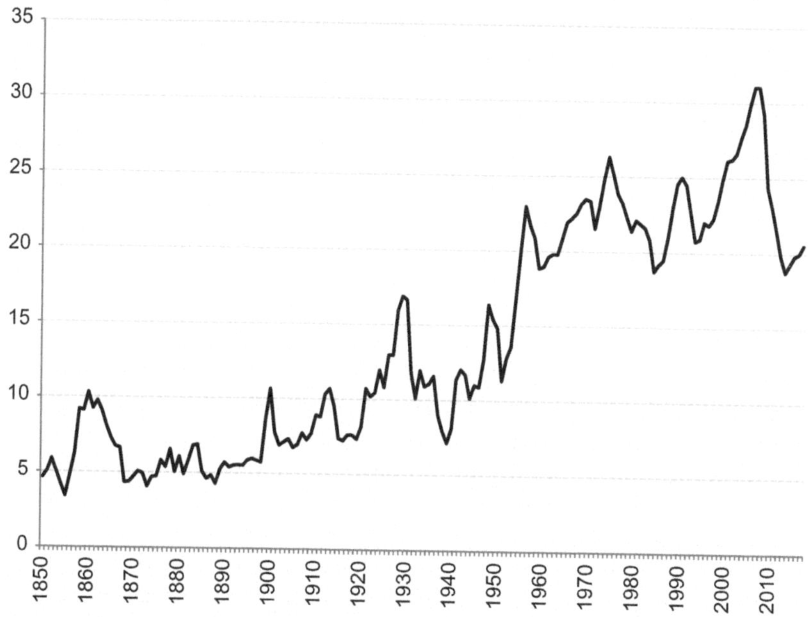

Fig. 12.1 Investment ratio (GFCF/GDP), in %, 1850–2017. *Source*: L. Prados de la Escosura (2017): *Spanish Economic Growth, 1850–2015*. London: Palgrave/Macmillan. Table S5. Data online at: https://www.palgrave.com/la/book/9783319580418

be imported than exported, led to increases in the share of private consumption and investment.

The most dynamic element, in the long term, has been the growth of gross capital formation, what we normally call "investment" (more precisely, gross fixed capital formation—GFCF). In all the benchmarks that we present, it has been growing, sometimes a lot and sometimes less. But there are three periods that display a clear reduction: 1913–1935, 1973–1985 and 1998–2017. In the first the fall is concentrated in the years 1929–1933 and in the last, from 2007 to 2013. The fall in investment after the railway boom of 1855–1866 has been left out of the focus.

In fact, since investment is the most dynamic and variable factor, it is useful to visualise its evolution, measured as a proportion of gross fixed capital formation to GDP. This is reproduced in the graph below (Fig. 12.1). Investment fluctuations are closely associated, as we have seen in detail in the preceding chapters, with the successive phases of the

Spanish economy. They are the driving force, both for the good—GDP expansions—and for the bad—its falls.

Finally, the balance of the foreign sector (last column of Table 12.2) reminds us that there have been periods when the economy has grown strongly dependent on imports. Annual data show that this has been the case from 1960 to 1973 and from 1998 to 2007, as we have seen in Chaps. 8 and 11.

1.2 *Productivity*

What are the determinants of economic growth? To answer this fundamental question, it would be necessary to know what the contribution of each productive factor has been to economic growth, as well as the contribution of total factor productivity (the unexplained residual). In a simplified approach, two factors are considered: labour and capital (each incorporating different categories and qualities). They should be extended to three, including land, if we are dealing with agrarian-based economies, as is the case in Spain in much of the contemporary era. Many authors insist on distinguishing the business factor from capital and labour, but it is very difficult to evaluate its contribution. Recently, growth theory has preferred to recombine the traditional classification and distinguish only two factors: human capital and physical capital. The first consists of labour in all its categories, from unskilled to highly skilled, which incorporates the most advanced knowledge, plus the entrepreneurial factor. The second incorporates land, and the various forms of capital in the traditional sense, from transport infrastructure to machinery. The estimation of the contribution of each factor sustains the estimation, by difference, of the total factor productivity (TFP). TFP is, in a broad sense, the improvement of efficiency: the extent to which an economy achieves higher growth through a better combination of available factors. The sustainability of income increases depends crucially on TFP developments.

Fortunately, we have research for Spain that has made exactly these calculations. In what follows we will make extensive use of their results. Before, we should note that the mentioned research covers the period 1850–2000 (panel C updates the data until 2015, but losing comparability with the previous century and a half), that the growth rates that follow are calculated as logarithmic growth rates and that the chronological divisions are those that the authors of the article have presented, as a consequence of previous research by L. Prados de la Escosura in which he was looking for the turning points of the GDP series. They do not always coincide with our periodization, but they are always very useful.

Economic growth consists, essentially, of applying more physical and human capital to the same units of labour. If we compare the Spain of 1850 with the Spain of 2000, the amount of labour (without considering its qualification) has multiplied by less than 1.6, while the Product has multiplied a little more than forty times. The difference comes from the growth of the stock of physical capital (3.8 times), human capital (1.6 times) and TFP (5.2 times). Labour productivity gains sustain increases in labour remuneration and, therefore, improvements in real income. It is certainly not the same to apply more land as to apply more machinery or to apply more knowledge. The former allows only for extensive growth, which can easily collapse if the amount of labour grows faster than the amount of land. Intensive growth, by applying more reproducible capital, is of higher quality because it is sustainable. Even so, there are times when limits are found to the application of more physical capital per unit of labour. An overcapitalized society can be very inefficient. All the old economies of real socialism are examples of over-capitalization. The combination of factors must be efficient. In fact, improvements in efficiency are essential. They usually come from improvements in allocative efficiency and improvements in available technologies.

With the estimates obtained by L. Prados de la Escosura and J. R. Rosés we can see the contribution of each factor to the growth of the economy. GDP growth is decomposed into growth of the productive factors and total factor productivity (obtained as a residual). Table 12.3 distinguishes between capital, quantity of work and quality of work. This does not mean that the contribution of land is ignored, but it happens to be quantitatively irrelevant. In the very long term, between 1850 and 2000, GDP has grown at a rate of 2.5% per year. The land factor has not contributed significantly to this growth. Capital has contributed 0.9 percentage points (35%). Labour contributed 0.6 percentage points (23%), equally between quantity and quality. Total factor productivity contributed 1.1 percentage points (42%). At a very high level of abstraction and quantification, these calculations summarise the experience of a century and a half. We can distinguish between the first century (1850–1950) and the following two quarters of a century. With its ups and downs, the first century is characterized by modest growth rates. From 1951 to 1974 the growth rates were, however, very high. In the last quarter of the twentieth century the rates were lower, but doubled those of 1850–1950. At this level of

Table 12.3 Sources of GDP growth, 1850–2015 (average growth rates, in percentage)

Years	*GDP*	*Capital*	*Labour (quantity)*	*Labour (quality)*	*TFP*
1850–2000	2.5	0.9	0.3	0.3	1.1
Panel A					
1850–1950	1.4	0.6	0.3	0.1	0.3
1951–1974	6.5	1.3	0.7	0.8	3.7
1975–2000	3.0	1.2	-0.4	0.5	1.7
Panel B					
1850–1883	1.8	0.7	0.5	0.0	0.6
1884–1920	1.3	0.6	0.1	0.1	0.2
1921–1929	3.8	1.1	1.1	0.5	1.1
1930–1952	0.8	0.5	0.4	0.0	-0.1
1953–1958	4.7	1.4	0.2	0.8	2.4
1959–1974	6.9	1.3	0.5	0.9	4.2
1975–1986	2.5	1.0	-2.8	0.9	3.4
1987–2000	3.5	1.6	1.6	0.2	0.2
Panel C					
2000–2015	1.1	1.0	0.1	n.d.	-0.1
2000–2007	3.2	1.3	2.1	n.d.	-0.2
2008–2015	-0.7	0.7	-1.4	n.d.	0.1

Note: Rounding off prevents final adjustment of the sums

Source: 1850–2000: L. Prados de la Escosura and J. R. Rosés (2009): "The Sources of Long-Run Growth in Spain, 1850–2000", *Journal of Economic History*, 4; 2000–2015 own elaboration using OECD database < https://data.oecd.org/economy.htm#profile-Productivity >

temporal disaggregation, several features stand out. First, the contribution of capital increased from 0.6 percentage points in the first century to 1.2 points in the last half of the twentieth century. Second, the amount of labour had a positive and growing contribution until 1974, to become very negative between 1975 and 1986 and then recover. Third, the quality of labour has always had a positive contribution. Fourth, TFP made a significant but lesser contribution (21%) from 1850 to 1950, to become the main source of growth in the last half of the twentieth century, at around 57%.

All these results are very interesting. They show that the Spanish growth model, from 1850 to 2000, has been more based on TFP than one might think. Capital contribution was more important than labour's until 1950, but the latter surpassed the former from 1951 to 1974. After 1975 the contribution of labour seems to have evaporated. In fact, within the last quarter of the twentieth century it has followed opposite evolutions, as can be seen in panel B of the table.

The authors of the table we are commenting on provide, in fact, a little more temporal detail in panel B, thanks to which we can come closer to the periodization established in our book. Regarding the period 1840–1890, which in Table 12.3 is captured from 1850 to 1883, the growth comes from three sources of similar importance: 0.7, capital; 0.5 labour; and 0.6, TFP. We have dealt extensively with the role played by the three sources, but now we know their relative importance. From 1884 to 1920, during the first globalization—but including the first world war—growth was reduced and it was labour and TFP—not capital—that reduced its contribution the most. The contrast is very revealing and confirms the costs in terms of efficiency of the nationalist involution—voluntary or forced—that we have shown in our explanation, as well as the importance of emigration. In the 1920s, growth was almost three times higher and, in line with our interpretation, was explained by all the components in a fairly balanced way (1.6, labour; 1.1, capital; and 1.1, TFP). Between 1930 and 1952, covering the years of economic depression, those of the Civil War and those of autarky, growth was reduced to less than a quarter. It will be the only time, until the year 2000, that the TFP has a negative contribution, which should not surprise us in a context of destruction—the war—and in one of autarky—the economic inefficiency par excellence. Capital and labour contributed in a rather similar way to the extremely weak growth of that period. In the central years of import-substitution industrialization, growth takes off again and will originate, for a little more than half, from TFP (2.4 points of annual GDP growth out of a total of 4.7), as we have underlined at various times. Capital contributes 1.4 points of growth per year and labour 1.0, but it comes mainly—pay attention—from quality and not quantity. During the years of fast economic development (1959–1974), almost all the increase in growth was explained by the TFP (1.8 additional points of GDP growth out of a total of 2.2). In line with what we have underlined in our interpretation of the period, 4.2 points out of the total 6.9 annual increase in GDP are TFP contributions. The rest will be more work than capital, with the quality of work remaining relevant, even if the quantity is also important. During the time of the economic crisis and the transition to democracy, growth contracted to just over a third and its origin was completely transformed. The quantity of work represents a very negative contribution (-2.8). The quality of labour and capital each contribute around 1 percentage point, and TFP 3.4

points. Obviously, these calculations perfectly portray the enormous destruction of labour that occurred at the time and how this disaster was countered with the greatest contribution ever made by the TFP (136%). Note that the quality of the work will have its greatest moment of absolute relevance between 1953 and 1986. In the last period considered, which includes the integration into the EEC and the first stages of EMU, the situation changes completely. The highest growth can hardly be explained by TFP (0.2 percentage points—one of the lowest values in a century and a half), but it can be explained by labour (1.8 points, but almost all of it in quantity and very little in quality) and capital (1.6 points).

Panel C, drawn from sources not strictly comparable with the rest of the table because of the absence of differentiated estimates of the quality of work, draws a remarkably accurate picture of the disaster of the first fifteen years of the twenty-first century, those dominated by integration into the euro. Not only was GDP growth in the cycle as a whole the lowest since 1930–1952, but TFP fell, as it had done in the same period, thus sharing its exceptionality since 1850. The first eight years (2000–2007) behaved similarly to the previous period (1987–2000), which basically corresponds to the first cycle of European integration, but with a greater contribution from the amount of work and less from the TFP. TFP fell (sic!) by 0.2% per year. From 2008 to 2015, GDP collapsed, and even more—the double—the amount of labour, without this being compensated by TFP growth, unlike what happened in 1975–1986. In the first years of the twenty-first century as a whole, GDP growth has been almost exclusively due to capital increases. In fact, this increase has consisted primarily of an excessive increase in the stock of capital in housing and infrastructure. The labour factor has been wasted and no efficiency gains have been achieved, quite the contrary.

TFP advances and setbacks can come from very different factors. The most frequent explanatory factor is technological change, which can hardly be fully reflected in the contribution of capital. The other major explanatory factor is improved allocative efficiency, which can result from better functioning markets or greater national and international integration. Structural change is another component that must be taken into account because it can bring about great improvements in TFP when intersectoral productivity imbalances are large and can be balanced by factor movements (see Sect. 1). Finally, the State can improve TFP through public policies that contribute to growth, or it can become a fundamental obstacle. Throughout the book we have highlighted when one or the other dominated.

As far as we know, in the Spanish nineteenth century technological improvements were very significant (industrial machinery, railways, telegraph, steam navigation, etc.) but allocative efficiency was also significant. This consisted of more trade—growth of markets, with its necessary consequences in terms of specialization. The reforms of the liberal revolution were all in this direction, and the developments of the second half of the century expanded them. The brakes that were put on were of lesser importance and proof of this is the growing integration of the Spanish market, the increasing integration into the international economy, the multiplication of markets, the advance of urbanization and, in general, the benefits obtained from economic freedom that will lead to more productive specialization.

Spain not only took advantage of efficiency improvements, but also suffered from them. Indeed, some significant advances in allocative efficiency worldwide came at its expense. The losses of the Continental American Empire and the Insular American Empire, at the beginning and end of the nineteenth century, respectively, constituted improvements in allocative efficiency for the former colonies, for the new reference metropolis and for the whole world in general, except for Spain. To the extent that Spain had monopolistic relations with its colonies, their independence was the most efficient solution on a global scale. But, without a doubt, Spain came out as the loser. In addition to the direct costs of the wars and their liquidation, there were the indirect costs of moving to a full market and to an open economy system. As it has been seen with the transitions from real socialist economies to market economies, these costs are not insignificant. Spain had to adapt, painfully, to a new situation in which its national product was lower. We do not know to what extent the improvements in efficiency mentioned in the previous paragraph compensated for the losses in income. The impoverishment and loss of markets are mechanisms that reduce allocative efficiency for the country suffering them, and have negative dynamic effects that can be significant: liquidation of highly productive economic activities, regression in productive specialization, de-urbanization, etc.

During much of the twentieth century, at least during its first half, Spain's economic progress depended above all on technological improvements. These improvements occurred in almost all areas. Electrification, the incipient motorization, the revolution in modern medication (sulphonamides and antibiotics) were examples of new technologies whose adoption increased productivity. In contrast, allocative efficiency did not cease to suffer. The Spanish economy moved away from the international economy; regional specialization patterns were altered; in some periods, the degree of industrialization was reduced and agrarianization increased; many markets were fragmented. All this contributed to limiting growth. In addition, the government increasingly imposed its preferences in many fields even though they had very high opportunity costs.

It was in the central years of the 1950s that the TFP took on, for the first time, a major role in explaining Spain's economic growth. The relaxation of the interventionist and autarkic corset returned, to some extent, the economy to the pre-war equilibria. This set in motion inverse migratory movements to those that had been activated by the impoverishment of the previous period. It returns to the growth model of the 1920s, but with a more markedly nationalistic orientation. The accumulated backwardness will allow great improvements in productivity. For the years of the "economic miracle", from 1960 to 1973, the interpretation that has been given to the high contribution of the TFP to growth is the same as that given to Western Europe: it enjoyed an enormous potential for structural change, transferring assets that were not very productive in the agricultural sector to much more productive jobs in the industrial and service sectors; furthermore, it enjoyed open destinations for labour migration, within each country and in the Western European area, and enjoyed a growing commercial integration.

The decade of crisis (1975–1985) is more complex and more susceptible to conflicting interpretations. All agree on the strong negative contribution of labour to GDP growth and the positive contribution of physical capital, but there is no agreement on the role of TFP. For some authors, TFP growth explains all the growth in GDP—which was modest. For others, TFP explains the negative growth differential with the countries in the OECD area. In other words, TFP contributed a lot to the really existing growth, but was unable to avoid the divergence of the Spanish economy. The depressive tendencies of labour and capital were too strong.

Since integration into the EEC, the contribution of factors to economic growth has changed completely. Until the outbreak of the crisis in 2008, and for twenty years, the contribution of the quantity of work dominated, responding to the progressive flexibilization of the labour market by means of a wide range of contracts that were becoming increasingly worse in terms of labour protection. The contribution of capital continues to be important, reflecting the permanent relevance of technological change. On the other hand—and as far as we have comparable data—the contribution of the quality of work is reduced and the contribution of the TFP, which has been practically nil since the entrance into the EEC, sinks. This has given rise to strong criticism to the production model, highlighting the low growth achieved in labour productivity.

Indeed, where it is clearest that in recent years Spain is facing a problem of stagnation is in labour productivity. Only in the crisis years, the destruction of employment has allowed productivity to increase. The trend towards a deceleration in labour productivity growth preceded the entry into the euro. It begins around 1980, associated with the introduction of new labour regulations in the transition to democracy. In contrast, the greatest growth in labour productivity occurred between 1960 and 1980, when population movements from the countryside to the city, between sectors of activity and between regions were more intense. The reallocation of labour allowed for spectacular increases in productivity. Obviously, these increases had high costs of personal suffering. Democratisation meant that they did not have to be repeated if not under more favourable conditions.

1.3 Amount of Labour: Participation and Employment

The amount of labour depends on demographic developments, combined with the participation rate, the employment rate and the number of hours worked per person per year. Over the last two centuries the population has increased by a factor of just under four, and from 1850 to 2000 by less than three. L. Prados de la Escosura and J. R. Rosés have estimated the other variables (participation, employment and hours worked per person per year), showing the importance of the fall in the number of hours worked per worker, especially in the interwar period and during the transition to democracy. Overall, there has been a shift from a situation in which some 2800 hours were worked annually to one in which they barely reached 1800. Participation and employment rates have also varied greatly, but in a more cyclical manner.

As we have already seen, a good understanding of the contribution of labour requires a distinction between quantity and quality. Both are important and both appear to have been of similar importance in the long term. The evolution of labour quantity is represented quite accurately by the historical series on employment. Recent research has allowed both J. Maluquer de Motes and L. Prados de la Escosura to propose long series of this variable. J. Maluquer de Motes is more pessimistic about employment growth (in full-time equivalent units) than L. Prados de la Escosura, and seems more linear in his pre-Civil War assumptions. The discrepancy hides an intense debate, about how much work was being done in Spain before official labour statistics became reliable. There is much discussion about the contribution of female labour and child labour, especially about the former, which is under-represented in the population censuses. This under-representation surely affects manufacturing activity. Seasonal employment is also under-represented, probably crafts and service employment. On the other hand, agricultural employment has always been easier to observe and to record. To the extent that the problem lies in capturing part-time or seasonal employment, we are very dependent on the assumptions used. In Fig. 12.2, displaying the employment rate over the total population, the trajectory of J. Maluquer de Motes' series seems more sensitive to capture these phenomena of changing (declining) participation in productive activity, while that of L. Prados de la Escosura may be too stable.

In any case, it would seem that the discrepancies end in the 1960s. Who knows if this is true or not. The fact that official statistics have triumphed does not necessarily mean that they are more true today than a century ago. Do we record accurately work that does not pay social contributions or taxes? We would be naive to think that this widespread fraud is adequately covered in our series. In fact, much of the official statistics effort is directed at tracking the enormous mass of informal employment. Even with this caveat, Fig. 12.2 is shocking as the last half century is concerned. From just over 11 million full-time equivalent jobs in 1985 to nearly 20 million in 2008, the range of experiences between 1965 and 2017 is surprisingly varied. The minimum employment rates are in the order of 29% and the maximum in the order of 43%. Whichever way you look at it, both in time and space, compared to previous times or to other economies, so much variability is not normal. The Spanish economy and society have settled into a system that multiplies the impact of the economic cycle on employment. The amount of labour is the adjustment variable. It is undoubtedly the most socially painful way to match economy and society. It could not be borne were it not for the softening impact of the modern welfare State, with its unemployment benefits, early retirements and other compensatory formulas; without the traditional welfare State, which was the family, with the pensions of the elderly and the intergenerational help

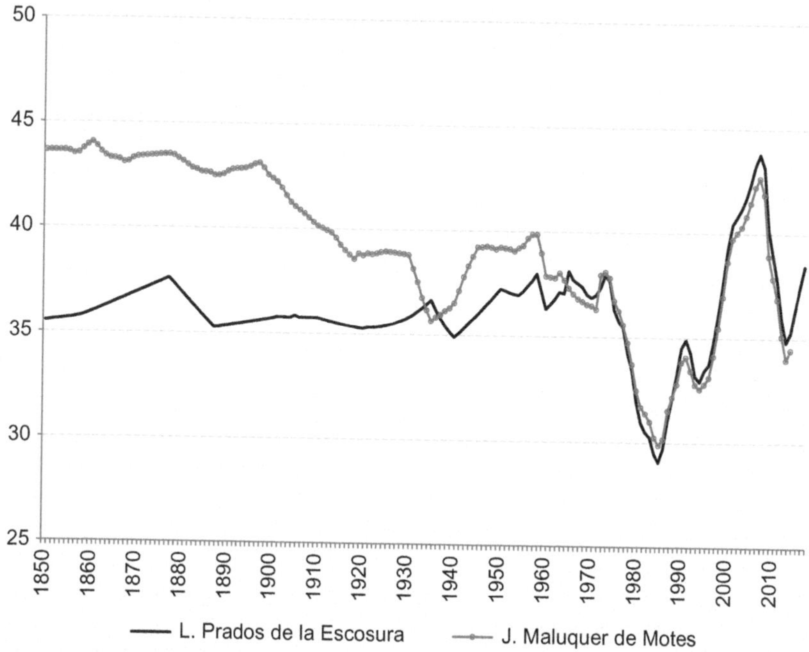

Fig. 12.2 Employment rate. Two estimates, 1850–2017 (in % on total population). *Sources*: L. Prados de la Escosura: Appendix, columns 1 and 2. The data are available, in their updated version, at https://espacioinvestiga.org/bbdd-chne/ ; J. Maluquer de Motes (2016): *España en la economía mundial. Series largas para la economia española (1850–2015)*, Madrid: Instituto de Estudios Económicos

in caring for the young and old, and without the absence of any State to correct permanent contractual and tax fraud on the part of employers and workers, widely consented by society at large. In other words: the data we present are the official image. But even if the reality is different, the official image is the one that counts to collect taxes and to compare Spain with other countries.

The structural under-utilisation (low participation rates) of the labour capacity of Spanish society can only be compared with that of other Latin societies, both in Europe and in the Americas. And in recent decades it has worsened with the high cyclicality of participation rates and employment. It is beyond the scope of this book to give a diagnosis of what is happening now and how it could be solved, but we cannot let the occasion pass to insist, as so many other economists and as we have already advanced in previous chapters, that the fierce duality of the labour market is at the root of these evils, and that few problems—if any—are more important than this for the future well-being of the inhabitants (citizens or not) of Spain. A labour system in which one part of society enjoys great protection while the other suffers from great lack of protection cannot be good and is not. All the incentives are badly placed. Neither the employers believe—invest—in their workers nor the workers in their employers. This is the basis of the economic model of low productivity and low remuneration in which Spain is installed.

1.4 Quality of Labour: Education

The skills are the economically relevant part of education. For many it is the least important. What would be important is the formation of individuals and citizens. We agree with the criterion and the concept, but neither in the Anglo-American world nor in the European do we ignore that good education usually solves both personal and social skills as well as labour and professional skills. To a large extent because they are all based on basic skills such as speaking, reading, writing, counting, socializing, empathizing, respecting, obeying, leading, cooperating and a long etcetera that ends up being indispensable, and often more than sufficient, for the great majority of labour and business trajectories. In addition, there is the strictly professional qualification, but that is hardly useful without all the above.

We have already seen, in Chap. 4, how much the absence of public expenditure on education in the nineteenth century had affected the schooling of Spanish children. Table 12.4 reminds us that illiteracy rates in Spain were still very high by 1850. At the same time when Spain had a 75% illiteracy rate, France had 42% and England 38%. It would be reduced progressively, at a very moderate speed at first—six percentage points from 1860 to 1875, five points from 1875 to 1890—which would then accelerate—seven points in the decade of 1890 and as many in that of 1900. By this time—in 1910, with a rate of 48%—England had already completely eradicated illiteracy, France had reduced it to 13% and Italy to 38%. In the following six decades it will continue to fall at a slower rate.

Just as important as the degree of literacy is the gender differential. Specialists have explained that it is the literacy level of the less literate sex that is important. The ability to change depends on it. In Spain, female

Table 12.4 Illiteracy rates, 1860–1990 (in percentage)

Years	*Total*	*Males*	*Females*	*GD*
1850	75			
1860	73	58	88	30
1875	67	53	81	28
1890	62	48	75	27
1900	55	43	67	24
1910	48	37	58	21
1920	39	30	47	17
1930	27	19	35	16
1940	23	17	29	12
1950	17	12	22	10
1960	13	8	18	10
1970	10	6	14	8
1980	7	4	10	6
1990	3			

Note: GD: gender illiteracy rate differential

Source: C. E. Núñez (1992); *La fuente de la riqueza. Educación y desarrollo económico en la España contemporánea*, Madrid, Alianza. For 1850 and 1990: G. Tortella (1994): *El desarrollo de la España contemporánea. Historia económica de los siglos XIX y* XX, Madrid, Alianza editorial

literacy has followed the progress of male literacy with a long delay. From C.E. Núñez's studies, it can be deduced that in Spain the problem of the gender differential was more pronounced in the southern regions, and could have represented a considerable brake on the possibilities of emigration that existed in the first globalization and in the 1920s.

The schooling deficit began to be corrected at the beginning of the twentieth century. It was not just a question of literacy, but of providing more years of schooling. It began to show results in the following decade and must have contributed to the progress of the Spanish economy in the 1920s and the first half of the 1930s. Similarly, the strong repression of school teachers during and after the Civil War decimated the Spanish teaching profession for many years. Schooling progressed slowly until sometime in the 1950s. Since then, education has once again attracted public resources and become a lever for growth. It will be more and more so. *A sensu contrario*, the great periods of divergence in Spain's GDP per capita are associated with periods of decline in schooling levels: between the 1880s and the outbreak of the First World War, and during the first Franco years. This relationship has yet to be studied and is certainly worthy of further attention. The data in Table 12.3 confirm these

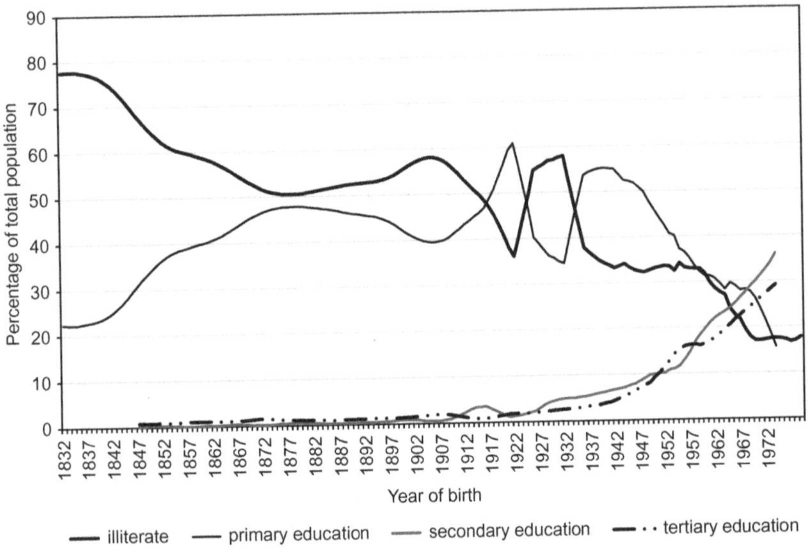

Fig. 12.3 Level of education of generations born between 1832 and 1979. *Source*: C.-E. Núñez (2005): "Educación", in A. Carreras and X. Tafunell (coords.): *Estadísticas históricas de España. Siglos XIX y XX*. Bilbao: Fundación BBVA, vol. I

diagnoses while underlining the strong dynamism of labour qualification between 1953 and 1986.

Figure 12.3, which describes the level of education of the generations born between 1832 and 1979, highlights some other significant features. The first is the reduction of the illiterate population—and the parallel advance of the one with primary education—in the first forty years of the new liberal regime. But it also shows how this progress stagnated and even reversed between the mid-1870s and the beginning of the twentieth century—the era of the Restoration. The generations that did not manage to improve their educational level were the ones that were sacrificed the most due to the lack of resources of the State and the administrations that used to provide elementary education—the municipalities and the parishes. During the following twenty years, this educational stagnation was vigorously corrected. The renewal was short-lived. The succession of economic crisis, war and autarky will generate a new generation less educated than the previous one. Two great steps back in three generations is a very heavy burden. Spanish society was only freed from this burden by the generations born in the 1950s. From then on, the educational levels accumulated after twenty years did not stop increasing. Higher education levels—those who completed their secondary education and university education—increased somewhat earlier.

A synthetic indicator of human capital is always difficult to calculate, and there is a dilemma between the following two options. One is to measure years of schooling, assuming that the longer the schooling, the greater the economic return obtained (hence the concept of human "capital"), which is statistically true. The other option is to measure income differentials—particularly wage differentials, assuming that economic returns to work are the best possible indicators of available human capital. Both strategies are complex in terms of measurement, and both are worth the attention. For a long term perspective, the best available series corresponds to the years of schooling of the adult population, as a "proxy" for human capital. It is a "stock" magnitude, since it does not distinguish by cohorts or generations but always considers the whole population. The series shows that from the start of the series in 1897 to 1949 human capital has grown little: 0.2% per year—just over half a year. The periods of improvement have been reversed twice, long enough to sterilize previous progress. It was only after 1949 that growth began to take place, and it will continue uninterrupted. Leaving aside the discontinuity of the series, the growth from 1949 to 2013 has been very constant, at an annual rate of 1.4%—seven years of schooling. According to the estimates of L. Prados de la Escosura and J.R. Rosés for 1850–2000, underlying their estimate of the quality of work in Table 12.3, the measurement via income differences, better to assess changing economic conditions, displays a greater rise in the interwar period, a more intense fall during the early Francoism, a more pronounced dynamism from the mid-fifties to the beginning of the nineties and a worrying stagnation until the year 2000. All this without fundamental differences in the underlying trends. These authors also evaluate that from 1850 to the beginning of the twentieth century human capital grows very slowly, in coherence with what Fig. 12.3 displays.

2 Performance of Economic Policies

As commercial policy, fiscal policy and monetary policy have been a central part in all the previous chapters, we provide a short review of their main features and highlights, always in reference to already presented figures.

2.1 Economic Internationalization—Foreign Accounts Balance

The reader will have noticed that the authors are firmly convinced that foreign trade has been a lever of contemporary Spanish economic growth. We have paid a lot of importance to changes in commercial policy up to the point of being a substantial part of the definition of the historical stages of Modern Spain. The naming of the chapters, and their chronology, stand for the economic relationship of Spain with the rest of the world and with the policies deployed on this issue. The openness series (value of foreign trade divided by GDP, see Chap. 3, Fig. 3.1) shows unequivocally that the best times for the Spanish economy are always linked to increases in the degree of openness. There may be chronologically limited exceptions. The prosperity of the 1920s, to take the most prominent example, was not linked to increased openness. In general, in times of peace, the opening up of trade has had very beneficial effects on the growth of the Spanish economy. Less obvious is her relative degree of openness.

Figure 3.2 on the degree of trade openness of Spain in relation to the EU-15 countries suggests that the period of trade liberalization from 1850 to 1880 was, in European terms, normal: all of Europe tended to open up simultaneously and in the same proportion. Surprisingly, from 1880 to 1900 Spain tended to open more (or rather, to close less) than its current European partners. This dissonance can be explained by the Spanish delay—one decade—in assuming and applying protectionist policies, and by the permanence—one more decade—of the export dynamism. During the first third of the twentieth century there were ups and downs. Spain was more closed than the average, but it did not became more closed. The protectionist shift was not as important as it has been used to assert. The real historical change was that of autarky. With such an objective—autarky—, it is not surprising that the degree of openness with respect to the rest of Western Europe collapsed. Autarky, with its more (1945–1947) and less (1951–1953) lasted until the economic liberalization turn of 1959. The Stabilization Plan and the new tariff brought Spain back to the relative levels of openness of before the Civil War. And it remained there for two decades, until, once in democracy, it made sustained efforts to open up commercially. Integration into the European Union has eased the way and has ended up generating a degree of trade openness similar, in relation to the European Union average, to that of the degree of convergence of per capita GDP.

In a very long-term assessment it is inevitable to refer to the role that real terms of trade (RToT), which reflect the purchasing power of exports measured as the price index of exports divided by the price index of imports, may have played. The growth or decline of many countries is inextricably linked to the trajectory of their RToT. No discussion of Latin American economic development can escape the hypothesis of declining RToT. For Spain, it was L. Prados de la Escosura who first estimated very long-term RToT with Great Britain and the United Kingdom, and who discovered the positive importance of these from the end of the eighteenth century to the third quarter of the nineteenth century. In Fig. 2.1 we also reproduce the longest and most homogeneous series currently available of Spain's real net terms of trade with rest of the world, from 1816 to 2017, and we superimpose on it the one available for the relationship between Spain and Great Britain, from 1784 to 1913. This captures the great dynamism of the first fifteen years of the nineteenth century, which we have already highlighted in Chap. 2.5. For its part, the series compiled by A. Tena, and which we have updated, documents the notable dynamism of the RToT from the beginning of the series in 1816 to the 1840s and, after a decline in the following quarter of a century, its strong growth in the 1870s culminating in a secular high in 1877. From then until the First World War the trend is downward, returning to the levels of the 1830s and 1850s. The Great War will be a positive but transitory shock for the RToT. The beneficial effects of the war will disappear in 1922, when the RToT will collapse, and will remain very low for the rest of the decade, returning to the levels of more than a century before. After the Civil War, for which we lack data, the Second World War will again be a period of very high RToT—so much so that we have chosen not to reproduce the 1942 value (345.9), because it was too high. As we have explained in Chap. 6, these exceptional values were hardly used because of Franco's commitments with Hitler. With the return to normality, Spain's RToT collapsed and reached a new historic low—below the 1816 value—between 1951 and 1956. After a brief recovery up to 1959, the declining trend that had been pointed out after the end of the Second World War resumed with ups and downs, reaching new historic lows in the 1980s, in this case due mainly to the explosion in oil prices, an essential commodity that was entirely imported and reached historic highs (see Chap. 9). The lowest point in the series happened in 1984. The fall in oil prices in 1986 and the simultaneous incorporation into the EEC will be a positive stimulus for Spain's RToT because it will significantly lower the price of imports.

The progressive trade liberalization subsequent to European integration, which coincides with rounds of trade liberalization worldwide, further lowers the cost of imports to a relative maximum of the RToT in 1993 (see Chap. 10). From then until 2017, in the period dominated by the second globalization, with an international environment dominated by stable trade regulations, the RToT remains largely unchanged. Overall, we can detect an upward trend until 1877, a downward trend until 1983—punctuated by the brief and intense upsurges of the two World Wars—and a thoughtful recovery and stability thereafter around the levels of two centuries earlier.

Figure 11.2 on the current account balance alerts us of Spain's extreme vulnerability due to its dependence on external financing. The endemic deficit on the external account of goods, services, transfers and income—with few exceptions at times of sharp contractionary adjustment—is a worrying structural weakness of the Spanish economy. Its growth is always associated with greater exposure—also in the sense of risk—to short-term international capital movements. This has been a painful experience during the worst moments of the euro crisis. In Chap. 11 we attach importance to very recent progress in the competitive capacity of exports, which is an encouraging trend although we fear that it is too fragile and too insufficient in view of the degree of net foreign indebtedness of the Spanish economy. Returning to previous periods in which the external sector has had to restructure completely, as happened with the loss of the American continental empire, it is worth remembering how complicated and slow the process of readapting domestic supply to the new opportunities of world markets has been. It is not that the change has not been made, but it takes a long time and the impoverishment suffered while the traditional sources of competitiveness are extinguished and new ones appear can be important. Nor can we forget that when the current account suffers, the external financial position suffers even more, causing maximum vulnerability. This is a challenge of the utmost importance for the entire Spanish economy and for future well-being. Fig. 4.3, on the Spanish risk premium, displays some of these moments. They have been at the core of the problems surveyed in Chaps. 2, 3, 4 and 5 and again in Chaps. 8, 9, 10 and 11. When they were not it was simply because data was not recorded because financial repression was at its highest. The evolution of the risk premium provides a bridge to the next issue.

2.2 The Role of the State—Public Accounts Balance

We will now consider the role of the State in the allocation of resources. Has its contribution to economic growth been positive or negative? We will first consider Government expenditure. Table 12.2 shows the evolution of public consumption in relation to GDP. We would have to add public investment to obtain the public expenditure.

For more than a century, from 1850 until well into the 1970s, central government spending—which until the last third of the twentieth century was the bulk of public spending—has been very stable at around 10% of GDP. There are exceptions, but they are linked to the mobilisation for war. We will have to wait until about 1976 to detect a powerful change with a strongly upward trend. If we were to consider all public administrations, we would note that the change in trend dates back to 1967, related to the first stages of Social Security (always considered a separate administration) and to the incipient deployment of the Welfare State. The Spanish government, first, and all public administrations, later, have weighed discreetly on the Spanish economy until the last third of the twentieth century. The transfers to the newly created (1978) Autonomous Communities had two high points: the educational ones, since the beginning of the autonomic system, in 1980, and the health ones, generalized since around the year 2000. Both "tempos" are related to the delay in the deployment of welfare policies by the government. While during Franco's regime, the educational expenditure, which was reduced during the two autarkic decades, grew strongly since 1960, the health expenditure, which was very insignificant, exploded later, from 1973.

Thanks to S. Espuelas we have summarized the expenses of a social nature, such as health, pensions, unemployment benefits and support for old age dependent people, extending them to the most recent date and also including those of the other public administrations in Fig. 9.3 on public social expenditure. The main novelty, beyond confirming the great delay in the emergence of the Welfare State in post-war Spain, is the strongly countercyclical nature of public social spending as it has been deployed and consolidated. This is something worth emphasising because it corresponds to what should be expected of public social spending—to cushion the falls in income of those who suffer the most in the event of economic crisis—but may not coincide with what the population feels has happened. Indeed, public social expenditure does not always provide for all those who consider themselves creditors of the same, in the unit amount—per person—, which may well be reduced even if the proportion of the collective effort has increased a lot.

As we have already commented on several occasions, the liberal Treasury suffered from a lack of resources. That is what can be seen in Fig. 3.3, which compares the deficit (budget balance) with the non-financial resources of the State. It turns out that there have been four major moments of deficit generation. The first corresponds to the 1860s and the first years of the following decade. It combines the high expenses of the military adventures during the reign of Isabel II with the abolition of consumption taxes following the Glorious Revolution in 1868. The Restoration (1874–1922) would be a period of considerable budgetary order. The exception is the Cuban war which, let us remember, did not initially burden the peninsula's budget but the Cuban one. The control of the deficit will be broken with the next colonial war, that of Morocco. Although it coincides temporarily with the European war, and this helps to keep military mobilisation high, the fact is that public money was spent, abundantly and for some fifteen years, on the Moroccan adventure. After the budgetary adjustment of Primo's dictatorship, and leaving aside the period of the Civil War for lack of data (not for lack of evidence: there is no doubt that much more was spent than the non-financial resources obtained), the deficits come back with the military mobilisation during the Second World War, which coincides with the panic of the Franco regime in the face of the possible foreign invasion and the threat of the Republican guerrillas. Once these dangers were eliminated, a long period of budgetary stability ensued. It will break down with democracy and the construction of the Welfare State, between the middle of the 1970s and the middle of the 1980s, to rebound strongly in the 1990s. It slows down in the first years of the twenty-first century, managing to provide three exceptional years of budget surplus (2005–2007). This was followed by the descent into the *inferno* of the financial crisis, which brought about a historic negative peak (-93.7%: the State's deficit was roughly equivalent to its revenue, i.e., half of its expenditure).

Nevertheless, with the exception of the exceptional episode of 2008–2012, the negative balances have been more modest proportions of non-financial resources than they had been in the first century of the series. By contrast, in terms of GDP (see Fig. 11.4), negative balances have reached historically high levels in the mid-1980s, in the mid-1990s and particularly since 2008, when they have surpassed year after year the peaks recorded since 1850.

Figure 3.3 also compares government deficits with debt burdens (amortization and interest payments). At first, we will contrast it with government expenditure, keeping a close eye on the profile of the public deficit (see Fig. 11.4). The dissonance between deficits and debt can be very surprising. Leaving aside the liquidation of the mass of debt accumulated before 1850, the figure fits very well the great episode of deficit centred in the *Sexenio* (1868-1874) with the unbridled accumulation of debt. Let no one be fooled: the amounts of new debt incurred have nothing to do with the income obtained by the Treasury. The government's credit was then so low that, in the worst moments of the *Sexenio* it became necessary to accept debts for amounts ten times higher than the liquid amounts obtained. As can be seen, the debt burden was substantially reduced in the early 1870s. It will be simply because the government will default. Shortly afterwards, in the early 1880s, there is a moderate reduction in the burden. This is Camacho's (the Treasury minister) "conversion" (i.e., another default). After a few years of bonanza, the Exchequer will go back into debt when the Cuban war is liquidated. There are no deficits, but when the war ends in defeat, Spain must recognize and settle the debt of its colonial administration, which is tantamount to making clear the costs of war. The following years of surplus will allow for a considerable reduction of the debt burden. Then we have the paradox that the high deficits accumulated during the Moroccan war have no effect on debt service. The Treasury has had extensive recourse to the issuance of pledged debt—a very inflationary procedure. We are in the years of the First World War, and the high inflation of those years was of little concern in a context of much higher inflation. Inflation ended up working like a special tax on debt. The same thing happened during the Second World War and well into the following decade with a deficit originating in military spending. The deficits of democracy appear to be not very dangerous from this point of view. In general, the tendency is to reduce the impact of the debt incurred. It is interesting to note the sharp rise in the debt burden in 1996-1998. This is due to the extraordinary debt repayments made by the government to comply with one of the conditions of the Maastricht treaty—that public debt should not exceed 60% of GDP. The privatizations of public enterprises carried out in those years mainly served to pay off debt. Even so, the large deficits and indebtedness will make it inevitable that the debt burden will systematically represent high proportions of non-financial expenditure.

The picture is similar when looking at the debt-to-GDP ratio (Fig. 4.2). Here again, the debt of the *Sexenio* is an all-time high (since 1850). It amounts to about 170% of GDP. During the Cuban war it will already be less than 130%. After the Civil War the level will be 70%. At the end of Franco's regime it had fallen to just over 10%. The inflation of the twentieth century has ended up reducing the burden of public debt. The holders of the debt—individuals or financial institutions—have had to contribute to the public coffers in this way. The inflation of 1914-1920 and the one that starts in 1936, to last until the launching of the Euro, are both taxes on debt holders. This is a feature that is by no means exclusive to Spain. Warlike inflation was common in all the countries around us, as well as moderate inflation after the Second World War. In fact, as we pointed out in the first chapter, Spain has not suffered any hyperinflation or anything like it. The comparison of the Spanish CPI with that of all the countries currently members of the European Union leaves no room for doubt. Spain was much less inflationary than its European neighbours both during (and after) the First World War and during (and after) the Second World War. Only after the period of post-war reconstruction can one speak of a differential inflation trend—with respect to the countries that will form the EU—being positive.

Since the beginning of the transition to democracy, public indebtment has been more the rule than the exception, in logical consequence of the behaviour of the public deficit. Only between 1998 and 2007 has there been a sustained period of debt reduction, shorter and less intense than that which occurred one century before from the Fernández Villaverde reform to the war in Morocco. Despite the massive nature of recent public debt, it should be stressed that before 2020 it has not reached, by any means, the maximum levels relative to GDP of the second half of the nineteenth century, although it has far exceeded the minimum levels, which were high (60%).

2.3 *Monetary Policy and the Management of the Exchange Rate*

As we have explained in Chap. 1.5, on the long-term evolution of money and prices, in the economic relationship with the rest of the world, not only trade policy counts but also, and very much so, exchange rate policy. Fig. 1.7 on the peseta nominal effective exchange rate compared with most developed countries was a good case in point. Going a step further it is possible to estimate the real effective exchange rate (REER) of the peseta with respect to the most developed countries (effective, by taking into account the weight of the different trading partners; real, by discounting differential inflation). The REER is an approximation of the purchasing power parity exchange rate. The result, visible in Fig. 6.7, is striking. From the creation of the peseta in 1868 until shortly before its disappearance, the trend in the real effective exchange rate has been substantially stable. However, the anomaly of the years from the Civil War to the mid-1950s stands out strongly. Since the outbreak of the war, the policy of the new regime had been to permanently strengthen the exchange rate of the peseta, and this led to a de facto appreciation that was simply exceptional. The apex of the appreciation movement occurred between 1947 and 1949, when the peseta was worth about two and a half times more than it should be. From that moment on, the silent reformism of the Franco regime began to take effect, consisting of correcting the most extreme interventions with another set of interventions. It will be the system of multiple changes, which will hide a true devaluation of the peseta. Note, however, that several interventions will be necessary to bring the peseta down to its true market value: 1949, 1951, 1957 and, the least important, 1959. The significance of 1959 lies in the fact that it means the complete acceptance of convertibility.

The real effective exchange rates ratify the impression that the degree of openness gave us: the exceptional moment of the relationship of the Spanish economy with the rest of the world was during the first years of Franco's regime. It is also worth noting that a tendency towards appreciation already existed since the early 1880s. It is interesting to insist on this point, as it is usually associated with the decision to abandon, de facto, the gold standard. In the light of Fig. 6.7, it can be considered that the Spanish monetary authorities tended to set a rather contractive monetary policy until 1936, which tended, decade after decade, to make the competitive position of the Spanish economy moderately more difficult. Undoubtedly, the high level of public debt (see Sect. 4.5 and the preceding Sect. 12.2.2) must have conditioned this contractive trend.

Let's come back to the risk premium (Fig. 4.3) to provide some final comments on monetary policy. For countries building large public debts, its cost is an essential financial issue, and the most crucial for its central bank. The long-term view on the Spanish risk premium displays perfectly well two critical junctures. The building of huge public indebtment in the late eighteen sixties and early eighteen seventies sent the risk premium to a historical maximum within yearly recorded financial history. It is very likely that higher marks were reached before 1850, as Chap. 2 suggests repeatedly for 1790-1840. At that critical point, in 1874, is when the Bank of Spain was given its monetary issuing monopoly at a very high price (see Chap. 3). The Figure does not provide data for the years when no risk premium was recorded as the whole Spanish money market was completely repressed (see Chaps. 6 and 7). Setting this undocumented period aside, the most turbulent risk premium years were those covered by Chaps. 9 and 10, between the establishment of a modern welfare State and the entry into the Economic and Monetary Union. Even with yearly data risk premium suffered many ups and downs. Let's think of daily data! The appeasement of the Euro years is simply spectacular, and strongly underlined by the Euro crisis that reached its critical point in 2012. The turbulent years were the last ones with the Bank of Spain in charge of the monetary policy. The appeasement years—with 2010-2013 exception, were those of the European Central Bank in charge.

3 The Outcome: Changing Inequalities

The deployment of policies aimed at macroeconomic stability, combined with structural reforms in the goods, services and factor markets, conditions economic growth and defines the patterns of distribution of its benefits. This perspective, which has always been present in sociological and political studies, was not very present in economic studies.

There are four elements that have captured the attention towards the inequality perspective. First, there is a widespread understanding that inequality worsens growth and well-being, both objective and subjective. Second, that globalization and, above all, the ongoing technological revolution have generated sharp increases in inequality. This is an ambivalent phenomenon, because inequality between countries—inequality on a global scale—has been greatly reduced. The enrichment of the large countries that were poor—China and India—has greatly reduced inequality on a global scale. But technological and business changes, combined with the spread of economic liberalism as a source of inspiration for public policy (even in communist China), have led to spectacular enrichment and impoverishment of entire strata of the population. Inequality in each country has increased dramatically. Thirdly, the great economic crisis, especially the crisis of the euro and the austerity policies that many countries on the periphery of the eurozone—such as Spain—have had to adopt, has generated a visible impoverishment and has given rise to a very lively debate, with political consequences, on inequality. Fourthly, some new and attractive academic narrative has appeared, expressed in T. Piketty and his *The Capital in the twenty-first Century* and *Capital and Ideology* that have fascinated both locals and outsiders, opening up the debate on long-term trends in inequality.

We do not want to finish our assessment of the two centuries without referring to what we know about inequality. We will refer to a few indicators of personal income distribution while exploring the main components of income distribution.

The great novelty in the studies of inequality is the series by L. Prados de la Escosura, which we represent below and which constitutes a great effort of statistical ingenuity (in sources and methods). The author measures inequality by means of a Gini coefficient, using data and estimates on property and its distribution and on wages and their distribution. The greater the weight of property and its income, the higher the coefficient. The smaller the weight, the lower the coefficient, or, in other words, the higher the weight of wages, the lower the coefficient. As of 1995, the estimate is the official one from Eurostat.

Unlike the vast majority of materials—tables and figures—that we reproduce in this book, this one is still under discussion. Why? Because of the peak in 1953 and what it implies about the evolution of inequality during the early Francoism. There is consensus on the trend towards increasing inequality in household income, as measured by the Gini coefficient, from the mid-1860s (the low is 1864) to the end of the First World War (the high is 1918). The fall in inequality in the migration-intensive years (see Sect. 4.1) fits in with theoretical predictions that the first globalization favoured, through migration, the remuneration of factors that were initially more abundant and less well paid. Even so, the general trend up to 1918 reflects the rise in non-wage income relative to wages, as suggested by the peaks of inequality coinciding with (capital-intensive) investment booms. As we have explained in Chap. 5, the First World War represented a real change of trend. The war deteriorated wage income, and multiplied profits. From 1917 onwards, labour was mobilised, strikes began, the negotiating capacity of the workers improved, and in a few years they regained purchasing power. Although the Primo de Rivera dictatorship stopped this trend, it did not completely reverse it. When the Second Republic arrived, and in spite of the great international depression, the position of wages in the national income improved again, and inequality was notably reduced. It should come as no surprise that inequality reached a minimum in 1936, when it returned to fin-de-siècle levels.

The subsequent trajectory, up to about 1980, raises questions for us. All the evidence we have (see Chap. 6) is that in the post-civil war period there was a redistribution of income against wage earners. A different issue is that we do not have the right measuring instruments. According to M. Vilar, the post-civil war period constitutes a period of sustained increase in inequality between benefits and wages. It begins with the collapse of real wages after the Civil War (see Fig. 6.1), which intensifies until 1951, during the height of autarchy (see Chap. 6), falling to between 40% and 50% of the pre-war real level. The recovery of real wages would not begin until after 1951, in parallel with the first flexibilization of the autarkic model, with the highlight of 1956, when the impact of the "gironazo"—the strong wage increase approved by Franco at the request of the Minister of Labour, Girón de Velasco—took place. M. Vilar's series is not fully comparable with that of L. Prados de la Escosura, but it fits better to what we know. After 1959, salaries recovered their weight in the national income simply because income grew through the massive absorption of work from rural activities—of low yield even if they were not wage-earning—moving towards urban activities, always better paid even if they were wage-earning. We assume than there must have been a continuous reduction in inequality from 1959 to 1974, reversing part of the path taken during the early Franco regime. As we have stressed in Chap. 9, the years of economic crisis and transition to democracy, between 1974 and 1980, meant a significant reduction in inequality. The series in Fig. 12.4 reflects this change, but extended between 1971 and 1983. From then on the trajectory of this figure is undisputed. It shows that inequality has fluctuated, in the years of democratic rule, around historically low levels (although high compared to the European environment). The range of the Gini coefficient has moved between 0.30 and 0.35, with a minimum before entering the EEC, and a maximum after full trade integration. The oscillation has been repeated, with minimums around 2002, and maximums at the end of the series, in 2016. This means that, within the narrow margins of inequality fluctuation, it has increased both in the years of the bubble and in the years of the depression and in the recovery of recent years. This decoupling from the cycle is worrying. It has often been said that inequality is mainly determined by unemployment, but this does not seem to be the case in recent experience: it has grown during the bubble because the highest incomes must have grown much more than the lowest; it has grown during the crisis because of rising unemployment, even if business incomes fell, and it has grown in the recovery because there has been internal devaluation—the fall in real wages.

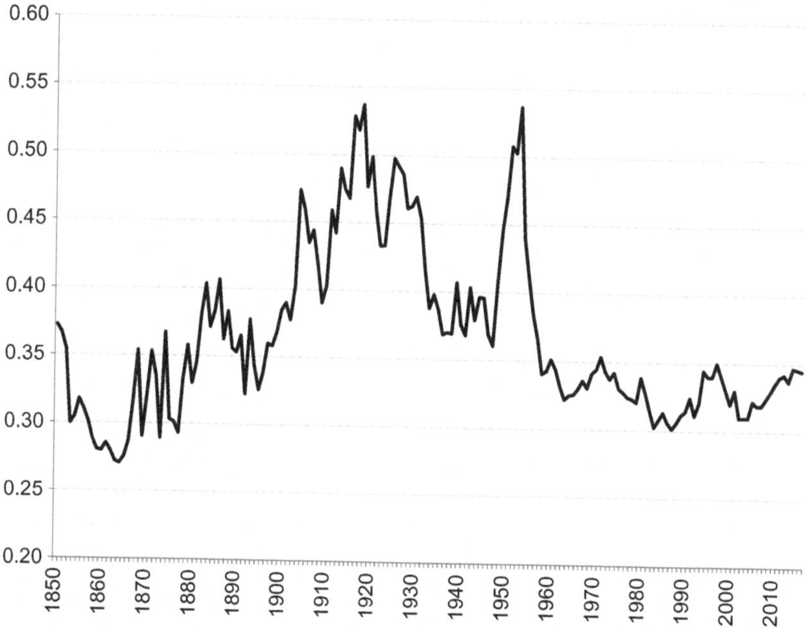

Fig. 12.4 Income distribution. Gini coefficient, 1850–2016. *Sources*: 1850–1995: L. Prados de la Escosura (2008): "Inequality, poverty and the Kuznets curve in Spain, 1850–2000", *European Review of Economic History* (12). We thank the author for his kindness in providing us with the data. For 1995–2016 data comes from EUROSTAT: http://ec.europa.eu/eurostat/data/database

For what we have explained, in the consideration of income distribution, business profits are very relevant. We have an indicator that can enlighten us on the behaviour of business profitability.

Figure 12.5 displays the evolution of corporate profitability (ROE-return on equity) from 1880 to 2017. There we see that around 1918 there was a maximum of business profitability, and around 1937 a minimum, which is consistent with the inequality index of L. Prados de la Escosura and with the real wages of M. Vilar. The other peaks before the Great War are also consistent with Fig. 12.4 as they correspond with the peaks in investment booms. With the end of the Civil War there was a strong recovery of profitability, particularly vigorous until 1945, and which extended until 1958. This profile seems very reasonable to us (and very different from the profile of Fig. 12.4 for those same years). We

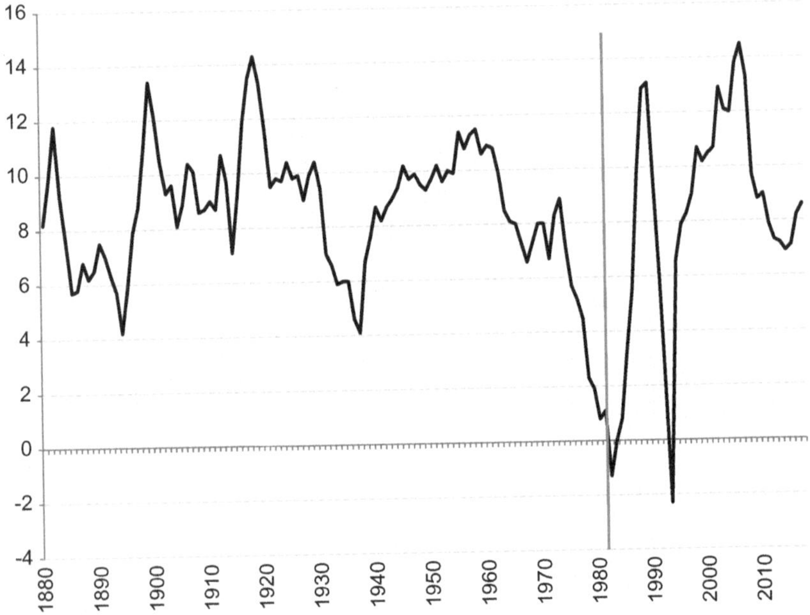

Fig. 12.5 Financial profitability (ROE) of the Spanish companies, 1880–2017 (in %). *Note*: We mark with a vertical line the change of sources between 1981 and 1982. *Sources*: Appendix, column 24

coincide with 1958 as a moment of change in the trend. The stabilization of 1959 and the trade liberalization will be a blow to existing Spanish capitalism, which will have to conform with lower rates of return in exchange for being able to significantly increase the volume of GDP and capital with which it can work. Profitability falls but profits increase. Spain is entering, albeit through the back door, the Europe of the golden age, characterised, among other things, by this trade-off between capital and labour.

A greater regulation of Spanish capitalism will allow the recovery of the rate of profit between 1967 and 1973. These were the years of "development planning". But what happens after 1973? The greatest collapse ever experienced by Spanish companies. As we explain in Chap. 9, the combination of economic crisis and political transition was lethal for business interests. Once democracy is consolidated and Spain joins the EEC, business profitability will be high, with the exception of the spectacular fall in 1993—a brief but intense crisis. The depression that begins in 2008 punishes profitability, but it seems that less than in other periods.

Collective action remains outside our interpretative chapter, but we believe we have contributed to a better understanding of the economic context in which it is deployed. We have concluded with a summary review of the evolution of income distribution in modern Spain. The treatment has been brief because it was not the central focus of the book and because there is not enough research to support factual and interpretative consensus. But we have ended up with inequality because it summarizes the great results and challenges of growth and public policies, in that space of collective action that is always more tense: the distribution of its fruits.

4 To Sum Up

In the foreword we state that the purpose of this work has been the study of economic growth and the factors that drive it, from a comparative perspective. The convergence or divergence of the Spanish economy with that of Western Europe has been our measurement standard. We have not neglected to consider other standards of comparison—the whole world or alternative measures of GDP such as the Human Development Index—which provide a much more rosy picture of Spain's comparative economic performance over the past two centuries. Between the Empire and globalization, the Spanish economy has performed better than the world as a whole, almost always well above the global average, and now more than twice as good. In terms of HDI, it has fully converged throughout the twentieth century with the most developed countries. Compared to Western Europe, it is where it was a disappointment as well as a reminder of the great benefits of dominance over a large empire. If we close the angle of observation to the last generations, the convergence has been spectacular in each of the last three. Indeed, the beneficial impact of open trade policies and of neighbourhood and integration into European institutions has produced one of the few undisputed global economic successes of the second half of the twentieth century.

In this last chapter we have taken up again growth analysis focusing the attention on structural change, contribution of the productive factors—especially, labour, both in quantity and in quality—as well as total factor productivity. These are the drivers of growth. We have made it clear that the more analytical view on the sources of productivity growth fits perfectly with the historical stages outlined throughout the book.

We have not yet reminded, although it appears continually in the background of our explanations, what has been the influence of the forces that alter the allocation of resources. These are crucial to understand the hard core of economic growth, the one that sustains improving levels of well-being: total factor productivity. Let us recall that in Chaps. 2 and 3 we devoted much space to the institutional and legislative changes—the liberal revolution—that completely changed the regulation of the markets for goods and productive factors (land, labour and capital) and the definition of major public policies. All were the consequence of the double revolution that inaugurated the contemporary age: the French Revolution and the Industrial Revolution. In the case of Spain, both movements resulted in a major consequence: the loss of the Empire, with all that it represented of privileges of all kinds. The revolutionary democratic ideals and the change of economic leadership, together with a change of economic model, inaugurated a new era, for which Spain was badly positioned. The reactions to adapt to the new situation were painful and slow. These changes, particularly intense in the period covered by Chap. 2 and the first decades of Chap. 3, shaped an institutional framework and public policies that remained stable for three or four generations to come, until the Civil War. Although they were conducive to the development of a flourishing capitalist economy, they did not prevent a continuous trend of economic divergence from Western Europe (but not from the world as a whole). The First World War—a completely exogenous phenomenon for Spain—altered many economic and social balances, giving rise to structural and regional changes that would modify the trajectory of the Spanish economy and society. A little less than a generation later, during the Second Republic, major institutional changes were reconsidered that aimed to correct some of those made during the liberal revolution. The reactions to these reformist policies were very intense. General Franco's *coup d'état* was carried out by combining diverse but converging interests in their profound discontent with the Second Republic and their outright rejection of the policies promoted by the Popular Front government. In doing so, the established institutional arrangements of the previous generations were turned upside down.

Indeed, since the First World War the Spanish economy has been exposed to a succession of political and regulatory impacts. The search for balance in the allocation of resources and the definition of public policies played a leading role in the temporal course of the Spanish economy until it joined the European Union. In all periods, institutional reforms were implemented that had a significant influence on the allocation of productive resources. In all of them, economic policy was reformulated in such a way that it had an undoubted allocative and distributive impact. We have also defined each chapter around these defining elements, providing a history of institutional change and regulation of goods and factor markets. It ranges from the break-up of the liberal pro market arrangements of the first third of the twentieth century to the radical autarchism of the 1940s, back to cautiously open markets and to the globalization of the first two decades of the twenty-first century. We have witnessed the disasters of the complete closure of the Spanish economy, the costs paid for unwise intervention in the era of developmentalism and the transition to democracy and, finally, the cost of too cheerful monetary integration in the Economic and Monetary Union.

When we define the periods, the characterizing elements are the great public policies. We have given interpretative priority to trade policy and, in general, to the opening up of the Spanish economy. The series linked to the degree of internationalization are a backbone of the book because they are a backbone of the evolution of the contemporary Spanish economy. Trade closure has tended to be a factor in curbing growth, while openness has promoted it. The other major public policy that has conditioned Spanish economic development is also a backbone: fiscal policy. It has usually limited the provision of public goods and services. But, underlying its failures in this field, the crucial thing about fiscal policy has been its recurrent tendency to incur into serious imbalances, which have generated large deficits and unmanageable debts. The relationship between the imbalances in the external accounts and those in the public accounts—what in macroeconomics is known as the "twin deficit"—constitutes the temporal nerve of the story we have explained. It was so during the period of the Old Regime crisis and it has been so during the stage of integration into the Eurozone, and in all the intermediate stages, without exception, always forcing controversial institutional changes. This is why monetary policy characterizes so well the stages of the Spanish economy and its greater or lesser success seen from the perspective of economic management—of economic policy. The struggle for stability in the foreign accounts, in the public accounts and in the exchange rates has been the calvary for most of the economic leaders of the Spanish governments and the bell of glory for a few. How much growth has been able to bring stability and how much stability, growth, is and will be an inexhaustible source of interest, and mobilises many more than economists. Politicians, jurists, businessmen, civil servants, scientists, workers or peasants, urban or rural, capital or peripheral, and with their very varied political and ideological orientations, they shape the balance between the trajectory of stability and the trajectory of growth.

Bibliographical Orientation

The sources of growth for a century and a half have been established by L. Prados de la Escosura and J. R. Rosés (2009): "The Sources of Long-Run Growth in Spain 1850–2000", *Journal of Economic History*, 69, 4. The stagnation of productivity is very present in L. Prados de la Escosura (2017): *Spanish Economic Growth 1850–2015*, London: Palgrave/Macmillan. On work and occupation we must refer to M. Llonch and J. Maluquer de Motes (2005): "Trabajo y relaciones laborales", in A. Carreras and X. Tafunell (coords.): *Estadísticas históricas de España. Siglos XIX y XX*, Bilbao: Fundación BBVA, III, and J. Maluquer de Motes (2016): *España en la economía mundial. Series largas para la economía española (1850–2015)*, Madrid: Instituto de Estudios Económicos. The criticism of the under-recording of female activity is summarized in C. Sarasúa (2006): "Trabajo y trabajadores en la España del siglo XIX", in A. González Enciso and J. M. Matés Barco (coords.): *Historia económica de España*, Barcelona: Ariel. The complicate issue of working hours is addressed by J. Doménech (2007): "Working Hours in the European Periphery. The Length of the Working Day in Spain, 1880–1920", *Explorations in Economic History*, 44 (3). For education and human capital one must read C. E. Núñez (1992): *La fuente de la riqueza. Educación y desarrollo económico en la España contemporánea*, Madrid: Alianza, and (2005): "Educación", in Carreras and X. Tafunell (coords.): *Estadísticas históricas de España. Siglos XIX y XX*, Bilbao: Fundación BBVA, I, and L. Prados de la Escosura and J. R. Rosés (2010): Human Capital and Economic Growth in Spain, 1850–2000, *Explorations in Economic History*, 47 (4).

The much studied internationalization of the economy is summarised in A. Tena (2005): "Sector exterior", in A. Carreras and X. Tafunell (coords.): *Estadísticas históricas de España. Siglos XIX y XX*, Bilbao: Fundación BBVA, II. The role of the State has been the speciality of F. Comín in numerous works, of which we highlight (1996): *Historia de la Hacienda Pública, II. España (1808-1995)*, Barcelona: Crítica; and F. Comín and D. Díaz (2005): "Sector público administrativo y estado del bienestar", in A. Carreras and X. Tafunell (coords.): *Estadísticas históricas de España. Siglos XIX y XX*, Bilbao: Fundación BBVA, II. On the Spanish public debt, see F. Comín (2013): "Apuros, ahogos, arreglos y bancarrotas. Las crisis de la deuda pública, 1504-2012" in F. Comín and M. Hernández (eds.): *Crisis económicas en España, 1300-2012. Lecciones de la Historia*, Madrid: Alianza.

Inequality studies are also indebted to L. Prados de la Escosura (2008): "Inequality, poverty and the Kuznets curve in Spain, 1850-2000", *European Review of Economic History*, 12, 3. For wages, M. Llonch and J. Maluquer de Motes, *op.cit.* On the most discussed years—those of Francoism—, M. Vilar Rodríguez (2009): *Los salarios del miedo. Mercado de trabajo y crecimiento económico en España durante el franquismo*, Santiago de Compostela: Fundación 10 de Marzo. For business profits and the stock market equity index, X. Tafunell (2005): "Empresa y Bolsa", in A. Carreras and X. Tafunell (coords.): *Estadísticas históricas de España. Siglos XIX y XX*, Bilbao: Fundación BBVA, II.

Statistical Appendix

Basic Economic Magnitudes of the Modern Spanish Economy

This appendix contains the twenty-four most significant and recurrent macroeconomic figures throughout the book. The electronic version of the data is available at https://www.aehe.es/apendice-carreras-tafunell/.

Notes on Sources and Procedures for the Production of the Series

1. Population

This is the resident population in the middle of the year (1 July). The source is L. Prados de la Escosura (2017): *Spanish Economic Growth 1850–2015*, London, Palgrave Macmillan, Table S3. The database, in its updated version until 2019, is freely accessible at https://espacioinvestiga.org/bbdd-chne/.

2. Full-Time Equivalent Employment

The source is the same as (1), Table S18.

3. Real GDP at Market Prices

The source is the same as (1), Table S3.

4. Real per capita GDP, in 1990 U.S. Dollars Gheary-Khamis

The source is the same as (1), Table S28.

5. GDP per capita of Spain in Relation to that of the European Union (EU-15)

A. Carreras, X. Tafunell, *Between Empire and Globalization*, Palgrave Studies in Economic History,
https://doi.org/10.1007/978-3-030-60504-9

For 1850–1949, calculated from (4) and A. Carreras and X. Tafunell (2005): "El crecimiento económico en la Unión Europea, 1830–2000", *Cuadernos Económicos de ICE*, 70, 2. For the post-1949 period, the population and GDP data for the EU-15 have been calculated by us from the Maddison Project database (https://www.rug.nl/ggdc/historicaldevelopment/maddison/), updated by the population data from the World Bank (https://data.worldbank.org/) and the GDP data from the International Monetary Fund (*World Economic Outlook* database, October 2017, at: https://www.imf.org/external/pubs/ft/weo/2017/02/weodata/index.aspx).

6. GDP per capita of Spain in Relation to that of the World

Own elaboration in an unpublished work based on the same sources as (5).

7. Productivity: Gross Value Added (GVA) per Worker

The source is the same as (1), Table S21.

8. Real Private Consumption per capita

The source is the same as (1), namely: Table S1, for private consumption in current values; Table S7, for the private consumption deflator; and Table S3 for the population.

9. Gross Fixed Capital Formation (GFCF)

The source is the same as (1), Table S6.

10. and 11. State and Public Administrations Deficit and Debt in Relation to GDP

Data on the State budget balance and public debt in circulation, in current values, can be found in F. Comín and D. Díaz (2005): "Sector público administrativo y estado del bienestar", in A. Carreras and X. Tafunell (coords.): *Estadísticas históricas de España . Siglos XIX y XX*, Bilbao, Fundación BBVA, Tables 12.17 and 12.34, respectively. From 1958 onwards—the first data available—we have replaced the State (government) budget balance with that of the Public Administrations as a whole. The source for 1958–1979 is the same. For the period 1980–1991 it is: Intervención General de la Administración del Estado, *Actuación económica y financiera de las Administraciones Públicas.* For the years 1991–2017: Banco de España, *Boletín Estadístico.* The resulting series has been divided by (3) at current prices (Table S3) until 1994. After this year, the percentage of the public deficit over GDP has been taken directly from the *Boletín Estadístico* of the Banco de España. For the Public Administrations debt as a whole, this source provides data from 1986.

12. Public Social Expenditure in Relation to GDP

For the period 1850–1980, the source is: S. Espuelas (2013): *La evolución del gasto social público en España, 1850–2005*. Madrid: Bank of Spain. We have completed the gaps in the series prepared by this author based on his own data on social spending by the State Administration. For the period after 1980 the source is the OECD's Social Expenditure Database (SOCX), accessible at: http://www.oecd.org/social/expenditure.htm.

13. and 14. Exports and Imports of Goods and Services

The data, in quantum indices, come from the same sources as (1, Table S1).

15. Degree of Openness of the Spanish Economy

It is the ratio of the sum of exports and imports of goods and services to GDP, all expressed in current values. Data for the numerator are in the sources used for (13) and (14); for the denominator, see (1), at current prices (Table S1).

16. Degree of Openness of the Spanish Economy in Relation to that of the European Union

Unlike the previous series, this one considers only the export and import of goods. A. Tena (2005): "Foreign sector", in A. Carreras and X. Tafunell (coords.): *Estadísticas históricas de España. Siglos XIX y XX*, Bilbao, Fundación BBVA, Table 8.4, provides data on Spain's foreign trade between 1850 and 2000. Those corresponding to 2001–2017 have been obtained from Instituto Nacional de Estadística (INE - Spanish Statistical Office) (http://www.ine.es). The coefficient of European trade openness for 1850–2000 has been estimated by A. Carreras and X. Tafunell (2005): "El crecimiento económico en la Unión Europea, 1830–2000", *Cuadernos Económicos de ICE*, 70, 2. We have updated this series based on the data on foreign trade and GDP at current prices provided by the International Monetary Fund in: *World Economic Outlook* database, October 2017 (https://www.imf.org/external/pubs/ft/weo/2017/02/weodata/index.aspx).

17. Current Account Balance in Relation to GDP

It is the ratio of the current account balance (sum of the balances of goods and services, income and transfers) to GDP at market prices, both expressed in current values. The data for the period 1850–1913 are an estimate, prepared by L. Prados De La Escosura (2010): "Spain's International Position, 1850–1913", *Revista de Historia Económica – Journal of Iberian and Latin American Economic History*, 1. From 1959 onwards they are official data, while between 1931 and 1958 they are elaborated by various authors based on official sources. They are compiled, for the years 1931–2000, in A. Tena (2005): "Sector exterior", in A. Carreras and X. Tafunell (coords.): *Estadísticas históricas de España* .

Siglos XIX y XX, Bilbao, Fundación BBVA, Table 8.9. The data for 2001–2017 come from the Bank of Spain, *Informe anual* (http://www.bde.es).

18. Nominal Effective Exchange Rate

Until 1998, this is the nominal effective exchange rate of the peseta in relation to the most developed countries. From 1850 to 1913 it consists only of the exchange rate against the pound sterling, as the exchange rate of the national currency against other reference currencies, such as the French franc, evolved in a virtually identical way. The sources are: for the period 1850–1889, P. Martín Aceña (1989): "Sistema financiero", in A. Carreras (coord.): *Estadísticas históricas de España. Siglos XIX y XX*, Madrid, Fundación Banco Exterior; for the period 1890–1899, Comisión del Patrón Oro (1929) *Dictamen de la comisión nombrada por Real Orden de 9 de enero de 1929, para el estudio de la implantación del patrón de oro.* From 1900 to 1913 we calculated the average annual contribution of the peseta to the pound from the average monthly contribution published by P. Martínez Méndez (1983) "Nuevos datos sobre la evolución de la peseta entre 1900 y 1936", in G. Anes, L. A. Rojo and P. Tedde (eds) (1983): *Historia económica y pensamiento social*, Madrid, Alianza/Banco de España. From 1914 to 1936 we have calculated the average annual exchange rate of the peseta to the pound, the dollar and the franc, also based on the monthly data provided by Martínez Méndez, and leaning towards the weighting he uses in table 18. For the period 1940–1958 we use the estimate of J. M. Serrano Sanz and M. J. Asensio (1997): "El ingenierismo cambiario. La peseta en los años del cambio múltiple, 1948–1959", *Revista de Historia Económica*, XV, 3, consisting of an average exchange rate for the basic balance that takes due account of the multiple exchange rate system. The basis for linking to the series ending in June 1936 is the dollar exchange rate (Table 3, by Martínez Méndez). Between 1959 and 1961 we have again used the data of P. Martin Aceña, now referring to the exchange rate of the peseta against the dollar. From 1962 onwards, the source is: Banco de España, *Boletín Estadístico.* It consists of an elaboration of the nominal effective exchange rate of the peseta with respect to a basket of currencies of developed countries, weighted by their weight in the Spanish foreign trade of goods and services.

19. and 20. Inflation and Inflation Rate

Year-on-year rate of change in the consumer price index (CPI) (19) and the consumer price index (1950 = 100) (20), Source: J. Maluquer de Motes (2013): *La inflación en España. Un índice de precios de consumo,*

1830–2012, Madrid, Banco de España. Since 2004, we have followed the CPI produced by the INE, base 2016. The data can be found at: INE (http://www.ine.es).

21. Long-Term Interest Rate

Following S. Homer and R. Sylla (1996): *A History of Interest Rates*, New Brunswick (N. J.), Rutgers University Press, we have used profitability data (internal rate of return—IRR) on public debt whenever it makes economic sense. It was lacking during the Franco era, when there was no free market for debt. For this period we have opted for the IRR of highly solvent private companies' bonds. For the years 1850–1882 the data refer to the average monthly closing quotations of the 3% consolidated internal debt on the Barcelona Stock Exchange, offered by X. Tafunell (2005): "Empresa y Bolsa", in A. Carreras and X. Tafunell (coords.): *Estadísticas históricas de España. Siglos XIX y XX*, Bilbao, Fundación BBVA, Table 10.34. For the period 1883–1935 the calculation refers to the average monthly quotation of the 4% perpetual domestic debt on the Madrid market. For 1884–1914 see P. Martín Aceña (1985): "La política monetaria durante la Restauración, 1874–1923", in J. L. García Delgado (ed.): *La España de la Restauración. Política, economía, legislación y cultura*, Madrid, Siglo XXI. Data from 1914 to 1918, in: *Anuario Financiero de Bilbao*. XXII (1935–1936), Banco de Vizcaya. For 1919–1935, in P. Martín Aceña (1984): *La política monetaria en España, 1919–1935*, Madrid, Instituto de Estudios Fiscales.

With respect to the 1960s and 1970s, we have opted for the IRR of company bonds. For 1960–1965 we use the estimate of I. Garrido (1974): *El rendimiento interno de las obligaciones, 1960–1973*, Madrid, Banco de España. We have linked this series in 1966 to the one prepared by the Banco de España—specifically: the weighted average of the IRR for bonds—published in the *Boletín Económico* of March 1981 ("New series of internal yield on private bonds"). In 1981 we replaced the previous indicator with the IRR of public debt at two or more years (weighted average), which is prepared by Banco de España itself and published regularly in the *Boletín Estadístico*. From 1981 to the end the series refers to this indicator and source, with the only exception that from 1989 it is calculated on the public debt at three or more years, and from 1995 on ten years public debt.

22. Risk Premium

This is the differential between Spanish long-term interest rates (21) and those of the leading country on international financial markets. We have considered that until 1936 this country was Great Britain, which then became the United States, and that since the incorporation of Spain into the European Monetary System (1989) the country of reference is Germany. The IRR data for the British public debt come from S. Homer and R. Sylla (1996): *A History of Interest Rates*, New Brunswick (N. J.), Rutgers University Press, Tables 19 and 59. Data on ten-year US and German bond yields can be found at Banco de España, *Boletín Estadístico*.

23. Stock Market Indices

These are two unlinked indices: the first ends in 1936, while the second starts in 1940 and can be followed to the present day. The first index is made up of two sections: 1850–1913 and 1913–1936. The first is a Dow Jones-type index (unweighted) on the equity values of the Barcelona Stock Exchange, estimated by L. Castañeda and X. Tafunell (2001): "La Bolsa de Barcelona entre 1849 y 1913: un nuevo índice", in C. Sudrià and D. Tirado (eds.): *Peseta y protección. Comercio exterior, moneda y crecimiento económico en la España de la Restauración*, Barcelona, Edicions Universitat de Barcelona. We have linked it to the stock exchange index, also of the Dow Jones type, calculated by the Madrid Stock Exchange Studies Service, published in *Bolsa de Madrid* (1994), no. 25, after obtaining the annual average from the monthly average values contained in this publication.

The index for the period after 1939 is the so-called total long index, based on 1940, until 1984, and based on December 1985 from that year onwards, prepared by the Madrid Stock Exchange Studies Service (see Bolsa De Madrid, *Índice de cotización de acciones*, http://www.bolsasymercados.es/esp/Estudios-Publicaciones/Estadisticas). It is a weighted index—according to stock market capitalization—and, unlike those prior to the Civil War, it takes into account dividends and subscription rights. The annual figures are the average of the monthly averages of the daily indices.

24. Financial Profitability of Companies (ROE)

Measured as the ratio of net profits to total equity. Refers to non-financial companies established in Spain. For the period 1880–1981, estimate made by X. Tafunell (2000): "La rentabilidad financiera de la empresa española, 1880–1981: Una estimación en perspectiva sectorial", *Revista de Historia Industrial*, 18. Since 1982, the financial profitability figures, referring to the ordinary return on equity, have been prepared by the Banco de España, in its annual monograph *Central de Balances*.

Table A

Year	Population	Full-time equivalent employment	Real GDP at market prices	Real per capita GDP	GDP per capita Spain vs EU-15	GDP per capita Spain vs World	Productivity: GVA per worker	Real private consumption per capita	Gross fixed capital formation	Public deficit	Public debt	Public social expenditure
	Thousands	Thousands	1950 = 100	1990 $ G-K	EU = 100	World = 100	1950 = 100	1950 = 100	1950 = 100	% GDP	% GDP	% GDP
	Col. 1	Col. 2	Col. 3	Col. 4	Col. 5	Col. 6	Col. 7	Col. 8	Col. 9	Col. 10	Col. 11	Col. 12
1850	14,754	5239	25.94	1155	78.9	153.6	52.68	61.25	5.60	0.3	91.7	1.14
1851	14,863	5281	26.37	1165	78.8	154.8	53.15	62.08	6.29	−0.3	85.0	0.89
1852	14,973	5324	27.57	1210	79.1	156.4	54.96	64.77	7.27	−0.1	83.6	1.11
1853	15,083	5367	27.78	1210	81.3	156.3	55.23	63.39	7.42	0.0	74.4	0.98
1854	15,193	5411	28.26	1222	79.2	158.7	55.92	64.31	6.20	−0.3	72.4	0.95
1855	15,176	5409	29.60	1281	84.4	166.9	59.31	67.36	6.20	−0.8	62.9	0.91
1856	15,273	5448	28.34	1219	76.6	154.4	56.34	64.92	7.65	−0.5	64.9	0.90
1857	15,463	5523	27.78	1180	71.9	148.9	53.69	61.68	10.25	−0.4	64.5	1.04
1858	15,505	5547	28.37	1202	72.6	148.5	54.76	61.96	15.74	−0.4	66.6	1.09
1859	15,550	5576	29.84	1261	76.5	157.3	57.13	62.93	15.84	0.4	63.3	1.01
1860	15,623	5616	31.09	1307	75.4	160.2	59.03	62.25	19.15	−0.9	59.3	0.98
1861	15,751	5676	31.37	1309	76.6	159.9	58.88	64.41	17.73	−1.8	57.6	1.01
1862	15,894	5742	31.66	1309	73.8	156.4	58.78	65.60	19.76	−1.8	64.6	1.00
1863	16,007	5798	32.33	1327	72.7	155.1	59.48	68.77	19.15	−1.5	58.5	0.96
1864	16,092	5844	32.28	1318	71.6	152.8	58.98	68.87	16.73	−2.5	61.1	0.96
1865	16,146	5879	31.04	1263	68.4	148.1	56.28	64.39	14.57	−1.8	70.5	1.04
1866	16,212	5919	33.05	1339	71.3	155.4	59.70	70.38	14.26	−0.8	69.4	1.02
1867	16,307	5969	32.72	1318	72.3	153.8	58.70	66.28	15.11	−0.8	80.5	1.00
1868	16,342	5998	28.66	1152	61.3	131.5	51.47	59.74	8.94	−1.5	102.8	1.20
1869	16,333	6010	29.64	1192	62.0	134.6	53.20	60.10	8.39	−2.6	130.8	1.31
1870	16,350	6032	30.49	1225	62.8	138.3	54.52	63.41	9.51	−3.4	122.1	1.18
1871	16,390	6062	32.92	1319	66.8	147.7	58.57	68.18	11.21	−2.6	115.0	1.07
1872	16,432	6094	38.05	1521	74.2	167.0	67.51	79.31	12.37	−2.3	117.8	0.94
1873	16,469	6124	41.21	1644	79.6	180.0	72.73	83.57	10.40	−2.2	121.4	0.91

(continued)

Table A (continued)

Year	*Population*	*Full-time equivalent employment*	*Real GDP at market prices*	*Real per capita GDP*	*GDP per capita Spain vs EU-15*	*GDP per capita Spain vs World*	*Productivity: GVA per worker*	*Real private consumption per capita*	*Gross fixed capital formation*	*Public deficit*	*Public debt*	*Public social expenditure*
	Thousands	*Thousands*	*1950 = 100*	*1990 $ G-K*	*EU = 100*	*World = 100*	*1950 = 100*	*1950 = 100*	*1950 = 100*	*% GDP*	*% GDP*	*% GDP*
	Col. 1	*Col. 2*	*Col. 3*	*Col. 4*	*Col. 5*	*Col. 6*	*Col. 7*	*Col. 8*	*Col. 9*	*Col. 10*	*Col. 11*	*Col. 12*
1874	16,503	6153	37.70	1501	70.3	163.3	65.14	76.01	11.15	−0.1	146.7	0.95
1875	16,538	6182	38.82	1542	71.2	164.5	66.87	75.28	11.35	−1.4	150.3	0.96
1876	16,575	6212	40.09	1589	75.1	169.4	68.45	83.55	15.84	0.1	169.0	0.91
1877	16,634	6251	44.62	1762	82.3	187.7	75.76	90.93	16.89	0.1	158.9	0.83
1878	16,732	6252	43.05	1690	78.8	177.9	73.06	84.77	20.57	−0.1	163.5	0.85
1879	16,848	6254	40.24	1569	75.4	163.6	68.04	80.25	16.63	−0.5	165.5	0.90
1880	16,968	6258	44.09	1707	79.0	172.6	74.51	83.24	20.27	0.0	152.5	0.87
1881	17,094	6263	44.73	1719	78.6	171.8	75.69	85.28	18.28	0.1	143.7	0.86
1882	17,201	6262	45.18	1726	76.7	169.6	76.45	83.48	22.42	0.4	112.2	0.84
1883	17,263	6244	45.98	1750	76.9	170.2	78.24	83.84	27.41	−0.4	73.4	0.85
1884	17,336	6230	46.30	1755	76.9	170.7	78.93	85.60	25.09	−0.2	70.8	0.88
1885	17,373	6204	44.67	1689	74.4	163.2	76.37	80.96	19.91	−0.8	71.3	0.90
1886	17,430	6185	43.76	1649	72.1	159.2	75.03	79.94	19.72	−0.1	70.0	0.88
1887	17,516	6176	43.01	1613	69.0	151.2	73.55	76.91	19.43	−0.7	75.8	0.98
1888	17,562	6195	44.82	1677	70.3	156.2	76.91	82.87	18.05	−1.0	72.1	0.96
1889	17,591	6211	44.78	1672	68.9	154.5	75.98	81.62	19.69	−0.4	79.0	1.04
1890	17,590	6216	44.67	1668	67.7	153.2	75.61	81.08	21.22	−0.4	77.9	1.03
1891	17,609	6229	45.56	1700	69.0	157.2	77.05	81.11	20.99	−0.4	76.8	1.01
1892	17,658	6252	49.53	1842	74.7	165.2	83.55	89.31	20.93	−0.7	80.3	1.00
1893	17,722	6281	47.56	1763	70.7	157.0	79.23	85.36	19.99	0.9	83.1	1.04
1894	17,780	6308	48.26	1783	69.6	155.1	80.28	86.93	19.50	−0.1	85.5	1.09
1895	17,848	6338	47.63	1753	67.5	149.4	78.97	83.13	22.11	0.8	86.1	1.09
1896	17,936	6376	43.11	1579	59.3	134.8	70.89	69.09	21.26	0.5	97.0	1.16
1897	18,072	6431	46.00	1672	62.8	138.8	75.42	74.82	21.95	−0.6	94.0	1.09
1898	18,254	6502	49.46	1780	64.2	144.3	80.19	81.64	20.52	0.1	110.7	1.03
1899	18,439	6575	50.11	1785	62.7	142.1	79.73	82.83	30.41	2.7	117.8	1.07

1900	18,584	6634	51.27	1812	63.3	142.6	81.03	81.81	36.46	1.0	124.1	1.05
1901	18,708	6690	55.65	1954	68.4	151.1	87.34	96.30	30.84	0.7	123.9	1.01
1902	18,882	6751	53.34	1856	64.8	140.7	83.06	89.70	27.21	0.7	128.0	1.05
1903	19,093	6825	53.39	1837	63.6	137.9	82.37	88.45	27.99	0.3	114.3	0.99
1904	19,268	6887	52.85	1802	61.8	133.9	80.96	84.95	29.31	0.5	107.5	0.94
1905	19,382	6945	52.40	1776	60.1	132.2	79.32	82.42	28.31	0.7	110.4	1.01
1906	19,471	6958	55.70	1879	62.0	134.7	83.94	87.98	29.92	0.9	108.4	0.98
1907	19,575	6995	57.07	1915	61.4	136.8	85.85	88.39	32.75	0.7	103.6	0.93
1908	19,694	7038	59.22	1975	63.4	142.4	88.65	94.35	31.97	0.6	103.7	0.94
1909	19,820	7083	60.86	2017	63.3	139.3	90.62	93.42	34.37	−0.3	102.1	0.94
1910	19,939	7127	58.03	1912	60.5	129.9	85.33	84.50	37.22	0.1	89.7	0.99
1911	20,036	7148	62.54	2051	62.2	137.9	92.27	91.87	39.57	0.2	82.6	0.93
1912	20,141	7173	60.53	1974	58.6	130.1	89.16	81.87	47.60	−0.3	80.6	0.93
1913	20,267	7207	64.09	2078	60.9	134.7	93.36	88.22	50.67	−0.1	75.2	0.88
1914	20,472	7269	62.52	2006	61.4	136.2	90.87	84.75	47.79	−1.0	76.5	0.89
1915	20,747	7356	63.58	2013	61.0	135.7	92.32	75.21	35.65	−3.0	70.0	0.81
1916	20,982	7430	66.56	2084	61.5	135.9	95.85	83.38	35.35	−1.2	63.2	0.71
1917	21,151	7480	65.73	2041	62.3	136.7	94.19	84.62	33.73	−1.5	59.7	0.67
1918	21,193	7487	65.10	2018	63.8	140.1	93.67	90.71	31.52	−1.8	50.7	0.57
1919	21,236	7494	66.23	2049	67.4	142.0	94.57	84.92	36.71	−1.8	48.7	0.82
1920	21,361	7532	71.44	2197	69.8	151.9	100.95	99.27	40.46	−2.4	44.4	0.50
1921	21,536	7604	73.77	2250	72.8	155.4	102.08	96.77	46.69	−3.3	51.1	0.60
1922	21,757	7683	76.89	2322	70.2	152.6	105.56	111.47	47.61	−2.3	57.2	0.64
1923	21,934	7749	77.64	2325	71.0	148.7	105.23	111.54	51.36	−1.9	59.0	0.71
1924	22,099	7814	80.17	2383	68.6	145.3	107.16	109.75	62.11	−1.8	57.3	0.73
1925	22,291	7891	85.61	2523	69.9	148.3	113.58	117.85	60.26	−1.2	56.6	0.73
1926	22,528	7987	84.79	2472	68.5	141.3	111.02	110.98	71.60	−0.6	59.5	0.81
1927	22,781	8092	93.00	2682	71.4	150.1	120.20	128.87	76.68	−0.5	57.3	0.83
1928	23,031	8199	92.77	2646	68.2	144.3	117.56	119.62	93.54	−0.3	60.2	0.87
1929	23,280	8309	100.18	2827	71.3	149.8	126.09	128.48	105.49	−0.1	57.1	0.87
1930	23,583	8443	95.40	2657	69.5	145.7	118.91	112.33	103.54	0.3	58.9	0.91
1931	23,967	8611	93.58	2565	71.8	147.3	114.54	115.83	71.11	0.1	62.5	1.35
1932	24,379	8798	96.92	2612	75.6	156.4	115.51	120.92	61.55	−0.3	63.1	1.82

(*continued*)

Table A (continued)

Year	Population	Full-time equivalent employment	Real GDP at market prices	Real per capita GDP	GDP per capita Spain vs EU-15	GDP per capita Spain vs World	Productivity: GVA per worker	Real private consumption per capita	Gross fixed capital formation	Public deficit	Public debt	Public social expenditure
	Thousands	*Thousands*	*1950 = 100*	*1990 $ G-K*	*EU = 100*	*World = 100*	*1950 = 100*	*1950 = 100*	*1950 = 100*	*% GDP*	*% GDP*	*% GDP*
	Col. 1	*Col. 2*	*Col. 3*	*Col. 4*	*Col. 5*	*Col. 6*	*Col. 7*	*Col. 8*	*Col. 9*	*Col. 10*	*Col. 11*	*Col. 12*
1933	24,792	8990	94.33	2500	70.3	147.9	110.17	115.11	67.43	−0.7	67.6	1.94
1934	25,177	9176	98.19	2562	69.5	148.1	112.91	120.69	66.51	−1.2	63.1	1.59
1935	25,543	9360	100.26	2579	67.3	143.0	112.81	120.99	68.93	−0.5	65.9	1.62
1936	25,875	9362	76.72	1948	49.4	102.2	86.81	71.28	55.24			
1937	26,047	9318	71.26	1797	43.3	91.3	81.06	62.90	40.12			
1938	26,123	9254	71.00	1785	43.1	90.6	81.29	68.94	36.97			
1939	25,929	9110	77.13	1954	45.3	94.9	89.67	79.71	37.80			
1940	25,700	8968	84.02	2148	50.3	103.8	99.71	98.50	48.21	−3.5	71.8	1.32
1941	25,660	9002	84.43	2162	49.2	102.4	97.88	93.95	63.92	−4.3	69.9	2.04
1942	25,633	9048	89.68	2298	52.3	108.2	102.94	97.26	74.99	−2.5	61.0	2.18
1943	25,796	9163	94.45	2405	54.1	108.2	105.71	94.70	73.24	−7.7	66.0	2.10
1944	26,039	9308	98.68	2490	60.7	111.2	109.33	102.70	70.85	−5.4	65.1	2.31
1945	26,294	9461	91.01	2274	64.6	112.5	99.84	90.00	74.28	−4.6	69.6	3.44
1946	26,558	9619	95.09	2352	68.2	127.1	103.17	107.44	74.73	−2.2	61.2	3.51
1947	26,838	9786	97.22	2380	65.1	124.0	103.28	105.94	79.50	−1.1	55.1	3.52
1948	27,249	10,004	97.73	2356	60.8	113.2	101.36	97.37	102.13	−1.2	55.6	3.51
1949	27,710	10,244	98.14	2327	55.6	115.1	98.65	95.94	102.76	−0.4	53.9	3.79
1950	28,000	10,424	100.00	2346	52.9	111.3	100.00	100.00	100.00	−0.4	46.2	3.73
1951	28,156	10,459	110.05	2568	54.9	116.9	110.17	113.69	88.45	−0.2	40.0	3.23
1952	28,342	10,500	119.94	2780	57.9	123.3	118.74	119.24	106.15	0.8	38.9	3.22
1953	28,571	10,567	119.81	2755	54.8	118.4	117.73	114.73	119.61	1.0	40.3	3.14
1954	28,801	10,645	128.50	2931	55.7	124.3	126.13	119.31	127.75	0.7	37.9	2.72
1955	29,027	10,782	132.95	3009	54.1	122.1	129.75	122.71	160.09	0.6	38.9	2.72
1956	29,255	10,947	143.88	3231	55.9	127.7	138.51	132.03	173.11	0.0	35.3	3.17
1957	29,499	11,109	149.03	3319	55.4	128.9	141.20	141.65	167.85	1.1	34.1	3.47

1958	29786	11,319	158.95	3506	57.5	134.7	144.98	153.00	189.26	1.2	30.0	3.33
1959	30100	11,184	157.83	3445	54.3	128.9	142.19	154.90	177.04	1.1	29.0	3.50
1960	30437	11,059	158.08	3412	50.8	123.1	145.14	148.15	190.12	1.2	29.3	3.52
1961	30773	11,245	177.29	3785	54.0	133.8	160.39	163.29	224.50	2.7	26.5	3.37
1962	31061	11,437	194.80	4120	56.7	141.5	175.16	176.61	250.22	1.8	24.3	3.28
1963	31326	11,635	214.43	4497	59.8	151.2	188.74	194.43	279.13	0.4	20.9	3.44
1964	31603	11,715	226.32	4705	59.4	150.4	206.64	202.32	321.31	0.7	19.3	3.74
1965	31949	12,187	244.41	5026	61.3	155.7	212.94	216.23	378.80	0.5	17.9	3.99
1966	32,368	12,210	263.01	5338	63.1	160.0	228.86	229.33	432.00	0.3	17.4	4.06
1967	32,799	12,318	277.81	5564	63.9	164.0	242.89	241.22	466.68	1.0	17.3	6.74
1968	33,206	12,414	294.67	5830	64.0	166.2	256.18	251.52	513.37	0.7	18.0	7.09
1969	33,553	12,427	321.99	6304	65.8	173.8	279.33	267.30	564.95	0.6	18.4	7.50
1970	33,878	12,494	332.22	6442	64.4	172.2	291.32	275.67	575.59	0.3	19.2	8.53
1971	34,217	12,667	349.03	6701	65.3	175.7	303.90	287.63	568.89	−0.9	17.9	9.38
1972	34,596	12,926	385.09	7312	68.5	186.6	326.99	309.68	684.19	0.6	17.2	9.98
1973	34,980	13,286	419.76	7883	70.2	192.2	348.48	330.85	798.30	1.1	15.9	10.34
1974	35,364	13,319	451.74	8392	73.3	203.8	374.68	344.69	876.50	0.3	13.3	10.55
1975	35,750	12,985	465.25	8549	75.2	208.2	399.37	353.19	867.37	0.2	11.7	11.66
1976	36,128	12,918	486.21	8841	74.6	208.8	419.26	367.74	870.22	−0.3	8.0	12.40
1977	36,507	12,948	502.17	9037	74.4	208.6	436.87	374.10	880.73	−0.5	8.5	12.88
1978	36,868	12,629	515.94	9193	73.8	206.7	463.42	381.08	874.74	−1.8	9.7	14.53
1979	37,194	12,434	524.66	9267	72.0	204.8	479.48	381.43	851.45	−1.9	9.6	15.34
1980	37,493	11,978	541.53	9488	72.9	209.2	509.67	386.28	877.33	−2.7	9.9	14.98
1981	37,764	11,686	541.05	9412	72.4	207.0	509.43	379.43	853.34	−3.9	10.5	16.09
1982	37,987	11,586	550.12	9514	72.7	210.2	523.23	377.47	872.00	−5.6	11.6	16.10
1983	38,160	11,548	560.21	9644	72.5	211.2	535.80	377.50	851.92	−4.8	13.0	16.83
1984	38,325	11,287	565.37	9691	71.2	206.3	554.17	375.76	793.47	−5.2	17.7	16.61
1985	38,467	11,175	582.65	9950	71.5	208.3	574.47	388.30	842.23	−6.9	30.4	17.14
1986	38,572	11,444	605.99	10,321	72.3	212.3	582.16	400.82	926.25	−6.0	45.1	16.89
1987	38,682	12,005	648.85	11,019	75.1	222.1	585.95	423.85	1068.76	−3.1	45.2	16.77
1988	38,764	12,438	690.36	11,699	76.8	230.0	597.22	444.80	1231.56	−3.2	41.3	17.25
1989	38,821	12,905	734.90	12,436	79.3	241.0	608.82	470.39	1415.39	−2.8	42.6	17.37
1990	38,861	13,413	769.93	13,015	82.5	251.4	613.04	488.20	1526.98	−4.2	44.2	19.20
1991	38,942	13,594	794.97	13,411	83.8	259.6	621.25	502.48	1569.98	−4.4	44.7	19.93

(continued)

Table A (continued)

Year	Population	Full-time equivalent employment	Real GDP at market prices	Real per capita GDP	GDP per capita Spain vs EU-15	GDP per capita Spain vs World	Productivity: GVA per worker	Real private consumption per capita	Gross fixed capital formation	Public deficit	Public debt	Public social expenditure
	Thousands	*Thousands*	*1950 = 100*	*1990 $ G-K*	*EU = 100*	*World = 100*	*1950 = 100*	*1950 = 100*	*1950 = 100*	*% GDP*	*% GDP*	*% GDP*
	Col. 1	*Col. 2*	*Col. 3*	*Col. 4*	*Col. 5*	*Col. 6*	*Col. 7*	*Col. 8*	*Col. 9*	*Col. 10*	*Col. 11*	*Col. 12*
1992	39,148	13,422	807.56	13,551	84.2	261.3	634.78	512.12	1517.86	–4.0	47.0	21.07
1993	39,356	13,055	794.54	13,262	83.0	253.8	649.47	499.33	1374.56	–6.8	58.5	22.32
1994	39,547	13,014	816.44	13,562	82.8	254.5	669.79	502.65	1425.97	–6.1	60.5	21.32
1995	39,719	13,285	846.81	14,006	83.4	256.1	678.78	509.68	1562.63	–6.5	61.7	20.69
1996	39,884	13,450	869.55	14,322	84.1	257.0	685.28	520.01	1601.18	–4.9	65.6	20.58
1997	40,050	13,928	902.42	14,802	84.4	259.1	683.39	532.69	1685.91	–3.4	64.4	20.01
1998	40,214	14,517	944.44	15,428	85.7	268.8	681.82	554.14	1866.98	–3.2	62.5	19.91
1999	40,370	15,187	989.53	16,102	87.1	274.2	680.02	579.06	2053.58	–1.4	60.9	19.75
2000	40,554	15,924	1041.93	16,878	88.2	277.6	683.57	602.46	2205.94	–1.0	58.0	19.48
2001	40,766	16,482	1083.58	17,462	89.8	282.3	688.12	621.79	2313.64	–0.7	54.2	19.11
2002	41,424	16,894	1115.55	17,691	90.3	279.6	690.57	630.39	2420.51	–0.5	51.3	19.34
2003	42,196	17,379	1151.11	17,928	90.9	273.6	690.29	633.54	2589.28	–0.2	47.6	19.93
2004	42,859	17,869	1187.56	18,218	90.8	267.6	690.89	648.87	2722.11	–0.3	45.3	20.14
2005	43,663	18,513	1231.77	18,552	91.4	263.9	690.82	662.67	2925.81	1.0	42.3	20.41
2006	44,361	19,193	1283.19	19,013	91.5	260.3	695.26	676.83	3141.01	2.4	38.9	20.43
2007	45,236	19,812	1332.47	19,351	91.2	256.8	702.42	685.59	3278.29	1.9	35.6	20.80
2008	45,983	19,850	1348.16	19,261	91.5	251.5	710.54	670.06	3149.56	–4.5	39.5	22.19
2009	46,368	18,642	1300.38	18,424	92.0	246.4	731.24	640.51	2618.17	–11.0	52.8	25.38
2010	46,562	18,148	1300.20	18,344	90.1	234.8	751.51	639.40	2490.77	–9.4	60.1	25.84
2011	46,736	17,647	1287.07	18,092	87.8	224.7	768.33	621.90	2317.96	–9.6	69.5	26.30

2012	46,766	16,797	1247.33	17,522	85.7	212.8	784.10	599.34	2118.40	−10.5	85.7	26.10
2013	46,592	16,226	1225.11	17,274	84.5	205.6	799.34	582.63	2045.40	−7.0	95.5	26.28
2014	46,455	16,393	1243.64	17,587	85.3	204.7	799.82	593.26	2141.30	−6.0	100.4	26.07
2015	46,410	16,911	1287.90	18,230	87.3	208.2	797.71	611.61	2280.67	−5.3	99.8	25.37
2016	46,450	17,418	1329.22	18,799	88.9	210.1	798.85	629.17	2356.61	−4.5	99.4	24.61
2017	46,549	17,908	1369.05	19,321	89.9	210.5	799.90	642.74	2474.69	−3.1	98.3	

Table B

Year	*Exports of goods and services*	*Imports of goods and services*	*Degree of openness*	*Degree of openness Spain vs EU-15*	*Current account balance*	*Nominal effective exchange rate*	*Inflation rate*	*Inflation*	*Long-term interest rate*	*Risk premium*	*Stock market indices*	*Financial profitability of companies (ROE)*
	1950 = 100	*1950 = 100*	*(X+M)/ GDP*100*	*UE = 100*	*% GDP*	*1950 = 100*	*%*	*1950 = 100*	*%*	*Basis points*	*1913 = 100 and 1940 = 100*	*%*
	Col. 13	*Col. 14*	*Col. 15*	*Col. 16*	*Col. 17*	*Col. 18*	*Col. 19*	*Col. 20*	*Col. 21*	*Col. 22*	*Col. 23*	*Col. 24*
1850	24.21	25.76	8.4	39.4	−1.6	262.12	6.6	7.3	9.2	609	82.8	
1851	24.16	29.41	8.1	35.7	−2.2	264.95	−0.7	7.3	8.3	526	93.2	
1852	21.82	29.94	8.1	35.5	−2.6	263.63	−2.1	7.1	6.9	383	101.2	
1853	29.23	29.02	8.1	30.7	−1.2	265.72	6.8	7.6	6.9	382	96.1	
1854	35.50	32.28	9.3	36.7	−0.8	265.39	6.8	8.1	8.5	523	93.9	
1855	44.57	35.32	10.9	43.6	0.4	264.95	0.5	8.2	9.1	582	89.1	
1856	40.63	42.97	12.3	44.7	−0.8	262.87	6.6	8.7	7.3	413	99.9	
1857	39.46	51.10	14.0	49.2	−1.9	261.58	2.5	9.0	7.6	433	93.3	
1858	27.14	52.65	11.7	43.1	−4.8	258.08	−10.4	8.0	7.4	426	62.9	
1859	35.44	43.24	10.7	36.2	−2.3	262.66	0.7	8.0	7.1	398	55.8	
1860	45.14	48.70	11.5	37.6	−1.3	268.41	7.6	8.6	6.3	306	71.1	
1861	43.02	49.10	11.4	43.2	−1.7	260.19	0.1	8.7	6.1	281	73.4	
1862	35.32	53.51	10.8	39.5	−3.4	262.87	−0.5	8.6	5.9	271	69.4	
1863	32.70	63.33	11.7	43.4	−4.5	262.87	6.9	9.2	5.7	243	66.3	
1864	30.70	58.57	11.5	40.2	−4.8	257.56	−0.9	9.1	6.0	262	56.6	
1865	37.58	53.14	11.6	35.0	−3.4	260.19	−3.7	8.8	7.1	379	40.6	
1866	38.76	54.98	11.0	32.0	−3.1	260.19	−0.5	8.7	8.5	514	28.6	
1867	50.74	46.36	10.4	31.4	−0.2	261.47	−1.1	8.7	8.9	571	27.5	
1868	51.20	55.63	13.5	41.5	−1.3	257.56	7.7	9.3	8.9	574	25.1	
1869	60.66	49.87	14.7	43.0	0.0	261.36	−8.7	9.0	11.5	822	25.4	
1870	53.66	54.11	12.2	36.0	−1.9	261.90	1.6	9.2	11.9	866	29.5	
1871	59.24	64.94	14.1	36.3	−1.3	265.94	3.5	9.2	10.8	754	38.7	
1872	63.93	73.58	14.6	38.4	−1.9	260.51	3.1	9.4	11.1	784	48.1	

1873	75.27	61.82	13.8	33.4	0.5	259.77	2.2	10.2	13.4	1.015	42.0	
1874	63.43	79.81	14.2	37.0	-2.5	259.34	0.5	10.1	17.3	1.408	43.6	
1875	67.44	70.01	13.6	35.3	-1.1	255.50	0.8	9.9	13.7	1.050	52.5	
1876	58.74	91.34	13.4	32.1	-2.4	255.09	-1.0	9.7	11.4	825	55.7	
1877	72.29	82.61	12.7	32.2	-0.2	252.36	3.5	9.8	8.6	549	55.4	
1878	73.83	81.93	12.2	32.4	-0.4	253.26	-2.8	9.8	7.3	417	66.8	
1879	78.38	93.33	13.5	31.1	-1.1	252.06	1.6	9.9	6.6	355	73.6	
1880	106.13	97.23	15.1	38.5	0.9	255.80	0.3	10.0	5.3	225	118.7	8.2
1881	111.98	106.17	15.5	35.1	-0.2	254.27	-0.8	10.0	3.9	87	138.7	9.8
1882	110.79	110.75	15.2	36.9	-0.5	248.52	2.2	10.3	4.4	138	104.0	11.8
1883	118.77	117.68	15.8	41.1	-0.5	249.20	2.6	10.1	6.4	343	80.2	9.2
1884	109.72	108.97	14.4	37.7	-0.6	250.28	0.3	10.2	6.6	365	79.5	7.5
1885	127.42	111.46	15.0	40.4	-0.2	247.94	-4.0	10.1	6.7	370	69.3	5.7
1886	120.69	116.36	15.5	42.3	0.3	248.04	-2.2	10.1	6.6	363	69.8	5.8
1887	135.95	119.39	16.1	41.9	0.1	250.48	3.0	10.3	6.1	316	65.3	6.8
1888	134.07	128.12	16.8	41.0	-0.2	248.82	0.1	10.3	5.7	274	72.4	6.2
1889	143.79	136.38	19.5	47.8	-0.5	245.27	-7.6	9.7	5.3	250	70.0	6.5
1890	136.50	129.70	19.4	49.5	-0.3	242.25	0.6	9.6	5.2	258	68.7	7.5
1891	147.33	123.46	19.4	48.4	1.0	236.74	4.0	10.0	5.3	259	65.0	7.0
1892	144.68	119.16	19.3	49.6	1.5	219.62	3.6	10.5	5.9	323	52.5	6.3
1893	140.62	117.34	19.3	47.8	1.2	212.72	-4.0	10.0	5.8	322	49.4	5.7
1894	147.25	128.50	20.1	54.7	1.1	211.68	0.3	9.9	5.7	321	50.1	4.2
1895	144.60	118.64	18.1	51.2	1.7	220.60	-1.0	9.8	5.7	332	48.4	5.9
1896	173.83	122.02	22.6	67.6	3.3	209.72	-4.5	9.6	6.3	403	48.3	7.9
1897	166.09	122.64	22.3	66.9	2.9	195.48	2.5	10.1	6.2	394	45.8	8.8
1898	152.42	102.25	22.4	60.0	3.6	162.44	3.2	10.4	7.2	492	48.6	10.9
1899	159.80	151.49	22.4	58.2	-1.2	202.88	0.6	10.2	6.3	398	68.6	13.4
1900	162.53	142.65	23.7	58.9	-0.5	195.74	0.1	10.3	5.6	306	79.3	12.1
1901	139.32	145.72	21.7	58.2	-1.3	183.25	4.3	10.5	5.6	290	87.7	10.4
1902	154.19	143.29	22.0	55.9	-0.8	186.68	2.6	10.7	5.5	284	90.7	9.3
1903	164.75	153.68	21.9	54.9	-1.0	187.51	0.8	10.8	5.2	245	85.8	9.6
1904	167.50	152.35	21.3	53.4	-0.5	183.92	-1.6	10.8	5.2	240	82.1	8.1
1905	194.17	168.01	23.8	55.1	0.5	193.68	0.3	10.9	5.1	232	77.7	8.9

(*continued*)

Table B (continued)

Year	*Exports of goods and services*	*Imports of goods and services*	*Degree of openness*	*Degree of openness Spain vs EU-15*	*Current account balance*	*Nominal effective exchange rate*	*Inflation rate*	*Inflation*	*Long-term interest rate*	*Risk premium*	*Stock market indices*	*Financial profitability of companies (ROE)*
	1950 = 100	*1950 = 100*	*(X+M)/ GDP*100*	*UE = 100*	*% GDP*	*1950 = 100*	*%*	*1950 = 100*	*%*	*Basis points*	*1913 = 100 and 1940 = 100*	*%*
	Col. 13	*Col. 14*	*Col. 15*	*Col. 16*	*Col. 17*	*Col. 18*	*Col. 19*	*Col. 20*	*Col. 21*	*Col. 22*	*Col. 23*	*Col. 24*
1906	187.25	160.90	21.6	48.5	1.5	224.31	−2.4	10.7	4.9	210	89.1	10.4
1907	190.43	152.62	21.3	46.2	2.0	226.90	0.5	10.7	4.9	189	85.8	10.1
1908	173.98	153.97	19.0	45.3	1.1	224.48	0.4	10.6	4.8	190	92.2	8.6
1909	177.34	145.97	17.7	41.6	1.7	229.99	−0.1	10.3	4.6	167	90.7	8.7
1910	193.14	156.47	20.5	44.9	2.5	235.82	−1.0	10.3	4.7	160	95.3	9.0
1911	207.62	181.91	21.7	46.9	2.3	233.02	1.7	10.6	4.7	159	95.9	8.7
1912	228.57	189.35	23.1	48.8	2.9	236.92	−1.0	10.4	4.7	144	103.1	10.7
1913	226.13	207.57	23.2	49.6	0.9	234.97	0.8	10.7	4.9	156	100.0	9.7
1914	187.56	154.39	17.1	36.7		242.98	1.1	10.8	5.2	177	91.3	7.1
1915	257.13	123.11	16.9	38.1		258.65	5.0	11.4	5.6	174	90.1	9.2
1916	274.26	143.35	18.2	43.1		273.68	6.8	12.2	5.4	105	102.6	11.9
1917	246.78	118.57	18.8	50.8		308.02	19.4	14.1	5.4	78	109.6	13.5
1918	177.29	89.41	13.1	40.5		329.94	15.3	16.7	5.1	72	135.6	14.3
1919	247.23	125.56	23.0	53.6		300.26	12.4	18.8	5.2	56	129.9	13.3
1920	226.25	206.71	24.1	51.6		337.65	8.3	20.3	5.5	19	124.0	11.6
1921	188.62	160.56	17.9	59.5		274.24	−6.6	19.0	5.9	65	110.3	9.5
1922	139.81	195.02	15.6	50.8		284.30	−3.9	18.3	5.7	131	113.7	9.8
1923	172.10	235.50	19.4	53.8		299.62	−0.3	18.2	5.6	133	120.8	9.7
1924	166.81	216.00	17.8	44.7		307.97	1.9	18.6	5.7	129	122.6	10.4
1925	196.01	226.40	17.3	44.8		334.76	0.1	18.6	5.7	126	125.6	9.8
1926	175.67	188.36	14.0	37.5		442.84	−3.9	17.9	5.8	130	129.4	9.9
1927	168.87	253.45	14.4	38.7		443.38	−0.5	17.8	5.7	117	153.3	9.0

1928	182.44	255.91	15.6	43.5		431.36	-1.8	17.5	5.3	86	197.2	9.9
1929	202.77	292.15	16.8	46.7		382.27	7.1	18.7	5.4	79	194.6	10.4
1930	225.21	222.53	16.9	53.6		303.28	-2.3	18.3	5.6	111	185.7	9.4
1931	215.82	184.45	15.1	55.6	-1.5	253.47	3.1	18.8	6.3	182	141.3	7.0
1932	229.19	198.84	15.3	70.2	-0.2	231.42	-1.0	18.6	6.2	249	119.7	6.6
1933	168.90	169.45	11.2	53.1	-0.3	250.83	-2.2	18.2	6.0	262	113.0	5.9
1934	162.14	178.57	10.2	49.5	1.5	261.01	3.2	18.8	5.7	261	112.5	6.0
1935	152.99	173.77	9.3	45.9		264.27	0.0	18.8	5.2	231	125.6	6.0
1936	153.36	128.02	10.3	47.4		263.31	0.6	18.9	5.3	238	118.8	4.6
1937	134.01	60.90	10.3	48.9			12.4	20.7				4.1
1938	95.56	58.25	8.5	56.1			12.6	23.7				6.7
1939	78.92	57.23	6.8	22.9			14.0	29.0				7.6
1940	56.73	81.28	5.0	21.5	-0.3	191.81	20.4	33.6			100.0	8.7
1941	53.24	32.41	4.5	21.6	1.6	188.13	29.9	43.7			130.1	8.2
1942	58.36	22.39	4.1	19.6	1.8	188.13	6.9	46.7			147.8	8.7
1943	94.13	59.32	5.8	25.0	0.3	188.13	-0.6	46.5			137.1	9.0
1944	105.87	56.16	6.2	21.2	1.7	188.13	4.4	48.6			139.8	9.4
1945	88.37	46.48	5.6	23.9	0.6	188.13	7.0	51.9			163.9	10.2
1946	63.46	93.69	5.7	21.2	-0.2	188.13	31.2	68.1			222.8	9.7
1947	81.84	73.67	6.4	17.0	-0.1	188.13	17.6	80.2			320.0	9.9
1948	91.40	64.89	6.3	20.1	-0.2	188.13	6.8	85.6			227.0	9.5
1949	97.94	79.35	7.9	25.3	-0.7	133.94	5.4	90.2			203.4	9.3
1950	100.00	100.00	8.3	22.5	-0.6	100.00	10.8	100.0			216.8	9.7
1951	175.89	148.26	13.7	31.4	-1.4	70.77	9.4	109.4			259.2	10.2
1952	197.19	158.20	14.1	36.4	-1.5	66.00	-2.0	107.2			284.2	9.6
1953	219.96	207.01	16.2	46.0	-1.0	64.05	1.6	109.0			295.9	10.0
1954	250.72	216.58	15.0	40.5	-0.3	62.44	1.2	110.3			373.0	9.9
1955	209.61	273.95	16.8	42.4	-2.0	60.39	4.0	114.8			513.6	11.4
1956	213.24	294.47	15.4	37.9	-2.1	60.02	5.9	121.5			767.4	10.8
1957	175.67	276.89	15.2	39.8	-2.3	51.19	10.8	134.5			838.1	11.3
1958	167.33	315.34	14.9	42.4	-1.6	47.70	13.4	152.6			739.1	11.5
1959	141.74	266.03	12.5	31.1	-0.3	34.33	7.3	163.7			699.3	10.6
1960	227.26	260.63	15.1	40.3	3.7	34.19	1.2	165.6	6.4	225	714.7	10.9

(*continued*)

Table B (continued)

Year	*Exports of goods and services*	*Imports of goods and services*	*Degree of openness*	*Degree of openness Spain vs EU-15*	*Current account balance*	*Nominal effective exchange rate*	*Inflation rate*	*Inflation*	*Long-term interest rate*	*Risk premium*	*Stock market indices*	*Financial profitability of companies (ROE)*
	1950 = 100	*1950 = 100*	*(X+M)/ GDP*100*	*UE = 100*	*% GDP*	*1950 = 100*	*%*	*1950 = 100*	*%*	*Basis points*	*1913 = 100 and 1940 = 100*	*%*
	Col. 13	*Col. 14*	*Col. 15*	*Col. 16*	*Col. 17*	*Col. 18*	*Col. 19*	*Col. 20*	*Col. 21*	*Col. 22*	*Col. 23*	*Col. 24*
1961	231.79	372.04	16.3	46.4	1.9	34.19	2.4	171.9	5.8	191	917.4	10.8
1962	256.80	506.57	18.1	51.5	0.3	34.40	5.7	181.7	5.2	129	1149.8	9.9
1963	250.64	613.90	17.6	49.8	-1.1	34.42	8.8	197.6	5.3	128	1252.0	8.5
1964	322.66	685.41	18.5	51.3	0.2	34.42	7.0	211.4	5.7	155	1272.0	8.1
1965	335.03	918.09	19.7	53.8	-2.2	34.43	13.2	239.3	6.0	168	1398.1	8.0
1966	400.47	1097.40	20.7	55.9	-2.2	34.45	6.2	254.2	6.8	190	1507.7	7.3
1967	407.45	1061.41	18.9	52.0	-0.9	33.92	6.4	267.1	7.2	213	1628.8	6.6
1968	514.43	1147.02	21.5	53.2	-0.9	30.21	4.9	283.9	7.4	173	1995.0	7.3
1969	630.69	1331.82	22.8	53.0	-1.2	30.29	2.2	290.1	7.8	111	3041.2	8.0
1970	747.01	1424.45	24.1	53.9	0.2	30.25	5.7	307.2	9.1	178	3330.9	8.0
1971	867.73	1436.73	23.7	54.0	1.9	29.89	8.2	332.0	9.4	322	3465.9	6.7
1972	1046.23	1799.59	25.2	57.0	1.1	30.44	8.3	359.4	8.7	248	4670.3	8.3
1973	1184.87	2104.64	26.5	53.8	0.8	30.96	11.4	400.5	8.8	194	6060.2	8.9
1974	1311.77	2303.66	31.7	56.1	-3.7	31.85	15.7	463.2	10.7	309	6310.0	7.1
1975	1346.07	2288.00	29.0	55.4	-3.9	30.93	16.9	541.8	11.0	302	5594.5	5.7
1976	1582.60	2535.87	31.1	54.6	-4.1	28.55	17.6	637.3	10.3	273	4982.7	5.2
1977	1782.91	2408.15	30.1	51.8	-1.6	25.18	24.5	793.6	10.2	281	3549.7	4.5
1978	2026.97	2402.37	28.7	50.7	1.1	22.82	19.8	950.5	11.4	296	3079.0	2.3
1979	2331.63	2676.79	29.5	49.2	0.1	24.87	15.7	1099.4	14.2	477	2858.8	1.9
1980	2442.28	2774.26	33.7	54.3	-2.4	23.10	15.6	1270.5	15.2	378	2886.3	0.8
1981	2613.02	2639.24	37.4	58.0	-2.5	21.23	14.5	1455.4	15.4	144	4110.6	1.1

1982	2743.70	2767.72	38.4	58.8	−2.7	20.00	14.4	1665.1	15.7	267	4110.7	−1.3
1983	3018.47	2762.10	41.9	63.5	−1.6	16.69	12.2	1867.8	16.5	543	4621.2	0.0
1984	3372.88	2715.06	43.4	64.4	1.3	16.41	11.3	2078.5	16.4	400	6779.8	0.8
1985	3463.89	2932.01	43.0	62.7	1.7	16.02	8.8	2261.7	13.4	275	9116.4	3.3
1986	3529.76	3358.36	37.1	59.9	1.7	15.90	8.8	2460.6	11.4	368	19,441.6	5.5
1987	3748.20	4036.12	37.9	62.9	0.0	16.01	5.2	2589.7	12.8	439	28,759.8	9.8
1988	3933.15	4621.08	37.9	64.0	−1.1	16.49	4.8	2715.0	11.7	289	32,896.4	12.9
1989	4045.66	5422.64	38.3	62.0	−3.0	17.19	6.8	2899.4	13.6	514	37,051.3	13.1
1990	4170.25	5848.66	36.2	61.5	−3.4	18.03	6.7	3094.3	14.6	593	32,680.2	9.4
1991	4492.38	6379.33	35.8	63.3	−3.1	18.07	5.9	3277.9	12.5	404	34,448.3	5.9
1992	4817.81	6825.45	36.2	65.4	−3.0	17.67	5.9	3472.1	12.6	471	31,663.9	1.9
1993	5220.92	6473.98	37.3	68.1	−0.8	15.62	4.6	3630.7	10.1	358	39,197.9	−2.3
1994	6086.07	7212.65	41.9	74.2	−1.4	14.57	4.7	3802.1	9.3	241	35,580.2	6.6
1995	6685.93	8010.12	44.8	74.7	0.2	14.48	4.7	3979.8	11.5	462	41,162.5	7.9
1996	7350.33	8602.99	46.3	79.0	0.1	14.57	3.6	4121.4	8.9	268	58,837.6	8.3
1997	8423.21	9713.24	51.3	82.4	0.4	13.92	2.0	4199.2	6.5	88	85,526.4	9.0
1998	9100.02	11,083.35	52.9	83.8	−0.5	13.87	1.8	4273.2	4.9	37	119,275.0	10.7
1999	9828.44	12,622.69	54.7	85.7	−2.1		2.3	4368.4	4.8	27	142,773.3	10.2
2000	10,858.81	13,820.71	60.2	85.5	−3.5		3.4	4520.8	5.6	30	127,905.7	10.5
2001	11,257.92	14,305.21	58.1	81.2	−4.4		3.6	4648.3	5.1	32	123,961.1	10.7
2002	11,411.80	14,816.53	55.0	79.9	−3.7		3.5	4815.4	5.0	20	98,023.8	12.9
2003	11,801.97	15,692.66	53.1	80.9	−3.9		3.0	4964.6	4.1	4	130,350.1	12.1
2004	12,303.80	17,274.05	54.2	79.8	−5.6		3.0	5116.4	4.0	−1	160,437.5	12.0
2005	12,521.75	18,487.99	54.3	76.9	−7.5		3.4	5289.3	3.4	9	201,802.9	13.8
2006	13,139.68	19,997.44	55.7	73.9	−9.0		3.5	5572.8	3.8	2	283,628.2	14.5
2007	14,224.28	21,709.86	57.4	74.0	−9.6		2.8	5633.7	4.2	3	309,614.4	13.3
2008	14,103.77	20,490.03	55.8	71.0	−9.3		4.1	5866.4	4.5	49	195,221.0	9.7
2009	12,549.10	16,737.31	46.5	67.1	−4.3		−0.3	5852.1	4.0	77	264,729.9	8.8
2010	13,731.70	17,895.97	52.3	68.3	−3.9		1.8	5971.7	4.2	146	225,895.1	9.0
2011	14,748.71	17,752.04	58.1	71.5	−3.2		3.2	6154.2	5.4	279	206,082.4	7.9
2012	14,905.73	16,624.28	59.9	73.4	−0.2		2.4	6303.8	5.8	431	216,408.8	7.3
2013	15,544.27	16,539.50	61.2	77.5	1.5		1.4	6392.1	4.6	303	281,072.4	7.2

(*continued*)

Table B (continued)

Year	*Exports of goods and services*	*Imports of goods and services*	*Degree of openness*	*Degree of openness Spain vs EU-15*	*Current account balance*	*Nominal effective exchange rate*	*Inflation rate*	*Inflation*	*Long-term interest rate*	*Risk premium*	*Stock market indices*	*Financial profitability of companies (ROE)*
	1950 = 100	*1950 = 100*	*(X+M)/ GDP*100*	*UE = 100*	*% GDP*	*1950 = 100*	*%*	*1950 = 100*	*%*	*Basis points*	*1913 = 100 and 1940 = 100*	*%*
	Col. 13	*Col. 14*	*Col. 15*	*Col. 16*	*Col. 17*	*Col. 18*	*Col. 19*	*Col. 20*	*Col. 21*	*Col. 22*	*Col. 23*	*Col. 24*
2014	16,210.96	17,629.66	63.0	82.5	1.1		−0.2	6379.3	2.7	154	306,606.8	6.9
2015	16,890.72	18,677.94	63.6	83.5	1.4		−0.5	6347.4	1.7	124	296,798.3	7.1
2016	17,693.63	19,179.57	62.9	82.7	2.0		−0.2	6334.7	1.4	131	304,916.5	8.2
2017	18,583.24	20,074.01	65.5		1.9		2.0	6461.4	1.6	123	341,930.7	8.6

Index[1]

[1] Note: Page numbers followed by 'n' refer to notes.

A. Carreras, X. Tafunell, *Between Empire and Globalization*, Palgrave Studies in Economic History,
https://doi.org/10.1007/978-3-030-60504-9

Q

R

The manufacturer's authorised representative in the EU is Springer Nature Customer Service Centre GmbH, Europaplatz 3, 69115 Heidelberg, Germany. If you have any concerns regarding our products, please contact ProductSafety@springernature.com

Printed and bound by CPI Group (UK) Ltd, Croydon, CR0 4YY
22/09/2026
02221066-0012